Governing European Communications

Critical Media Studies

Series Editor
Andrew Calabrese, University of Colorado

This series covers a broad range of critical research and theory about media in the modern world. It includes work about the changing structures of the media, focusing particularly on work about the political and economic forces and social relations which shape and are shaped by media institutions, structural changes in policy formation and enforcement, technological transformations in the means of communication, and the relationships of all these to public and private cultures worldwide. Historical research about the media and intellectual histories pertaining to media research and theory are particularly welcome. Emphasizing the role of social and political theory for informing and shaping research about communications media, Critical Media Studies addresses the politics of media institutions at national, subnational, and transnational levels. The series is also interested in short, synthetic texts on key thinkers and concepts in critical media studies.

Titles in the series

Governing European Communications: From Unification to Coordination by Maria Michalis
Knowledge Workers in the Information Society edited by Catherine McKercher and Vincent Mosco

Governing European Communications

From Unification to Coordination

Maria Michalis

LEXINGTON BOOKS

A division of
ROWMAN & LITTLEFIELD PUBLISHERS, INC.
Lanham • Boulder • New York • Toronto • Plymouth, UK

LEXINGTON BOOKS

A division of Rowman & Littlefield Publishers, Inc.
A wholly owned subsidiary of The Rowman & Littlefield Publishing Group, Inc.
4501 Forbes Boulevard, Suite 200
Lanham, MD 20706

Estover Road
Plymouth PL6 7PY
United Kingdom

British Library Cataloguing in Publication Information Available

Library of Congress Cataloging-in-Publication Data

Michalis, Maria, 1969–
  Governing European communications : from unification to coordination /
Maria Michalis.
      p. cm. — (Critical media studies)
  Includes bibliographical references and index.
  ISBN-13: 978-0-7391-1735-4 (cloth : alk. paper)
  ISBN-10: 0-7391-1735-1 (cloth : alk. paper)
  ISBN-13: 978-0-7391-1736-1 (pbk. : alk. paper)
  ISBN-10: 0-7391-1736-X (pbk. : alk. paper)
  1. Communication policy—Europe—History—20th century. I. Title.
  P95.82.E85M53 2007
  302.2094—dc22   2007017517

Printed in the United States of America

Contents

List of Figures and Tables

Acknowledgments

Many people have helped me with this book. To start with, I would like to thank all those who graciously gave up their time to respond to my questions and to discuss a wide range of topics, in the knowledge that without their contribution it would have perhaps been impossible to understand the complexity of the issues involved.

I would also like to thank the Communication and Media Research Institute and the Department for Journalism and Mass Communication at the University of Westminster for giving me a semester's research leave as well as my colleagues who covered for me in my absence. Special thanks to Jill Hills, my mentor and now friend, who has stood by me throughout this project.

My thanks also go to Andrew Calabrese, the series editor, for his long-distance but unfailing encouragement and to Joseph Parry, associate editor at Lexington Books, for his support and advice.

Finally, on a personal note, I would like to thank Spyros and my family for always being there for me.

Abbreviations

3G	Third Generation mobile system
3GPP	Third [mobile phone] Generation Partnership Project promoting the UMTS/W-CDMA standard
3GPP2	3GPP's opposite grouping promoting the cdma2000 standard
ACT	Association of Commercial Television broadcasters
AEG	Allgemeine Elektrizitäts Gesellschaft
AT&T	American Telephone & Telegraph
BBC	British Broadcasting Corporation
BEUC	The European Consumers' Organization
BSB	British Satellite Broadcasting
BT	British Telecommunications plc
CCITT	International Telegraph and Telephone Consultative Committee (one of the permanent organs of the ITU responsible for technical, operational and tariff issues). Now the ITU-T
CDMA	Code Division Multiple Access
CEPT	European Conference of Postal and Telecommunications administrations
CII	Compagnie Internationale pour l' Informatique
CLT	Compagnie Luxembourgeoise de Télédiffusion
CoCom	Communications Committee (EU)
COST program	COoperation in the Scientific and Technical Field
DBS	Direct Broadcasting by Satellite

DCMS	Department for Culture Media and Sport (UK)
DG	Directorate General (of the European Commission)
DSL	Digital Subscriber Line
EBU	European Broadcasting Union
ECSC	European Coal and Steel Community
ECTA	European Competitive Telecommunications Association
ECU	European Currency Unit
EEC	European Economic Community
EPRA	European Platform of Regulatory Authorities in broadcasting
ERG	European Regulators' Group (EU)
ERT	European Round Table of industrialists
ESPRIT	European Strategic Program in Information Technologies
ETNO	European Telecommunications Network Operators' association
ETSI	European Telecommunications Standards Institute
EU	European Union
EURATOM	European Atomic Energy Community
EUREKA	European Research Coordinating Agency
GATS	General Agreement on Trade in Services
GATT	General Agreement on Tariffs and Trade
GDP	Gross Domestic Product
GSM	Global System for Mobile Communications
HDTV	High Definition Television
IBM	International Business Machines corporation
IBO	International Broadcasting Organization
IBU	International Broadcasting Union
ICL	International Computers Limited
ICT	Information and Communication Technology
Intelsat	International Telecommunications Satellite consortium
INTUG	International Telecommunications Users' Group
IP	Internet Protocol
IRG	Independent Regulators' Group
ISDN	Integrated Services Digital Network
ITC	Independent Television Commission (UK). Now Ofcom
ITFF	Information Technologies Task Force
ITU	International Telecommunication Union (affiliated with the United Nations)
ITU-R	ITU-Radiocommunications Sector
ITV	Independent Television (UK)
MAC	Multiplexed Analogue Components (family of high-definition standards for satellite analog transmission proposed by Europe)

MEDIA	Measures to Encourage the Development of an Audiovisual Industry in Europe
MHP	Multimedia Home Platform
MPAA	Motion Picture Association of America
MUSE	(high-definition standard for satellite analog transmission proposed by Japan)
NATO	North Atlantic Treaty Organization
NMT	Nordic Mobile Telephone (analog cellular mobile standard)
NTSC	National Television System Committee (color TV standard)
OECD	Organization for Economic Cooperation and Development
OEEC	Organization for European Economic Cooperation
Ofcom	Office of Communications (UK)
Oftel	Office of Telecommunications (UK). Now Ofcom
OIRT	International Radio and Television Organization
ONP	Open Network Provision
OSI	Open Systems Interconnection
PAL	Phrase Alternating Line (color TV standard)
PTO	Public Telecommunications Operator (former PTT; administration or private operating agency providing public telecommunications services)
PTT	Post, Telegraph and Telephone administrations (generic term for European Telecommunications Administrations in the monopoly era)
R&D	Research and Development
R&TTE	Radio & Telecommunications Terminal Equipment
RACE	Research for Advanced Communications in Europe
RCA	Radio Corporation of America
RSC	Radio Spectrum Committee (EU)
RSPG	Radio Spectrum Policy Group (EU)
RTD	Research and Technological Development
RTL	Radio Télévision Luxembourg
SECAM	Séquentiel Couleur à Mémoire (color TV standard)
The Six	The founding six members of the three European Communities (ECSC, Euratom, EEC), that is, France, Italy, West Germany, Belgium, the Netherlands, and Luxembourg.
SMG	Special Mobile Group (ETSI committee)
SMS	Short Message Service (to a mobile phone)
SNA	Systems Network Architecture (IBM)
SWIFT	Society for Worldwide Interbank Financial Telecommunications

TABD	TransAtlantic Business Dialogue
TCP/IP	Transmission Control Protocol/Internet Protocol
UGG	UMTS Globalization Group
UMTS	Universal Mobile Telecommunications System (third generation mobile phone standard)
UN	United Nations
UNESCO	United Nations Educational, Scientific and Cultural Organization
UNICE	Union of Industrial and Employers' Confederation of Europe
USSR	Union of Soviet Socialist Republics
VHS	Vertical Helical Scan (de facto analog format for video cassette recorders)
VLSI	Very Large Scale Integrated circuits
W-CDMA	Wideband CDMA
WEF	World Economic Forum
Wi-Max	World Inter-operability for Microwave Access
WTO	World Trade Organization

1

Introduction

This book documents and critically assesses the emergence of European governance in the area of communications in the postwar era and its subsequent evolution and dynamics, paying particular attention to telecommunications and television policies and regulation and their technological convergence. Why has a European system of governance come about? What have been the main forces and objectives? Has it changed over time, how and why? These are the central questions that the following chapters endeavor to address.

In recent decades, the field of Information and Communication Technology (ICT) has attracted growing interest from academics, industry and policy makers at national and international levels. Broadly speaking, this interest can be attributed to four major interrelated factors. First, technological advances have revolutionized three previously distinct sectors—information technology, telecommunications and the media—blurring the boundaries between them. Digitalization together with the advent of new transmission technologies—such as satellites, optic fibers and wireless—have altered the economics of the sectors concerned and, in turn, have challenged the former national monopolistic, or at best oligopolistic, market structures in broadcasting and telecommunications.

These techno-economic developments, and this is the second main factor behind the increased interest in ICT, have contributed to the liberalization and internationalization of the relevant markets by having progressively defied the principal justifications on which market structure and regulation

1

had traditionally been premised, notably spectrum scarcity in broadcasting and the natural monopoly argument in telecommunications.

Third, ICT, experiencing high growth rates, is not just an important sector in its own right but in addition, and more significantly, it has steadily, from the late 1960s onward, gained political saliency and is posited as *the* engine of broader economic growth and competitiveness. The revival of information society visions around the world since the 1990s focusing on the internet and broadband communications has rested upon this assumption. Communication policy has moved into the mainstream of economic planning and development. In the European Union (EU), political leaders at the Lisbon Summit in March 2000 committed to an ambitious ten-year plan aiming at transforming Europe into the world's most competitive and dynamic knowledge-based economy.[1]

Fourth, the liberalization of communication markets, especially from the mid-1980s onward, has been accompanied by increased regulatory activity at the national level but also a process of regionalization and internationalization of regulatory regimes. At the national level, country after country has set up a sector-based regulatory authority (e.g., the Office of Telecommunications—Oftel—in Britain from 1984 till 2003) or, more recently, a converged regulatory authority with responsibility over the entire electronic communications sector (e.g., the Italian Communications Regulatory Authority—Agcom—and the British Office of Communications—Ofcom—formed in 1997 and 2003 respectively) or with responsibility over utilities in general (e.g., the German Federal Network Agency—BnetzA—created in July 2005).[2] At the regional level an example is the intergovernmental Asia-Pacific Economic Cooperation, established in 1989 and bringing together twenty-one countries from the region, that deals among other things with telecommunications regulatory reform. In Europe, the EU has assumed various responsibilities in the field of ICT, as this study analyzes. At the international level, in the area of telecommunications, this shift of regulation beyond national states culminated in the 1997 World Trade Organization agreement on basic telecommunications.

Of course, international cooperation on certain technical and operational aspects has always been necessary for the actual establishment of communication links across national borders, as for instance in the spheres of radio frequencies, technical standards and tariffs for international calls. Such cooperation, however, dictated for pragmatic reasons would stop at national borders. The difference is that now—in the context of liberalization, privatization, international trade agreements, and the process of European integration—above-the-national-state regulation has increased in both scope and depth. It has moved inside national borders and deals with a much wider range of issues, such as universal service and public service broadcasting. Arguably, above-the-national-state regulation has become more contested as it touches on the domestic political and social structures of national states.

This study takes into account the main European organizations involved in the governance of communications although, in view of its importance, the overall focus is on the EU. By concentrating on the most advanced actual example of regionalism we have at present, the aim is to contribute to a better understanding of processes of regionalization and internationalization of regulatory regimes, their drivers and constraints, as well as implications for public policy, harmonization and legitimacy.

In addition to the European experience being useful for other studies on regionalism and globalization, another reason for examining the EU regulatory framework for electronic communications is that it may serve as a model for other regions. In October 2005, for instance, regulators from fifteen West African countries agreed on a common procompetitive regulatory framework for their national ICT markets aiming at creating a single market as per the EU example.[3]

It is in this context, as just described, that the present study on European-level governance of communications is located. It differs from existing accounts in three main respects. First, it offers a fresh analytical perspective. Available studies provide national comparative accounts examining the interplay between European and national policies.[4] National variations are attributed to diverse policy styles, the embeddedness or path dependency of institutional idiosyncrasies and national configurations of interests. These studies assume predominantly a state-centric theoretical perspective and focus on the traditional territorial dichotomy between the EU and national states.[5] Adopting a broader political economy perspective, this book argues that the decisive issue in the European governance of communications has been not more-or-less Europe but primarily what kind of Europe. It places the Europeanization of communication policy within the wider processes of globalization and the restructuring of the state, and explores its links to broader economic and industrial policy goals, ideas and thinking. The analysis depicts European communications as a field of contestation where the actual balance of interests has varied over the years and with differing visions being supported by different parts of the industry, national governments and European institutions.

Existing accounts are sector specific, examining either broadcasting or telecommunications or single issues thereof or offering a normative reading of the EU media policy and the public sphere.[6] A second aim of the book is to offer an up-to-date account of the European governance of both broadcasting and telecommunications and their technological convergence that is currently a major policy theme. In 2002, the EU moved from the regulation of telecommunications to the regulation of electronic communications, covering all networks and associated facilities but leaving outside broadcast content and electronic commerce. This framework is at the time of writing (March 2007) in the process of being revised. Equally, a regulatory framework for all audiovisual media services has been proposed as part of the second review of the Television without Frontiers directive, the principal EU legislative instrument in the field. We will examine how the EU has dealt with the regulation of the technologically converging sectors of broadcasting and telecommunications, the two sectors that arguably present the most contentious regulatory issues and are at the heart of the information revolution.

The available literature emphasizes formal regulation and institutions.[7] However, and this is the third aim of this work, we contend that the opening up of communication markets has been accompanied by changes in not only the level but also the form of regulation. In other words, the character of European governance has evolved through the years. In addition to formal legislative measures, we examine the increasing importance of and reliance on "soft" non-binding policy instruments—such as recommendations, benchmarks, sharing of experiences and best practice models—and "soft" institutions, in particular new transnational groupings of regulators. The analysis explains the rise of such instruments and institutions, and assesses their implications for the governance of communications. It maintains that these newer modes of governance favor policy coordination rather than strict policy convergence. Another notable and related change in European governance that has been overlooked concerns the role of the European Commission, in particular its transformation from direct planner to enabler and supporter of other modes of governance. We argue that this change and the associated reassessment of policy instruments are the result of the failures and limitations of the former hierarchical command-and-control system of governance as well as the result of broader political economy transformations embedded in the process of globalization.

UNDERSTANDING GOVERNANCE

Governance is a concept that has been the subject of many debates, especially from the 1980s onward, in a variety of social sciences disciplines.[8] Still, there is not one agreed definition. Rather uses vary from "good governance" as coined by the World Bank to stress prudent fiscal policies and an array of reforms as preconditions for the promotion of the private sector and sustainable development, to the minimal state, corporate governance, and the new public management, to mention a few.[9]

Even within the discipline of political science there are differences in the debate on governance. From an international relations perspective, "governance without government" refers to the efforts toward cooperation of collectivities in an anarchic international system that lacks a locus of power but is characterized by a complex web of interdependencies.[10] From a comparative politics perspective, governance has been associated with explorations within the theory of the state, mainly in Germany, and the shift of analytical focus away from the functionalist imperatives of state actions to the actual actors involved in governing—but also with developments in public administration, notably in Britain, where Rhodes, for instance, uses governance to refer to the "hollowing out" of the state, namely the decline of central authority and the concomitant rise of self-organizing and resource-dependent networks.[11]

Despite the diversity of uses, there is one common element. The notion of governance denotes changes "in the nature of the state." This transformation of statehood refers to changes in politics (actor constellations and power relations, for instance, the involvement of and balance between public and private actors), polity (institutional structures, for instance, the degree to which interactions among policy actors and associated procedures are institutionalized) and policy (instruments, for instance, legal bindingness and presence of sanctions).[12]

From a political economy perspective, governance refers to "the steering capacities of a political system."[13] It involves actors and institutions other than the state, including markets, hierarchies (e.g., firm) and networks comprising various combinations of public and private actors. In this broad sense, and contrasting the understandings above, governance is not a new phenomenon. Rather, different modes of governance have always characterized the global economy of modern times; "[w]hat has changed has been the balance between them, and the territorial and political circumstances in which they have operated."[14]

This study adopts the political economy understanding of governance as steering for four main reasons. First and foremost, a political economy perspective situates governance into broader transformations of capitalism and the modern state. For instance, Gamble explains that the progressive ascendancy of the neoliberal constitution since the 1970s, which culminated in the 1990s, altered the role of the state from direct administration to regulation while it strengthened the importance of other modes of governance such as markets. The state is still expected to assume "an active role" but now it is perceived more as an enabler and less as planner, acting to facilitate and support, rather than direct, other modes of governance.[15] It is argued here that it is only when governance is embedded in an analytical framework that it makes sense. This wider context of transformations and its relevance to European governance is analyzed below.

Second, from a political economy view, governance is neither associated with nor prioritizes specific agents (public or private), structures (formal or informal) or arenas (e.g., national—European). It makes no assumptions as to who does the governing, how and where. Governance includes not just hierarchical top-down legislation but also soft policy measures (e.g., recommendations) and light institutional arrangements (e.g., groupings of national regulators). Governance is agnostic on the outcome of the process and, in what interests us, does not *ipso facto* assume that European governance arrangements operate at the expense of domestic arrangements and vice versa. Rather governance is an uneven, multi-dimensional process and it is not necessary for all dimensions to move together.

Third, governance is not a static condition but an evolving process characterized by particular combinations of the main forms of governance. Indeed, as this study demonstrates, governance arrangements, structures and instruments have varied over time as well as across and within the examined sectors. And when we talk about greater reliance on "new" non-legislative forms in the current phase of European governance of communication, "new" should be interpreted in relative not absolute terms.

Finally, and closely related, a political economy perspective of governance has also the benefit of moving beyond a state versus market interpretation since all major modes of governance are always present albeit in different configurations. Contra neoliberal thinking, therefore, here markets are conceptualized "not [as] natural phenomena but [. . . as] politically constructed and politically maintained."[16] An illustrative example of markets as constructs comes from the 2002 EU regulatory framework of electronic communications, which correlates the degree of regulation to the degree of competition in a relevant market. Its starting point, the definition of markets, was a highly contested issue. The degree of competition in the market—the trigger for regulatory intervention—clearly differs depending on how one defines the market. This is why incumbent telecommunications operators, in contrast to new market entrants, were favoring a wide definition of the nascent broadband market with important implications for the need or not for regulatory intervention (chapter 6).

꙳

THE GOVERNANCE TURN IN EUROPEAN STUDIES

In the field of European studies, the notion of governance emerged in the 1980s in response to developments in the progress of European integration, in particular the launch of the single market project and the associated rise of European policy-making. The so-called governance turn came to underline the interpenetration and interdependency of the European and (sub)national spheres, though somewhat overlooking wider international forces.[17]

The governance approach is not a single coherent theoretical proposition but rather brings together various analytical perspectives. The most representative perspective among them is the understanding of the EU as a system of multilevel governance associated with Gary Marks who, in his study of structural policy, drew attention to subnational actors and their potential in establishing direct links not just with their counterparts in other member states but also with European institutions, thereby undermining national governments.[18] Other perspectives describe the EU as a system of "supranational" or "network" governance. According to the former, the EU represents a series of distinct sectoral policy regimes, rather than a single one, in turn the result of intense cross-border transactions as well as the actions of EU institutions.[19] According to the latter, the EU is a unique political system, and "network governance," referring to the dispersed network character of EU policy-making with no clear center, is its most notable feature.[20] It follows that, like the first one, these two latter governance perspectives assume the weakening of the state.

Another strand of governance analyzes the EU as a "regulatory state." The rise of regulation at the European level, associated with the work of Giandomenico Majone, has been understood mainly in the context of the institutional peculiarities of the EU. Using Lowi's well-known categorization of policies, Majone has tried to explain the considerable regulatory activity at the European level.[21] He attributes the regulatory bias of the European Commission to five main factors. First, unlike (re)distributive policies, regulation does not require significant administrative and financial resources. Regulatory policies are therefore ideal for the under-staffed and financially under resourced European Commission. Second, under such constraints, regulation is a highly effective means for the entrepreneurial Commission to increase her powers. Third, transnational actors prefer a common regulatory framework rather than an array of disparate, and probably incompatible, national rules. Thus, multinational actors (e.g., large scale firms) support in principle the expansion of the Commission's regulatory competence at the expense of member states' competence. Fourth, the poor credibility of intergovernmental agreements explains why national governments are willing to delegate regulatory authority to the Commission although, finally, the highly technocratic nature of regulatory policy makes this not an unconditional but rather a cautious delegation since the Commission has to cooperate with national experts to gain access to knowledge and information.

Majone's explanation of the considerable increase in the regulatory competence of the European Commission is highly relevant to our argument in that it implies the continuing, rather than diminishing, importance of the national state. Nevertheless, instead of understanding the rise of regulation at the EU level as primarily due to its institutional peculiarities, here it is viewed as a distinct mode of governance embedded in broader transformations, as the next section analyzes.[22]

This view contrasts with narrow economic understandings of regulation that perceive it as the imposition of rules aimed at promoting public policy goals, such as public safety and at correcting market failures, such as economies of scale and scope, abuse of market power, information asymmetries, and externalities.[23] In essence, an economic perspective proclaims regulation to be "in the public interest" and depicts it as a positive-sum game, as opposed to (re)distributive policies which are inherently zero-sum. It further suggests that regulation is an ephemeral phenomenon that will wither away once competition has been effectively established in the market, public policy objectives have been achieved and there no longer are any market failures.

The view of regulation as a mode of governance also qualifies the critique on Majone's account of the EU as a regulatory state on the ground that it cannot explain the failure of the Commission to regulate highly political issues such as media ownership.[24] Be that as it may, the singling out of specific "political" cases suggests that regulatory policy, as per Majone, is effectively synonymous with technocratic policy in a way that obfuscates the distributive consequences of regulation. Contrasting the economic and technocratic perspectives and their underlying functionalist rationale, this study understands regulation as "part of a political process."[25] It defines and (re)structures markets, influences outcomes, affects the balance of power and has distributional implications as to who wins and who loses. It is neither neutral nor objective but defines, to borrow Lasswell's famous questions, "Who gets what, when and how?"[26]

Despite their differences, the brief exposition of key governance perspectives suggests that they all share one core aim. They all aim to transcend the hitherto dominant explanatory models of European integration from the field of international relations and overcome the long-standing dichotomy between supranational and intergovernmental interpretations that focused on the question of national sovereignty—as if it ever existed as more than an ideal and a legal concept—and, in particular, on whether European integration strengthens (intergovernmentalism) or weakens (neofunctionalism) member states.[27] The so-called governance turn in European studies has signalled a disaggregation of analysis as attention moved away from the question of "why integration?," its drivers and nature, to the study of specific policy domains and everyday politics.[28] Governance has come to highlight the growing incorporation of primarily business interests into the European policy process since the 1980s, thereby challenging the previous view of integration as the exclusive domain of national governments and European institutions. Indeed, as we will see, the European Round Table of industrialists and the Big Twelve forum of leading European firms in electronics and information technology, both formed in the 1980s, came to challenge the tight nexus between national governments and the EU, and were instrumental in promoting European integration and in shaping its character (chapter 4).

The fact that the EU neither is a state nor has a government has helped the notion of governance to progressively gain greater prominence in European studies and policy discourse.[29] But whereas in the 1980s, the term governance was used primarily as an argument against traditional state-centric explanations of European integration, increasingly since the late 1990s, "new governance" has come to denote growing reliance on flexible voluntary forms of governance and networks bringing together public and private actors aiming at socialization, sharing of experiences and identification of best practice.[30] In the early 2000s, under the newly appointed European Commission President Romano Prodi, the notion of governance was officially put on the EU agenda in response to the rigidities of the "old" formal hierarchical governance and as part of the major rethink of European integration in the post-single market post–Cold War era.[31] The rise of flexible governance instruments has been a key element of the Commission's efforts to improve EU governance, although it interprets governance narrowly to refer to procedural elements such as increased transparency, openness, consultation, accountability and effectiveness of policy-making rather than to broader substantial aspects in terms of a demos.

Hix has criticized governance approaches for treating the EU as a unique case, the study of which requires a *sui generis* theory.[32] Nevertheless, various governance studies apply and refine theoretical explanations and concepts from the fields of comparative politics and public policy and in doing so counter the parochialism of much of the European studies field. Similar to "governance" research at the national level, European governance studies too have drawn on new institutionalism to stress the importance of institutions and on actor-based concepts, notably policy networks.[33]

Separately and more recently, other studies have aimed to widen European studies by explicitly taking into account the broader international context. Two main lines of inquiry can be identified here. One analytical strand has been to examine the relationship between European integration and globalization.[34] A second strand studies the EU from primarily a critical international political economy perspective.[35] Both these theoretical explorations highlight the interrelationship between domestic, European and international developments.

The present study aims to add to research that challenges state-centric accounts and the insularity of much of the European studies literature. Hence, while the concept of governance is useful in that it brings attention to the plurality of coordination structures where there is no clear hierarchy but rather a complex system of often overlapping structures with different functional and territorial jurisdictions, left at that, governance turns out to be a primarily descriptive rather than analytical concept. To address this, we adopt the political economy conceptualization of governance as steering and place the process of European governance of communications in the context of more general developments concerning the political economy of capitalism and the modern state. This analytical framework can capture the dynamism of European governance, explain its evolution and also reflect on its democratic and legitimation aspects.

GOVERNANCE IN THE EUROPEAN REGULATORY STATE

Instead of understanding the rise of regulation at the EU level as primarily due to its institutional peculiarities, this study embeds it in wider developments in global capitalism, in particular the crisis of Keynesianism, the advent of the national regulatory state and growing economic globalization. Two main arguments follow from this. First, the main contestation in European governance has to do with its form and character rather than its level. And second, European governance exhibits and, at the same time, reinforces the fundamental problem of governmentality characterizing the national state, in particular the bias in favor of output as opposed to input legitimacy which is, in turn, reflected in the choice of governance instruments. These points are analyzed in turn.

Focusing on general transformations in capitalism and the modern state, Jessop identifies two main European state forms. The Keynesian welfare national state, dominant from the 1950s until the 1970s, was closely linked to the fordist model of mass production and consumption. It was an interventionist state aiming at promoting economic growth and, at the same time, securing full employment in a relatively closed national economy primarily through demand-side policies and infrastructural provision.[36] This state form came under pressure beginning in the mid-1970s and increasingly through the 1980s. Mounting skepticism about the ability of the state to deal with the tasks it was facing contributed to the ascendancy of the "government failure" discourse.[37] The state was perceived as being "overloaded" and a feeling of "ungovernability" began to sink in.[38] Growing economic interdependence, the rise of neoliberal ideology, the deregulation of capital markets in the 1980s and the attendant process of economic globalization together with a worsening fiscal climate in the 1980s and 1990s for many advanced economies compounded this feeling. In response, the positive, actively interventionist and protectionist national state transformed into the regulatory enabling and internationalizing state.

This transformation refers to changes of emphases in state responsibilities. Although variations in national capitalist economic systems and regulatory states remain, the point is that from the 1980s onward, the state in advanced Western European countries has moved away from directly producing and supplying goods and services to regulating their provision by private competing suppliers.[39] In the field of telecommunications, for example, the positive interventionist state was typically the monopolist provider of infrastructure, customer equipment and services. With the shift to the regulatory state, former publicly owned telecommunications operators have been privatized, the market has been gradually opened up to competition and regulatory reform has taken place.[40] It is worth stressing that to point out that in certain domains state power has eroded is different from saying that it is powerless or about to retreat or even that it is less interventionist.[41]

Significantly, under the new state form, the relationship of the state to the international political economy has altered too. Cox explains:

> Formerly, the state's role was conceived as bulwark or buffer protecting the domestic economy from harmful exogenous influences. Latterly [in the last half of the twentieth century], the state's role has been understood more as helping to adjust the domestic economy to the perceived exigencies of the world economy. "Competitiveness" is the key word indicative of this shift in perspective.[42]

Cox calls this new enabling role the internationalization of the state. This understanding is similar to Cerny's "competition state," a state that is increasingly concerned with international competitiveness, with "promoting the competitive advantages of particular production and service sectors in a more open and integrated world economy."[43] Jessop takes this point further and talks of the emergence of a specifically Schumpeterian version of the competition state.[44] The emphasis of this new state form on innovation and related new understandings about economic growth and competitive advantage (chapters 3–6) have contributed to raise the political saliency of information and communication technology. At the heart of the competitiveness discourse is the notion of the information society—for Garnham the dominant ideology of our times—and, more generally, the adoption of technological advances by societies.[45]

Hence, in contrast to the multilevel, supranational and network governance notions, in this study European governance is associated with the transformation not the decline of the state. Changes in state forms and the related processes of regionalism and globalization are all seen as part of the modern capitalist state's efforts to survive and accommodate capital accumulation. We agree with Armstrong and Bulmer who, in their study of the European single market, understand "governance beyond the state [. . . as] a response to the inability of traditional formal state institutions to manage the size and complexity of tasks facing them."[46] Similarly, Scharpf explains the rise of European governance and the evolution of integration on the basis of the decreasing problem-solving capacity of national governments and their inability to promote efficiency.[47]

States are increasingly competing "for the means to create wealth within their territory."[48] The problem is that in this process states have arguably become more efficient, and they have therefore managed to fend off a possible system crisis, but, at the same time, their legitimacy has increasingly come under question.[49] "Output-oriented effectiveness (government for the people)" has been advanced at the expense of "input-oriented authenticity" (government by the people)."[50] Put differently, the emphasis is on policy "outcome legitimacy" rather than "process legitimacy."[51]

In turn, the prioritization of the economic over the political sphere has contributed to the marginalization of non-economic interests and considerations since these cannot establish a strong direct link to the overriding objective of economic wealth creation.[52] The regulatory state accentuates the disjuncture between the economic and political spheres. It involves "the marketization of the state" bringing about a radical alteration in state-society relations by converting the public citizens of the welfare state to private customers in the regulatory state.[53] Ultimately, society "is reduced to an aggregation of competing 'associations of consumer.'"[54] In this context, to borrow from Streeck's study on the European social model and employability, the primary objective of communication policies and universal service measures is the "creation of *equal opportunities for commodification.* [. . . They are policies] of *equal marketability.*"[55] For instance, in the field of digital interactive television in the current European governance phase, competitiveness and innovation are valued higher than interoperability at the level of the consumer, media pluralism and diversity (chapter 6). Vertically integrated commercial broadcasters support proprietary standards which are integral elements of their business models and are willing to promote the interoperability of only commercially attractive services.

This marketization creates tensions between "market" and "social" citizenship. In effect, the former—entailing processes of individualization, privatization and economization—subverts the latter, linked to public, social and communitarian conceptions and practices of citizenship.[56] As Pierre observes,

> the introduction of the concept of the customer opens up the possibility of inequalities between individuals, which essentially run counter to the equal and universalistic entitlements and obligations associated with citizenship.[57]

Indeed, the fundamental contradiction between political equality and economic exclusion in representative democracies within market economies is at the heart of the crisis of governmentality.[58]

The foregoing analysis points to two arguments. First, the broader political economy conceptualization that views the European regulatory state as neither primarily due to the institutional characteristics of the EU nor primarily technocratic in nature, but rather sees European regulation as a mode of governance and its rise and evolution embedded in broader transformations concerning the restructuring of the state and the process of globalization, draws attention to a different aspect of governance. From this perspective, the decisive cleavage has been not the territorial more-or-less Europe but rather what kind of Europe, that is socioeconomic tensions over which values, interests, sectors and issues should be promoted and the power to influence such choices. As Hix remarks, the allocation of values by the EU means that the positions of policy actors relate not only to their views on European integration (at which level to regulate?) but also to their views about specific issues, such as "why" regulate, "what" and "how," intervention versus free markets, public versus private actors.[59] The influence of such value judgments is often neglected in European studies overshadowed by the more emotive question of more-or-less integration.

To argue that conventional socioeconomic conflicts concerning in particular the relationship between state and market provide a better explanation of European governance than explanations focusing on conflicts concerning the division of powers between European-level institutions and member states is, of course, different from arguing that the latter tensions do not exist. Often, different views about the relationship between market and regulation, its necessity and form, entail assumptions about the territorial division of powers between the European and the (sub)national level. The question of regulation in the era of technological convergence between information technology, internet, telecommunications and broadcasting is a case in point (chapters 5 and 6). The proposed European Commission redefinition of markets in the late 1990s, supported by telecommunications and internet interests, aimed to bring the technologically converging sectors under the lightest possible regulatory regime and forego content regulation which, effectively, would have negated public service broadcasting. This regulatory scenario also implied a redistribution of regulatory powers in favor of the EU at the expense of member states.

The second and related main argument is that the rise, contestations and difficulties of European governance all reflect and, at the same time, reinforce the fundamental contradiction of governmentality between output and input legitimacy that characterizes the capitalist state. The tension, though undeniable, between the increasing significance of European governance structures that lack democratic accountability and the continuing importance of the national-state level as the locus of democracy and collective identities is not a specifically "European" problem but rather a symptom of and a contributor to the crisis of the national state, in turn embedded within the broader political economy of capitalism. It is not therefore their European dimension that makes policy issues contentious and difficult to solve. The difference is that, for European countries and policy actors, international

pressures and policy issues have to be negotiated through the European institutional framework as well and the specific opportunities and constraints
that presents. And in this sense, European institutions matter.

Like the national level, at the European level there is an attempt to redefine and prioritize the "economic" at the expense of the "political" whereby
the "economic" is projected as objective, neutral and technocratic. For Sbragia, the EU acts as a "coxswain." It

> governs in the sense of 'steering' because it is structurally designed [to keep]
> certain substantive questions off the table while insisting that others be kept
> on the table.[60]

Regulation as a mode of European governance is largely of an economic,
negative integration kind (breaking down market barriers) and is biased in
favor of economic actors interested in international competitiveness and
the creation of the internal market.[61] Regulatory governance has reinforced
"[t]he predominance of interest-driven, élite-level politics."[62] Non-economic issues, such as media pluralism and ownership, typically manage to
get support from European Commission departments with low standing
and the less influential European Parliament to form "'a coalition of the
weak,'" and from politically weaker European organizations such as the
Council of Europe.[63] For Scharpf, the fact that the EU finds it hard to address non-market issues and to adopt (re)distributive policies is related to
its limited legitimation basis. Ironically then, European decisions "are legitimate only because they do in fact respect the limitations of their legitimacy base—which implies that European public policy is, in principle, only
able to deal with a narrower range of problems [. . .] than is generally true
for national polities."[64] Put differently, the marginalization of cultural issues and public service considerations from the EU domain is by design
rather than default and, paradoxically, this makes EU pro-market policies
legitimate.

The present study confirms the argument that European regulatory governance presents substantial opportunities for primarily economic actors to
influence policies, with the caveat that differing economic actors, in alliance
with parts of European institutions, may favor different solutions depending on their position and perceived vulnerabilities in international markets.
Hence, whereas in the 1980s, leading European electronics and information technology firms, still mostly contained within small national
economies, in the face of intensifying international competitive pressures
were seeking direct intervention and protection at the European level and
perceived integration as a shield from the wider globalization process, in
the 1990s European cellular mobile manufacturers and operators, already
integrated in the international market, regarded established European in-

stitutional structures as limiting their global expansion and managed to successfully challenge them. And, similar to Cox's analysis of the changing role and internationalization of the national state mentioned above, at the European level too there has been a shift away from the Commission acting as a direct planner toward acting as an enabler and facilitator. Whereas in the 1980s, the Commission took over former national state roles, adapted to promote European champions and was involved in direct support policies and defensive initiatives (such as collaborative research and development projects, coordinated network planning, common infrastructure and standardization), since the 1990s, the Commission has been acting as an enabler assisting the transformation of European into global champions, as for example in the third generation standards race (chapters 4 and 6). Equally, whereas in the 1980s the Commission acted as an active planner by, for instance, mandating technical standards for analog high-definition satellite television, in the 1990s and early 2000s in the era of digital interactive television, in response to the manifest failure of the former strategy and pressures from technological progress and globalization, the Commission has assumed an enabling role. It no longer dictates standards but rather aims to facilitate the introduction and take-up of new technologies (chapters 5 and 6).

In the post–Cold War order of the 1990s, the accession of many ex-communist countries, the controversy between negative integration (market-creating measures) and positive integration (market-shaping and market-correcting measures), persistently slow economic growth and high unemployment and strong public discontent led the EU to explicitly recognize the importance of public policy objectives and citizens' rights and, among other things, it attempted to safeguard public service broadcasting from the competition and economic imperatives of the EU Treaty (chapter 5). However, and though these considerations managed to enter the EU policy debate in their own right and thus broke with past practice when policy was reactive and centered on negative integration, arguably, the importance of this change is compromised since these considerations have not in effect challenged the substantive policy output of the EU, which has remained premised on competition, economic and trade considerations, all the more important under the current orthodoxy of competitiveness. It is informal governance tools—such as non-binding recommendations, guidelines, declarations, sharing of experiences, benchmarking and dissemination of best practice models—and "transnational regulatory networks" that aim to address the regulatory gap between negative and positive integration (chapter 6).[65]

Soft governance instruments cut across the national-European dichotomy and attempt to promote policy coordination, as opposed to policy convergence, in a complex multilevel system of governance. They are a

means of accommodating diversity as opposed to uniform European policies and one-size-fits-all solutions. Indeed, it is precisely areas that exhibit
strong conflicts, for instance cost methodologies and cost accounting in
telecommunications, that are more amenable to softer governance instruments where agreements are not binding and there are no sanctions for
non-implementation.[66] But the effectiveness of soft governance mechanisms is doubtful precisely because of the presence of strong conflicts of
interest.

The policy coordination model that soft policy tools promote bears
similarities to the notion of framing integration, the weakest Europeanization mechanism identified by Knill and Lehmkul to account for
ways in which European governance may impact upon the domestic
level.[67] Here, European policies neither prescribe policy solutions nor affect domestic political opportunity structures but instead seek to trigger
domestic adjustment indirectly by framing domestic beliefs and expectations. Policy transfer and harmonization take place through socialization,
deliberation, persuasion, learning and cognitive convergence. Framing
policies may prepare the ground for subsequent policy reform, and they
can stimulate support for formal European policy initiatives. Knill and
Lehmkul contrast framing integration to institutional compliance associated with prescriptive EU policy measures typically, though not exclusively, pronounced in policies of positive integration (market-shaping or
market-correcting policies), which stipulate outcomes, imply coercion
and require top-down enforcement. The third and last Europeanization
mechanism refers to changes in domestic opportunity structures and relates to, in particular, negative integration (market-making policies).
Rather than prescribing a distinct policy model, market-making policies
exclude certain policy options, for instance monopoly rights, and domestic administrative and technical rules that hinder the functioning of the
internal market. European governance output addressing public policy
objectives and non-economic considerations has increased, but that is
based on the weakest Europeanization mechanism.

In sum, this study argues that the emergence of the European regulatory
state is inextricably bound up with the rise of the national regulatory state,
itself part of broader transformations in the political economy of capitalism, in a process that is still evolving. European governance is understood
in the context of the constant adaptation, rather than decline, of the modern state. It accentuates the problem of governmentality since it cannot fully
compensate for the loss of the policy-making capacities of the national state
in the face of internationalization and is biased toward market-creating
measures (negative integration) as opposed to market-correcting and -shap-
ing measures (positive integration).

IDEAS AND DISCOURSE MATTER

Although, as explained, regulation is political, its portrayal as *a*political, technocratic and objective enhances its chances of being accepted. Ideas and discourse play an important role in justifying and legitimating regulatory (non)intervention in markets. The rise of neoliberalism increasingly since the 1980s, strongly identified with the Reagan Administration in the USA and the Thatcher government in Britain, and calls for more market — less state, spread rapidly internationally, creating a so-called bandwagon effect, and contributed to a radical privatization and pro-competition policy reform program. Neoliberal ideology has greatly influenced reforms in the media and telecommunications sectors.[68] International institutions, including the Organization for Economic Cooperation and Development and, as this study demonstrates, the EU, played an important role in the diffusion and legitimation of the neoliberal policy paradigm.

However, it is not just neoliberal ideology that has influenced the restructuring of communication markets and their European governance. Drawing on constructivist insights, we attempt to understand how new theoretical understandings about economic growth and industrial policy have helped shape European policy discourse and reform, and how they have been endorsed by various economic and institutional interests to promote their own agendas.

Constructivist insights direct attention to the role of ideas, discourses, knowledge and beliefs and the construction of reality, in ways that add to the credibility and acceptability of proposed measures, making them appear as commonsensical, often phrased in technocratic and deterministic terms, and thus neutral, obscuring winners and losers. The deterministic framing is used to disguise the real interests behind such policy proposals. But ideas are not neutral. They reflect specific interests and can help legitimate certain policy options put forward over others. Ideas, therefore, "have important distributional consequences in influencing problem definition and policy outcomes."[69] In turn

> [t]he discourse serves to alter perceptions and influence preferences through cognitive arguments about the logic and necessity of new policies in the face of the failures of the previous ones and normative appeal to values [. . .] that suggest why the new policies are not only sound but appropriate.[70]

Very often the proposed course of (in)action is presented as technology-driven, non-negotiable and thus unavoidable. The technical nature of telecommunications has often helped the European Commission to put forward policy and regulatory proposals in ostensibly neutral terms.[71] The Commission uses access to knowledge and scientific expertise to increase its legitimacy and to be seen as "independent," what Héritier has called "policy making by subterfuge."[72] This de-politicizing practice strengthens the inevitability of the proposed policy reform and moderates associated political responsibility. The more technical a particular issue, the more influential an "epistemic community" of experts can be and the more susceptible to "capture" by it the Commission becomes.[73] For instance, similar to the debate in the late 1990s (chapter 5), in 2006 and early 2007 during the second review of the Television without Frontiers directive, technological convergence was again used by telecommunications/internet interests and certain parts of the European Commission as an argument to forego regulatory intervention in the emerging electronic communications era (chapter 6).

Besides ideas and discourse, social constructivists are also interested in how the external and internal spheres interlink.[74] This is in contrast to mainstream rationalist accounts, which depict the external environment as a given structure, overlooking the actors and their interests behind its formation and, ultimately, the dialectical relationship between the two, structure and agency. Rationalist explanations take the external environment for granted and are interested in how actors react to it. The conceptualization of the external sphere as an independent, powerful force serves to politically neutralize responses by portraying, for example, technological advances and globalization as "processes[es] to which no actors are linked."[75] Indeed, the interests that stand to benefit from such conceptualizations are best served by a strong delineation of the internal and the external spheres whereby the latter is construed as irrefutable.

Unlike rationalist accounts, social constructivists are interested in how the external context might constitute actors' interests and preferences—in this sense, interests and preferences are not exogenous but endogenous—and in turn how these interests and preferences may contribute to shape the external environment. For social constructivists the external (e.g., globalization) is neither given nor structural. Rather, there is a dialectical relationship between the internal and the external.[76]

Hence, although European integration itself and associated policies are shaped by the wider process of economic internationalization, it would be wrong to conclude that European organizations and their institutions simply react to exogenous forces. In this study, institutions are not construed simply as conditioning structures but also as actors in their own right who can in turn shape structures.[77] The very process of Europeanization influences the process of globalization. The relationship between the EU and broader transformations is not a linear one whereby Europe passively adapts. Rather, as will be examined, at times the EU has accommodated (telecommunications) and at others it has resisted (audiovisual) the process of globalization.

In many cases, an "external threat" has played a key role in calls for European common action. In the technology gap discourse from the 1960s until the 1980s, the "Other"—U.S. computing and data processing firms subsequently joined by the Japanese consumer electronics industry—helped justify common European research collaborative projects, infrastructure initiatives and coordinated network planning in the context of the European single market. But as the analysis will demonstrate, this construction of the external environment served the interests of specific economic (ICT manufacturers and monopolist telecommunications operators) and institutional (parts of the European Commission) actors.

More recently, the competitiveness gap discourse, closely linked to information society/knowledge economy visions, has been used by various economic actors to advocate solutions to this external "threat" that promote their narrow interests. It is in this sense, as constructivist insights explain, that the external becomes an important element in the construction of actors' interests and preferences. Thus, incumbent fixed telecommunications operators have taken advantage of the dominant orthodoxy of competitiveness and called for the rollback of regulatory obligations that require them to share their infrastructure with new market entrants in exchange for investing in new broadband networks perceived as key contributors to Europe's economic growth. Opposition to regulatory intervention by appeals to the ultimate values of innovation and competitiveness, understood in Schumpeterian terms, actually implies the foreclosure of competition, at least for the short term.

The current orthodoxy of competitiveness, therefore, should not obscure the fact that the very concept of competitiveness and its drivers are contested and that, on the basis of different, even conflicting, definitions of problems, different solutions are put forward (chapter 6). Various interests appeal to the same values but for different purposes. For some innovation and competitiveness demand regulatory intervention, while for others such intervention serves only to stifle them. It is suggested here that competitiveness policies may still be associated with efforts to support specific industries and/or market players and are not synonymous with non-intervention and free markets and trade.

Overall, the construction of the external environment and associated official discourse, in particular the emphasis on real (or perceived) threats of economic, industrial and/or cultural nature, have facilitated the constitution of a "European"—be it technological, industrial, economic or audiovisual/cultural—space and, in turn, have served to justify European-level action. In these constructions, it does not so much matter whether the perceived threats are "real" as long as they can be portrayed as given "external" threats which demand European-level action. The external environment is depicted as objective and as such constraining the available policy options. The aim is to conceal not only the interests behind such conceptualizations but also the contestations that each and every conceptualization contains. We thus agree with Stråth, for whom

> Europe is a discourse which is translated into a political and ideological project [. . .] Both as politics and ideology, Europe must be seen in the plural, always contested and contradictory.[78]

In this study then the external environment and "Europe" are construed not as conditioning structures but rather as arenas of contestation with competing claims made upon them.

THE PLAN OF THE BOOK

This chapter has set out the analytical framework of the book on which the ensuing chapters are based. The empirical part demonstrates that the European governance of communications has always been a space of contestation and provides explanations for its changing character. It relies principally on primary sources from the 1940s onward, insights from participant observation in policy consultations, informal discussions and twenty-five semi-structured interviews conducted since the 1990s with key national and international policy officials and stakeholders.

The organization of the material and the arguments put forward are developed along two dimensions: chronologically and thematically. This is for analytical purposes. As is usually the case, the delineation of different periods and the separation of different themes are largely artificial. In practice, the various periods and threads have been intimately interwoven.

Chapter 2 traces the roots of (West) European-level cooperation in the field of communications in the postwar order, covering the period from the late 1940s to the 1960s. The analysis is placed within the broader postwar international context, in particular the emergence of the USA as the hegemonic power in the West having a direct influence over European postwar reconstruction, the onset of the Cold War and the ensuing dense framework of institutional multilateralism witnessed in Western Europe. From the start, European cooperation was riddled with divisions. The chapter shows how these divisions had less to do with the communications sector as such and more with fundamental political and economic questions concerning the very need for, character and purpose of any cooperation scheme. This period witnessed the establishment of the main politico-economic and professional European organizations, the same ones that continue to shape, albeit with differing powers, the European communications scene today. At the time, European-level cooperation in the fields of television and telecommunications was confined to cross-border technical, commercial and operational matters. The loose professional character of the established arrangements among national (near) monopolist organizations under state control resonated with the nationally based communications order.

Chapter 3 examines developments during the crisis years from the late 1960s throughout the 1970s. The turmoil in international political economy, the levelling out of the postwar economic boom and new explanations about the drivers of economic growth against the background of fast technological advances served to highlight Europe's weakness in high technologies. Concerns about technological disparities between Europe and the USA in particular soon gave way to the technological gap discourse, which was used as an argument in favor of European collaboration. The chapter argues that the EU was called upon to intervene in general industrial and economic affairs and define a European identity in response to the upheaval in the postwar international order and the crisis of the national Keynesian model of socioeconomic management. The chapter assesses the EU's attempts to deal with the (inter)national crisis and the difficulties it encountered due to its own politico-institutional problems, lack of powers, the rise in national protectionism and, importantly, the absence of either political or industrial support. Responses were reactive, and although the EU initiatives did not result in concrete action, they were important in that they allowed the EU to discover the field of telecommunications and, quite independently, that of television.

Chapter 4 documents the emergence of the EU as an actor in ICT against growing economic, trade and commercial considerations. The period from the late 1970s to the mid-/late 1980s is the period of defensive Europeanization. Intensifying competitive pressures from the USA and South East Asia, the rising political saliency of ICT and the inadequacy of disparate nationally based solutions contributed to a climate favorable to European-level solutions. Industrialists, many from the ICT sector, feeling increasingly vulnerable in the context of new technologies and globalizing market conditions, turned to Europe and saw in the creation of the single market—to be premised on internal liberalization, active industrial policy and temporary external trade protection—the answer to their own decline. The move of emphasis from national to European champions reinvigorated the integration process. The chapter argues that the EU was able to play an interventionist industrial policy role—a role formerly assumed by national states alone—precisely because it served to promote and defend the interests of established market players. In contrast to the previous period, EU technology-push initiatives now had the strong support of the existing interests in the fields of ICT (major European information technology and electronics manufacturers), telecommunications (PTTs) and television (public service broadcasters), that is, the interests feeling most threatened by the new techno-economic developments. The chapter finally examines the contradictions surrounding the first pan-European television initiatives pursued at the same time for democratic, industrial and cultural aims.

Chapter 5 explores the period from the mid-1980s to the late 1990s, the most intensive one in terms of market restructuring, regulatory reform and Europeanization of communication policies. It examines the role of political economy factors and shows how these were mediated through institutional parameters. Market restructuring brought to the fore the fundamental contestation concerning the balance between state and market, and the conflict between the neomercantilist (chapter 4) and neoliberal visions of the single market, each with its own supporters within the industry, national governments and European institutions. These two visions came to a head in the 1990s but, as the chapter demonstrates, neither faction prevailed. The chapter documents the rise of the European regulatory state based on prescriptive rules, although more so in telecommunications than in television, and assesses its limits and implementation. It shows how the procompetitive policy turn came to challenge the former mutually supportive relationship between (parts of) the European Commission and established interests and examines the role of EU competition rules in that process. With the collapse of communism, the European Broadcasting Union and the Council of Europe, emphasizing the cultural and democratic aspects of the media, regained importance, challenging the EU's mainly economically focused regulatory output. Within the EU context, during the 1990s, the overall emphasis on market-creating rules was somewhat redressed through the explicit recognition of the importance of public service objectives and the move toward a civic conceptualization of European citizenship and identity. Still, the chapter points to the imbalance in governance whereby legally binding and enforceable measures support market-making policies while informal non-binding measures are used for market-shaping and market-correcting policy areas. The reemergence of the information society metaphor, the technological convergence between telecommunications and the media and the move to a competitiveness industrial policy served to further stress the importance of market-making measures, and to move the policy agenda toward infrastructure and telecommunications related issues and away from politically sensitive broadcasting and cultural concerns.

Chapter 6 investigates the latest and current phase of European governance of communications from the late 1990s till early 2007, characterized by growing globalization and technological convergence. It critically assesses the rising political saliency of competitiveness and its endorsement as the new EU strategic goal. It shows that while defining and measuring productivity and competitiveness remain controversial, various interests within the electronic communications sector use the dominant orthodoxy of competitiveness to promote their own narrow interests. The chapter argues that the latest phase in European governance of communications is characterized by two main trends. First, a move away from prescriptive sector-specific toward sector-neutral (horizontal) regulation, including greater reliance on general competition rules. It explains that this "move" has been relatively easier in relation to electronic communications infrastructure compared to audiovisual content and services. Yet, as the analysis of the 2002 electronic communications regulatory framework demonstrates, increased emphasis on competition rules does not make regulation less controversial or less burdensome. The chapter also examines the growing resort by commercial interests to the EU state aid rules to challenge the expansion of public service broadcasters into online and neighboring activities in order to assess the role and impact of the EU competition rules upon public services which are all the more important in the absence of distinct positive rules. The second trend characterizing the current phase of European governance of communications is greater reliance on less formal policy instruments and transnational regulatory groupings. The chapter discusses their role in relation to harmonization. It argues that although the greater flexibility afforded is more conducive to policy coordination as opposed to strict policy convergence, paradoxically, this flexibility, by allowing member states to adjust regulatory responses to national circumstances, may increase the legitimacy of the new regulatory regime. The last section of the chapter turns to examine by means of three selected examples some of the main challenges in the latest phase of European governance of communications. The focus is on the new enabling role of the Commission in the context of the increased political salience of competitiveness, the tension in the age of technological convergence surrounding the artificial distinction between the regulation of infrastructure and associated services at the European level and the regulation of content at the national level, and on ways in which the broader process of globalization and the international aspirations of European economic interests may impact upon the structures of European governance and limit EU-level regulatory intervention.

The concluding chapter summarizes the main arguments and contributions of the study and assesses recent developments in the European governance of communications, focusing on its character, impact so far and questions of legitimacy.

NOTES

1. For simplicity and consistency we use throughout the book the term European Union (EU), even though it formally came into being in 1992 with the Treaty on

European Union, commonly known as the Maastricht Treaty, except where specific reference needs to be made to individual European Communities.

2. For an overview see OECD, *Telecommunication Regulatory Institutional Structures and Responsibilities*, DSTI/ICCP/TISP(2005)6/FINAL (Paris: OECD, 2006).

3. ITU, "West African Regulators Agree on Common Regulatory Framework: Region Takes a Big Step Towards a Common ICT Market," *ITU Press Release* (7 October 2005) <http://www.itu.int> (10 Oct. 2005).

4. Willem Hulsink, *Privatisation and Liberalisation in European Telecommunications: Comparing Britain, the Netherlands and France* (London and New York: Routledge, 1999). Giorgio Natalicchi, *Wiring Europe: Reshaping the European Telecommunications Regime* (Lanham, Md., and Oxford: Rowman & Littlefield, 2001). Mark Thatcher, *The Politics of Telecommunications: National Institutions, Convergence and Change* (Oxford: Oxford University Press, 1999). David Levy, *Europe's Digital Revolution: Broadcasting Regulation, the EU and the Nation State* (London and New York: Routledge, 1999). Alison Harcourt, *The European Union and the Regulation of Media Markets* (Manchester: Manchester University Press, 2005).

5. Though see Peter Humphreys and Seamus Simpson, *Globalisation, Convergence and European Telecommunications Regulation* (Cheltenham and Northampton, Mass.: Edward Elgar, 2005).

6. See respectively: Richard Collins, *Broadcasting and Audio-visual Policy in the Single European Market* (London: John Libbey, 1994). Kjell A. Eliassen and Marit Sjøvaag, eds., *European Telecommunications Liberalisation* (London and New York: Routledge, 1999). Daniel Krebber, *Europeanisation of Regulatory Television Policy: The Decision-making Process of the Television without Frontiers Directives from 1989 & 1997* (Baden-Baden: Nomos Verlagsgesellschaft, 2002). Shalini Venturelli, *Liberalizing the European Media: Politics, Regulation, and the Public Sphere* (Oxford, New York: Clarendon Press; 1998). David Ward, *The European Union Democratic Deficit and the Public Sphere: An Evaluation of EU Media Policy* (Amsterdam and Oxford: IOS Press, 2002).

7. Though see Harcourt, *The European* and Humphreys and Simpson, *Globalisation*.

8. See Jon Pierre, ed., *Debating Governance: Authority, Steering, and Democracy* (Oxford and New York: Oxford University Press, 2000). Martin Hewson and Timothy J. Sinclair, eds., *Approaches to Global Governance Theory* (New York: State University of New York Press, 1999). Kees van Waarden and Frans van Waarden, "'Governance' as a Bridge between Disciplines: Cross-disciplinary Inspiration Regarding Shifts in Governance and Problems of Governability, Accountability and Legitimacy," *European Journal of Political Research* 43 (2004): 143–71.

9. World Bank, *Governance and Development* (Washington, D.C.: World Bank, 1992). R. A. W. Rhodes, "Governance and Public Administration," in *Debating Governance. Authority, Steering, and Democracy*, ed. Jon Pierre (Oxford and New York: Oxford University Press, 2000), 54–90.

10. James N. Rosenau and Ernst-Otto Czempiel, eds., *Governance without Government: Order and Change in World Politics* (Cambridge: Cambridge University Press, 1992).

11. Volker Schneider, "State Theory, Governance and the Logic of Regulation and Administrative Control," in *Governance in Europe: The Role of Interest Groups*, ed. Andreas Warntjen and Arndt Wonka (Baden-Baden: Nomos Verlagsgesellschaft, 2004), 25–41. R. A. W. Rhodes, *Understanding Governance: Policy Networks, Governance, Re-*

flexivity and Accountability (Buckingham and Philadelphia: Open University Press, 1997).

12. Oliver Treib, Holger Bähr and Gerda Falkner, "Modes of Governance: Towards a Conceptual Clarification," *Journal of European Public Policy* 14, no. 1 (2007): 3, 1–20. For the communications sector see: Michael Latzer, Natascha Just, Florian Saurwein and Peter Slominski, "Institutional Variety in Communications Regulation. Classification and Empirical Evidence from Austria," *Telecommunications Policy* 30 (2006): 152–70.

13. Andrew Gamble, "Economic Governance," in *Debating Governance: Authority, Steering, and Democracy*, ed. Jon Pierre (Oxford and New York: Oxford University Press, 2000), 110.

14. Gamble, "Economic," 113.

15. Gamble, "Economic," 114.

16. Andrew Gamble, "The New Political Economy," *Political Studies* 43 (1995): 523. See also Charles E. Lindblom, *The Market System: What It Is, How It Works, and What to Make of It* (New Haven and London: Yale University Press, 2001).

17. For useful reviews of the "governance turn" see Markus Jachtenfuchs, "The Governance Approach to European Integration," *Journal of Common Market Studies* 39, no. 2 (2001): 245–64. Beate Kohler-Koch and Berthold Rittberger, "Review Article: The 'Governance Turn' in European Studies," *Journal of Common Market Studies—Annual Review* 44 (2006): 27–49.

18. Gary Marks, "Structural Policy and Multilevel Governance in the EC," in *The State of the European Community. Vol. II: The Maastricht Debates and Beyond*, ed. Alan Cafruny and Glenda Rosenthal (Boulder: Lynne Rienner; Harlow: Longman, 1993), 391–410. See also Liesbet Hooghe and Gary Marks, *Multi-Level Governance and European Integration* (Lanham, Md.: Rowman & Littlefield, 2001).

19. Wayne Sandholtz and Alec Stone Sweet, eds., *European Integration and Supranational Governance* (Oxford: Oxford University Press, 1998).

20. Rainer Eising and Beate Kohler-Koch, "Introduction. Network Governance in the European Union," in *The Transformation of Governance in the European Union*, ed. Beate Kohler-Koch and Rainer Eising. (London and New York: Routledge, 1999), 3–13.

21. Theodore J. Lowi, "American Business, Public Policy, Case Studies and Political Theory," *World Politics* 16, no. 4 (1964): 677–715. Giandomenico Majone, "The Rise of the Regulatory State in Europe," *West European Politics* 17, no. 3 (1994): 77–101. Giandomenico Majone, "The European Commission as Regulator," in *Regulating Europe*, ed. Giandomenico Majone (London: Routledge, 1996), 60–79.

22. For a similar view see Lee McGowan and Helen Wallace, "Towards a European Regulatory State," *Journal of European Public Policy* 3, no. 4 (1996): 560–76.

23. Iain Begg, "Introduction: Regulation in the European Union," *Journal of European Public Policy* 3, no. 4 (1996): 527.

24. See Alison Harcourt and Claudio Radaelli, "Limits to EU Technocratic Regulation?" *European Journal of Political Research* 35 (1999): 107–22. Levy, *Europe's Digital*, 50–59. See also James Caporaso, "The European Union and Forms of State: Westphalian, Regulatory or Post-Modern?" *Journal of Common Market Studies* 34, no. 1 (1996): 29–52.

25. Jill Hills and Maria Michalis, "Restructuring Regulation: Technological Convergence and European Telecommunications and Broadcasting Markets," *Review of International Political Economy* 7, no. 3 (2000): 438.

26. Harold D. Lasswell, *Politics: Who Gets What, When and How* (New York: Peter Smith, 1950 [1936]).

27. Still, although neofunctionalism and intergovernmentalism concentrate on the nature of integration as a whole, both have been extensively applied to examine single case studies which in turn concluded with the vindication of one theory at the expense of the other. For a critique see Susanne K. Schmidt, "Sterile Debates and Dubious Generalisations: European Integration Theory Tested by Telecommunications and Electricity," *Journal of Public Policy* 16, no. 3 (1997): 233–71.

28. For a discussion see John Peterson, "The Choice for EU Theorists: Establishing a Common Framework for Analysis," *European Journal of Political Research* 39 (2001): 289–318.

29. Simon Bulmer, "New Institutionalism and the Governance of the Single European Market," *Journal of European Public Policy* 5, no. 3 (1998), 366.

30. See Burkard Eberlein and Dieter Kerwer, "New Governance in the European Union: A Theoretical Perspective," *Journal of Common Market Studies* 42, no. 1 (2004): 121–42. Susana Borrás and Krestin Jacobsson, "The Open Method of Coordination and New Governance Patterns in the EU," *Journal of European Public Policy* Special issue 11, no. 2 (2004): 185–208. David M. Trubek and James S. Mosher, "New Governance, EU Employment Policy, and the European Social Model," New York University School of Law, Jean Monnet Chair Working Paper 15/01, 2001 <http://www.jeanmonnetprogram.org/papers/01/011501.html> (13 July 2006).

31. See indicatively European Commission, *European Governance: A White Paper*, COM (2001) 428 (Brussels, 25 July 2001).

32. Simon Hix, "The Study of the European Union II: The 'New Governance' Agenda and Its Rival," *Journal of European Public Policy* 5, no. 1 (1998): 38–65. ECSA, "Does the European Union Represent an *n* of 1?" *ECSA Review* X, no. 3 (1997): 1–5, <http://www.eustudies.org/N1debate.htm> (21 Nov. 2003).

33. See indicatively Bulmer, "New Institutionalism," 365–86. J. Jupille and J. A. Caporaso, "Institutionalism and the European Union: Beyond International Relations and Comparative Politics," *Annual Review of Political Science* 2, no. 1 (1999): 429–44. Mark D. Aspinwall and Gerald Schneider, "Same Menu, Separate Tables: The Institutionalist Turn in Political Science and the Study of European Integration," *European Journal of Political Research* 38, no. 1 (2000): 1–36. Paul Pierson, "The Path to European Integration: A Historical Institutionalist Analysis," *Comparative Political Studies* 29, no. 2 (1996): 123–63. Jeremy Richardson, "Actor Based Models of National and EU Policy-Making," in *The European Union and National Industrial Policy*, ed. Hussein Kassim and Anand Menon (London and New York: Routledge, 1996), 26–51. For an application of these concepts to the field of communications, see indicatively Laura Cram, *Policy-Making in the EU: Conceptual Lenses and the Integration Process* (London and New York: Routledge, 1997). Godefroy Dang-Nguyen, Volker Schneider and Raymund Werle, "Networks in European Policy-making: Europeification of Telecommunications Policy," in *Making Policy in Europe: The Europeification of National Policy-making*, ed. Svein S. Andersen and Kjell A. Eliassen (London: Sage, 1993), 93–114. John Peterson, "The European Technol-

ogy Community: Policy Networks in a Supranational Setting," in *Policy Networks in British Government*, ed. David Marsh and R. A. W. Rhodes (Oxford: Oxford University Press, 1992), 226–48.

34. For instance, Marjoleine Hennis, "Europeanization and Globalization: The Missing Link," *Journal of Common Market Studies* 39, no. 5 (2001): 829–50. Helen Wallace, "Europeanisation and Globalisation: Complementary or Contradictory Trends?" *New Political Economy* 5, no. 3 (2000): 369–82.

35. For instance, Bastiaan van Apeldoorn, *Transnational Capitalism and the Struggle over European Integration* (London and New York: Routledge, 2002). Andreas Bieler and Adam David Morton, eds., *Social Forces in the Making of the New Europe: The Restructuring of European Social Relations in the Global Political Economy* (London: Palgrave, 2001). Alan Cafruny and Magnus Ryner, eds., *A Ruined Fortress? Neoliberal Hegemony and Transformation in Europe* (Lanham, Md.: Rowman & Littlefield. 2003). Erik Jones and Amy Verdun, guest eds., "Political Economy and the Study of European Integration," *Journal of European Public Policy* 10, no. 1 (2003).

36. Bob Jessop, "The European Union and Recent Transformations in Statehood," 2004, <http://eprints.lancs.ac.uk/217/02/F-2004g_vienna-state-best.doc> (3 Aug. 2006).

37. Gamble, "Economic," 126.

38. Anthony King, "Overload: Problems of Governing in the 1970s," *Political Studies* 23, nos. 2/3 (1975): 284–96. Michel Crozier, Samuel P. Huntington and Joji Watanuki, *The Crisis of Democracy* (New York: New York University Press, 1975).

39. Harold Seidman and Robert Gilmour, *Politics, Position and Power: From the Positive to the Regulatory State* (4th ed. Oxford: Oxford University Press, 1986), 119. For the variety of capitalisms see indicatively Michel Albert, *Capitalism against Capitalism* (London: Whurr, 1993). Peter A. Hall and David Soskice, *Varieties of Capitalism: The Institutional Foundations of Comparative Advantage* (Oxford: Oxford University Press, 2001). Fritz W. Scharpf, and Vivien Schmidt, eds., *Welfare and Work in the Open Economy, Vol. 2: Diverse Responses to Common Challenges* (Oxford: Oxford University Press, 2000). Mark Thatcher, "Analysing Regulatory Reform in Europe," *Journal of European Public Policy* 9, no. 6 (2002): 859–72. John Zysman, *Governments, Markets, and Growth: Financial Systems and the Politics of Industrial Change* (Ithaca: Cornell University Press, 1983).

40. Edgar Grande, "The New Role of the State in Telecommunications: An International Comparison," *West European Politics* 17, no. 3 (1994): 138–57.

41. Graham Wilson, "In a State?" *Governance: An International Journal of Policy and Administration* 13, no. 2 (2000): 235–42. Alberta Sbragia, "Governance, the State, and the Market: What Is Going On?," *Governance: An International Journal of Policy and Administration* 13, no. 2 (2000): 243–50. Michael Moran, *The British Regulatory State: High Modernism and Hyper-innovation* (Oxford: Oxford University Press, 2003).

42. Robert Cox, "Towards a Post-Hegemonic Conceptualization of World Order: Reflections on the Relevancy of Ibn Khaldun," in *Governance without Government: Order and Change in World Politics*, ed. James N. Rosenau and Ernst-Otto Czempiel (Cambridge: Cambridge University Press, 1992), 143.

43. Philip Cerny, "Structuring the Political Arena. Public Goods, States and Governance in a Globalizing World," in *Global Political Economy: Contemporary Theories*, ed. Ronen Palan (London and New York: Routledge, 2000), 22.

44. Bob Jessop, *The Future of the Capitalist State* (Cambridge: Polity, 2002), 95–139.

45. Nicholas Garnham, "The Information Society Debate Revisited," in *Mass Media and* Society, ed. James Curran and Michael Gurevitch (4th ed. London: Hodder Arnold, 2005): 287–302.

46. Kenneth Armstrong and Simon Bulmer, *The Governance of the Single European Market* (Manchester: Manchester University Press, 1998), 259.

47. Fritz W. Scharpf, *Governing in Europe: Effective and Democratic?* (Oxford: Oxford University Press, 1999).

48. John M. Stopford and Susan Strange with John S. Henley, *Rival States, Rival Firms: Competition for World Market Shares* (Cambridge and New York: Cambridge University Press, 1991), 1.

49. David Held, "Democracy, the Nation-State and the Global System," in *Political Theory Today*, ed. David Held (Cambridge: Polity Press, 1991), 197–235.

50. Scharpf, *Governing*, 2 (emphasis deleted).

51. Sophie Meunier, "Trade Policy and Political Legitimacy in the European Union," *Comparative European Politics* 1, no. 1 (2003): 67–90.

52. Edward S. Cohen, "Globalization and the Boundaries of the State: A Framework for Analyzing the Changing Practice of Sovereignty," *Governance: An International Journal of Policy and Administration* 14, no. 1 (2001): 85. Joel D. Wolfe, "Power and Regulation in Britain," *Political Studies* 47, no. 5 (1999): 905. Stephen Gill, "Constitutionalising Capital: EMU and Disciplinary Neo-Liberalism," in *Social Forces in the Making of the New Europe: The Restructuring of European Social Relations in the Global Political Economy*, ed. Andreas Bieler and Adam David Morton (London: Palgrave, 2000), 47–69.

53. Jon Pierre, "The Marketization of the State: Citizens, Consumers, and the Emergence of the Public Market," in *Governance in a Changing Environment*, ed. Guy B. Peters and Donald J. Savoie (Montreal and Kingston: McGill-Queen's University Press, 1995), 55–81.

54. Cerny, "Structuring," 24.

55. Wolfgang Streeck, "Competitive Solidarity: Rethinking the 'European Social Model,' *Max Planck Institute for the Study of Societies Working Paper*, no. 8 (1999), 6 (original emphasis), <http://www.mpi-fg-koeln.mpg.de/pu/workpap/wp99-8/wp99-8.html> (5 Feb. 2007).

56. Mark Freedland, "The Marketization of Public Services," in *Citizenship, Markets, and the State*, ed. Colin Crouch, Klaus Eder and Damian Tambini (Oxford and New York: Oxford University Press, 2001), 90–110. See also Andrew Calabrese and Jean-Claude Burgleman, eds., *Communication, Citizenship, and Social Policy* (Lanham, MD: Rowman & Littlefield, 1999).

57. Pierre, "The Marketization," 57.

58. David J. Bailey, "Governance or the Crisis of Governmentality? Applying Critical State Theory at the European Level," *Journal of European Public Policy* 13, no. 1 (2006): 16–33.

59. Hix, "The Study," 42–43. Simon Hix, *The Political System of the European Union* (London: Macmillan, 1999), 133–65.

60. Alberta Sbragia, "The European Union as Coxswain: Governance by Steering," in *Debating Governance: Authority, Steering, and Democracy*, ed. Jon Pierre (Oxford and New York: Oxford University Press, 2000), 236.

61. Helen Wallace, "An Institutional Anatomy and Five Policy Modes," in *Policy-Making in the European Union*, ed. Helen Wallace, William Wallace and Mark Pollack (5th ed. Oxford and New York: Oxford University Press, 2005), 81.

62. Bulmer, "New Institutionalism," 381.

63. Rainer Eising and Beate Kohler-Koch, "Governance in the European Union," in *The Transformation of Governance in the European Union*, ed. Beate Kohler-Koch and Rainer Eising (London and New York: Routledge, 1999), 282.

64. Scharpf, *Governing*, 23 (emphasis deleted).

65. Burkard Eberlein and Edgar Grande, "Beyond Delegation: Transnational Regulatory Regimes and the EU Regulatory State," *Journal of European Public Policy* 12, no. 1 (2005): 100.

66. Adrienne Héritier, "New Modes of Governance in Europe: Increasing Political Capacity and Policy Effectiveness?" in *The State of the European Union, 6. Law, Politics, and Society*, ed. Tanja Börzel and Rachel Cichowski (Oxford: Oxford University Press, 2003), 105–26. Martin Rhodes, "The Scientific Objectives of the NEWGOV project. A Revised Framework" (paper presented at the NEWGOV Consortium Conference, Florence, 30 May 2005).

67. Christoph Knill and Dirk Lehmkuhl, "The National Impact of European Union Regulatory Policy: Three Europeanization Mechanisms," *European Journal of Political Research* 41, no. 2 (2002): 255-80. Although they analyze the domestic impact of EU policies, one can widen the concept of Europeanization beyond the EU and easily apply these analytical concepts in relation to other European organizations. This is in line with one of the aims of this book, to contribute to the broadening of European studies.

68. For the influence of neoliberal ideology on European telecommunications policy see Johannes Bauer, "Normative Foundations of Electronic Communications Policy in the European Union," in *Governing Telecommunications and the New Information Society in Europe*, ed. Jacint Jordana (Cheltenham and Northampton, MA: Edward Elgar, 2002), 110–33, and Ian Bartle, "When Institutions No Longer Matter: Reform of Telecommunications and Institutions in Germany, France and Britain," *Journal of Public Policy* 22, no. 1 (2002): 1–27. For the media see Venturelli, *Liberalizing*.

69. J. J. Richardson and R. M. Lindley, "Editorial," *Journal of European Public Policy* 1, no. 1 (1994): 3.

70. Vivien Schmidt, *The Futures of European Capitalism* (Oxford and New York: Oxford University Press, 2002), 66.

71. Peter F. Cowhey, "The International Telecommunications Regime: The Political Roots of Regimes for High Technology," *International Organization* 44, no. 2 (1990): 169–99. Hills and Michalis, "Restructuring."

72. Andrienne Héritier, "Policy-making by Subterfuge: Interest Accommodation, Innovation and Substitute Democratic Legitimation in Europe—Perspectives From Distinct Policy Areas," *Journal of European Public Policy* 4, no. 2 (1997): 171–89.

73. Peter Haas, "Introduction: Epistemic Communities and International Policy Co-ordination," *International Organization* 46, no. 1 (1992): 3.

74. See indicatively Thomas Diez, "Riding the AM-track through Europe; or, The Pitfalls of a Rationalist Journey Through European Integration," *Millennium: Journal of International Studies* 28, no. 2 (1999): 355–69. *Journal of European Public Policy* 6, "Special Issue on Social Constructivism," no. 4 (1999). Colin Hay and Ben Rosamond "Globalization, European Integration and the Discursive Construction of Economic Imperatives," *Journal of European Public Policy* 9, no. 2 (2002): 147–67. Jeffrey Checkel, "Review Article. The Constructivist Turn in International Relations Theory," *World Politics* 50, no. 2 (1998): 324–48.

75. Colin Hay, *Political Analysis: A Critical Introduction* (Basingstoke: Palgrave, 2002), 254.

76. See also Anthony Giddens, *Central Problems of Social Theory: Action, Structure, and Contradiction in Social Analysis* (Basingstoke: Macmillan, 1979). Philip Cerny, *The Changing Architecture of Politics: Structure, Agency, and the Future of the State* (London: Sage, 1990).

77. Ben Rosamond, *Theories of European Integration* (Basingstoke and New York: Palgrave, 2000), 122.

78. Bo Stråth, "Introduction: Europe as a Discourse," in *Europe and the Other and Europe as the Other*, ed. Bo Stråth (Brussels: PIE-Peter Lang, 2000), 14.

2

Origins of European Governance in Communications

The Formative Years (Late 1940s to Late 1960s)

INTRODUCTION

This chapter analyzes the beginning of the European governance process in the field of communications in the postwar period. The origins of European cooperation are generally traced back to a number of initiatives taken in the late 1940s and 1950s. This process, which as will be briefly explained is itself rooted deeper into history than the period examined here, was linked to the broader postwar international context as well as the debate on and the process of European integration.[1]

The postwar European reconstruction effort witnessed the creation of several organizations in almost all spheres of activity. Developments were intergovernmental and riddled with divisions, in particular between those interested in greater politico-economic integration (strongly supported by the USA) and those interested in looser economic cooperation (notably Britain).

This chapter examines the formation and main characteristics of the major European organizations that, since their establishment or subsequently, would become involved in the field of communications. The order is chronological but, as will become clear, developments were intertwined. The chapter explores how these developments were embedded in the broader context of international and European political economy. In particular, three main elements of the postwar order shaped West European developments: the question of Germany and Franco-German relations, the incipient Cold War and the containment of communism and the U.S.

hegemony of the capitalist world. In this light, the chapter explains that within the context of European integration, communications was not a priority sector. In Western Europe at the time, in line with the Keynesian welfare order, telecommunications was considered a natural monopoly and was typically the responsibility of a state-owned public administration, while television was organized nationally along public service broadcasting lines. The limited European-level cooperation arrangements were primarily the result of technical and operational functional necessities. These arrangements would stop at, and not penetrate within, national borders. As such, they did not upset the established nationally based communications order. Still, as this chapter demonstrates, even this narrow technical and functional cooperation was highly contested and political precisely because it was part of the European postwar reconstruction effort whose aims and character were disputed.

U.S. HEGEMONY AND EUROPEAN RECONSTRUCTION

The incipient Cold War in 1946–1947 forced the USA to review its postwar strategy and abandon its initial reluctance to become involved in European reconstruction. The USA shifted away from institutional multilateralism pursued in the immediate aftermath of World War II—through for instance the creation of the United Nations and the Bretton Woods institutions—toward active support of regionalism, especially in Western Europe.[2] Through the creation of regional organizations in every possible sphere, from defense to economic affairs, the USA cemented its hegemony in the capitalist West.

In 1947 two defining episodes in the Cold War formally sealed this change of U.S. strategy. The Truman Doctrine and the European Recovery Program, commonly known as the Marshall plan, committed the USA to active involvement in world, and in particular European, affairs. It was in the U.S. strategic political and economic interests to assume a leading role in European reconstruction and integration since a strong and united ally was essential not just for containing the communist threat from the East but also for eventually providing valuable export markets for American products, thereby sustaining American economic growth.

The Organization for European Economic Cooperation (OEEC), set up in 1948 to help administer the Marshall plan, was, unsurprisingly since it contributed all the funds, effectively controlled by the USA. However, despite U.S. hopes, the OEEC did not become the principal organization in European integration. Resistance from West European countries but also disagreements among them regarding the character of European economic cooperation meant that integration was not going to progress under the auspices of the OEEC.

More specifically, it became evident to the USA that Britain, on which it had primarily placed its hopes, was not interested in, let alone prepared to lead, European integration. Britain, the only non-invaded and undefeated power in Europe, perceived its priorities as not lying with Europe but rather that economically its future lay with the Commonwealth, and strategically and politically with the USA. U.S. hopes were subsequently placed on France.[3] During 1948–1949, the idea of a customs union, first raised by the British but rejected as economically unfavorable, found strong support in France, which was seriously concerned about the emerging sovereign and rapidly growing West German state. Disagreements about the nature of European cooperation eventually led to the economic division of Western Europe, as will be seen.

Besides the Cold War and the hegemony of the USA in the West, strong economic and political drivers and, despite the rhetoric, to a lesser extent idealistic aims, all shaped the process and character of European integration. Postwar revival served to strengthen, not suppress, the national state as the most appropriate form of political organization.[4]

Generally speaking, postwar European reconstruction relied on national Keynesianism and international trade. The U.S. financing of European reconstruction was conditioned on West European cooperation and on free market and trade principles.[5] Nationally, the state assumed a highly interventionist role and became associated with economic growth, cohesion and the provision of social welfare. During the *trente glorieuses*—the thirty glorious years between 1945 and 1975 of unprecedented international economic growth—the national state was consolidated and became the main sphere of political, economic and social action. In turn, the success of national policies put limits to the European integration process, especially to its more ambitious federalist-supranational version.

A major element of U.S. foreign policy was the enhancement of productivity in Western Europe. The export of the commitment to productivity aimed to ensure "the primacy of economics over politics, [and] to de-ideologize issues of political economy into questions of output and efficiency."[6] For Maier, the politics of productivity, in turn rooted in the domestic U.S. experience, depended upon the super-session of distributive and class conflict with aggregate economic growth and emphasized the transition of a society from scarcity to relative abundance. Originally one of the primary tasks of the Organization for European Economic Cooperation (OEEC), when the Marshall plan came to an end, the emphasis on productivity was quickly resumed with the creation of the European Productivity Agency in 1953 as a semi-independent body within the OEEC framework.[7] The aim was to reform established socioeconomic structures by exporting U.S. management techniques and business practices in order to assist West European reconstruction and thereby contribute to the twin objectives of acting as a bulwark against the Soviet threat and supporting U.S. economic development and expansion.

By the mid-1950s, productivity had become a key concept in economic growth theory and Keynesianism. It was thought that, provided there were productivity improvements, the high rates of national income growth could be sustained. State action was believed to be instrumental in boosting productivity by, for instance, encouraging technological innovation and undertaking investment. As Milward explains, "the ideology of growth" came to justify ex post policies that had emerged from the realities of the postwar context and served to legitimize a range of interventionist policies associated with the postwar state.[8]

The Keynesian welfare consensus on which postwar European reconstruction was based also manifested itself in the organization of telecommunications and television. In the postwar era in most of Western Europe, postal, telegraph and telephony services and equally broadcasting were mainly government sanctioned monopolies to be operated by state or public entities.

In sharp contrast to the USA, in Western Europe—with the notable exception of Luxembourg, which had a commercial monopoly—broadcasting was considered not a commercial competitive industry but a public service "to be produced and distributed by institutions and by mechanisms guaranteed by the state and other than that of a market economy."[9] Having said that, there has never existed a single European public service broadcasting model but rather diverse national models, some closer than others to the public service ideals. Even in the few cases where commercially funded broadcasting existed, such as Britain introduced in the early 1950s, it was subject to public service obligations. Public service monopolies remained the norm up until the 1980s, when a confluence of technological, economic, political, ideological and social factors resulted in the liberalization and commercialization of television markets.

Equally, unlike the USA, telecommunications was a state, not private, monopoly and regarded as the textbook case of natural monopoly. Similarly to broadcasting, it was mainly from the 1980s onward that the interplay of several factors contributed to the progressive liberalization and privatization of telecommunications markets.

THE COUNCIL OF EUROPE:
AN INTERGOVERNMENTALIST START

Origins

In the aftermath of World War II, various movements sprang up in Europe sharing a commitment to European unity. It is important to note that, at the time, the idea of European unity was not associated with a European identity. These movements were convinced that federalism was the answer to the nationalism that had been the source of military conflict so often in the recent past and with catastrophic effects. The International Committee of the Movements for European Unity, the umbrella of all these movements, organized a congress that was held in The Hague in May 1948, bringing together over a thousand delegates, including existing and former national ministers, parliamentarians, academics and intellectuals.

The "Congress of Europe," as this historic meeting is known, established the main themes on which Europe was to be built and, in effect, it set out the main objectives to be assumed a year later by the Council of Europe. Among other things, it called for

> the creation of an economic and political union to guarantee security, economic independence and social progress, the establishment of a consultative assembly elected by national parliaments, the drafting of a European charter for human rights and the setting up of a court to enforce its decisions.[10]

But despite these general common aims, the Congress of Europe revealed strong disagreements about the character of European unity. On the one side, federalists—supported notably by France, Belgium and Luxembourg—wanted to create a European Assembly, composed of members of national parliaments, that would decide by a majority vote. On the other side, intergovernmentalists—notably Britain, Ireland and the Scandinavian countries—favored loose intergovernmental cooperation. The compromise reached allowed for the creation of the Council of Europe. As Milward remarks, Britain "reluctantly accepted" its formation on the ground that it "should remain entirely powerless."[11] A ministerial committee meeting in private would be the decision-making body, whereas the Assembly meeting in public would assume a purely consultative role. Not only national foreign ministers would decide, but their Committee could not impose decisions, thus leaving member states free to ratify, and thereby be bound by, agreements and conventions.

Ironically, since it was the only European organization with which the European federalist movement was closely associated, the Council of Europe has been created as a typical intergovernmental organization.

Objectives

On 5 May 1949, the Treaty of London established the Council of Europe with the central objective

> to achieve a greater unity between its members for the purpose of safeguarding and realising the ideals and principles which are their common heritage and facilitating their economic and social progress.[12]

This ambitious and wide-ranging remit was to be achieved

> by discussion of questions of common concern and by agreements and common action in economic, social, cultural, scientific, legal and administrative matters and in the maintenance and further realisation of human rights and fundamental freedoms.[13]

In contrast to the almost immediate involvement of the Council in postal and telecommunications matters analyzed below, it was not until the mid-1970s that the media became a distinct area of activity. Before that, in the first decades of its existence the Council of Europe did not deal with media and respective policy issues in their own right but on a reactive ad hoc basis. The media was a strictly national responsibility and the Council approached only certain legal, cultural and human rights aspects as a subfield of these respective main fields of its activity.[14]

The Council was the first European political organization to be formed in the postwar era and, unsurprisingly, its main aim has been to defend and strengthen human rights, parliamentary democracy and the rule of law. The European Convention for the Protection of Human Rights, adopted in 1950, is perhaps the most important and most known Convention to be produced by the Council of Europe. It is assisted by the independent European Court of Human Rights. The legal guarantees of this Convention—especially article 10 on freedom of expression and information, vital in its own right but also in the exercise of other rights in democratic societies—have been invoked regularly.

The Council of Europe has continued to work to achieve policy coordination in various, often controversial, areas. It has adopted nearly 200 conventions that are legally binding on the countries that ratify them. In addition, it has issued a large body of recommendations and resolutions to national governments. These non-binding agreements complement the conventions and lay down policy guidelines. The intergovernmental character of the Council of Europe, coupled with the fact that its policy instruments respect national sovereignty, makes it easier for it to work on politically sensitive areas.

THE EUROPEAN BROADCASTING UNION: THE COLD WAR DICTATES THE ORGANIZATION OF THE EUROPEAN BROADCASTING ORDER

Origins

The organization of the postwar European broadcasting order is rooted in the pre-war order and subsequent developments. International cooperation in the field of broadcasting started in the 1920s, shortly after the introduction of radio. In the first half of the 1920s, in response to the rapid rise of radio broadcasting and technical interference, and in an effort to prevent a repeat elsewhere of the chaotic development of radio broadcasting in the USA, where there was no control over frequency assignments up until the enactment of the Radio Act and the establishment of the Federal Radio Commission in 1927, various initiatives originated in Europe aiming at the international regulation of radio frequencies.

At the time, the only international legal instrument dealing with radio, the pre-war International Radiotelegraph Convention of 1912, was mainly concerned with ship-to-ship and maritime communications.[15] In view of a likely International Radio-Telegraphic Convention in Washington in 1925, the BBC in particular, the largest and most powerful broadcaster in Europe, was anxious to ensure that the Convention would not neglect broadcasting needs.[16]

To this effect, in April 1925, following a conference in London organized by the BBC the previous month, the delegates of eleven broadcasting organizations from ten European countries set up the International Broadcasting Union (IBU) with administrative headquarters in Geneva and a technical center in Brussels.[17] The creation of the IBU was crucial in giving broadcasters a voice in the international negotiations of radio frequency allocation under the auspices of the International Telegraph Union and later the International Telecommunication Union (ITU). The IBU aimed to operate as a liaison between European broadcasters, protect their interests, centralize the study of issues of common concern and pursue plans favorable to them.[18]

But the IBU was weakened by its nongovernmental status. Agreements were voluntary and the IBU did not have power to impose sanctions. Implementation therefore depended on the cooperation and goodwill of its members who, in addition, had to submit any allocation plans developed within the IBU to their competent national telecommunications administration for approval.[19] In effect, despite the creation of the IBU, the radio spectrum remained the primary responsibility of national governments while interference problems persisted. In 1929, for instance, 72 of the 209 radio stations operating in Europe were not observing the agreed frequency plan.[20] Countries regularly exceeded their frequency assignments and used powerful transmitters in order to illegally broadcast either advertisements (e.g., Radio Luxembourg) or propaganda to audiences in neighboring countries.[21] Besides compliance problems with its agreements, its narrow membership, notably the absence of the USSR, meant that the IBU could not put order in the European broadcasting scene. Yet, despite these problems, the IBU was instrumental in aiding the growth of broadcasting. It pioneered many techniques with regard to radio spectrum management, program rights and exchanges later taken on by the European Broadcasting Union and the International Radio and Television Organization.

But it was the IBU's role during World War II that discredited the organization and led to its eventual dissolution. The IBU was brought into disrepute because the occupying authorities took control of its technical facilities and used them to monitor allied radio traffic. The IBU survived the war but it was left seriously compromised. In the eyes of most of its original members it could no longer be trusted.

Upon the conclusion of World War II, there immediately followed an intense debate about the future of the organization. As an illustration of their distrust, the broadcasting entities and their governments, not prepared to attend a formal meeting under the IBU, decided to go ahead with an informal meeting to be held in Brussels—not in Geneva, the seat of the IBU.[22] Ironically, it was the USSR, which had never joined the IBU, that was to prove the catalyst to future developments that dealt the fatal blow to the organization. At the meeting in March 1946, the USSR proposed the dissolution of the IBU and the institution of a new International Broadcasting Organization (IBO) to assume its responsibilities. National governments and broadcasters were faced with a dilemma: either support the discredited IBU or allow for it to be dissolved in favor of a new body.

Two issues were most contentious: voting rights and the international control of broadcasting. The debate on and resolution of these issues had more to do with politics and diplomacy and less with the needs of broadcasting as such.

More specifically, according to the proposed Statutes of the IBO, each broadcaster would have one vote. But upon closer examination, it was clear that the proposed voting procedure would have given the USSR eight votes since it would have had the right to vote on behalf of its autonomous republics. Similarly, France would get to vote for its North-African colonies and have four votes. The Netherlands and Belgium too would have enjoyed more than one vote. In sharp contrast, Britain, with the powerful BBC, would be left with just one vote and hardly any influence in the new organization.[23]

The British, in particular, were very skeptical about these proposals and proceeded cautiously. The BBC, though it had suspended its collaboration with the IBU since 1941, was not ready to support the creation of an alternative association, especially one that would effectively be controlled by the USSR. In June 1946, despite strong British-led opposition, twenty-six countries under the leadership of the USSR and France signed the Statutes founding the International Broadcasting Organization (IBO). But in effect, the controversial question of voting rights was left unresolved, to be settled at a world conference that the IBO was now legally committed to call later that year. This tactical manoeuvre, on the one hand, allowed the creation of the IBO and, on the other, left open the possibility of more broadcasting entities joining the new organization upon successful resolution of the voting procedure.

A day after the IBO constitutive assembly met, the IBU General Assembly failed to obtain the needed majority to dissolve the IBU. The stalemate prolonged the uncertainty over the international organization of broadcasting. Neither organization—not the IBU nor the newly created IBO—could take the lead in the allocation of radio frequencies, whereas to be credible, either solution needed to secure the participation of the BBC, Europe's largest broadcaster.

The second contentious issue, the international control of broadcasting, was a conflict, already visible in the pre-war era, between broadcasters and governments.[24] The IBO world conference was never convened. In 1946, in preparation for the ITU conference in Atlantic City due the following year, two meetings were held among the five great powers. National governments, notably Britain and the USA, intended to regain full and sole control over broadcasting. Broadcasters would need to comply fully with the international decisions taken by the intergovernmental ITU.[25]

More specifically, the British Foreign Office, backed by the Post Office (the state-owned telecommunications administration with responsibility over radio frequencies) preferred that broadcasting be organized at the international rather than European level. The Foreign Office therefore recommended restraint, waiting for the planned ITU radio conference in Atlantic City. It wanted the United Nations to assume responsibility for all broadcasting matters, with the ITU and another UN agency, possibly UNESCO, responsible for the technical and non-technical aspects respectively.[26] Broadcasters were against such a scenario, believing that a division of tasks would adversely affect and weaken them. Broadcasters, who in the pre-war period had set up their own international professional organization, the IBU, and had striven for the recognition of broadcasting in its own right at international frequency allocation conferences, were now, in the postwar period, faced with new political and diplomatic realities, realities that would sidestep their needs.

Following the ITU Atlantic City conference that was eventually held in 1947, a European Broadcasting Conference was convened in 1948 in Copenhagen. The aim of this intergovernmental conference was the elaboration of a detailed radio frequency plan for Europe. Such a plan, however, required an "expert" organization that would assume responsibility for its implementation, a task taken on by the IBU in the pre-war period. The Copenhagen conference failed to appoint either the IBU or the IBO as an expert organization.

To the refusal of Britain to back either organization and its failure in June 1949 to amend the voting procedure of the IBO to the effect that only one broadcasting organization from a country belonging to the ITU would be entitled to vote, thereby placing the IBO under Western control, were added the escalation of political rivalries between East and West, as well as strong internal disagreements within the IBO itself with France, the Netherlands, Italy and Belgium in August 1949, prepared to quit the IBO. It was out of these divisions and the Cold War context that the European Broadcasting Union was founded in 1950 and the IBU was officially dissolved in May 1950. Cold War politics divided the European broadcasting area in two.

Objectives and Structure

The European Broadcasting Union (EBU) was founded in February 1950 by twenty-two broadcasting organizations from Western Europe, but including Yugoslavia, and the Mediterranean basin, meeting at Torquay, England.[27] As explained in the preceding section, the EBU was set up in direct response to the onset of the Cold War and the break up of the International Broadcasting Union, which had been established at the initiative of European countries in 1925. On the other side of the Iron Curtain, the IBO—in 1960 renamed the International Radio and Television Organization (OIRT per French initials)—continued its operations headquartered in Prague and comprising the East European broadcasting institutions. Thus, from 1950 to 1992 there existed two broadcasting associations in Europe. The EBU and the OIRT merged in 1993 in the aftermath of the collapse of communist regimes in Europe.

Although its Statutes provided for almost every aspect of broadcasting, originally, similar to the IBU work, early priorities for the EBU were technical and legal questions, in particular international frequency management and copyright. It was a few years later that the EBU got involved in program matters, as will be discussed.

The EBU has been established as a nongovernmental professional association of broadcasters. Upon the insistence of Britain, EBU membership has been conditional upon ITU membership. This link has meant that governments, not broadcasters, decide who can join the EBU. This was particularly significant in the immediate postwar context. For instance, West Germany and Austria had been excluded as founding members. Whether they were to be allowed to join the EBU at a later stage would be the responsibility of national governments within the ITU.[28] National governments have assumed responsibility for the politically sensitive issue of EBU membership but thereafter have not intervened in the operation of the EBU and so the latter has functioned as a professional association.

In addition to ITU affiliation, the other two original conditions for EBU membership were authorization by the competent authority to operate a broadcasting service, and production and general responsibility for the programs broadcast from transmitters permanently at its disposal.[29]

Initially, there were two categories of EBU members. Active members were those that belonged to the European Broadcasting Area as defined by the ITU. Broadcasting organizations from outside that area could become associate members. When the EBU was set up in 1950 a monopoly broadcaster was the norm in the countries within the European Broadcasting Area. However, when competition in broadcasting markets began to emerge slowly, the EBU's membership structure became a problem. At issue was not so much the admission of commercial broadcasters—after all Luxembourg's RTL was a founding active member—but rather that these new broadcasters were competing with an already active EBU member.[30] An example here is from Britain. In 1956, the commercial, though subject to public service obligations, broadcaster Independent Broadcasting Authority (IBA) was admitted as an associate member due to resistance from the BBC and fear that its admission as an active member would threaten the EBU's noncommerical character. In 1959, however, following IBA pressure, the EBU Statutes were amended to allow for more than one active member from the same country.[31] In 1981, with the growth of television broadcasting and the rise in broadcasting entities, supplementary active membership was abolished.[32] There are now two categories of EBU members, active and associate.

Moving now to the present organization of the EBU, the General Assembly is its Supreme body and has ultimate responsibility for the organization. All members can participate but only active members have voting rights and can hold office. It normally meets on an annual basis. Among other functions, it elects from active membership the president and vice presidents, and members of the Administrative Council.

The original Statutes of the EBU provided that assembly decisions were binding on all members. However, in 1969, in response to criticism from associate members, who even though they had no voting rights had to comply with decisions, but also in view of the diversity of interests among member organizations, this provision was amended.[33] The General Assembly (and since 1992 the Administrative Council) may grant derogations or temporary exemptions in the event a member is unable to conform to decisions "for imperative reasons."[34] In other words, similar to its sister association in telecommunications (CEPT) examined below, member and national sovereignty takes precedence. Only decisions related to the administrative and financial operation of the EBU are binding on all members, active and associate.

The Administrative Council is in effect the executive body of the EBU. It implements the decisions of the General Assembly and reports to it. It meets at least twice annually. Its main duties include the consideration of reports of study groups and committees, the organization of committees making recommendations to the Assembly and the drafting of the budget.

The Statutes stipulate that decisions by the General Assembly and the Administrative Council are taken by majority. However, and similar to the CEPT in telecommunications, decisions are consensual with actual voting taking place only in the case of electing members of the Administrative Council, the president and vice-presidents.

The EBU's Secretariat, known as the "Permanent Services," is located in Geneva. It is directed by the Secretary General, supported by the heads of departments. The Secretariat has evolved over the years. When the EBU was originally set up in 1950, the EBU's Permanent Services, as per the earlier IBU example, included the Administrative Office and the Technical Center.[35] In 1966, the Department for Legal Affairs was formally acknowledged in the EBU Statutes and in 1976 the Administrative Office was replaced by the General Affairs Service, and two program Departments, one for radio and one for television. The same year, for the first time, a Secretary General assumed responsibility for these five offices.[36]

Finally, the General Assembly of the EBU, upon recommendation of the Administrative Council, can establish committees comprising national experts to investigate particular issues. Their role is advisory. Reflecting the main priorities at the time of creation, the founding members established just two specialized committees, the Technical Committee and the Legal Committee. Although such an aim had been identified by the IBU since the pre-war period, the expansion of the EBU activities into programming matters was controversial and met the resistance of its members and their national governments, in particular Britain and France, who saw this as a threat to national sovereignty.[37] It was eventually in 1954 that the radio and broadcasting program committees were formed. They proved instrumental in the institutionalization of program exchanges through the Eurovision and Euroradio systems.

Eurovision

Program cooperation and exchanges among European broadcasting organizations did not start with the EBU. They have a long history that goes back to the early days of radio in the pre-World War II era. Initially, exchanges were informal and bilateral and later organized along geographical and linguistic areas.[38] The idea of an international clearing house of television programs was discussed within the IBU. The discussion continued under the auspices of the EBU and eventually resulted in the creation of Eurovision in 1954.

Under the Eurovision system, program exchanges supplement national programming and they benefit in particular smaller broadcasters from less wealthy and small language countries faced with a smaller pool of financial resources and talent. Besides benefits for broadcasters, the Eurovision initially benefited television manufacturers too as more and better programs boosted the sale of television sets.[39] Finally, another more idealistic aim of program exchanges, identified quite early on in discussions under the auspices of the IBU, has been the promotion of international understanding and the enrichment of the cultural experience of audiences.[40]

Despite the long history of program exchanges, the main novelty of the EBU Eurovision system is that it has "institutionalized program control."[41] Eurovision does not challenge the national organization of broadcasting. Governments and broadcasting entities precisely due to national sovereignty concerns did not allow the EBU to produce programs itself. National broadcasters retain complete control over what to offer, and whether to accept or reject programs.

FROM POLITICO-ECONOMIC INTEGRATION TO INTEGRATION BY SECTOR AND BACK AGAIN

One tension that has characterized the European integration process from the very beginning has been the balance between integration by sector based on functional necessities (functionalism) and broader politico-economic integration.[42] Further to the formation of the OEEC and the Council of Europe in the 1940s, the 1950s witnessed the creation of several other European organizations. But whereas the OEEC and the Council of Europe were broadly about politico-economic cooperation, most initiatives in the 1950s were sector-specific, concentrating on cooperation in distinct areas.

The Limits of Integration by Sector

Shortly after the formation of the Council of Europe, in May 1950, French Foreign Minister Robert Schuman presented a plan calling for the creation of a European coal and steel community. The choice of coal and steel as the first two sectors to launch European integration of a supranational kind was no accident. They had been at the center of Franco-German conflicts ever since the 1920s. Besides, coal and steel provided the basic element of any war effort but were also essential raw materials for postwar economic reconstruction. The supranational control of these sectors under a High Authority would on the one hand prevent another war while on the other guarantee France adequate supplies of coal from the Ruhr region. For France the gains were primarily economic, while for West Germany they were primarily political since it got recognition as an equal negotiating partner.[43]

For economic and political reasons, Britain decided from the outset not to participate in the negotiations. Supranationality was non-negotiable for the French, and Britain was unwilling to participate under those terms. In addition, Britain possessed adequate domestic supplies of coal and steel, two industries, moreover, that the Labour government had just nationalized.[44]

The European Coal and Steel Community (ECSC), founded in 1951 among the "Six," was the first organization concerned with functional integration of two economic sectors.[45] The ECSC, however, remained effectively under the control of national governments wary of relinquishing control over domestic affairs. Even Haas's seminal study—one of the original formulations of neofunctionalism and the view of integration as a process driven by major economic interest groups—effectively explains the formation of the ECSC on the basis of intergovernmental bargaining with variable input from domestic interests in national positions.[46] Governments and national discriminatory practices were putting limits to the development of the common market in coal and steel and to the work of the ECSC and, in turn, to integration by sector. Things came to a head in 1959, when coal surpluses in Europe coincided with a drop in demand, cheap coal imports from the USA and growing use of oil. National governments rejected calls by the supranational High Authority for increased emergency powers as provided for in the Treaty.

The experience of the ECSC in the 1950s starkly demonstrated that the road to sectoral integration was a difficult one.[47] In view of the difficulties that the ECSC experienced, some governments, as will be seen, thought it would be easier to pursue broader economic, not sectoral, integration. Nevertheless, in response to Cold War developments, sectoral integration was to be given another chance, this time in the highly politically sensitive area of defense.

The intensification of the Cold War in June 1950 when the Korean War broke forced the USA to review its defense strategy. At once, containment policy became internationalized and militarized. With the U.S. military heavily committed in Korea, Britain burdened with international responsibilities and France involved in the colonial war in Indo-China, German rearmament appeared essential for containing communism in Europe.[48] At the same time, however, full West German sovereignty just five years after World War II was a disturbing proposition to neighboring countries and France in particular.

The idea for a European Defense Community in October 1950 was the French response to that latest turn in the Cold War hostilities and the alarming prospect for a fully sovereign West Germany.[49] But despite it being a French initiative, it was the French National Assembly that rejected it in August 1954, serving a severe blow to aspirations for political integration.

The rejection of the European Defense Community and the experience with the ECSC manifested the limits of integration by sector. It was not just that there was national hostility to integration in a sensitive political field such as defense, but in addition, and more significantly, the experience with the ECSC, in particular the problems and difficulties it faced due to conflicting national interests and persistent national discriminatory policies, indicated that even integrative steps concerning economic sectors were not working.

Reviving European Integration

In June 1955, the foreign ministers of the Six ECSC countries met in Messina to discuss the problems and possible revival of European integration. The importance of the Messina conference lies in the fact that, despite the difficulties of the ECSC and the recent rejection of the European Defense Community, it underlined the commitment of the Six to continue to explore integrative plans. They concluded that the circumstances were not favorable for big integrative steps especially if touching on politically sensitive areas. Rather, they held, integration should focus on the economic front. In their propositions, they referred, among other things, to the development of common communication channels and the expansion of trade. Although the final resolution made no mention of posts and telecommunications, it proved a catalyst for subsequent developments.[50]

An intergovernmental committee was formed, chaired by Paul-Henri Spaak of Belgium and charged with examining the prospects for European integration. The so-called Spaak report, delivered in April 1956, signalled the resumption of the European integration process.[51] The report studied in particular the choice between general economic integration and the creation of a common market, and sectoral integration as per the ECSC model. The report reaffirmed the conclusion of the Messina conference that integration among the Six should focus on the economic front. Sectoral integration was rejected as a more difficult exercise. It was to take place only in relation to atomic energy.

In the mid-1950s, atomic energy was a good candidate for European cooperation and France was its strongest advocate. Besides, international events, especially the Suez crisis in 1956 and the attendant energy crisis, made cooperation in atomic energy, seen as a cheap future energy source that would reduce reliance on imports, attractive.[52] Furthermore, it was relatively easy to discuss integration in nuclear energy because national interests and positions had not yet become ossified in this nascent sector, although this was to change fast and eventually national interests stalled the European Atomic Energy Community (Euratom).[53]

It is ironic that the second and more ambitious scheme concerning general economic integration, the scheme less supported initially and on which fewer hopes had been placed, the scheme which "was lucky to get onto the Messina agenda in the first place," has turned out to be not just the most important European Community but the most advanced regionalist movement in world politics.[54] The common market was an idea first raised by the Netherlands in 1952 at an ECSC ministerial gathering.[55] In Messina, it was Belgium, the Netherlands and Luxembourg—the Benelux countries already on the road to forming a customs union—that advocated the creation of a common market rather than integration by sector. They believed that such a step would assist and expand international trade, essential for sustainable economic recovery.

The more ambitious European Economic Community (EEC) was based on a series of compromises among the Six, in particular between France and West Germany. The former was originally hostile to the idea of a common market on grounds that its economy was not ready yet to face competition. In the end, after gaining important concessions, France agreed to support it. For West Germany, the main attraction of the common market was that it would provide a big market for its industrial products.

Europe at Sixes and Sevens

Britain participated in the first phase of the intergovernmental Spaak negotiations, always expressing its preference for a free trade area over a common market. When it was clear that the Six were determined to proceed with their plans for closer integration, Britain decided to play no further part in the negotiations. Prioritizing once again its relations with the USA and the Commonwealth, Britain wrongly assumed that the French would never agree to a common market whereas Germany could possibly be persuaded to join a free trade area.[56]

In May 1956, the Six approved the Spaak Committee's report and the drafting of the Treaties to institute the EEC and the Euratom got underway. Reacting to these developments and the real prospect for a trading division of Western Europe, Britain sought to establish a free trade area for manufactured goods within the Organization for European Economic Cooperation (OEEC) including the Six. If the idea were to gather enough support, then that could have signalled the end of the common market that was at the time awaiting ratification by national parliaments. The Six, however, were not prepared to start any talks until the common market had been established. France in particular, concerned about its insufficiently competitive economy, strongly resisted calls to turn the OEEC into a free trade area.

The conflict between a loose European free trade area, supported by Britain, and a regulated common market, supported by the Six, came to a head in 1957 in discussions within the OEEC. The USA, despite the perceived commercial disadvantages, was in favor of the second option of closer cooperation, for the potential political advantages.[57] It was neutral regarding the creation of a free trade area because it lacked a political dimension, crucial for containing communism, but also because, by 1958, the idea had shifted far away from "a pure, ideal-type free trade area."[58] In any case, the USA was against the division of Western Europe into trading blocs, which is precisely what happened.

In November 1960, after the failure to establish a free trading zone within the OEEC and with the Six proceeding with the creation of a common market, the outer Seven set up the European Free Trade Area.[59] The latter was set up as an alternative looser organization to the EEC, symbolizing deeper economic and potentially political integration. With the formation of two rival economic organizations, Europe was now formally at "sixes and sevens." It is worth noting that the tension between free and regulated liberalization and trade has been rehearsed numerous times throughout the history of European integration.

The eventual collapse of the OEEC negotiations and the emergence of an economically divided Western Europe signaled the beginning of the end of the OEEC.[60] European integration was to evolve outside it. In 1960, with the accession of the first non-European countries, Canada and the USA, the OEEC was reformed into the Organization of Economic Cooperation and Development (OECD) with a wider remit beyond European reconstruction. By virtue of its extended membership, the OECD could not stand for genuinely European cooperation. The OECD now brings together thirty advanced industrialized liberal democracies and is concerned with national and international economic development and growth. It has played a prominent role in the institutionalization and dissemination of the debate on the role of science and technology in economic development and in the liberalization of telecommunications markets, as will be seen.

EEC: Objectives and Structure

The Spaak report revived European integration. It led to the Treaties of Rome in 1957 instituting the Euratom and the EEC among the six countries that had earlier formed the European Coal and Steel Community. Despite being an economic community, the political objectives of the EEC were laid out in the preamble of the Treaty:

DETERMINED to lay the foundations of an ever-closer union among the peoples of Europe,
RESOLVED to ensure the economic and social progress of their countries by common action to eliminate the barriers which divide Europe,

AFFIRMING as the essential objective of their efforts the constant improvements of the living and working conditions of their peoples.[61]

The main objective of the EEC was

by establishing a common market and progressively approximating the economic policies of Member States, to promote throughout the Community a
harmonious development of economic activities, a continuous and balanced
expansion, an increase in stability, an accelerated raising of the standard of living and closer relations between the States belonging to it.[62]

Not surprisingly, in view of the stated aims, the founding EEC Treaty is
long. The common market is based on the free movement of goods, services, persons and capital. The EEC Treaty has bestowed the European
Commission direct competition policy powers aiming at ending competitive distortions.[63] While the provisions concerning the creation of a customs union were quite clear, other provisions concerning controversial
areas, such as the harmonization of fiscal and social policies, were vague,
left to be resolved at a later stage. The lack of details illustrated the limits
of political consensus at the time of the EEC's formation and implied disagreement on the character of European integration. In the absence of a
pre-existing consensus on the main economic and political goals of European integration, fundamental conflicts and contestations on the very
nature and future course of European integration have been rehearsed in
several policy fields, including telecommunications and television, at various times.

Moving from the EEC days to the present, the institutional organization
of what is now called the European Union (EU) reflects the complexity of
its tasks.[64] The European Commission is the executive arm. It initiates the
policy-making process and forwards proposals to the European Parliament
and the Council of Ministers. As guardian of the Treaties, it monitors policy implementation. Compared to its tasks, the Commission is over-
stretched and understaffed. Its resources include "the capability to build up
expertise; the potential for developing policy networks and coalitions; the
scope for acquiring grateful or dependent clients; and the chance to help
member governments to resolve their own policy predicaments."[65] The
Commission is neither a homogenous nor a monolithic institution but
rather a complex organization itself. It is organized into Directorates General (DGs), each headed by a Commissioner. Commissioners are chosen by
national governments but they are supposed to promote the common European, not national, interest. The Commission acts collectively but often
the blurring of boundaries and accountabilities as well as the diverse, even
conflicting, interests distinct DGs represent result in rivalries and infighting.
The sectoral organization of the Commission produces the potential for

fragmentation in the formulation and coordination of policies, as will be seen. The Commission enjoys strong powers over some areas—notably competition—and less over others, such as culture. These strengths and weaknesses are in turn reflected in the power of the various DGs.

The Council of Ministers, representing the governments and comprising national ministers, is the principal decision making body. In the past most issues were decided unanimously. But, especially since the Single European Act in 1986 launching the single market project, most decisions covering economic integration, including the issues examined here, are reached by qualified majority voting, a system under which each member state has a number of votes relevant to its size.[66] Even so, the norm is for decisions to be reached by consensus and very rarely are they put to vote.[67]

The Council of Ministers is different from the European Council or simply the Summit, that is, the gatherings of the EU Heads of state or government. Starting with an informal existence, the European Council has, increasingly since the late 1980s, provided political impetus on major issues and has laid down strategic guidelines in key areas.

The third major EU institution is the European Parliament, originally called the Parliamentary Assembly. Unlike national Parliaments, the European Parliament was not meant to be a legislature. Before direct elections were introduced in 1979, it was effectively functioning like a talk-shop. Its role has subsequently been strengthened and it has assumed various (co)-legislative and budgetary powers but it still remains less powerful compared to national parliaments.

The European Court of Justice is the judicial authority. It arbitrates and interprets the EU Treaty. Since the early 1960s, the Court has established important principles, notably the direct effect of EU law and its supremacy over national law, that effectively render the European Court a supreme court.[68] Together with the Commission, the Court has made significant contributions to the road of European integration.[69] As we will examine, it was the Court that gave legitimacy to the Commission to intervene in the sectors of television and telecommunications. The Court also acts as the regulator of last resort, often used by interests who did not manage to get their way during the policy-making process and/or are dissatisfied with the national implementation of EU rules.

The EU has three main legal instruments. Regulations are directly applicable in all member states upon approval by EU institutions. Directives are binding in terms of the result to be achieved but leave the choice of form and methods to national authorities to deal with during the transposition of directives into national legislation. Directives are the most common policy instrument in the field of communications. Finally, decisions can be addressed to member states or legal entities and are binding in their entirety. They are common in competition cases.

TOWARD EUROPEAN COOPERATION IN
POSTS AND TELEPHONY

The debate about European cooperation in the field of telegraphy and telephony has a long history that goes back to the early days of these inventions. It was in Europe that the first regional organizations concerning telegraphy emerged in the 1850s. The International Telegraph Union, the first international organization and forerunner of the ITU, was created in 1865 by twenty European countries.[70] In turn, the International Telegraph Union itself was premised on the earlier Austro-German Telegraph Union set up in 1850 by Austria, Prussia, Bavaria and Saxony and the West European Telegraph Union, formed in 1855 by Belgium, France, Sardinia, Spain and Switzerland.

The discussion and initiatives concerning cooperation in the fields of posts and telecommunications in the postwar period need to be understood within the broader context of the debate on European integration and the series of functional integration plans launched in the early 1950s, analyzed above. Following the creation of the ECSC various proposals for the future of European integration were debated, many of which supported sectoral integration, in particular in the energy and transport sectors. At the time, posts and telecommunications were two closely linked sectors, typically operated by the same state-owned monopolist administration, the so-called PTT. Their cross-border character made them ideal candidates for European cooperation initiatives. But there were strong divisions among West European PTTs and their respective governments about the nature, scope and structure of such cooperation. These divisions mirrored broader disagreements about the purpose and desired path of European integration in general, in particular between federalist aspirations stressing close cooperation among a small group of countries and larger and looser cooperation propositions. Another question was whether to create a distinct organization to cover the two fields or whether such cooperation should take place within the structures of an existing organization, such as the Council of Europe and subsequently the EEC.

Plans for European cooperation in posts and telecommunications were being discussed in parallel under the auspices of the Council of Europe and the ECSC/EEC. Overall, the debate in the former aimed at creating a looser intergovernmental organization covering the wider Western Europe, while the latter aspired to closer cooperation but just among the Six ECSC/EEC countries.

The Idea of a European Postal Union

Only a couple of months after its creation in 1949, as part of a broader economic debate, the Council of Europe launched the idea of a European postal union among all its countries. To this effect, in December 1951, the Consultative Assembly called for the establishment of a European postal union aiming, among other things, at a reduction in postal charges between member countries that were to be calculated on the basis of the distance covered, not national frontiers crossed, and called for the extension of this arrangement to telephony services. The improvement of postal and telecommunication services, the introduction of new facilities and lower prices were all deemed as "measures of incalculable value to intra-European trade."[71]

But although the general climate for European functional integration was favorable—the Treaty of Paris instituting the ECSC had been signed just a few months earlier—in May 1953, the Committee of Ministers representing the national governments rejected the proposal on various political, technical and financial grounds.[72] Political because posts and telecommunications were under direct national government control. Technical because of the complexities involved. Financial because the proposed postal union and the lower prices for services it entailed would also have resulted in a correspondingly appreciable decrease in profits, thereby threatening the financial viability of national PTTs.

In the mid-1950s France, that as noted had initiated various sectoral integration initiatives, took the lead again. In July 1955, a month after the conference in Messina assessing the prospects for European integration, Édouard Bonnefous, a French member of the Consultative Assembly and ardent supporter of intergovernmental cooperation, proposed the creation of a European Postal and Telecommunications Ministerial Conference. While calling for the institutionalization of cooperation, Bonnefous suggested that the organization in question should assume a purely consultative role so as not to impinge on national sovereignty.[73]

In addition, Bonnefous, in his capacity as the French Minister of Posts, Telephones and Telegraphs, participated in the ECSC deliberations. His ideas therefore were concurrently being discussed in the two major European organizations. In July 1955, the intergovernmental committee under Spaak established in Messina instructed the ECSC Commission for transport to form a subcommittee to examine the Bonnefous proposal and to assess the prospect for European cooperation in posts and telecommunications among the Six.

At the two first meetings of the ECSC subcommittee on posts and telecommunications during August-September 1955, disagreements were revealed, with Belgium favoring close cooperation confined to the Six ECSC countries and France preferring cooperation among as many Council of Europe countries as possible, as per the Bonnefous plan.[74] Despite strong advantages, notably the potential for common investment in infrastructure and lower communication tariffs, the subcommittee rejected the idea of a new sector-specific European organization on the ground that national governments would never accept it since it concerned areas under their direct authority. The subcommittee also recalled the earlier rejection of the European Defense Community and the Messina resolution, where foreign ministers had ruled out supranational projects. In the end, the subcommittee unanimously recommended the creation of a postal union among, at least initially, the Six. This was hardly a bold or new recommendation.[75]

The subsequent Spaak report in April 1956 endorsed the Committee's recommendation. But although it concluded that there was no consensus in favor of functional integration except for atomic energy, the report singled out air transport, energy (beyond atomic power) and posts and telecommunications as "sectors requiring urgent action" and called for further studies to explore the possibility of cooperation.[76] In relation to telecommunications and television, the Spaak report envisaged three areas for possible common action: the development of (semi)automatic telegraphic and telephony connections (mentioned in the Bonnefous plan), common research in the field of telecommunications (significantly cut down version from the objective in the Bonnefous memorandum that stated common investment) and, lastly, extension of the television transmission network. In short, the Spaak report envisaged cooperation along technical functional lines.[77]

TOWARD A EUROPEAN CONFERENCE OF POSTAL AND TELECOMMUNICATIONS ADMINISTRATIONS

Origins

Following the adoption of the Spaak report, the debate on European cooperation in posts and telecommunications resumed in earnest in two main arenas. Between 1956 and 1959, senior representatives from the PTTs of the Six ECSC/EEC countries held a series of meetings in which their British and Swiss counterparts also participated as observers.[78] Concurrently, the Council of Europe relaunched its proposals for cooperation. At issue were the nature and scope of cooperation. Would cooperation be intergovernmental or not, and to which countries would it be open?

The first informal meeting among PTTs focused on the postal sector. In October 1956, just days before the second informal meeting of PTTs, the Council of Europe reemerged as a key forum. Its Consultative Assembly once again called for intergovernmental cooperation to include as many of its members as possible.[79] This proposal was a repeat of its earlier recommendation in 1951 and, indeed, it had the same fate.

When the PTT administrations met for the second time in October 1956 the question of closer cooperation among the Six versus wider cooperation among a larger number of West European countries came to the fore. The British and Swiss delegations, fearing exclusion from any cooperation scheme confined to the ECSC Six, requested that the meetings be opened to any administration interested and that the distinction between "members" and "observers" be abandoned. With no consensus in sight, it was agreed to refer the matter to the national PTT Ministers.

Meeting for the third time in February 1957, the PTTs of the Six decided to set up a permanent secretariat. The British and Swiss administrations objected to this and resolved not to attend the PTT conference the following year.[80] The secretariat was established after the signing of the EEC Treaty in July 1957. It was the first formal institutional link among the PTT administrations of the Six EEC member states.

In March 1957, the Council of Europe became the main arena again. However, in line with past practice, the Committee of Ministers rejected the Assembly's recommendation on cooperation in the fields of posts and telecommunications on two grounds. First, in view of the work already being carried out separately by the PTTs of the Six in conjunction with Britain and Switzerland and noting that by that time there already had been three meetings, the Ministers contended that there was no point in acting on the Assembly's recommendation. The second objection was in effect a misinterpretation of the recommendation. More specifically, the Ministers took the proposal to mean the creation of a body within the structures of the Council of Europe. However, the recommendation envisaged a European Conference of Ministers of Posts and Telecommunications as an independent organization outside the Council of Europe framework, similar to the European Conference of Ministers of Transport.[81]

Believing that the Committee of Ministers' rejection was based on a misunderstanding, the Consultative Assembly resubmitted its recommendation.[82] Ignoring the divisions among the PTTs evident at their meetings, the Assembly argued that its proposals were actually in agreement with the PTTs' wishes since they too wanted cooperation to be institutionalized and embrace as many countries as possible. And equally, the Assembly continued, the PTTs had recognized that decisions on these matters were political and therefore outside their competence.

With a deadlock in sight and aiming to prevent the establishment of two rival organizations—one among the PTTs of the Six EEC countries and another comprising the outer countries—the Council of Europe decided to convene a conference to resolve the matter and invited all OEEC countries to participate. Eventually, only thirteen countries attended the meeting in September 1958: the Six, Austria, Britain, Denmark, Greece, Ireland, Spain and Turkey.[83] The Council of Europe favored cooperation with the broadest membership possible and explained that as long as there was agreement for such cooperation, even if that were to take place outside its structures, it would accept it.[84]

In parallel, and independently of the Council of Europe conference, representatives from the PTTs of the Six EEC countries met once again to discuss the two alternatives for European cooperation.[85] France was the most fervent advocate of the creation of an organization drawing from the broader membership of the Council of Europe. The French delegation went as far as to present draft statutes for such an organization which were to serve the basis for the European Conference of Postal and Telecommunications Administrations (CEPT), which eventually institutionalized cooperation among West European PTTs in 1959.

The second alternative, strongly supported by Belgium, concerned the creation of an organization confined to the Six and within the EEC structures. In the end, the Six PTTs decided to go ahead with this second proposition of closer cooperation and present it to their Ministers due to meet in November 1958. However, this meeting, owing to ministerial changes in several EEC countries, was postponed. It had not been convened by the time the PTTs of the Six met for the fifth time in The Hague in March 1959.

Two weeks before that meeting was due, it transpired that the PTTs' decision to pursue close cooperation within the EEC structures presented serious legal and procedural problems. In addition, the PTTs became aware that the Ministers, fearing that the planned organization would curb their powers, wished to place it under their control and thus compromise its autonomy.[86]

In the face of these difficulties—legal and procedural problems and the prospect for diminished independence—France and Britain (the latter attending The Hague meeting as an observer), which opposed closer collaboration, seized the opportunity to reopen the debate, and indeed they were instrumental in altering the basis of European cooperation.

More specifically, were the planned organization to be set up within the EEC framework, then automatically Britain, which did not belong to the EEC at the time, would be left out. Taking into account the internationally powerful position that Britain then held in telecommunications, its exclusion would have severely weakened that cooperation scheme.[87] Equally, it was in Britain's strategic interests to push for an organization outside the EEC institutional structures that would have allowed it to participate in it. Moreover, domestic political developments changed France's position on European integration. In June 1958, six months after the entry into force of the EEC Treaty, Charles De Gaulle was called to form a government and was inaugurated as President in 1959. Under De Gaulle, the emphasis was on national independence and loose intergovernmental cooperation. France, hitherto a fervent advocate and indeed the instigator of several European integration plans, including that of a European Postal and Telecommunications Conference, was now resisting supranational efforts that would suppress national sovereignty.

In a volte-face in March 1959, the PTTs of the Six abandoned their plan for cooperation within the EEC structures in favor of an organization independent of the EEC and with wider membership, the solution long promoted by the Council of Europe and in line with the Bonnefous plan. In June 1959, in Montreux in Switzerland, PTT delegations from nineteen West European countries signed the statutes setting up the European Conference of Postal and Telecommunications Administrations (CEPT as per French initials).[88]

The Council of Europe welcomed the progress made in European coop eration but was dissatisfied with its nongovernmental character. In September 1959, its Consultative Assembly asked the Committee of Ministers to treat the CEPT "as preparatory to a European Conference of Ministers of Posts and Telecommunications, to be set up as soon as possible and to be linked with the O.E.E.C. in the same way as the [European Conference of Ministers of Transport]."[89]

However, broader European integration was undergoing important changes. Soon after PTT cooperation was crystallized in the CEPT, disagreements about economic cooperation, visible for some time, divided Western Europe in Sixes and Sevens. The OEEC was about to expand and admit non-European countries, the USA and Canada. The danger therefore was that any kind of cooperation under its auspices would be political and not purely European. The Committee of Ministers rejected the recommendation.

Objectives and Structure

The CEPT was set up in 1959 as an independent nongovernmental organization among PTTs from wider Western Europe with a simple structure. It was the culmination of efforts going back to the late 1940s. Similarly to the European Broadcasting Union, although membership was open to all European postal and telecommunications administrations of the member countries of the Universal Postal Union or ITU, the CEPT up until the fall of the Iron Curtain in the early 1990s remained an organization of West European PTTs.[90]

The CEPT was effectively "a club of telecommunications civil servants."[91] Initially, it was concerned with operational matters, such as tariffs of international telecommunications services, rather than with regulatory issues. Its primary aims were the promotion of professional cooperation among its members and the harmonization and improvement of their administration and technical services.[92] Later, in the early 1980s, it got involved in technical matters such as standardization.

The Plenary Assembly is the supreme organ of the CEPT. It decides on recommendations and the general organization of the CEPT. In its early days, it would normally meet every two years, an indication of the slow pace of developments that characterized the telecommunications sector during the analog-monopoly phase.

In line with the original intention to keep the organization as simple as possible, originally, the CEPT did not have a permanent secretariat. It was the 1977 Plenary in Stockholm that decided to establish a small but permanent secretariat located in Berne, where the UPU and ITU were also located. The Plenary would decide the working plan of the two main subcommittees on "Posts" and "Telecommunications" comprising PTT delegates and typically meeting every six months. Based on the work of their working groups, the subcommittees would adopt non-binding recommendations on the tariffs, and the technical supply and usage conditions of international services.

The Statutes provided that decisions should be taken by simple majority and that each PTT administration would have one vote. Nevertheless, the members rarely resorted to voting. Instead, decisions were reached by consensus, rendering the decision-making process lengthy.

Similarly to the EBU, the only mandatory decisions were those concerning the internal organization of the CEPT. Unlike EEC legislation therefore, but in line with the practice of most international organizations, the vast majority of CEPT's decisions were not legally binding on its members; rather they simply had the character of recommendations. Implementation of CEPT agreements would take place gradually and with great discretion, if at all. All member administrations were required to do was inform the Presidency whether they had adopted a specific recommendation or not, and indicate whether they were planning to do so. In this way, PTT autonomy within domestic territory would remain intact. By extension, the CEPT did not undermine national sovereignty. The issues that the CEPT would deal with touched on cross-border communications and did not penetrate within national borders. In short, the CEPT was a loose organization of technical and commercial co-operation among PTTs.[93]

Up until the 1980s, European cooperation in telecommunications was conducted exclusively among PTTs within the auspices of the CEPT. The EEC context was not significant. For many years, the EEC, in its efforts to enter the telecommunications field, had to work closely with this European forum of PTTs.

Similarly to the EBU, especially since the second half of the 1970s, the CEPT had to face two main challenges: new technologies and the EEC competition powers. More specifically, since in most cases the administrations participating in the work of the CEPT were the monopoly operators in their respective countries, with the first signs of liberalization and private networks in the 1970s, they resorted to using the organization to protect their monopolies. Hence, although it was not an overt goal, the CEPT contributed to delaying the introduction of competition in telecommunications markets. This aim was facilitated by the fact that the only internationally recognized entities with competence over regulatory matters, for instance the CEPT and the ITU, were controlled by the monopolist PTTs. Beginning in the mid-1970s, the cartel-like behavior of the CEPT brought it into conflict with the competition services of the European Commission, as explained later. Thus, although initially the EEC in order to gain legitimacy was forced to cooperate with the professional associations of monopoly operators in broadcasting and telecommunications, the EBU and the CEPT respectively, subsequent technological developments and procompetitive market restructuring challenged the close relationship between them and led to the reorganization of the two professional associations.

CONCLUSIONS

This chapter examined the foundations of cooperation in broadcasting and telecommunications at the (West) European level in the postwar period. It has been argued that initiatives were intimately linked to the broader process of European integration, itself part of the postwar reconstruction efforts in the shadow of the U.S. hegemony and in the wake of the Cold War.

A few observations can be made. The first and most obvious concerns the large number of European organizations formed as a result of intense intergovernmental bargaining in various fields of activity, only a handful of which are mentioned here. Diverse motives and aims drove their formation, but the main point is that West European reconstruction was conditioned on multilateralism and the development of institutionalized economic interdependence.[94]

The decade from the late 1940s until the late 1950s marked the establishment of the main political and economic European organizations, notably the Council of Europe and the EEC, and the main professional nongovernmental associations, the European Broadcasting Union and the European Conference for Posts and Telecommunications. Although they have evolved through the years, these organizations have shaped European communications to various degrees ever since.

A second observation relates to the long time required to set up these organizations. For instance, ideas on European cooperation in the fields of posts and telecommunications were first raised in the late 1940s, first plans were presented at the beginning of the 1950s, and the European Conference for Posts and Telecommunications was eventually created in 1959. In broadcasting, high politics took over the process. The onset of the Cold War accelerated developments and was instrumental in the creation of the European Broadcasting Union in 1950 among the national monopolist broadcasting entities of mainly West European countries.

A third and related observation is that, from the start, the process of European integration was riddled with divisions about its character and purpose. Similar conflicts and disagreements characterized the cooperation initiatives in broadcasting and telecommunications. Should cooperation have an intergovernmental or professional character? What would be the aims of and limits to European cooperation? In the case of telecommunications, did cooperation warrant the creation of a distinct sectoral organization, or could an existing politico-economic organization, such as the Council of Europe or the EEC, assume responsibility for it? The answers to these questions had direct implications for the scope of cooperation, and the countries and administrations that would agree to participate.

During this phase, cooperation in television and telecommunications beyond national borders was limited and even that was within the intergovernmental structures of the Council of Europe or between state-owned, or at least controlled, national monopolist administrations—a typical characteristic of the Keynesian welfare order—working within their professional associations, the European Broadcasting Union and the European Conference for Postal and Telecommunications administrations. European cooperation was very specific and narrow in scope, addressing technical, operational and commercial cross-border issues. Importantly, it challenged neither national sovereignty nor the national organization of broadcasting and telecommunications. Even within its limited scope, European cooperation was not restrictive but afforded great latitude to national administrations and governments. Any agreements reached within the professional associations had the character of recommendations, leaving national administrations and governments free to decide whether to implement them.

In the broader context of European integration, communications was not a priority. Initiatives were piecemeal and reactive rather than part of a coherent strategy. Compared to later periods characterized by major technological and market developments, the communications landscape in the period examined in this chapter was quite stable. European cooperation was defined to a large extent by broader developments outside the immediate sectors examined.

NOTES

1. There is no room here to discuss in detail the process of European integration. Only important aspects that are relevant for our purposes are analyzed. For useful

accounts see indicatively Desmond Dinan, *Ever Closer Union? An Introduction to the European Community* (Basingstoke: Macmillan: 1994). Keith Middlemas, *Orchestrating Europe: The Informal Politics of European Union 1973–1995* (London: Fontana Press, 1995). Loukas Tsoukalis, *The New European Economy Revisited* (3rd ed. Oxford and New York: Oxford University Press, 1997). For an up-to-date overview as well as policy cases see Helen Wallace, William Wallace and Mark Pollack, *Policy-Making in the European Union* (5th ed., Oxford and New York: Oxford University Press, 2005). Ian Bache and Stephen George, *Politics in the European Union* (2nd ed. Oxford and New York: Oxford University Press, 2006).

2. Mario Telò, "Introduction: Globalization, New Regionalism and the Role of the European Union," in *European Union and New Regionalism: Regional Actors and Global Governance in a Post-Hegemonic Era,* ed. Mario Telò (Aldershot: Ashgate, 2001), 2–3.

3. Alan Milward, *The Reconstruction of Western Europe 1945–1951* (London: Methuen, 1984), 391–92.

4. Alan Milward, *The European Rescue of the Nation-State* (2nd ed. London and New York: Routledge, 2000).

5. Derek Urwin, *The Community of Europe: A History of European Integration since 1945* (London and New York: Longman, 1995), 17.

6. Charles Maier, "The Politics of Productivity: Foundations of American International Economic Policy after Word War II," in *Between Power and Plenty: Foreign Economic Policies of Advanced Industrial States,* ed. Peter Katzenstein (Madison: University of Wisconsin Press, 1978), 45.

7. The Agency was wound up when the OECD took over the OEEC; see below. For a detailed analysis see Bent Boel, *The European Productivity Agency and Transatlantic Relations 1953–1961* (Copenhagen: Museum Tusculanum Press, 2003)

8. Alan Milward, *The European Rescue of the Nation-State* (London and New York: Routledge, 1992), 41–42.

9. Kees Brants and Els de Bens, "The Status of TV Broadcasting in Europe," in *Television Across Europe: A Comparative Introduction,* ed. Jan Wieten, Graham Murdock and Peter Dahlgren (London: Sage, 2000), 8. There are many sources on the organization of broadcasting and telecommunications in Europe and the USA. Indicatively see Eli Noam, *Telecommunications in Europe* (New York: Oxford University Press, 1992). For a historical comparative analysis, see Peter Humphreys, *Mass Media and Media Policy in Western Europe* (Manchester and New York: Manchester University Press, 1996), 111–58. For the original economic, technological and politico-institutional factors that determined the organization of broadcasting in the USA on a commercial basis see Hernan Galperin, *New Television, Old Politics: The Transition to Digital TV in the United States and Britain* (Cambridge University Press, 2004), 55–70. See also Burton Paulu, *Radio and Television Broadcasting on the European Continent* (Minneapolis: University of Minnesota Press, 1967). Eli Noam, *Television in Europe* (New York: Oxford University Press, 1991). William Boddy, "The Beginnings of American Television," and Anthony Smith, "Television as a Public Service Medium," in *Television. An International History,* ed. Anthony Smith (Oxford: Oxford University Press, 1995), 35–61 and 62–91.

10. Council of Europe, "A Brief History of the Council of Europe," 1998, <http://www.coe.fr/eng/present/history.htm> (23 Oct. 1998).

11. Milward, *The Reconstruction*, 393.

12. The ten founding states were Belgium, Britain, Denmark, France, Ireland, Italy, Luxembourg, the Netherlands, Norway and Sweden. Council of Europe, *Statute of the Council of Europe: London 5.V.1949*, Article 1(a), <http://conventions.coe.int/Treaty/EN/Treaties/Html/001.htm> (23 Mar. 2006).

13. Council of Europe, *Statute*, article 1(b).

14. For instance, Council of Europe, *European Agreement on the Protection of Television Broadcasts*, (22 June 1960), <http://conventions.coe.int/Treaty/EN/treaties/Html/034.htm>. *European Agreement for the Prevention of Broadcasts transmitted from Stations Outside National Territories*, (22 Jan. 1965), <http://conventions.coe.int/Treaty/EN/treaties/Html/053.htm>. Council of Europe—Committee of Ministers, *Resolution (69) 6 on Cinema and the Protection of Youth*, (7 March 1969), <https://wcd.coe.int/com.instranet.InstraServlet?Command=com.instranet.CmdBlobGet&DocId=635222&SecMode=1&Admin=0&Usage=4&InstranetImage=50011> (23 March 2006). For an overview of these early initiatives see Bernd Möwes, *Fifty Years of Media Policy in the Council of Europe—A review* (Strasbourg: Council of Europe, 2000), Section A, <http://www.coe.int/T/E/human_rights/media/4_Documentary_Resources/MCM%282000%29003_en.asp#TopOfPage> (23 Mar. 2006).

15. John Tomlinson, *The International Control of Radiocommunications* (Ann Arbor, MI: J. W. Edwards, 1945), 12–44.

16. Asa Briggs, *The History of Broadcasting in the United Kingdom. Volume 1: The Birth of Broadcasting* (London: Oxford University Press, 1961), 313. The Washington conference was eventually held in 1927.

17. For the influence of the British see Briggs, *Volume I*, 308–22. The founding members of the IBU were the broadcasting organizations of Austria, Belgium, Czechoslovakia, France (with two organizations), Germany, the Netherlands, Norway, Spain, Switzerland and Britain. Ernest Eugster, *Television Programming Across National Boundaries: The EBU and OIRT experience* (Dedham, Mass.: Artech House, 1983), 209–13, Appendix A.

18. IBU, *Union Internationale de Radiophonie. Statutes Submitted to the General Assembly Meeting at the League of Nations on the 4th April 1925*, Article 2. The Statutes of the IBU are reproduced in Appendix III in Briggs, *Volume I*.

19. Charles Sherman, "The International Broadcasting Union: A Study in Practical Internationalism," *EBU Review* XXV, no. 3 (1974): 33.

20. Tomlinson, *The International Control*, 181.

21. Asa Briggs, *The History of Broadcasting in the United Kingdom. Volume II. The Golden Age of Wireless* (London: Oxford University Press, 1965), 339–56, 360–67. It was for this reason that Luxembourg never joined the IBU.

22. Léo Wallenborn, "From IBU to EBU. The Great European Broadcasting Crisis. (Part I)," *EBU Review* XXIX, no. 1, (1978): 29.

23. EBU, "Before Torquay," *EBU Diffusion* (Winter 1999/2000): 12.

24. In 1929, following the Washington conference, European national PTT administrations met in Prague. This was the first official conference to allocate specific frequencies to European broadcasting stations. Due to the voluntary nature of the IBU's frequency plans and persistent interference problems, the governments at the Prague Radiocommunications conference agreed to relegate the role of the IBU to

expert technical advisors and to supplement the IBU's plans with intergovernmental agreements. Tomlinson, *The International Control*, 185–88.

25. Wallenborn, "From IBU," 32.

26. Asa Briggs, *The History of Broadcasting in the United Kingdom. Volume IV: Sound & Vision* (London: Oxford University Press, 1979), 479. Wallenborn, "From IBU," 32.

27. The founding members of the EBU were the broadcasting organizations of Belgium, Denmark, Egypt, France, Greece, Ireland, Italy, Lebanon, Luxembourg, Monaco, Morocco, Norway, the Netherlands, Portugal, Sweden, Switzerland, Syria, Tunisia, Turkey, Britain, Vatican City and Yugoslavia. Finland joined in June 1950. Finland was a member of both the EBU and the corresponding East European association the OIRT and participated in the program exchange systems of both associations.

28. Both countries were admitted to the ITU and subsequently to the EBU in 1951–1952.

29. Russell B. Barber, "The European Broadcasting Union," *Journal of Broadcasting* 6, no. 2 (1962): 113.

30. Eugster, *Television*, 60.

31. Hans Brack, *The Evolution of the EBU Through Its Statutes from 1950 to 1976* (Geneva: EBU, 1976), 32–33.

32. Eugster, *Television*, 62.

33. Brack, *The Evolution*, 46–48.

34. In the latest Statutes this provision is art. 13(1). EBU. *Statutes of the EBU 2003* (Geneva: EBU, 2003).

35. EBU, "25 Years of the European Broadcasting Union: A Retrospect," *EBU Review* XXVI, no. 1 (1975): 20. In 1993, the Technical Center moved to Geneva from Brussels.

36. Eugster, *Television*, 66.

37. See EBU, "25 Years," 10–13. For the reluctance of some broadcasting organizations and governments to give the EBU competence over programming and the birth of the EBU's Eurovision program exchange system see Eugster, *Television*, 95–104 and EBU, "50 Years of Eurovision," *EBU Dossiers* (May 2004).

38. Paulu, *Radio*, 135.

39. Stig Hjarvard, "Pan-European Television News: Towards a European Political Public Sphere?," in *National Identity and Europe*, ed. Phillip Drummond, Richard Patterson and Janet Willis (London: British Film Institute, 1993), 76.

40. EBU, "50 Years," 8.

41. Eugster, *Television*, 19.

42. The principal exponent of functionalism is Mitrany. See David Mitrany, *A Working Peace System* (London: Royal Institute of International Affairs, 1943). David Mitrany, "The Functional Approach to World Organisation," in *The New International Actors: The UN and the EEC*, ed. C. A. Cosgrove and K. J. Twitchett (London: Macmillan, 1970), 65–75.

43. Martin J. Dedman, *The Origins and Development of the European Union 1945–1995: A History of European Integration* (London and New York: Routledge, 1996), 64–65.

44. Urwin, *The Community*, 28.

45. The so-called Six—Belgium, France, Italy, Luxembourg, the Netherlands and West Germany—interested in closer economic and potentially political integration were the founding members of all three European Communities.

46. Ernst B. Haas, *The Uniting of Europe: Political, Social and Economic Forces, 1950–1957* (2nd ed. Stanford Calif.: Stanford University Press, 1968 [1958]).

47. For details see Milward, *The European Rescue*, (2000), 46–118; Urwin, *The Community*, 47–57.

48. Dedman, *The Origins*, 73.

49. For the EDC see indicatively Dedman, *The* Origins, 70–92; Middlemas, *Orchestrating*, 24–28.

50. ECSC, *Resolution Adopted by the Ministers of Foreign Affairs of the Member States of the ECSC at Their Meeting at Messina on June 1 and 2, 1955*, <http://www.ena.lu/mce.cfm> (3 Oct. 2005).

51. Spaak, Paul-Henri, (21 April 1956), *Report of the Heads of Delegation to the Ministers of Foreign Affairs.* (In French) [Spaak Report], <http://aei.pitt.edu/> (10 Apr. 2006).

52. Dedman, *The Origins*, 98.

53. Urwin, *The Community*, 75.

54. Middlemas, *Orchestrating*, 31.

55. Urwin, *The Community*, 73–74.

56. Dedman, *The Origins*, 109.

57. Milward, *The European Rescue* (1992), 427.

58. Richard T. Griffiths, " 'An Act of Creative Leadership': The End of the OEEC and the Birth of the OECD," in *Explorations in OEEC History*, ed. Richard T. Griffiths (Paris: OECD, 1997), 237.

59. The "outer Seven" were Austria, Britain, Denmark, Norway, Portugal, Sweden and Switzerland. Finland and Iceland joined the EFTA in 1961 and 1970 respectively. The Free Trade Area was completed in December 1966.

60. For details about these negotiations see Griffiths, "An Act of Creative Leadership," 235–56.

61. Treaty of Rome establishing the European Economic Community. 1957, <http://www.eurotreaties.com/eurotexts.html#rometreaty> (10 Apr. 2006).

62. Article 2. Treaty of Rome EEC.

63. The competition provisions in the EEC treaty are article 81 [ex 85]: prohibition of anti-competitive agreements; article 82 [ex 86]: prohibition of *abuse* of sole or joint dominant positions; article 86 [ex 90]: abolition of special or exclusive rights where they induce abuse; articles 87–89 [ex 92–94] outlaw public subsidies to industries that threaten competition and trade between the Member States. These were complemented in 1989 by the Merger Control regulation as amended.

64. Only the core institutions are briefly mentioned here. For an overview see Helen Wallace, "An Institutional Anatomy and Five Policy Modes," in *Policy-Making in the European Union*, ed. Helen Wallace, William Wallace and Mark Pollack (5th ed. Oxford and New York: Oxford University Press, 2005), 49–90.

65. Wallace, "An Institutional," 53.

66. Cultural matters require unanimity, thereby restricting EU-level intervention.

67. Fiona Hayes-Renshaw and Helen Wallace, *The Council of Ministers* (2nd ed. London: Palgrave Macmillan, 2005.)

68. Weiler refers to the "constitutionalization" of the EC legal structure. J. H. H. Weiler, *The Constitution of Europe: "Do the New Clothes Have an Emperor?" And Other Essays on European Integration* (Cambridge: Cambridge University Press, 1999), 10-101.

69. Karen J. Alter, "Who Are the 'Masters of the Treaty'? European Governments and the European Court of Justice," *International Organization* 52, no. 1 (1998): 121–47. Walter Mattli and Anne-Marie Slaughter, "Revisiting the European Court of Justice," *International Organization* 52, no. 1 (1998): 177–209. Renaud Dehousse, *The European Court of Justice: The Politics of Judicial Integration* (Basingstoke: Macmillan, 1998).

70. William Drake, "The Rise and Decline of the International Telecommunications Regime," in *Regulating the Global Information Society*, ed. Christopher Marsden (London and New York: Routledge, 2000), 125–27.

71. Council of Europe—Consultative Assembly, *Recommendation 9 for the Establishment of a Postal Union between the Member States of the Council of Europe*, 5 December 1951, <http://assembly.coe.int/Main.asp?link=/Documents/AdoptedText/ta51/EREC9.htm> (9 Apr. 2006).

72. Council of Europe—Committee of Ministers, *Report of the Committee of Ministers REC 9 (1951). Doc.2 (Report). To the Consultative Assembly in Pursuance of Article 19 of the Statute. 12 May 1952*, (Strasbourg, 12 March 1952).

73. Claude Labarrère, *L' Europe des Postes et des Télécommunications* (Paris: Masson, 1985), 46.

74. For details of these two subcommittee meetings see Labarrère, *L' Europe*, 47–50.

75. See Council of Europe—Consultative Assembly, *Recommendation 9* (1951).

76. Spaak, *Report of the Heads*, 124–35. The subsequent Treaty of Rome establishing the EEC reflected these thoughts. Transport was explicitly included in the Treaty, thereby giving the Commission strong legal powers to intervene. Energy, posts and telecommunications were left out.

77. Spaak, *Report of the Heads*, 134–35.

78. For details of these meetings see Labarrère, *L' Europe*, 50–52, and D. Van den Berg, "The European Conference of Postal and Telecommunications Administrations (CEPT)," *EBU Review* (March 1966): 28–29.

79. Council of Europe—Consultative Assembly. *Recommendation 102 on European Co-operation in the Field of Posts and Telecommunications* (Strasbourg, 24 October 1956).

80. Van den Berg, "The European," 29.

81. It was Bonnefous who in 1950 proposed to the Council of Europe the creation of a consultative European transport authority. The European Conference of Ministers of Transport was eventually formed in 1953 as an international body, part of the OEEC.

82. Council of Europe—Consultative Assembly, *Recommendation 143 on the Institution of a European Conference of Posts and Telecommunications*, Strasbourg, 4 May 1957.

83. Van den Berg, "The European," 29.

84. Council of Europe—Committee of Ministers, *Resolution (58) 21: Posts and Telecommunications—European Cooperation in This Field. Recommendation 143*, Strasbourg, 18 November 1958.

85. For details see Labarrère, *L' Europe*, 54–55.

86. Labarrère, *L' Europe*, 59, 61.

87. For Britain as a leading international telecommunications player see Jill Hills, *The Struggle for Control of Global Communication: The Formative Century* (Urbana and Chicago: University of Illinois Press, 2002).

88. The founding members were the EEC Six, Austria, Britain, Denmark, Spain, Finland, Greece, Ireland, Iceland, Norway, Portugal, Sweden, Switzerland and Turkey.

89. Council of Europe—Consultative Assembly, *Recommendation 206 on a Proposed European Conference of Ministers of Posts and Telecommunications*, Strasbourg, 15 September 1959, point (i).

90. The only exception was Yugoslavia, which had attended the constitutive conference in 1959 and became a member in 1969.

91. Godefroy Dang-Nguyen, "The European Telecommunications Policy or the Awakening of a Sleeping Beauty" (paper presented at the European Consortium of Political Research, Amsterdam, April 1987), 9.

92. Michel Toutan, "CEPT Recommandations," *IEEE Communications Magazine* 23, no 1 (1985): 28.

93. These remarks are from a former CEPT high official interviewed in London, 6 February 1995. See also Volker Schneider and Raymund Werle, "International Regime or Corporate Actor?: The European Community in Telecommunications Policy," in *The Political Economy of Communications: International and European Dimensions*, ed. Kenneth Dyson and Peter Humphreys (London: Routledge, 1990), 87.

94. Milward, *The Reconstruction*, 463.

3

The Crisis Years

National Capital and the Search for European Solutions and Identity (Late 1960s to Late 1970s)

INTRODUCTION

The period from the late 1960s up until the early 1980s and the launch of the single market project has been described as the "doldrums era" of European integration.[1] The European Union (EU), a relatively new organization that was perceived as an experiment in European integration and with which fewer hopes had been originally placed, was soon faced with several interlocking crises. Some of these crises were international, in particular the financial and economic turmoil, the consequent recession and the challenge to the established postwar Keynesian national order. Other crises were closer to home. The EU was in the midst of its own political and institutional crisis. It was unprepared and lacked the powers to tackle the problems arising from these circumstances.

This chapter explains how the changing international context, the consequent economic crisis and Cold War rivalries all served to expose Western Europe's weakness in high-technology sectors. Fast technological changes in the field of electronics in particular, coupled with new theoretical explanations about economic growth emphasizing the role of Information and Communication Technology (ICT), accentuated this weakness. The chapter then examines how "technological disparities" and later the "technological gap" discourse were used to promote European cooperation and integration. It explores the uncoordinated and reactive European responses to these challenges whereby individual countries separately resorted to protecting the interests of national capital, fragmenting markets and obstructing the creation of the common market. Yet, despite the emphasis on national solutions, it is in this period that the EU stumbled upon the sectors of telecommunications and television, not in pursuit of a comprehensive communication policy but by accident. Finally, the chapter explains how, in direct response to the massive turbulence in the established (inter)national order, the concept of a European identity emerged for the first time.

THE TURMOIL

Postwar reconstruction and European integration were in general progressing well and relatively fast. However, the 1960s were to prove controversial. Within the EU, there were two main issues. The first was Britain's application for membership, pitting France under De Gaulle against its EU partners, Britain and the USA. The French government twice unilaterally rejected the British application, in 1963 and in 1967.

The question of British membership has tended to obscure the second major issue facing the EU, namely fundamental disagreements about the nature and future of the integration process. As soon as the Six EU countries began working on the detailed implementation of the objectives of the founding Treaty, itself a political compromise containing both intergovernmental and supranational elements, serious differences were revealed. De Gaulle's coming to power in France in June 1958 was not the primary cause of these differences; it "merely served to crystallise them."[2] The collapse of the so-called Fouchet plan in 1962—basically advocating de Gaulle's position of *L'Europe des parties*, a confederation of states with responsibilities over economics, education and culture as well as foreign policy and defense that would have weakened established structures like NATO and the EU—was a first taste of developments to come.[3] Disputes over specific Treaty objectives—such as a common agricultural policy, the EU budget and the transition from unanimity to qualified majority voting—eventually led to the "empty chair" crisis when for seven months from July 1965 France boycotted all Council of Ministers meetings, bringing the EU to a standstill.

Having survived these internal politico-institutional crises, in the late 1960s, the EU and its members were caught in an international monetary turbulence. In 1967, the British pound was devalued. Similarly, worsening domestic economic conditions led the French government in 1969 to devalue the franc, a move that was followed by an upward revaluation of the German mark. Concomitantly, the growing U.S. balance of payments deficit was putting pressure on the dollar and eroding the credibility of the international postwar monetary system, the Bretton Woods. The inflationary financing of the Vietnam war aggravated pressure on the U.S. currency. For the first time in the postwar era, the USA now also ran a trade deficit.

The crisis culminated in 1971 when the U.S. Nixon administration suspended the dollar's convertibility into gold, the foundation of the Bretton Woods system. The collapse of the international monetary system ushered in the era of floating exchange rates. The ensuing monetary instability pushed the six EU countries to create their own so-called snake monetary system aimed at guaranteeing stability by limiting the fluctuation of exchange rates between European currencies. Nevertheless, crises persisted. Between 1972 and 1976 all the major European currencies were forced to leave the system. U.S. expansionary policies led to a new devaluation of the dollar in 1973, which coincided with the first oil crisis. The second oil crisis—rapidly raising further prices for energy and raw materials—aggravated the consequent recession. EU countries were individually seeking a way out and struggling to protect their domestic economies. The established national Keynesian order under which the state had assumed a central role in socioeconomic life and had become associated with economic growth, stability and social cohesion was now being questioned in the face of economic stagnation, rising unemployment and inflation.

Still, for the EU, the 1960s were not all doom and gloom. In July 1968, with the abolition of internal tariff barriers and the adoption of common external tariffs, the customs union was completed. But in view of the circumstances just described, the success was short-lived and it did not automatically induce further integration.

NEW ECONOMIC THINKING:
THE RISE OF ICT AND THE TECHNOLOGICAL GAP

Economic Growth and the Residual Factor

Growing concern about economic recession following the monetary crises in the late 1960s and the international turmoil of the 1970s, but also the inadequate insights of conventional economic thinking, rendered new explanations about the drivers of economic growth imperative. These new explanations came at a time when the fields of information and communications, in particular electronics, were experiencing fast technological change. Economic development came to be closely associated with these fields. It is in these new theoretical explorations starting as early as the late 1950s/early 1960s that one can trace the origins of explicit preoccupation with a distinct "information sector" and of the growing perception that Information and Communication Technology (ICT) is a key determinant of economic growth and competitiveness.[4]

More specifically, it was becoming increasingly apparent that the neoclassical economic growth theory, dominant in the immediate postwar period, would describe that a: economy grows but could not fully explain why it grows.[5] Economists would note changes in output that could not be attributed to changes in the two identified inputs, labor and capital. The theory could account for the effects of technological progress but not its causes. Technology was considered an exogenous driver of growth. The crucial implication of this assumption was that intervention by governments, firms or individuals could do little to influence growth since that was conditioned on external factors.

The principal body in Western Europe concerned with the question of economic growth and the role of technology, that has proved instrumental in the eventual worldwide dissemination of this debate, was the OECD. In October 1963, in view of the differing speed at which countries appeared to grow economically, the OECD science ministers met for the first time to discuss the importance of science and technology and their contribution to economic and social development.[6] The Ministers commissioned a comparative study of national research and development initiatives (R&D) and of differences in the technological potential among OECD countries, to be presented at their next meeting in January 1966.[7] In 1964, the OECD concluded that although capital and labor contributed too, these two elements alone could not account for economic growth. Technological progress, "knowledge, education, research and development" became progressively identified as major parameters to economic wealth and referred to as "investment in human resources" and "the 'third' or 'residual' factor."[8]

This emphasis on factors other than capital and labor was in turn reflected in international trade and competitiveness statistics. Up until the late 1950s, one of the key indicators used to measure the competitiveness of countries was the balance of payments.[9] Based on the comparative advantage model, the indicator would classify a country as competitive if its exports exceeded its imports. However, in the late 1960s additional indicators started to be used to reflect recognition of the fact that a country's growth was not narrowly to its own resources (labor and capital) but rather other factors were important too, such as technology, science and research and development. Indeed, terms such as "structural" or "systemic competitiveness" and the "competitive advantage" of nations underscore precisely the significance of such additional factors deemed previously "non-economic."[10]

The general concern with economic growth and eventually the emphasis on technology and scientific knowledge became intertwined with the debate on the so-called technological gap.

Cold War Rivalries and Technological Disparities

Reflecting the preoccupation of national governments and the European scientific community at the time, but also in reaction to the Cold War and the rivalry between the USA and the USSR for technological, scientific and military supremacy, the first European collaborative efforts concerned advanced technologies in the energy, space and civil aviation sectors. Examples here include Concorde, the joint supersonic passenger aircraft program between France and Britain agreed to in 1962, and Airbus, the joint aircraft venture formed in 1969 initially between France and Germany to challenge the dominance of the U.S. Boeing in the large civil aircraft market. Both these examples of technological cooperation took place outside the EU structures.

On the one hand, there existed strong drivers for European cooperation in these strategic fields, not least the enormous investment required and the strategic need to establish European capabilities independent of the two superpowers. Scientific and technological cooperation was linked to economic and industrial modernization and development. The launch of cooperation coincided with the postwar West European economic miracle, making public funding of these schemes, especially in the 1960s, unproblematic. But on the other hand, it was precisely because these sectors concerned "prestige technologies" and were closely associated with national sovereignty and defense that national egoisms often put limits on cross-national collaboration.[11]

One of the first areas raising concerns about technological defeat was space. Questions of technological power and international prestige came to the fore in the late 1950s when the USSR launched *Sputnik*. Technological disparities became more pronounced as Western Europe got caught up in the space race between the two superpowers. Although West European history in space was marred by national political, industrial and scientific tensions, collaboration was successful and resulted in the creation of the European Space Research Organization and the European Launcher Development Organization in 1964, forerunners of the European Space Agency established in 1975, and in the development of independent European communication satellite launching facilities.[12]

In addition to an independent European presence in space, West European countries skilfully managed to use the "technological disparities" discourse for political and eventually economic advantage as they succeeded in negotiating better terms in Intelsat, the International Telecommunications Satellite consortium. Intelsat was a central strategic element of U.S. geopolitical concerns during the Cold War and the space race.[13] It was conceived by the USA as a single global commercial communications satellite system to be effectively controlled by it—the dominant power in satellite technology and launchers at the time—through Comsat, a U.S. company purposely created for that reason. The interim agreements of Intelsat were signed in 1964, with negotiations for the final agreement due to resume five years later. In this interim period, West European efforts in communication satellites intensified and agreement was finally achieved for the development of an independent West European satellite launcher. West European cooperation was in reaction to U.S. technological leadership and the reflection of this dominance in the interim agreements of Intelsat. Besides, initially, West European PTTs were at best cautious about the establishment of Intelsat for two main reasons. First, they lacked technological capability in satellites, a technology, moreover, that was unproven, economically uncertain and therefore risky. Second, Intelsat was a threat to the PTTs' investment in terrestrial networks. West European PTTs already had strong financial interests in cable transmission systems in which they owned much larger stakes than what the USA was prepared to give them in the global commercial communications satellite system, Intelsat.[14]

Hence, technological and political considerations but also industrial policy concerns regarding West European participation in the building of the Intelsat system and procurement contracts resulted in Western Europe being strongly dissatisfied with the interim agreements. U.S. officials were aware of this. "Major continental European nations are critical of the 'excessively dominant' position of the United States in the decisions of the International Consortium," wrote President Johnson's Special Assistant for Telecommunications, adding that the lack of European interest could threaten the commercial viability of the venture.[15] The USA needed to have Western Europe on board, a valuable ally in the Cold War context. In the end, the Europeans used the interim period to develop the necessary technological capabilities in order to be treated as equal partners by the USA and reduce the latter's influence in Intelsat.

In the second half of the 1960s, the issue of technological disparities moved beyond a handful of prestige technologies to become a much wider and serious politico-economic concern. The alarming "technological gap," in particular in computers and data processing, between Western Europe and the USA reached the highest political levels but, unlike space, it did not immediately result in concerted action.

From Technological Disparities to the Technological Gap

It was in France under De Gaulle that the term "technological gap" was coined and progressively came to dominate the transatlantic political agenda. In the second half of the 1960s, there was widespread uneasiness that the gap was growing and concern about accelerating inward U.S. investment. The picture was one of giant U.S. corporations swallowing up West European national companies. More worryingly, U.S. companies investing in Europe were carrying out neither advanced production nor R&D. The following passage is indicative of the sentiments of that period:

FIFTEEN years from now the world's third greatest industrial power, just after the United States and Russia, may not be Europe, but American industry in Europe.[16]

The Freeman and Young study, prepared at the request of the OECD science ministers and presented at their second meeting in January 1966, documented significant technological disparities between the USA and the major West European countries.[17] The study noted the undoubtedly "very large and growing" favorable technological balance of payments (i.e., receipts for payments for technological know-how, licenses and patents) of the USA compared to the main West European nations. Regarding R&D investment, the report found that the USA spent both a higher percentage of its Gross National Product (3.1 percent) and a much greater amount per capita ($93.7) for R&D than any West European country. The study also acknowledged the pivotal role of government spending in technological progress, which was estimated at 63 percent in the USA compared to a West European (France, Germany, Netherlands, UK) average of 57 percent, ranging from 70 percent in France to 35 percent in the Netherlands.

In the second half of the 1960s, numerous studies were published analyzing the transatlantic "technological gap." Several of these went beyond an emphasis on the role of technology and scientific knowledge in economic growth to specify further integration within the context of the EU as the solution.[18] In short, the technological gap discourse was used to promote European integration. The argument put forward was that a large economic and political European entity was needed in order to offset and emulate *Le Défi Américain*.[19]

Servan-Schreiber's and Layton's analyses in particular were important, not so much in stating the obvious, that is the technological leadership of the USA, but in the solution they both forcefully espoused.[20] For them, the solution no longer lay with national champion policies, the response of the major industrialized West European countries so far, but rather with the creation of a European technological community. Action was urgently required and European-level initiatives were imperative if Europe was not to be condemned to an inevitable and irreversible decline. It was in this sense—the need to think and act beyond national frontiers—that the technological challenge was a political challenge.

Servan-Schreiber's book, providing an alarmist account, contributed to the popularization of the debate on the technological gap and the associated brain drain referring to the migration of scientists. Layton, who subsequently became Altiero Spinelli's (European Commissioner for industrial affairs) Chef de Cabinet, supported European solutions in an enlarged EU that was to include Britain. Among the proposals he put forward, it is worth noting two. Regarding the computing sector, Layton suggested that governments should encourage the formation of big European consortia able to take on American companies, in particular IBM. He also supported the end of national procurement policies favoring national champions and the launch of a "Buy European Policy" which would create a big enough market for the proposed European companies. Both proposals influenced the European debate.

The technological gap was being discussed in parallel bilaterally between the USA and individual West European states, and within multilateral organizations such as the OECD and NATO. There was disagreement among national governments concerning the form European cooperation should take. The issue became entangled with Britain's entry into the EU.[21] Britain did not want to commit to any specific arrangements or institutions, preferring to use advanced technology as a lever in its attempts to join the EU. But France in particular was wary of Britain's close relation to the USA and therefore not convinced of Britain's commitment to European integration. De Gaulle was also wary of the OECD—of which the USA was a member—assuming formal science policy activities, preferring instead purely European solutions.[22] Conversely, the USA preferred the OECD to which it belonged and which it could influence and saw Britain's technological power and its accession to the EU as key to alleviating the technological gap.

The political saliency that the technological gap had reached by the second half of the 1960s and the widespread concerns shared by various commentators but also the general public triggered an official response from the USA, quick to appease its valuable West European allies. The U.S. strategy had three aims: to dispel the perception that it itself was somehow responsible for the gap, to transform European concerns into a lever to promote European integration and the accession of Britain into the EU, and, finally, to rely on NATO and the OECD in order to improve transatlantic relations. Significantly, in what illustrates the U.S. influence in the work of the OECD, the U.S. government foretold the outcome of the OECD studies on the technological gap:

> U.S. is already fully committed to support basic study of composition and characteristics of gap by OECD. Results of this OECD analysis may remove mystique of "gap" and demonstrate that many aspects of solution lie in European actions such as scales of market, organization, education, corporate structure, management techniques, etc.[23]

In January 1967, the Interdepartmental Committee on the technological gap—set up by U.S. President Johnson and headed by Donald Honig, the President's Science and Technology Advisor—delivered its interim report.[24] Three observations are worth making. First, for the USA the technological gap was not a technological but primarily a political problem with potentially adverse economic effects for itself. Second, the roots of the problem lay squarely with Europe and it was up to Europe itself to find solutions. In addition to further European integration and Britain's accession to the EU, for the USA bold socioeconomic structural reforms too—concerning among other things education, "work habits," management and marketing practices—would greatly alleviate technological disparities. Lastly, while the USA was eager to play down the scale of the problem by suggesting possible solutions and U.S. style reforms, it was also wary that European initiatives to overcome the technological gap would not ultimately threaten the U.S. competitive advantage: "a substantial part of our favorable trade balance with the world depends upon our technological superiority and we should not give it away for nothing."[25]

When Honig delivered the final report of the Interdepartmental Committee on the technological gap in December 1967, he noted that in general the U.S. strategy had been successful and pointed out that much of the sensitivity surrounding the issue had been removed. Significantly, the issue was now framed differently. The report argued that the gap was only to a limited degree technological and that psychological, political, economic and social factors were more important. It conceded that the perceived gap concerned largely a handful of advance technology sectors, "principally those that have benefited from U.S. military, space, and atomic energy programs" including computers, advanced aircraft, electronic components and communications.[26]

The U.S. strategy coupled with various reports produced, *inter alia*, by the OECD succeeded in diffusing the blame from the USA.[27] In particular, as the Honig report noted, there was growing recognition of the complexity of the technological gap that eventually became conceptualized as a European problem of rapidly applying technological know-how due to several long-standing structural factors. Similar to the U.S. official response, U.S. scholars attributed the technological gap to the small size of European firms and national markets, inadequate economies of scale, duplication of R&D, lack of risk finance, weak entrepreneurship in exploiting basic research and lack of managerial skills, and contrasted this picture to the USA of big corporations, entrepreneurial spirit, venture capital, commercial technological inventions and labor mobility.[28] Thus, for the USA the gap was not technological but rather just a symptom of an extremely complex problem involving various interrelated economic, financial, political, educational, managerial and cultural factors.

In sum, from the 1960s onward, technology in general and ICT have come to figure prominently on national and international political agendas. And, crucially, since its origins, the technological gap has been interpreted differently by various policy stakeholders seeking to promote their interests. For instance, whereas Europeans would largely perceive the gap as a technological problem and some would use it to advocate further integration, the U.S. official and unofficial response was that the roots of the problem were not technological but rather political and therefore the solution lay with broader socioeconomic structural reforms.

PROMOTION OF NATIONAL CAPITAL: PROTECTIONISM AND THE SEARCH FOR NATIONAL CHAMPIONS

By the mid-1950s, the U.S. computer industry was well ahead internationally. Generous federal funding and military spending fuelled by Cold War rivalries, a dynamic entrepreneurial spirit and strong domestic market demand further nurtured in a thriving economy all contributed to this lead. West European firms—with their small national markets, latent domestic demand, growing competitive pressure from the USA and national austerity programs to lift war-ridden economies—simply could not afford the high R&D funding required to establish themselves in domestic markets let alone compete on the international stage. Moreover, whereas the industry in Western Europe placed emphasis on scientific applications, IBM, the undisputed leader in computer mainframe technology, was racing ahead, having realized that growth potential lay with data processing.[29]

In an attempt to stay abreast of technological advances, European companies began establishing alliances with U.S. companies. For instance, in 1964, the West German Siemens got into alliance with the U.S. Radio Corporation of America (RCA). The same year, the U.S. General Electric bought the computer arm of Italian Olivetti and French Bull. For U.S. companies, alliances with and acquisitions of European companies were crucial in finding new markets at a time when competition at home was intensifying. In effect, competition between IBM and other U.S. computer companies was being played out on West European soil.

In the mid-1960s, IBM controlled over 60 percent of the European and half of the British computer markets despite the latter's earlier lead in computer technology.[30] The penetration of U.S. computing companies in European markets, the buying out and closing down of European companies' production facilities (e.g., General Electric in France after the takeover of Bull) pushed European governments to intervene, ushering in the era of national champions. The USA was entrenching its dominance in advanced technology fields and was showing no willingness to allow its West European allies access to critical technology. Nor was the U.S. administration or industry prepared to forge a more equal relationship with Western Europe. The Intelsat case and the U.S. attitude toward the "technological gap," discussed above, provided clear evidence of this unequal relation. Western Europe had to respond to the growing U.S. economic and political domination.

Individual European countries turned inward in an attempt to build indigenous capabilities in advanced technological sectors, sectors increasingly perceived as major contributors to economic growth. In addition, especially in the context of the Cold War, technological prowess was intimately linked to national sovereignty and seen as a symbol of independence and global power. Under De Gaulle in particular, industrial and technological strength and independence from the USA became matters of national prestige. The search for national solutions went hand-in-hand with hostility toward supranational initiatives seen as impinging upon national sovereignty. In the second half of the 1960s, the major West European countries (notably Britain, France and West Germany) responded to the "technological gap" through a mix of new institutional structures (e.g., a Ministry for research in West Germany), specific projects (e.g., *Plan Calcul* in France), public funding (though the amounts given by the British government were smaller) and "buy national" policies.

The massive changes in the world economy in the 1970s, noted above, and the ensuing economic recession led to a proliferation of nontariff barriers to trade and a resurgence of protectionism. The 1970s witnessed industry restructuring in West Europe with a number of mergers and withdrawals. Part of this restructuring was triggered by the recession of the computer industry in the USA that, coupled with IBM's growing power, forced U.S. computer companies with investments in Europe, such as General Electric and RCA, out of the market. For instance, following General Electric's withdrawal from computers, France decided to allow Honeywell, which had taken over the computer activities of General Electric, to take General Electric's stake in Bull.[31]

During this period, efforts to establish cross-national groupings to face competition from the USA were doomed to failure as they were not compatible with the interests of the powerful national champions. A noteworthy example here is the Eurodata venture, formed in 1969 among major European information technology firms: the British International Computers Limited (ICL), the French Compagnie Internationale pour l'Informatique (CII subsequently Bull), the Dutch Philips, the German AEG-Telefunken, the Swedish Saab and the Italian Olivetti. The aim was that Eurodata, not IBM, should supply computers to the European space research organization. The venture failed because of German government resistance due to Siemens being excluded from the consortium.[32] The contract went to IBM.

Equally, Unidata, a joint venture between the German Siemens, the Dutch Philips and the French CII formed in 1973 to produce a new common range of computers in order to challenge IBM, officially collapsed in 1975 when the French government under President Giscard d' Estaing decided not to approve it but instead pursue an agreement with U.S. Honeywell.[33] In effect, the venture was a non-starter since from its inception there was fierce domestic lobbying in France by Honeywell-Bull, the largest computer manufacturer with French interests, seeing in Unidata a potential competitor, but also lobbying by Compagnie Générale d' Electricité, the French telecommunications equipment manufacturer and a shareholder in CII, who feared that the venture would strengthen the German Siemens, one of its main competitors. In the end, Honeywell-Bull rescued CII in France and Siemens rescued the ailing computer manufacturer Telefunken-AEG in Germany. The collapse of Unidata together with these two national rescue plans confirmed the return of national champions. Unidata, and with it the attempt to establish a European dimension in computer related industries, failed.

Once again, it was evident that national European companies would see each other as competitors—earning the label "hostile brothers"—and would prefer to establish cooperation with their counterparts across the Atlantic.[34] Strategically of course, cooperation with technologically advanced companies from the USA, where there was also the expectation of access to the large, fast-growing U.S. domestic market, and later from Japan made more sense, but it served to prolong the fragmentation of the European market.

The recession following the oil crises brought extensive state intervention. Besides, capital in Western Europe in the postwar period, with the partial exception of Britain, was essentially state-contained and that exacerbated interventionism.[35] CII-Honeywell-Bull in France, Siemens in Germany and, though to a lesser extent, ICL in Britain, all benefited from public funding and procurement. However, the growth these companies experienced in the late 1970s turned out to be short-lived. Similarly, the entry of other European companies, like the Italian Olivetti, the Dutch Philips and the German Nixdorf, into the promising market for mid-range computers was not meant to last.[36] It was becoming clear that national champion solutions were inadequate. Not only had they failed to assist individual European computer companies to take on the world leader IBM, but another strong competitor began to emerge, Japan.

Since the late 1950s, the Japanese government working in concert with the industry had launched a series of policy measures—including tariffs to control import competition, various programs backed by generous public funding—with the aim to assist the development of the domestic computer industry to a level at which it could credibly challenge IBM. Japanese computer policy, though not lacking internal conflicts, became an example of cooperative research.[37] Government efforts intensified in the first half of the 1970s and in 1975, the year of the aborted Unidata venture aimed at forming a European computer champion, Japan launched its Very Large Scale Integrated circuits program, which propelled Japan to the forefront of integrated circuit technology worldwide. Japan's cooperative research strategy that proved so successful and allowed the Japanese industry to attack IBM's leadership attracted a lot of attention and, as will be seen, was repeatedly referred to in European Commission policy documents as a strategy that Europe itself needed to emulate.

In sum, government intervention in the electronics and computing sectors was not a feature unique to the large West European countries. On the contrary, the governments of both the USA and, later, Japan were doing exactly the same. These governments sought through subsidies, generous funding and other measures to support their domestic industries. However, there were crucial differences between West European countries and their main competitors. For besides such industrial support measures, neither the U.S. nor Japanese governments actively shaped industry structure. The USA and Japan sought to support their domestic industries but they did not deliberately seek to favor one specific market player or to create a single domestic company. In sharp contrast, government intervention in individual West European countries was not so much industry- but more accurately company-specific. European governments were convinced that the solution to the technological gap was the creation of one big domestic company, a national champion. To this end, European governments would actively induce industry restructuring and encourage mergers between domestic companies. For example, both the British ICL (1968) and the French CII (1970) were products of such strategies. Having strangled any elements of domestic competition in the process, governments would then erect several trade barriers to protect their national champions from external competition as well. This created a vicious circle of government intervention and protection and diminishing competitiveness. In Western Europe, each national champion was expected to individually attack IBM. In contrast, much of the industry dynamism in the USA, for instance in the production of integrated circuits, came from small start-up companies. The latter (such as Fairchild and Texas Instruments in the late 1950s) would choose not to compete head on with IBM but rather target segments outside its dominance and act as suppliers to IBM.[38] In Western Europe, the governments' twin strategy of national champions and protectionism coupled with the lack of venture capital, small domestic markets and absence of strong domestic demand all served to kill off any entrepreneurial spirit. And although there were no start-ups in Japan and, like West European countries, vertical integration was the norm with the components industry concentrated in big electronic groups, the components production arms of these diversified companies had to be internationally competitive, not least because they would provide inputs to other parts of their business, notably the Japanese consumer electronics sector, parts which were already fiercely competing on world markets.[39]

In view of the patent failure of national protectionist policies, the European Commission intervened aiming to stimulate cross-border trade and, in turn, the growth of national computer firms and also started to urge the national champions to merge in order to create European champions.

AIMS WITH NO MEANS: THE EU STRATEGY

In the 1960s and 1970s, information and communication technology and telecommunications started to figure within the EU context. Handicapped by the lack of specific competence in this field and caught in its own institutional and political stalemate, the European Commission attempted to intervene but, without the support of either national governments or the European industry, its efforts failed. The Commission's strategy focused on three areas: total harmonization through the development of uniform European technical standards and administrative rules, a broad economic and industrial planning role which included science and technology, and, finally, common network planning and development. The relevant developments are examined in turn.

Total Harmonization

Roughly until the 1980s, telecommunications in the EU was under the sovereign control of national monopolies and national governments. Co-operation and regulation beyond national states was confined to commercial operational and technical matters necessary for the establishment of cross-border communication, which in Europe the PTTs themselves, working under the auspices of the European Conference of Postal and Telecommunications administrations, would address. In this light, the EU context was not significant and, in any case, the founding treaty did not grant the EU specific competence in telecommunications.

The EU initially came across telecommunications by accident as part of its principal objective concerning the creation of a common market rather than in pursuit of sector-specific policy objectives. The general aim was to eliminate trade barriers within the EU, allow the free movement of factors of production and stimulate trade by replacing national administrative rules and technical standards with uniform European ones.[40] The challenge was of great magnitude. The EU followed a two-pronged strategy.

The first key policy tool of the creation of the single market has been the development of common European rules and standards. Originally, the EU conceptualized harmonization as uniformity: the mosaic of incompatible national rules and standards would be replaced by new pan-European ones. This evidently discredited strategy was subsequently abandoned in favor of measures promoting approximation, not uniformity, and mutual recognition of rules. But it was after the path breaking case of Cassis de Dijon in 1979 that the Commission succeeded in raising the principle of mutual recognition among national rules on the basis of minimum harmonization from the confines of technical norms and administrative rules to the main driver of the internal market.[41] This "new strategy for regulatory coordination" allows for national differences and competition between national rules but, importantly, ensures that these do not act as barriers to trade and thus it promotes open markets.[42] As will be discussed, in 1989 with the adoption of the Television without Frontiers directive, harmonization of minimum requirements and mutual recognition of national rules expanded to television services.

The second key policy tool of the creation of the single market has been the prevention of new national rules and standards through a process of mutual notification whereby national regulators are required to notify the European Commission and their counterparts in the other member states of any planned new measures. The early notification system was first introduced in 1965.[43] The aim was to preempt the adoption of new rules that could act as trade barriers further fragmenting the market. However, the success of this initiative depended on the cooperation of member states, which proved not forthcoming. Little progress was achieved and in May 1968, amidst the monetary turmoil, the member states signed a "gentlemen's agreement" to respect the notification provision and allow for a standstill period.[44] But the agreement failed to promote harmonization. For besides political resistance and the real difficulties encountered, the agreement covered only a small number of national technical regulations. The following year, the national governments inserted a provision on early notification in the General Program for the elimination of technical barriers to trade, but they then proceeded to interpret widely exemptions on grounds of health and safety thereby, once again, rendering the provision ineffective.[45] It took fifteen years for a breakthrough to be achieved, this time with a stronger legislative instrument covering industrial standards.[46] The most recent expression of the mutual notification principle is the notification procedure under the 2002 electronic communications regulatory framework, examined in chapter 6.

It was within this general context of eliminating trade barriers through the adoption of uniform technical standards and rules that the EU originally got involved in telecommunications. More specifically, at their first meeting in September 1964, the six EU Ministers responsible for posts and telecommunications expressed the view that certain issues, such as technical standards acting as nontariff trade barriers and public procurement, could be addressed under the auspices of the EU.[47] The fact that it took thirteen years for the posts and telecommunications Ministers to meet again illustrates the lack of political stimulus for concrete action in the area of telecommunications.

In sum, as was to be expected, the process of removing barriers to trade proved complex and slow. Little progress had been achieved by 1970, the deadline for the establishment of a customs union. The problem was compounded by the international economic upheaval of the 1970s, the consequent recession, and the first enlargement of the EU in 1973 with the accession of Britain, Ireland and Denmark, that increased the number of member states needed to reach agreement. As noted, during the recessionary years, national governments became progressively more protectionist. Unable to raise tariffs or quotas—which the customs union and the GATT had lowered—they resorted to nontariff barriers in an attempt to fragment and thus protect domestic markets. Throughout the 1970s, national approaches to technical standards and rules persisted, thwarting the creation of a common market. Total harmonization had clearly failed. Under these circumstances, the Commission resorted to the pursuit of an abstract industrial policy.

Abstract Industrial Policy

One of the first initiatives of the medium-term economic policy committee, comprising national experts and European Commission representatives, was the establishment in March 1965 of a working party for Scientific and Technical Research Policy, known as PREST.[48] Its creation was an indication of the political recognition of the role of science and technology in economic development as well as concern about the growing European dependency on the USA for high technology. But the "empty chair" crisis that broke out a few months later put initiatives on hold. This crisis was effectively a continuation of the fundamental tension over the character of integration, a tension that is as old as European integration itself and has been repeated numerous times, a conflict about "what kind of Europe?"

In October 1967, PREST, the working party for Scientific and Technical Research Policy, submitted its report to the first ever Council of Ministers for Scientific Affairs.[49] Based on this Maréchal report, known by the name of the working party's chairman and director of the French science policy agency, the Council agreed on measures aiming at encouraging the formation of European firms big enough to compete with the American giants. To this end, it recommended the adoption of European standards, the introduction of European patents, and the harmonization of company tax rules. The Council agreed for a second study to assess the prospects for European-level scientific research cooperation in seven priority areas (data processing, telecommunications, transport, oceanography, metallurgy, the environment and meteorology) with the participation of nine non-EU members: Austria, Britain, Denmark, Ireland, Norway, Portugal, Spain, Sweden, and Switzerland. Britain's participation was strongly resisted by France but was deemed essential by the other EU member states since Britain was at the time the most advanced West European country in many technological areas.

But the Maréchal report's proposals were not destined to go any further. In December 1967, France vetoed Britain's entry to the EU for the second time, creating a standstill in plans for European scientific collaboration. It was only after De Gaulle was succeeded by Georges Pompidou in the summer of 1969 that the debate on European scientific research resumed. Eventually, in October 1969, member states endorsed most of the proposals in the second PREST report for collaborative research among European firms. But unlike the first one, the second report advocated intergovernmental cooperation. It led to the COST program (COoperation in the Scientific and Technical Field), the oldest European intergovernmental scientific and technical research collaborative network involving countries from wider Europe.

Since intergovernmentalism reigned in the 1960s, it is not surprising that ultimately national governments had to put the integration process back on track. Their summit in The Hague in December 1969 was "the most significant event within the [Union] since its inception."[50] It signaled the end of the political impasse that had put the EU on hold. National governments agreed to open full membership negotiations with the four applicant countries (Britain, Ireland, Denmark and Norway) and to set up two committees to examine the prospects for economic and monetary union and political cooperation respectively.[51] In addition, in what interests us, the political leaders reaffirmed their support for European R&D efforts as a means to promote industrial development.[52]

The Hague Summit pushed the Commission's DG for industrial affairs—headed by Altiero Spinelli, a fervent federalist—into action. Established in 1967, the DG for industrial affairs had failed to function properly not least because—like all Commission services—it got bogged down by the merger of the institutions of the three European Communities that same year.[53] But the need for common action was felt quite strongly as the completion of the customs union in July 1968 had significantly increased the exposure of European industry to external competition. In addition, the perceived European technological backwardness and the imminent accession of countries with strong industrial and technological potential made a common industrial policy central to the strengthening and enlargement of the Union.[54] Developments were fast underlying the emphasis that the Commission placed on assuming a general economic and industrial role and the importance attached to advanced technology as a key element of any such effort.

However, as explained, industrial policy was the domain of national governments. Any European-level initiatives, for example Airbus, were selective and intergovernmental. Even though it lacked explicit powers in this field, the European Commission seized the opportunity to move beyond ad hoc action and develop a general economic and industrial policy. Indeed, its memorandum in 1970 stressed the need for a pan-European industrial policy to advance economic integration and technological independence.[55] In the end no action stemmed from it but the Colonna memorandum, as is known, was very important. It was the first EU document to provide a synoptic analysis of the European industry and outline general principles and guidelines for a common industrial policy.

The starting points of the memorandum were the inadequate competitiveness of the EU industry, especially when compared to the USA, and the small size of national markets for growth industries in particular. It called for the elimination of technical barriers to trade and the liberalization of public procurement; the harmonization of the legal, fiscal and financial frameworks within which firms had to operate in order to promote transnational activities; industrial restructuring notably through European cross-border mergers; measures to facilitate change and adjustment such as industrial exploitation of scientific research; and solidarity in external economic relations.

The memorandum repeatedly emphasized the importance of advanced technological sectors and singled out electro-nuclear, aerospace and information technology. The Commission advocated industrial consolidation but warned against the "very serious danger" of consolidation taking place exclusively at the national level within individual member states. If they remained national, it explained, firms would be small and weak, easy takeover targets by rival non-EU firms. European-level industrial consolidation, however, could strengthen their competitiveness and contribute to technological independence thereby discouraging further U.S. penetration. To this end, the Commission urged national governments to rid themselves of their hitherto hostile attitude—illustrated, for instance, in the cases of Eurodata and Unidata—and instead look favorably into the creation of transnational European industrial groupings. The message was that European, not national, champions could face competition under international oligopolistic market conditions. It is evident that the Colonna memorandum contained a fundamental contradiction. On the one hand it called for initiatives to foster liberalization and increase competition and on the other it recommended European mergers and industrial concentration.

The Colonna memorandum on industrial policy represents a failed attempt by the Commission to claim a role in general macroeconomic and industrial planning. Neither national governments nor, importantly, the European high-technology firms were yet convinced that coordinated action was needed. In short, there was lack of consensus on the need for, let alone the possible character of, a European-level industrial policy. Indeed, the Colonna memorandum revealed fundamental disagreements between the member states about the principles underpinning industrial policy.[56] With Britain at the time not an EU member, the two camps were represented by France, supported by Italy, in favor of direct intervention and planning and Germany, supported by the Netherlands, advocating a general strategy for economic and industrial development with the emphasis on competition and on the basis of a liberal noninterventionist approach. These diametrically opposing views were also a reflection of the exposure of the respective domestic industries to competitive pressures and perceived vulnerabilities. Whereas in the early 1970s the German industry was at a peak, the French industry was facing serious challenges.

The massive changes in the world economy in the 1970s, the internal conflicts concerning industrial policy and the stark heterogeneity in industrial structures and issues among the EU countries forced the Commission to abandon its ambitious macroeconomic and industrial policy plans. Instead, it concentrated on the creation of the common market, the assumption being that the common market (negative integration) would force the industry to restructure itself in order to take advantage of it.

Government leaders were once again to provide the impetus. In the aftermath of the collapse of Bretton Woods in 1971 and in view of the imminent enlargement, EU political leaders met in Paris in October 1972.[57] The focus of this summit was on the economic and monetary union, institutional changes, and the international role of the EU. Among other things, political leaders expressed their determination to develop a common science and technology policy. Following the Paris summit, the Commission concentrated on the data processing sector where European weakness and IBM dominance were uncontested facts, the opening up of public procurement, and the harmonization of telecommunications equipment and services.

In 1974, for the first time, national governments accepted the principle of industrial policy action not in a declining but in the growth sector of data processing though, despite the rise of inward, primarily U.S., investment no concrete action resulted from the proposals until 1979.[58]

In the field of telecommunications, the Commission worked on reviving its links with the national PTTs, first established when the question of opening up public procurement arose in the early 1970s. Between March and September 1974, a series of meetings took place between the Commission and the PTTs to discuss the technical, economic and administrative issues surrounding the liberalization of public procurement.[59] The problem was big. It was estimated that, in 1972, only 5 percent of telecommunications equipment was purchased across Union borders. The PTTs agreed in principle on the opening up of public procurement but were against legally binding deadlines, arguing instead that the envisaged ad hoc committee, comprising PTTs representatives, should assume responsibility for the gradual implementation of this measure. The opposition of the PTTs led to the exclusion of the telecommunications sector from the eventual public procurement European directive in 1977 and, two years later, its exclusion also from the GATT multilateral code on government procurement.[60]

With regard to the harmonization of equipment and services, the PTTs recognized the importance of this measure for the creation of the internal market, the potential for significant economies of scale in research and production, and, in turn, the strengthening of the international competitiveness of the European industry. However, once again protecting their interests, the PTTs were quick to emphasize that the best forum to address harmonization was their own professional association, the CEPT, embracing then twenty-five countries compared to the nine of the EU. In an attempt to avoid a direct confrontation with the powerful PTTs, the Commission accepted the loose cooperation framework of the CEPT and called for better links between herself, the CEPT and the European industry.

Besides the resistance of the PTTs, developments in the broader international context—the collapse of the Bretton Woods, the oil shocks, the consequent recession and the resurgence of protectionism—undermined the weak political commitment to create a single market through the harmonization of technical standards and the opening up of public procurement. It is not that the Commission was not active during the examined period. Rather, with the international political and economic order in disarray, hardly any proposals were adopted let alone acted upon. Government and industry support for European action was forthcoming only in relation to the industrial sectors in crisis (in particular steel, textiles and shipbuilding) facing strong international competitive pressures and in urgent need for structural adjustment. The Commission got preoccupied with declining, as opposed to future growth, industries.[61] This situation was to change toward the end of the 1970s, as the next chapter explains.

Network Planning and Development

In the first half of the 1970s, the EU got involved in network planning and development with two major initiatives. The first concerned network planning and standards and was part of the long-standing effort of Europe to fight IBM's market power. The second initiative concerned future network development.

In 1974, IBM created a proprietary network architecture called Systems Network Architecture (SNA). Its fundamental principle was hierarchical centralized control provided by mainframes. This way IBM, controlling the mainframe computers, would effectively control the entire network system, thereby protecting and strengthening its market power.

In Europe, there was a concerted effort to advance Open Systems Inter-connection (OSI), a set of public standards for interconnecting computer systems, products and networks of different manufacturers and therefore a direct attack on IBM's dominance based on its proprietary architecture. European computer manufacturers and national governments strongly supported the OSI reference model which, moreover, had the potential to create a much needed pan-European market for computer products.[62] The European Commission's DG for Competition also promoted OSI as part of its investigation into the marketing practices of IBM, which was launched in 1974 in response to complaints from competitors alleging that IBM was abusing its dominant power by deliberately delaying servicing and updating its software running on non-IBM machines and unnecessarily delaying the release of technical information on new products, information that was crucial for competitors to innovate and produce compatible equipment.[63]

Despite such strong support, implementation of OSI experienced many delays and was not as straightforward as initially anticipated. But above all, and with the benefit of hindsight, the biggest failure in European efforts to back the OSI model was overlooking the emerging Transmission Control Protocol/Internet Protocol (TCP/IP), which originated in the USA through defense spending during the Cold War but whose protocols were to form the basis of the internet and become the internationally accepted internet-working model.[64] Ironically, therefore, although it contributed to curbing IBM's dominance, European preoccupation with OSI reflected, and at the same time served to sustain, the strength and influence of the telecommunications industry, and for a long time of monopolist public telecommunications operators, in the broader field of electronic communications.[65] In turn, support for OSI at the expense of the TCP/IP protocols contributed to European weakness in the computing and internet sectors. It was in the late 1990s that Europe, overtaken by the unprecedented growth of the internet, launched a catching-up race.

The second major initiative, and perhaps the most significant EU action in the field in the 1970s, was the establishment of the first European data network, Euronet. In the first half of the decade, as noted, the Commission was eager to promote tighter cooperation among national PTT administrations, especially in the most advanced technological sectors of the future. The assumption was that consensus on future generations of equipment and networks would be relatively easier to build and would avoid further disparities.

More specifically, the Commission became concerned at the number of uncoordinated information and documentation networks that were being introduced in individual EU countries. Euronet, the first European network envisaged to provide direct access to databases, was part of the initial three-year (1975–1977) Union action plan in the area of scientific and technical information.[66] The Commission, in an effort to prompt the national PTT administrations to cooperate, highlighted several benefits. Besides the significantly lower cost in building one common network as opposed to several, other advantages mentioned included intercommunication between existing documentation systems (at the time the different systems were incompatible), wider access to databases, greater reliability and the possibility of interconnection with other networks.[67] Prices would be based on volume of data rather than distance or fixed subscription and it was expected that, as a result, prices would drop by up to one-third.[68]

Euronet was more important than it appears at first sight. For the first time, a single European network for data transmission was to be set up under the Commission's sponsorship; there was agreement on the use of a single technology; the PTTs closely collaborated and formed a consortium for implementing a joint program; common standards for equipment were to be developed; and lastly Euronet represented the first ever agreement between the EU and the national PTTs. Moreover, Euronet was fundamentally linked with other EU policies, in particular the building of the internal market and the elimination of technical barriers to trade. The Commission expected to assume an active role in the operation and management of the network.[69] The politically salient idea was that it would gain footing in the telecommunications sector.

Inside the Commission, the main advocate of Euronet was DG XIII, at the time responsible for the dissemination of information, and in particular its committee for scientific and technical information and documentation. The Commission had the support of information centers and public administrations. Euronet was also part of the PTTs' efforts to preempt competition from private data networks by offering a public monopoly alternative.

However, in parallel with the implementation of Euronet and in line with the historical focus on national network development, the majority of EU countries individually started implementing national data networks. Instead of a common European data network the result was fragmentation. By the mid-1980s, there were several national data networks with differing pricing models and technical capabilities, connecting to other national networks on a bilateral basis. In the end, Euronet, the vision of a common European public data network, was reduced to the interconnection of national data networks, similar to telephony networks. Telecommunications therefore retained their country-to-country character. Not only had the old model of national telecommunications networks and markets not been disrupted but it was strengthened and replicated in the nascent data communications market.

In short, the Euronet venture failed as national interests proved too resilient to accept cooperation. The only tangible result was PTT cooperation in standards, which led to the X.25 standard family (packet switching) becoming the main standard for public data networks in Europe. Again, this standard has to be understood in the context of the wider efforts to promote Open System Interconnection—X.25 was just one standard for the implementation of this networking paradigm—to counteract IBM's dominance. The implicit assumption in these efforts, driven primarily by European PTTs and pursued simultaneously at European and international arenas—in particular the ITU's International Telegraphy and Telephony Consultative Committee (CCITT) representing predominantly the interests of PTTs which eventually approved the standard in 1976—was that "'networks' meant national public switched networks configured as closed hierarchies and controlled by monopoly [public telecommunications operators]."[70]

In sum, in the 1970s, the third main strategy of the EU concerned common open standards to counter IBM's power and collaboration among national PTTs in future generation networks. For the first time, cooperation in telecommunications moved beyond the confines of national PTTs and embraced the European Commission. Indeed, the links between the Commission and the PTTs were strengthened in the first half of the 1980s, as the next chapter examines. However, the main result of these actions in network planning and development was the entrenchment of the power of the PTTs not just in the plain-old-telephony market but in the broader electronic communications market. These initiatives contributed to the belated recognition and acceptance in Europe of the Internet, the de facto internetworking model.

REGULATION BY INVITATION: LAYING THE GROUND FOR THE LIBERALIZATION OF TELEVISION

During the 1970s, when the turmoil of the international political economy and the severe economic recession had put a brake on European integration, one EU institution, the European Court of Justice, became particularly active. For Middlemas, "[the European Court's] continuous activity throughout the 1970s was probably the most important single factor in keeping the sense of 'Community' alive in an era of intergovernmentalism."[71]

The European Court is a policy actor by invitation. In contrast to the European Commission, which has the right to initiate policies, the Court cannot intervene unless it is specifically asked to do so. But, having been asked to intervene, the Court has significant powers to shape markets and regulation. It has been instrumental in expanding the scope of European law and associated Commission competencies.

The case of television confirms the central role of the Court in European integration. The Court was the first EU institution to intervene as early as 1974. More specifically, at the onset of the accidental, and what proved to be chaotic, television deregulation in Italy which led to a great proliferation of television channels especially between 1974–1978, Guiseppe Sacchi, a private local cable operator redistributing television signals from outside its reception area, lodged a complaint with the Biella Court against the monopoly granted by the Italian state to the public broadcaster RAI over all kinds of television transmissions and in particular over advertising revenue. In turn, the Italian Court referred the case to the European Court, asking it to rule on two main issues. First, whether the principle of the free movement of goods within the common market applied to television signals and in particular to advertising. And second, whether the monopoly rights granted by the state to the public broadcaster (RAI) covering all kinds of television transmissions and advertising was in breach of the principle of the free movement of goods.

The Court held that the granting of monopoly rights as such "for considerations of public interest, of a non-economic nature" was not incompatible with the EU Treaty and dismissed the claim that a public service broadcaster's monopoly over television constituted in itself a breach of the principle of the free movement of goods.[72] The Court referred to the Italian and West German governments' submissions, which stated that public service broadcasters were entrusted with specific public interest tasks related to the "cultural and informative nature" of broadcasting and as such they could not be treated like any other "undertakings" and be obliged to fully observe the provisions of the EU Treaty.

Nonetheless, the Court ruled that the transmission of television signals, including advertisements, constituted services and hence came under the rules of the EU Treaty, although it confirmed that limits to competition and hence derogations from the Treaty provisions on competition were acceptable insofar as their full application would obstruct the performance of their particular duties. This is the most significant legal element of the Sacchi case. By defining television as a tradeable service, the Court at the same time established that it comes under EU jurisdiction. Crucially, the conceptualization of television broadcasting as one type of telecommunications service to be transmitted, as a result of technological convergence, by means of telecommunications facilities (e.g., cable network) signaled a similar change in policy emphasis that was eventually crystallized in the 1984 Green Paper on Television without Frontiers.

IN SEARCH OF A EUROPEAN IDENTITY

In the 1960s, the EU was trying to establish itself as an actor on the world stage. This was most obvious in external economic relations. For instance, despite tensions, the Six negotiated as a bloc in the GATT Kennedy Round that ended in 1967 and concluded trading agreements with ex-colonies. Later, in the 1970s, the EU began the search for a European identity, no longer unity, in response to the new international political economy order and the concomitant breakdown of the postwar Keynesian consensus.

For the first time, in December 1973, the EU political leaders put the concept of a European identity on the political agenda when they adopted a Declaration in order to enable member states "to achieve a better definition of their relations with other countries and of their responsibilities and the place which they occupy in world affairs."[73] For the Declaration, the unity of the EU countries was based on common ideals and objectives, on representative democracy, the rule of law, social justice and respect for human rights.[74] It stressed that international developments, namely the Cold War and the turmoil in international political economy, meant that West European countries could no longer individually assume a major role on the international scene; only united could they do so.

Two observations are worth making here. First, although the Declaration was on "European identity," it interpreted this narrowly as EU identity. Indeed, the same is true for the EU official rhetoric in general and subsequent debates that tend to equate EU identity with European identity. Both concepts, "Europe" and "identity," are ambiguous and fluid in terms of what they represent and who belongs to them. European identity is neither an essentialist nor a natural phenomenon but rather a historical construct discursively shaped.[75]

Second, it is important to note the context in which the concept of European identity emerged. The 1973 Declaration was primarily concerned with external European identity. European identity was launched at a time when the EU was attempting to revive integration after the politico-institutional stalemate that had emerged in the 1960s with the empty chair crisis and the rejection twice of Britain's application for membership, and when the demise of the postwar international monetary system resulted in the collapse of the established international political economy order. The international environment, in particular the worsening relations with the USA, pushed the EU to think about its international image and role, to think about what it stood for internationally.[76] And, finally, in these circumstances the first enlargement of the EU took place which, similarly to subsequent enlargements, threw the EU into an identity crisis, pushing it and its members to reflect about the nature and ultimate goals of European integration. It was in this turbulent and uncertain context that European identity became a concern. It was launched by EU political leaders "as a key concept in order to re-establish [. . .] order, and the place of Europe within it."[77]

In parallel to the search of an external European identity, concerns about public support for the European project arose. Ironically, it was the breakdown in the elite consensus on the character of integration during the 1965–1966 empty chair crisis that raised the issue of public support. The absence of consensus effectively put at risk the elite driven process of integration. It was a major setback since—according to neofunctionalism, the dominant theoretical explanation at the time—integration was supposed to rely on political and economic elites who, having perceived a common interest, were expected to collaborate with their counterparts in other countries and progressively transfer their activities and loyalties from the national to the supranational level.[78] This so-called Monnet method of gradual integration has been justified as follows:

> The people weren't ready to agree to integration, so you had to get on without telling them too much about what was happening.[79]

But the breakdown in political consensus in the mid-1960s forced European Union officials to recognize "the need actively to stimulate support for the European project."[80] For if support was not forthcoming from political elites, it could be cultivated in strong economic interests and the European public at large.

Popular support increasingly became an issue in the 1970s with the levelling out of the postwar economic growth and the crisis of the Keynesian national order. It is indicative that since 1973, the European Commission has begun measuring public opinion to inform itself and the general public about the views of EU people, the so-called Eurobarometer surveys. In 1975, a report to the Commission called for EU-wide rights to be enjoyed by all member states' citizens.[81] The introduction of direct elections to the European Parliament in 1979 was another attempt to stimulate public support. Finally, the European Commission actively sought to co-opt established economic interests—such as European information technology manufacturers, PTTs and public service broadcasters—and encouraged the creation of pan-European interest groups such as the European Round Table of industrialists, as the next chapter explores.

Interestingly, responding to concerns about inadequate popular support, another European organization, the Council of Europe, contended that broadcasting could further European unity. To this end, and noting the underreporting of major European organizations' activities on national television, it called upon national broadcasters to provide "regular and serious (rather than sensational) coverage" of their activities and recommended to member governments to pursue "a more active policy" of program exchanges.[82]

These themes—concern about inadequate public support and underreporting of major European organizations' activities on national television in particular, and in general a more active policy in the field of television in order to increase the exposure of European viewers to non-domestic Euro-

UNIVERSITY OF WESTMINSTER※

University of Westminster
Harrow Library

Title: Telecommunications policies for Sub-
Saharan Africa /
ID: 2600756809
Due: 11 March 2016

Title: World development report.
ID: 2600764046
Due: 11 March 2016

Title: Governing European communications :
ID: 2601561486
Due: 11 March 2016

Total items: 3
04/03/2016 16:11
Checked out: 4
Overdue: 0
Hold requests: 5
Ready for pickup: 3

pean content—have continued to figure highly on the European political agenda ever since. New technological developments, especially the advent of transfrontier television, gave a fresh impetus to this debate in the 1980s, pushing the European Parliament and the Commission into the fields of culture and television, fields that prior to the 1970s were the domain of the Council of Europe.

CONCLUSIONS

The international political economic upheaval and the associated crisis of the national Keynesian order explain developments in the period from the late 1960s up until the late 1970s.

The end of the postwar economic miracle, rising Cold War tensions and growing recognition that a "residual factor," technological progress, was a key contributor to economic growth accentuated Western Europe's weakness in high-technology sectors. It is in this period that Europe's preoccupation with the technological gap can be traced. The risk of technological dependency on the USA becoming permanent and the associated serious implications for the economic, political and strategic interests of Western Europe pushed some analysts to argue in favor of common European solutions. An external threat, the technological gap, was used by pro-integration forces as an argument to promote common European action. Again, this subterfuge has been used at various points throughout the history of European integration, as will be discussed later.

Developments in this period were either intergovernmental outside the EU context—for instance technological collaboration in aerospace and space—or national, within states, as was the case in the computing sector. This can be attributed to the predominantly national organization of capital in the postwar era in Western Europe, the Keynesian interventionist national order and the associated close relation between state and industry, and the fact that ICT industry itself was broadly satisfied with the status quo and the protection it afforded it. The response of West European governments to the new circumstances was to individually turn inward in an effort to protect national markets and promote national capital. The policy mix was active intervention in the market and a surge in nontariff barriers to trade. Governments would pick winners to create national champions. This nationally centered response impeded industry restructuring at the European level, hindered the emergence of coherent European initiatives, fragmented the internal market and, most importantly, did not enhance the industry's competitiveness.

The EU was unable to provide a way out of the international crisis. It was facing serious political-institutional challenges, was handicapped because it had no explicit powers to intervene in industrial or technological affairs, and, more importantly, lacked the support of either national governments or the industry to do so. The economic recession served to expose and emphasize on the one hand the differences of interests among the member states, and on the other hand the weakness of the EU system. The EU, a relatively new European organization, was called on to assume responsibilities which went beyond the bounds of its establishing Treaty. The EU pursued a three-pronged strategy.

First, in an effort to eliminate barriers to trade, the Commission sought the adoption of uniform technical norms and administrative rules. It was this strategy, soon abandoned as unrealistic, that first got the EU involved in telecommunications. The quest for uniformity was subsequently rejected in favor of two principles that have become the cornerstones of the entire single market project including communication policy: total harmonization gave way to mutual recognition among national rules on the basis of minimal essential harmonization and to mutual notification of planned new rules. Second, the Commission attempted, but failed, to play a role in general economic and industrial planning. Still, in these efforts one can trace the conflict between liberalization and industrial restructuring at the European level aimed at the creation of European champions who would take advantage of the substantial economies of scale of the internal market to become internationally competitive. Third, the Commission promoted pan-European network planning and development concerning new generations of technology and a set of standards for interconnecting different computer systems (OSI), in order to counter the dominance of IBM. Although, out of the three, these last initiatives were the most successful in that they allowed the Commission for the first time to establish links with the national PTTs, these initiatives reflected and at the same time served to entrench the power of the telecommunications industry, and for a long time that of monopolist public telecommunications operators, in the broader field of electronic communications and contributed to the disregard of the emerging internet protocols and, in turn, to the weakening of the European computing sector.

While the Commission's efforts largely failed, another EU institution, the European Court of Justice, the policy actor by invitation, in a key judgment granted the Commission competence to intervene in television and sowed the seeds of liberalization. This would prove crucial in subsequent developments.

As economic growth began to level out in the late 1960s and 1970s, in the context of massive turmoil in the world economy, worsening relations between Western Europe and the USA, economic recession, rising unemployment and the crisis of the postwar Keynesian paradigm, for the first time the question of a European identity arose together with concerns

about weak public support for the integration process. European identity emerged in the context of, and as a means to deal with, the crisis of the established (inter)national order. Again, similar to the technological gap, a European identity and inadequate public support have been recurring themes in the process of European integration.

In sum, in the period examined in this chapter, from the late 1960s to the late 1970s, the EU discovered the fields of telecommunications and television by accident—the former through the pursuit of broader objectives and the latter as a result of a legal case—rather than as part of a coherent communication policy framework. European efforts were curtailed by national governments eager to pursue individual solutions and promote national champions and by the adverse international economic situation. Overall, although EU initiatives largely failed—they were mired in institutional weakness, lacked legitimacy and the support of either national governments or the European industry—they were important in that they established fundamental principles on which subsequent liberalization and harmonization initiatives would be based. It was not long before the failure of national protectionism, technological developments and intensifying international pressures would alter the perceptions of major European industrial players.

NOTES

1. James Caporaso and John Keeler, "The European Union and Regional Integration Theory," in *The State of the European Union, 3: Building a European Polity?*, ed. Carolyn Rhodes and Sonia Mazey (Boulder, Colo.: Lynne Rienner, 1995), 37.

2. Derek Urwin, *The Community of Europe: A History of European Integration since 1945* (London and New York: Longman, 1995), 104.

3. Keith Middlemas, *Orchestrating Europe: The Informal Politics of European Union 1973–1995* (London: Fontana Press, 1995), 44–45.

4. Paschal Preston, *Reshaping Communications: Technology, Information and Social Change* (London: Sage, 2001), 43.

5. For the standard neoclassical growth theory see, for instance, Robert Solow, "A Contribution to the Theory of Economic Growth," *Quarterly Journal of Economics* 70, no. 1 (1956): 65–94.

6. For the early involvement of the OECD in science policy see Alexander King, *Science and Policy: The International Stimulus* (London: Oxford University Press, 1974).

7. The Freeman and Young study discussed below.

8. OECD, *The Residual Factor and Economic Growth* (Paris: OECD, 1964), 5. These theoretical explorations led in the 1980s to the endogenous economic growth theory.

9. Benoît Godin, "The Obsession for Competitiveness and Its Impact on Statistics: The Construction of High-Technology Indicators," Project on the History and Sociology of S&T Statistics, Working Paper 25, 2004, <http://www.csiic.ca/PDF/Godin_25.pdf> (24 Apr. 2006).

10. Bob Jessop, "The Future of the State in an Era of Globalization," *International Politics and Society*, no. 3 (2003): 38, <http://www.fes.de/ipg/ONLINE3_2003/ARTJESSOP.PDF> (18 July 2006).

11. For details see John Peterson and Margaret Sharp, *Technology Policy in the European Union* (London: Macmillan, 1998), 26–28.

12. For an excellent history of Europe in space see John Krige and Arturo Russo, *A History of the European Space Agency 1958–1987. Volume I: The Story of ESRO and ELDO, 1958–1973*, and *Volume II: The Story of ESA, 1973–1987* (Noordwijk: ESA Publications Division, 2000).

13. See, for instance, Milton Mueller, "Intelsat and the Separate System Policy: Toward Competitive International Telecommunications," *Cato Policy Analysis*, no. 150 (1991), <http://www.cato.org/pubs/pas/pa-150.html> (1 Nov. 2004).

14. Krige and Russo, *A History*, Vol. I, 263–74.

15. Memoranda from the President's Special Assistant for Telecommunications (O'Connell) to President Johnson. Washington, February 17, 1967 and September 21, 1965. For European concerns on U.S. dominance in Intelsat see also Letter from the Deputy Under Secretary of State for Political Affairs (Johnson) to the President's Special Assistant for Telecommunications (O'Connell), Washington, September 3, 1966. All in *FRUS* XXXIV, "1964–1968, Energy, Diplomacy and Global Issues" (Washington, D.C.: Government Printing Office, 1999).

16. Jean-Jacques Servan-Schreiber, *The American Challenge*, trans. Ronald Steel (New York: Atheneum, 1968 [1967]), 35, emphasis deleted.

17. For the data referred to in the text see Christopher Freeman and Anthony Young, *The Research and Development Effort in Western Europe, North America and the Soviet Union: An Experimental International Comparison of Research Expenditures and Manpower in 1962* (Paris: OECD, 1965), 52, 71–72 and tables 6 and 7. The Freeman-Young study used 1962 exchange rates and data based on available national statistics.

18. For instance, Eric Moonman, ed., *Science and Technology in Europe* (Harmondsworth, Middl.: Penguin, 1968).

19. *Le Défi Américain* (*The American Challenge*) is the original title of Servan-Schreiber's popular book, first published in French in 1967.

20. Servan-Schreiber, *The American*. Christopher Layton, *European Advanced Technology: A Programme for Integration* (London: Allen & Unwin, 1969).

21. John W. Young, *Britain, France and the Unity of Europe 1945–1951* (Leicester: Leicester University Press, 1984). Hubert Zimmerman, "Western Europe and the American Challenge: Conflict and Cooperation in Technology and Monetary Policy, 1965–1973," *Journal of European Integration History* 6, no. 2 (2000): 85–110.

22. Telegram from the Embassy in France to the Department of State Paris, January 14, 1966, 2013Z. In *FRUS*. XXXIV, "1964–1968, Energy, Diplomacy and Global Issues" (Washington, D.C.: Government Printing Office, 1999).

23. Circular Telegram from the Department of State to the Embassy in France, Washington, January 13, 1967. In *FRUS* XXXIV, "1964–1968, Energy, Diplomacy and Global Issues" (Washington, D.C.: Government Printing Office, 1999). See also OECD, *Gaps in Technology: General Report*. Committee for Science Policy (Paris: OECD, 1968).

24. For a summary see Letter from the President's Special Assistant for Science and Technology (Honig) to President Johnson. Washington, January 31, 1967. In *FRUS* XXXIV, "1964–1968, Energy, Diplomacy and Global Issues" (Washington, DC: Government Printing Office, 1999).

25. Telegram from the Department of State to Secretary of State Rusk in Belgium, Washington, June 6, 1966. In *FRUS*. XXXIV, "1964–1968, Energy, Diplomacy and Global Issues" (Washington, D.C.: Government Printing Office, 1999).

26. Memorandum from the Interdepartmental Committee on the Technological Gap to President Johnson. Washington, December 22, 1967. In *FRUS* XXXIV, "1964–1968, Energy, Diplomacy and Global Issues" (Washington, D.C.: Government Printing Office, 1999).

27. In accordance with the U.S. strategy, the OECD institutional framework became central to the debate on the technological gap. As noted, the OECD was already involved in the associated question of the role of technology in economic growth and competitiveness and was instrumental in the development of high-technology indicators. See indicatively OECD, *Gaps in Technology*. To this day the OECD continues to produce data and comparative studies on this issue.

28. For instance, John Diebold, "Is the Gap Technological?" *Foreign Affairs* (1968): 276–91. James Brian Quinn, "Technological Competition: Europe vs. USA," *Harvard Business Review* (July–August 1966): 113–30. For a European account see Ian Mackintosh, *Sunrise Europe: The Dynamics of Information Technology* (Oxford: Blackwell, 1986).

29. Paul Gannon, *Trojan Horses & National Champions: The Crisis in the European Computing and Telecommunications Industry* (London: Apt-Amatic Books, 1997), 114–19.

30. Diebold, "Is the Gap," 286.

31. Gannon, *Trojan Horses*, 171–72.

32. Roger Williams, *European Technology: The Politics of Collaboration* (London: Croom Helm, 1973), 89.

33. For details see Jean-Michel Quatrepoint, Jacques Jublin and Danielle Arnaud, *French Ordinateurs: de l' Affaire Bull a l' Assassinat du Plan Calcul* (Paris: Alain Moreau, 1976).

34. Alan Cawson, Kevin Morgan, Douglas Webber, Peter Holmes and Anne Stevens, *Hostile Brothers: Competition and Closure in the European Electronics Industry* (Oxford: Clarendon Press, 1990).

35. Otto Holman and Kees van der Pilj, "Structure and Process in Transnational European Business," in *A Ruined Fortress?: Neoliberal Hegemony and Transformation in Europe*, ed. Alan Cafruny and Magnus Ryner (Lanham, MD: Rowman & Littlefield, 2003), 76.

36. Gannon, *Trojan Horses*, 181–185.

37. For details see Marie Anchordoguy, *Computers Inc.: Japan's Challenge to IBM* (Cambridge, MA.: Council on East Asian Studies, Harvard University, 1989). Martin Fransman, *Japan's Computer and Communications Industry* (Oxford: Oxford University Press, 1995). Jill Hills, *Information Technology and Industrial Policy* (London: Croom Helm, 1984), 225–62.

38. Gannon, *Trojan Horses*, 192.

39. Richard N. Langlois and W. Edward Steinmueller, "The Evolution of Competitive Advantage in the Worldwide Semiconductor Industry, 1947–1996," in *Sources of Industrial Leadership*, ed. David C. Mowery and Richard R. Nelson (Cambridge and New York: Cambridge University Press, 1999), 19–78.

40. Michelle Egan, *Constructing a European Market: Standards, Regulation, and Governance* (Oxford and New York: Oxford University Press, 2001), 61–82. Alan Dashwood, "Hastening Slowly: The Community's Path Toward Harmonisation," in *Policy-Making in the European mmunity*, ed. Helen Wallace, William Wallace and Carole Webb (Chichester: John Wiley, 1983), 177–208.

41. For a discussion of the mutual recognition principle see Calypso Nicolaidis, "Mutual Recognition of Regulatory Regimes: Some Lessons and Prospects," *Jean Monnet Paper Series* (New York University School of Law Jean Monnet Center, 1997), <http://www.jeanmonnetprogram.org/papers/97/97–07.html> (18 July 2006).

42. Stephen Woolcock, "Competition among Rules in the Single European Market," in *International Regulatory Competition and Coordination: Perspectives on Economic Regulation in Europe and the United States*, ed. William Bratton, Joseph McCahery, Sol Picciotto and Colin Scott (Oxford: Clarendon Press, 1996), 295.

43. European Commission, "Recommandation de la Commission 65/428/CEE, du 20 Septembre 1965, aux États membres, relative à la communication préalable à la Commission, à l'état de projets, de certaines dispositions législatives réglementaires et administratives," *Official Journal* 160/2611 (29 September 1965).

44. Council, "Resolution of 28 May 1969 on the Adaptation to Technical Progress of the Directives for the Elimination of Technical Barriers to Trade Which Result from Disparities between the Provisions Laid Down by Law, Regulation or Administrative Action in Member States," *Official Journal* C76/8 (17 June 1969). See "Accord."

45. European Commission, "General Programme of 28 May 1969 for the Elimination of Technical Barriers to Trade Which Result from Disparities Between Provisions Laid Down by Law, Regulation or Administrative Action in Member States," *Official Journal* C76/1 (17 June 1969), in French.

46. This was achieved in 1983 with the so-called Mutual Information Council directive.

47. Claude Labarrère, *L' Europe des Postes et des Télécommunications* (Paris: Masson, 1985), 149.

48. Council, "Décision du 15 avril 1964 créant un Comité de politique économique à moyen terme (64/247/CEE)," *Official Journal* 64/1031 (22 April 1964).

49. The Maréchal report is published as an appendix to Council, "Conseil 69/157/CEE: Second programme de politique économique à moyen terme," *Official Journal* L129 (30 May 1969).

50. Urwin, *The Community*. 138.

51. The first three countries officially joined in 1973. Norway in a referendum rejected joining the EU.

52. EC, "Meetings of the Heads of State or Government, The Hague, 1–2 December 1969," *Bulletin of the European Communities*, no.1 (1970).

53. David Coombes, *Politics and Bureaucracy in the European Community: A Portrait of the Commission of the E.E.C.* (London: George Allen and Unwin, 1970), 264–71.

54. Industrial policy is defined here "as the set of measures applied by governments to deal with the process of structural adjustment associated with changes in comparative advantage. It includes measures aimed at declining sectors as well as policies oriented towards the future." Pierre Buigues and André Sapir, "Community Industrial Policies," in *Industrial Policy in the European Community: A Necessary Response to Economic Integration?* ed. Phedon Nicolaides (Dordrecht: Martinus Nijhoff Publishers, 1993), 21.

55. European Commission, "La politique industrielle de la Communauté. Mémorandum de la Commission au Conseil," COM 70 (100) (Brussels, 18 March 1970).

56. Stephen Woolcock, "Information Technology: The Challenge to Europe," *Journal of Common Market Studies* XXII, no. 4 (1984): 324–26.

57. EC, "Meetings of the Heads of State or Government, Paris, 19 21 October 1972," *Bulletin of the European Communities*, no.10 (1972).

58. Council, "Resolution of 15 July 1974 on a Community Policy on Data Processing," *Official Journal* C86/1 (20 July 1974).

59. EC, *Bulletin of the European Communities*, no. 9 (1974): 43–44.

60. Council, "Directive 77/62/EEC of 21 December 1976 Coordinating Procedures for the Award of Public Supply Contracts," *Official Journal* L13/1 (15 January 1977). Woolcock, "Information Technology," 327.

61. Michael Hodges, "Industrial Policy: Hard Times or Great Expectations?" in *Policy-Making in the European Community*, ed. Helen Wallace, William Wallace and Carole Webb (Chichester: John Wiley, 1983), 265–93.

62. The British ICL was one of the most fervent proponents of OSI. Its efforts to support open standards intensified in the early 1980s with the arrival of Robb Wilmot as chief executive. Martin Campbell-Kelly, *ICL: A Business and Technical History* (Oxford: Clarendon, 1989), 339–45.

63. The settlement reached in August 1984 referred to OSI. IBM agreed to release technical details to its competitors in order to allow non-IBM products to interconnect

with IBM products. The settlement was reproduced in EC, *Bulletin of the European Communities*, no. 10 (1984), point 3.4.1.

64. For details about the "religious war" between the two models (OSI and TCP/IP) see William Drake, "The Internet Religious War," *Telecommunications Policy* 17, no. 9 (1993): 643–49, and Jane Abbate, *Inventing the Internet* (Cambridge, Mass., and London: MIT Press, 1999), 147–79.

65. Raymund Werle, "Internet @ Europe: Overcoming Institutional Fragmentation and Policy Failure," in *Governing Telecommunications and the New Information Society in Europe*, ed. Jacint Jordana (Cheltenham and Northampton, MA: Edward Elgar, 2002), 137–58.

66. Council, "Decision 75/200/EEC of 18 March 1975 Adopting an Initial Three-year Plan of Action in the Field of Scientific and Technical Information and Cocumentation," *Official Journal* L100/18 (21 April 1975).

67. EC, *Ninth General Report on the Activities of the European Communities in 1975* (Brussels: European Commission, 1976), 321–22. Annex 4 to chapter III.

68. EC, *Bulletin of the European Communities*, no. 2 (1978), point 2.1.86.

69. EC, *Ninth General*, 323–24.

70. Drake, "The Internet," 643

71. Middlemas, *Orchestrating Europe*, 92.

72. European Court of Justice "Judgment of 30 April 1974 in Case 155/73. Giuseppe Sacchi. Tribunale civile e penale di Biella—Italy," *European Court Reports* (1974): 409. Ground 14.

73. EC, "Declaration on European Identity," *Bulletin of the European Communities*, no. 12 (1973): 118–22.

74. EC, "Declaration," para. I(1).

75. See Bo Stråth, "A European Identity: To the Historical Limits of a Concept," *European Journal of Social Theory* 5, no. 4 (2002): 387–401. Anthony Pagden, "Europe: Conceptualizing a Continent," in *The Idea of Europe: From Antiquity to the European Union*, ed. Anthony Pagden (Cambridge: Cambridge University Press, 2002), 33–54.

76. The transatlantic tension is evident in the 1973 Declaration. Under the section of EC relations with the world the USA is mentioned way down the list of countries.

77. Bo Stråth, "Multiple Europes: Integration, Identity and Demarcation to the Other," in *Europe and the Other and Europe as the Other*, ed. Bo Stråth (Brussels: PIE-Peter Lang, 2000), 385.

78. Ernst B. Haas, *The Uniting of Europe: Political, Social and Economic Forces, 1950–1957* (2nd ed. Stanford, Calif.: Stanford University Press, 1968 [1958]), 16.

79. Paschal Lamy, then Chief de Cabinet of the Commission President Delors, quoted in George Ross, *Jacques Delors and European Integration* (Cambridge: Polity, 1995), 194.

80. Charlotte Bretherton and John Vogle, *The European Union as a Global Actor* (London and New york: Routlege, 1999), 231.

81. EC, "Report on European Union. [Tindemans report]," *Bulletin of the European Communities Supplement* 1 (1976): 11–35. The national governments never approved the report.

82. Council of Europe, *Recommendation 749 on European Broadcasting* (Strasbourg, 23 January 1975).

4

Defensive Europeanization

Industrial Policy Moves to Europe (Late 1970s to Mid-/Late 1980s)

( )

INTRODUCTION

In a climate of worsening economic crisis, rapid developments took place in the late 1970s and early 1980s. The momentum is an illustration of greater political awareness of the technological changes in the field of information technology, increasing concern about perceived European weakness and the belief that technologically advanced sectors would lift European economies out of the malaise they had plunged into.

This chapter explains how technological developments, associated trade and commercial considerations and the rising political saliency of Information and Communication Technology (ICT) contributed to the EU entering the fields of telecommunications and television. In the course of the 1980s, industrial policy moved to Europe in the form of sponsored R&D programs, network planning and defensive standardization. The objective was not yet liberalization. The chapter argues that EU intervention was possible precisely because it aimed to promote, not challenge, established interests. A mutually supportive relationship developed between the Commission and leading information technology and electronics manufacturers, PTTs, public service broadcasters and their professional associations. Intervention was part of the single market project, itself the defensive response of those sections of the European industry most threatened by intensifying international competition. The chapter moves on to explore the competing aims and contradictions in the first pan-European television initiatives pursued at the same time for democratic, industrial and cultural reasons. Intervention was linked to the construction of "Europe," the promotion of cultural unity and a European identity and EU state-building efforts.

THE RISING POLITICAL SALIENCY OF ICT

During the recessionary 1970s, Japan, the USA and Western Europe progressively turned their attention to the "information sector." This mutually reinforcing preoccupation arose from concern about falling rates of productivity and growth, and belief that the application of information technology was instrumental to socioeconomic development and international competitiveness. From the start, most studies centered on perceived developments in the USA, a core theme being how quantitative shifts, such as the growing percentage of the workforce in the services sector, automatically engendered broader and far-reaching qualitative socioeconomic changes.[1] By the late 1970s and early 1980s, the "information society" notion encapsulating these ideas had become commonplace.[2] Attention turned to the revolutionary technological changes underway, in particular the plethora of new services coming out of the merging of data processing and telecommunications, and the high growth potential of the nascent telematic sector. In the wake of the Nora-Minc report to the French President on the emergence of telematics, the EU political leaders meeting in November 1979 endorsed the "information society" as the answer to Europe's socioeconomic challenges.[3]

In the course of the 1980s, new economic growth and trade theories reinforced the link between technology, public policy and economic growth. These theories were instrumental in justifying policy intervention in high-technology sectors and, in turn, with their emphasis on economies of scale, in lending support to the European single market project.

More specifically, elaborating on earlier insights concerning the "residual factor," endogenous (or else new) growth theory developed as a critique of the dominant neoclassical theory explained in the last chapter. The theory is important for our purposes for two reasons. First, whereas for the neoclassical model growth is exogenous and so there is little, if anything, policies can do to accelerate its rate, for the new theory growth is driven by endogenous factors such as technological innovation and human capital. The logical consequence of that is that government policies are important and may play a role in enhancing growth.[4] Competitive advantage then is not given but instead created.[5] Intervention aims at nurturing an innovation-friendly environment through measures that influence the behavior and motives of economic agents by, for instance, creating incentives and rewards for innovation through strong intellectual property rights, R&D subsidies and so on.[6]

Second, whereas previous economic explanations relied on the fundamental but unrealistic notion of perfect competition, an underlying assumption of new growth theory is that of market imperfections and oligopolies.[7] This is particularly pertinent to high-technology sectors in which

> [o]ligopolistic competition and strategic interaction rather than the "invisible hand" of market forces condition today competitive advantages and the international division of labour.[8]

If growth and competitiveness depend on innovation, the problem is that the benefits of innovation are short-lived. Flamm, drawing on Schumpeter, explains competition in the computer industry as

> continuous investments in technology creating a sequence of temporary monopolies on new products, with rents [profits] earned on current products financing the investments in the next round of innovation.[9]

This creates a vicious circle whereby the targeting of oligopolistic industries creates strong incentives for first-mover advantage and measures that will sustain, if not strengthen, the oligopolistic characteristics on which government intervention and international competitiveness are based. The picture that emerges is not one of free markets and free trade but one of oligopolies trying to stymie competitive pressures.

Whereas new growth theories point to the role of public policy in economic growth, new trade theory draws attention to the role of trade policy. New trade theory originated in the 1970s to address the inadequacies of the old Ricardian model of comparative advantage, which could not explain actual trade practices, in particular why a significant amount of trade is intra-, not inter-, industry and takes place between industrialized countries. New trade theory is a critique of international free trade and emphasizes the role of economies of scale, increasing returns and imperfect competition.[10]

For new trade theory, some industries matter more than others in maximizing a country's welfare. Industrialized countries facing mounting competition from low-wage economies cannot compete in labor-intensive sectors. The solution is for them to move up the value-added chain and specialize in technology-intensive sectors where competition is based on innovation not lower cost.[11] New trade theory provides a forceful justification for sectoral industrial policy and has contributed to "technological nationalism."[12] In the 1970s and 1980s, many national governments and the EU became engaged in "high-tech neo-mercantilism" using an array of policy instruments in efforts to create or sustain technological and market leadership.[13]

It is worth noting here that the rediscovery of industrial policy for high growth critical sectors emerged in the USA as part of the Democrats' efforts in the late 1970s and early 1980s to come up with an alternative economic policy proposal in response to the rise of the Republicans.[14] Strategic industrial policy subsided in the 1980s with the two electoral defeats for the Democrats only to revive in the early 1990s again as an answer to supply-side economics.[15] These ideas were prominent in the Clinton-Gore presidential campaign and, this time, they led them to electoral victory.

In sum, the basic assumption of these new theoretical understandings is that industrial and trade policy can stimulate economic growth. The emphasis domestically is away from traditional sunset toward technology-intensive sunrise industries[16] and is combined in international trade relations with a focus on sectors that exhibit significant economies of scale which governments can help cultivate to gain competitive advantage.

New growth and trade theories have drawn attention to technology and research policy. Crucially, whereas industrial policy is anathema to some, nobody can challenge technology and research policies, initiatives in sectors believed to be able to promote economic growth and competitiveness. Old conflicts about states and markets, the need for and character of industrial policy become effectively meaningless. Political and industrial leaders can now espouse intervention dressed as technology policy for strategic sectors believed to be able to solve deep-seated socioeconomic problems. For instance, whereas during the relative decline of the USA in the late 1970s and early 1980s "'industrial policy' became a label for policy packages to avoid, the same was not true of 'critical technologies,' or 'high-tech industries.'"[17] Similarly in Europe, in the first half of the 1980s,

> [s]everal R&D projects which had originally been conceived in the context of industrial policy, a policy which some Member States rejected as a matter of principle, could now be redefined in a new context, that of scientific and technological policy.[18]

Unsurprisingly, the high-technology industry, which stood to benefit directly, embraced the new thinking of strategic industrial sectors and new trade policies and the related vision of the information society. The debate would be seen to be about "new" ideas and initiatives, not old-hat controversial industrial policy. Unlike industrial policy, therefore, technology policy could yield broad support.

INDUSTRIALISTS MOVE TO EUROPE: DEFENSIVE EUROPEANIZATION

In the early 1980s, there was still no visible way out of the economic malaise that the European economy had plunged into with political elites unable or unwilling to take the lead. The impetus this time came from Europe's industrialists, with many from the ICT sector playing a leading role. They became the most prominent advocates of the single market that had been not only neglected throughout the recessionary 1970s but fragmented further with the surge in national protectionism and nontariff trade barriers.

One of the first groups to be formed in the early 1980s to promote the single market was the European Parliament's Kangaroo Group.[19] Its name was meant to emphasize free movement across national borders. The British Basil de Ferranti, of the pioneering Ferranti computers and subsequently of ICL, at the time a member of the Parliament's economic and monetary affairs committee, was instrumental in the creation of that group. But by far, the group that was most influential in setting the agenda for the single market program and then selling the idea to national governments was the European Round Table for industrialists (ERT).[20] Set up in 1983, the ERT is "a club of giants," a collection of top European industrialists in various sectors with significant multinational activities.[21] Membership is personal, not corporate, and by invitation only.

The creation of the ERT was an effort to have effective representation of industrialists' interests at the European level. Hitherto, UNICE, the European peak business association, torn by divisions among national industrial federations and the tendency of companies to approach their home governments, had been unable to act as the voice of the European industry.[22] Other European industrial groupings representing specific sectors were often seeking measures that would serve their own narrow interests and were of little use to the Commission's efforts to map out a general industrial development policy.[23]

Two key differences between UNICE and ERT help explain the latter's instrumental role in European integration. First, whereas UNICE has to work through the national industry associations it represents, the ERT bypasses them. It therefore challenges traditional business-government relations and strengthens the position of the European Commission vis-à-vis national governments. The European Commission has found in the big European manufacturers a much needed strong ally in favor of European-level solutions that at the same time serve its own institutional interests. From the start, the instigator of the idea of a European forum of industrialists, Pehr Gyllenhammer, chairman of the Swedish automotive group Volvo and subsequently first chairman of the ERT, established a close working relationship with Davignon, European Commissioner for industry. Second, unlike UNICE that deals with the details of legislative proposals, since inception the ERT has been interested in setting the overall strategic orientation of the EU and in shaping a coherent economic, monetary and industrial policy.[24] ERT's first aim, in close alliance with the Commission, was not simply the creation of the single market but, crucially, a new European socioeconomic order "conducive to the 'reindustrialization of Europe.'"[25] The goal was to relaunch Europe on the basis of the needs of European industrial capital.

However, the needs of various segments of industrial capital within the emergent European transnational capitalist élite differed on account of their geographical spread and degree of incorporation into the international economy, sectoral characteristics and vulnerability to international competitive pressures, and finally, the national institutional context and state-society complexes in which capital operated.[26] In other words, the internal market project was contested. But despite divisions, it was the French-inspired protectionist faction of European capital that managed to control the ERT and the European economic policy agenda in the 1980s.[27] In response, the three original British members (Unilever, ICI and Shell), representing some of the most internationalized parts of European capital, all left the ERT within a few months, to return later in the decade.[28] It was in the late 1980s/early 1990s that the interventionist industrial policy promoted by the ERT in concert with (parts of) the European Commission openly came under attack from the more globalized transnational segments of European capital, as the next chapter explains.

From the outset, the ERT enjoyed very close links with the French political establishment and France dominated the ERT's original membership.[29] It is not surprising, therefore, that the views of France and the ERT largely coincided. These views were elaborated in detail in the French memorandum for a European industrial space in September 1983.[30]

The French memorandum came after the failure of "socialism in one country" and the move of the French government under Mitterrand toward a more market and European direction. In effect, it signaled the transfer of French national policy objectives, and to an extent policy instruments too, to the European level.[31] Having become redundant nationally, the aim was to initiate neomercantilist projects on a larger scale. French capital, still more national in its organization and less competitive compared to British and German capital, perceived the ERT as a key element to its internationalization efforts. The French memorandum linked the creation of the internal market through liberalization and active industrial policy to temporary external trade protection, raising fears at the time about the building of a Fortress Europe. The thinking was that European industry, not ready to face international competition yet, should start facing competition internally within the EU market, which would be temporarily closed to outside competition until the point when European companies would be strong enough, having reaped substantial economies of scale and scope, to launch their worldwide expansion.

The memorandum was also a reflection of the gradual Europeanization of French national identity beginning in the 1980s whereby France started to incorporate "Europe" into its national identity by exporting to Europe some of the defining features of its historical nation-state identity based on visions of grandeur and independence.[32] In the emerging globalizing world order, French values and norms were to be safeguarded and promoted through Europe. France abandoned its dirigiste industrial policy entailing the active support of national champions only when it had managed to export it to the European level in the pursuit of European champions. Similarly, as will be seen, in the early 1990s during the Uruguay trade negotiations, French cultural exceptionalism was exported and fought as European cultural exceptionalism.[33]

The ERT membership was originally dominated by firms, many of them national champions, feeling increasingly vulnerable to intensifying international competition. In the early 1980s, large sections of the European industrial capital, particularly in the electronics and car sectors, were concerned about escalating international competition. One of the most influential reports in the launch of the single market project, "Europe 1990: An Agenda for Action," was written by Wisse Dekker, head of Philips, as an internal company document and was subsequently adopted by the ERT.[34] The report, among other things, called for technical harmonization and the opening up of public procurement.

The creation of the internal market as a defensive response to intensifying competitive pressures was enthusiastically espoused by European firms in information technology and electronics, two fields experiencing rapid technological change and where economies of scale and access to a large market are essential to competitive advantage. In the 1980s, European IT and electronics producers were not ready to take on world competitors while the latter's presence was increasingly being felt in domestic markets. The idea was that the single market coupled with temporary external trade protection would turn national champions into European and, ultimately, global champions.

RINGING THE CHANGES

After the second oil crisis in 1978–1979, the continuing stagnation of the European economy and the decline of intra-EU trade were coupled with gradual loss of international competitiveness especially in critical growth potential sectors.[35] In the fast-growing fields of computers, semiconductors and consumer electronics Europe was not only falling behind the USA, the original source of competitive pressure, but was now being surpassed by Japan and the emerging Asian Tigers. Looking at the electronics sector as a whole, in the first quarter of 1980, the EU imported 26.8 percent, up from 19.1 percent in 1978–1979. Imports of electronic microcircuits witnessed the largest rise during that period, going up two and a half times to reach

65 percent, followed by data processing equipment (31.4 percent in the first quarter of 1980 compared to 26.2 percent in 1978–1979), and finally, by telecommunications equipment (30.6 percent in the first quarter of 1980 compared to 17.8 percent in 1978–1979).[36] The EU market was increasingly penetrated by foreign-owned manufacturers while the EU world market shares in these sectors were being reduced. Within their domestic markets, national champions were dominant, but this was the result of fragmentation and protection rather than technological leadership and competitiveness. Years of government support and public funding had failed to reverse the situation. More correctly, government intervention had contributed to the weakness of Europe in these fields since protectionism insulated domestic producers from competition. By the early 1980s, it was obvious that the nationally focused industrial policies had not produced results.

To make matters worse, the USA and Japan were racing ahead. In 1981, as a follow-up to the success of its Very Large Scale Integrated circuits project, Japan launched the Fifth Generation program, creating shock waves in Europe. Equally, the USA launched several collaborative programs in the broader information technology sector, channelling substantial financial aid through the Department of Defense. Action was urgent if Europe's weakness in information technology was not to become irreversible.

In addition, there were growing concerns about the implications of technological convergence and market restructuring in the USA. The telecommunications liberalization process, on course since the 1950s, culminated in the Consent Decree of January 1982, which freed AT&T to expand internationally and enter the adjunct information technology market. At the same time, a second long-running anti-trust case was settled, allowing IBM to enter telecommunications, thereby augmenting the competitive threat it represented on world markets. These developments sent shivers to European policy-makers and industrialists fearing that U.S. leadership in information technology would now expand into telecommunications, an area where Europe had traditionally been performing relatively well. The competitive fight between the biggest U.S. companies in information technology and telecommunications was played out on European soil. Early signals included AT&T's joint ventures with Italy's Olivetti (1983) and the Dutch Philips (1984).[37] Similarly, IBM was making further inroads into European markets, building the German videotex system and gaining a contract to provide telephone centers to the British Post Office. But in October 1984, the British Department of Trade and Industry rejected the proposed joint venture between IBM and British Telecom (*JOVE*) for a managed data network using IBM's proprietary standards on grounds of the dominant position it would have occupied in the market. This was an important decision.

Were the deal to go ahead Britain, and Europe, would have lost any chance of "getting back into the technology game."[38]

These developments sparked a new round of individual national responses in major EU countries. National governments launched research programs and intervened to assist industry restructuring through mergers and/or nationalizations. This is the time of the "Mission filière Electronique" program in electronics and computers in France under the new Socialist government of President Mitterrand elected in 1981. The French government also proceeded with a wave of nationalizations in the first half of the 1980s, including that of CII-Honeywell-Bull to create Groupe Bull and that of Thomson-CSF to concentrate on semiconductors and consumer electronics.[39] In 1983, Britain launched the Alvey program though, in contrast to French and German initiatives, less public money was committed.[40]

In information technology and computers, Europe's main competitor was the USA. In consumer electronics, it was Japan. The Japanese industry built a competitive advantage in the production of television sets, assisted in the process by the adoption of the same color television standard (NTSC) as the USA. A common standard meant that Japanese sets would be immediately suitable for the vast U.S. home market and the Japanese industry would stand to benefit from significant economies of scale. Unlike the Japanese, European countries not only decided to reject the U.S./Japanese standard but they fragmented their market further by choosing two different standards: PAL to be used in most West European countries and SECAM to be used in France, Greece and Eastern Europe.[41] The decision on standards was to act as a nontariff trade barrier thereby protecting the European industry from outside competition. But the result was that European manufacturers were caught at a disadvantage having to serve relatively small and fragmented markets. The problems of the European consumer electronics manufacturers were soon augmented by three developments.[42] First, the Japanese started encroaching on European markets by establishing assembly facilities in the EU, proving in the process that standards alone could not provide an adequate form of protection. Second, European manufacturers underestimated the latent demand for smaller second television sets, a demand that manufacturers from Japan, together with the rising Asian Tigers, were only too ready to satisfy. Third, European manufacturers were further weakened in the video-format war in the late 1970s and early 1980s when the V2000 standard backed principally by Philips failed to win market acceptance. The Japanese VHS standard developed by JVC became the *de facto* international standard, boosting the competitiveness of Japanese manufacturers.

Under these circumstances of renewed national intervention and growing international competition, the Commission opted to nurture links with the industry, rather than governments. The crisis of the European information technology and electronics sectors was intimately linked to the cost of non-Europe.[43] The latter referred to the fragmentation and small size of domestic EU markets. Technological advances, digitalization in particular, and the associated rising R&D costs coupled with ever shortening product life-cycles further accentuated the structural weaknesses of the EU market. Domestic markets could simply not carry the European electronics industry into the digital era. As an illustration, a digital switching system needed to secure at least 8 percent of the world market to recoup the huge R&D costs. But no EU national market represented more than 6 percent of the world telecommunications market, whereas the U.S. and Japanese domestic markets accounted for over 35 and 11 percent respectively.[44] Hence, a single telecommunications market was regarded as vital for the competitiveness of the European industry. Higher market shares were a matter of survival and so European industrialists turned their attention beyond the confines of national markets to European and international markets.

In short, the failure of national protectionism, intensifying international competition and a new sectoral political economy—the result of technological advances—provided the building blocks for European initiatives. No longer was the European Commission a lone voice urging common action in the field of advanced technologies. It could now count on support from the industry and subsequently national governments.

EU TECHNOLOGY-PUSH INITIATIVES: COLLABORATING WITH MANUFACTURERS AND PTTS

The 1980s witnessed the gradual rise of the EU as a key policy actor in the field of ICT. The Commission, notably the DG Industry fostered by Commissioner Davignon, initiated an active industrial policy focusing on technology-push initiatives—mainly R&D, network development and standardization—to counter the perceived threat of American and Japanese technological superiority and invigorate the European economy through market integration and the promotion of European champions.

R&D

In the early 1980s, leading European electronics and information technology firms were shifting their efforts to Europe. Contrasted with past practice, they would now start to actively push for the creation of the internal market and European-level cooperation in R&D. Commissioner Davignon, determined to shift emphasis away from the industrial sectors in crisis toward new technology growth sectors, sponsored the formation of Europe-wide associations and cultivated links with the senior executives of

European information technology and electronic firms to discuss the outlook of the industry. As a result, the Information Technologies Task Force (ITTF) was formed, charged with proposing EU strategy for the telematics industry and, emphasizing its political saliency, reporting directly to the Commissioners. At the end of 1981, the first "Big Twelve Round Table" of top European industrialists in information technology and electronics was convened.[45] Attention focused on the promotion of R&D collaboration among EU companies based on the experience of the industrial synergy that characterized Japan in particular. R&D programs were first introduced in the field of information technology (ESPRIT) and then in that of broadband communications (RACE).

In 1984, after an initial pilot phase, the European Strategic Program in Information Technologies (Esprit), a ten-year collaborative R&D initiative, was launched, concentrating on information technology development and applications.[46] Esprit was the first major EU research program and it provided a model for pre-competitive cooperation. Whereas technological cooperation so far had been intergovernmental, for the first time in Esprit the industry itself got involved. That was a watershed in European R&D policy. In actual fact, it was the leading European firms in electronics and information technology, working closely with the Commission, that drafted the lines of the program. Predictably, the "Big Twelve" firms were the main beneficiaries.[47] The direct and strong contacts between the Commission and leading European companies disrupted the tight nexus between national governments and national champions and challenged the traditional national R&D model, thereby encroaching on national sovereignty.[48] Nevertheless, in view of the failure of national policies, public budgets under pressure from stagflation and high unemployment, technological developments, growing international competition, and the fact that the very essence of the Esprit program was to continue the support of national champions but at the European level and on terms set by the industry itself, national governments had no option but to back this collaborative effort.

Still, Esprit did not signal the end of intergovernmental R&D ventures. Eureka, launched in 1985, was the European response, orchestrated by French President Mitterrand, to the U.S. Strategic Defense Initiative.[49] Unlike EU programs, Eureka is not about pre-competitive but rather near-market research. It operates outside the EU institutional framework, though the European Commission may participate in its projects.

What Esprit was in the field of information technology, RACE (Research for Advanced Communications in Europe) was in the field of telecommunications. Launched a few days after Eureka, the main objective of RACE was the definition of technologies for the introduction of integrated broadband networks by 1995.[50] As noted, Europe was weak in information technology but strong in telecommunications. Hence, in contrast to Esprit, the aim of RACE was not to close the technological gap vis-à-vis the USA and Japan but rather to enable European industry to construct in common future products and networks in order to strengthen its competitiveness in new technologies. Similar to Esprit, RACE was drafted by the leading European telecommunication manufacturers (e.g., CIT-Alcatel, Siemens).[51] Its ultimate objective was "to create a climate of trust and co-operation between the various telecommunications administrations, and between these and the industry."[52]

The aim of these R&D initiatives was to transform national champions into European champions, or else to move from national monopolies to a European oligopoly. In this scenario, it was crucial to determine which companies were "European" enough to be allowed to participate in the joint collaborative R&D efforts. The most controversial issue was how to treat European subsidiaries of foreign firms. An illustrative example of the protectionist sentiments of that period was when ICL, following its takeover by the Japanese Fujitsu in 1990, was temporarily thrown out of Esprit, lending support to the "Fortress Europe" scenario, a Europe, for the short term at least, for European companies only. Such fears were very strong at the time especially in the USA but turned out to be misplaced.[53]

Network Planning

Unlike information technology and electronics, EU intervention in telecommunications, a traditionally strong European sector controlled by national monopolies and national governments, was to prove more difficult. Here, the Commission needed to gain the consensus of public authorities, the PTTs.

As seen in the preceding chapter, the PTTs were hostile to the Commission's early efforts regarding the harmonization of technical standards and type approvals and the gradual opening up of public procurement, seeing them as an encroachment on their competence. PTTs tended to emphasize the technical and operational aspects of the sector and the value of the existing European-level cooperative framework within the CEPT, the organization representing only their interests. The Commission realized that it could not win a head-on fight with the PTTs and changed its strategy accordingly.

In 1980, in renewed attempts to intervene in the field of telecommunications, the Commission chose not to antagonize but instead rely on the national PTTs, whose agreement was vital.[54] But although the greater involvement of the national PTTs was essential and resulted in the Commission gaining better understanding of the sector, it served to strengthen the position of the PTTs in European policy. Indeed, the European Parliament, with additional legitimacy following the 1979 first direct elections, in a demonstration of rhetorical force—at the time the Parliament had a purely consultative role—strongly criticized the Commission's strategy and questioned the effectiveness of heavy reliance on the national PTTs.[55]

In the 1980s, the Commission became increasingly active in telecommunications. It set up several committees and advisory groups and published several reports, using what Dang-Nguyen has called its "rhetoric of persuasion," in which the Commission highlighted the need for common EU-level action.[56]

But the power of the PTTs was evident in the committees and advisory groups formed in 1983. A Special Task Force on Information Technologies and Telecommunications was set up within the DG Industry headed by Michel Carpentier and comprising Commission officials and national industrial experts.[57] In 1986, the Task Force was incorporated into the European Commission's organizational structure and merged into DG XIII (DG for Telecommunications, Information Industry and Innovation) with Michel Carpentier as Director General. Not surprisingly, DG XIII has been "engineering-driven" and has enjoyed close links with the European industry.[58] A Senior Officials Group for Telecommunications was formed to advise the Commission on telecommunications policy. Both it and its subcommittee, the Analysis and Forecasting Group, were heavily dominated by PTTs' representatives. Both were instrumental in advocating a common advanced telecommunications infrastructure based on the ISDN standard, examined below.

In its reports prepared by the DG Industry, the Commission aimed at drawing the attention of political leaders to the growing and urgent problems of the telecommunications sector, and emphasized the need for European solutions.[59] It was time, it argued, that the Union stopped treating telecommunications like any other sector intervening on a selective basis and instead adopt a comprehensive common policy in order to reap significant economic and social benefits. To counter opposition, the Commission linked its proposed telecommunications policy to the more politically salient market of information technology products, where fear of the "technology gap" could provide a spur to action.[60] Accordingly, the creation of a common market for telecommunications equipment was now viewed as a necessary condition for the strengthening of European manufacturers. Europe's competitive position was precarious. European manufacturers had mostly concentrated on traditional products and were at risk of being left out of emerging technologically advanced markets. Although still maintaining a strong position vis-à-vis developing countries, the EU was witnessing a growing deficit with both the USA and Japan. Indicatively, its persistent trade deficit with the USA in telecommunications equipment soared to US$418 million in 1984. The EU, with a share of 15.4 percent of U.S. exports, had become together with Latin America, the largest U.S. export market. In contrast, the EU share in U.S. imports had dropped to just 3.6 percent.[61] In this context, an industrial policy consensus with information technology at its core was relatively easy to build.

In 1984, the EU for the first time set out comprehensive action lines for a European telecommunications policy.[62] A couple of observations are worth making. First, the proposed policy was not procompetitive. The Action Lines focused on standardization and network development, priorities which reflected limited political consensus. Second, not only did the Action Lines not challenge the status quo but they effectively accommodated the interests of the major policy stakeholders, that is leading European manufacturers and the national PTTs. In fact, the PTTs were instrumental in advocating the primary objective: the coordinated introduction of future telecommunications infrastructure (ISDN). To effect this, an R&D program, RACE mentioned above, would be instituted and a redistributive program would assist less-economically advanced member states (STAR, Special Telecommunication Action of Regional Development).

In view of the increasing acceptance of the contribution of telecommunications to economic growth but also competitive pressures made stronger by digitalization, an industrial policy consensus was relatively easy to build in telecommunications too. In contrast to the situation before, increased European-level activity especially in 1983/4 illustrates the urgent priority attached now to the sector. Gradually but steadily the idea of EU-level intervention in the area of telecommunications, with the Commission as a central actor, was gaining political currency.

ISDN

The 1984 Action Lines mentioned ISDN (Integrated Services Digital Network)—a single network to support all types of communication—for the first time as an area that required immediate coordination and action, and which was to boost the competitiveness of the European industry. The idea of ISDN came from the PTT-dominated Analysis and Forecasting Group, subcommittee of the Senior Officials Group for Telecommunications.[63]

Historically, whenever their monopoly has been threatened, PTTs have emphasized the importance of unified infrastructure.[64] ISDN was precisely such a proposition. It was the product of a tightly knit group of experts that dealt with network development and standardization and was being promoted concurrently at national, European and international levels, all arenas dominated at the time by state-owned PTTs.[65] This group effectively functioned as an "epistemic community" whereby its authority and legitimacy, grounded on its members' technical and engineering expertise, rendered it an influential policy actor.[66]

ISDN was the PTTs' defensive response, an effort to assert control in the emerging era of advanced digital communications at a time when traditional telephony markets were becoming saturated and in the face of growing competitive threats from new telematic services and the growth of private networks. The concept of ISDN—a single network—provided it turned out to be the right technological platform, also implied fewer risks and costs for the PTTs since they would not have to build separate networks to provide different services.[67]

The Analysis and Forecasting Group's recommendations on ISDN were designed on the one hand to protect PTTs' market power and on the other to maintain the close relation between PTTs and telecommunications manufacturers. The implementation of ISDN would create new markets for PTTs and equipment manufacturers and assist both in retaining their dominant positions. The Commission, eager to gain a footing in the telecommunications sector, supported the engineering-based consensus on ISDN and linked this industrial policy initiative to European economic recovery. The rollout of a pan-European network was expected in the short-term to provide substantial economies of scale for the telecommunications equipment industry and in the long-term to boost Europe's industrial competitiveness in world markets. In addition to the technological and economic benefits, the politically salient idea was the centralization of policy-making power in the hands of the Commission since ISDN would require central planning and control.[68]

The strong influence of the PTTs and leading European equipment manufacturers, the latter controlling the RACE R&D program on integrated broadband networks, is also supported by the fact that initially ISDN was perceived as a universal rather than a specialized network for corporate users. It was expected that by 1993 territorial coverage in each member state should be sufficient to permit 80 percent of telecommunications users to have the option of ISDN access.[69]

In short, the vision behind ISDN was the implementation of a single technological platform throughout Europe. It was a supply-led process driven by state-owned PTTs and European manufacturers. However, despite initial strong support, ISDN was slow to take off, not least because incumbent telecommunications operators realized that it was more profitable to continue to lease lines to private corporate users and competitors rather than invest in the rollout of ISDN.[70] It was in the mid-1990s, at the time the internet began to grow fast in the USA, that ISDN became broadly available in major European markets. Ironically, ISDN, a circuit-switched technology, would be used to access the internet, a packet switched network (explained below).

The engineering-led vision of ISDN and the strong influence of PTTs and equipment manufacturers over network development were also evident in the case of second generation mobile telephony.

GSM

In 1981, France and Germany agreed to develop a common cellular radio-telephone system to rival the established Scandinavian system (NMT).[71] Upon the insistence of the Scandinavian PTTs, that stood to lose from such an eventuality, the professional association of PTTs, CEPT, took over responsibility for the creation of a new digital pan-European cellular system. To this end, the Groupe Speciale Mobile (GSM) committee was formed inside the CEPT. All its members were from state-owned PTTs. It was only with the creation of the European Telecommunications Standards Institute (ETSI) in 1988 and the transfer of all CEPT standardization activities to it that manufacturers and other operators got involved.[72] In other words, the GSM standard was effectively developed by fixed state-controlled telecommunications operators.

When the GSM group was established in 1982, the telecommunications environment was undergoing a major transformation. The previous year, IBM had introduced the first personal computer. Britain was about to privatize British Telecom, its monopolist telecommunications operator, and introduce competition in the market. In the USA, AT&T was in the process of being divested. Telecommunications operators in advanced countries were proceeding with the digitalization of networks. This transformation, notably the technological convergence between telecommunications and information technology, generated a debate within the industry on circuit switching, dominant in the analog telephone world, and packet switching, dominant in the digital computer, and subsequently internet, world. In Europe, similar to ISDN, the national PTTs, in control of the standardization process, supported the implementation of GSM on the basis of circuit switching, the paradigm in the traditional telephony sector.[73] No packet switching services were envisaged as such. It is ironic, given the resistance toward packet switching in the formulating stages of GSM, that the short message service, the only low rate packet service in GSM, has become immensely popular among users and hugely lucrative for operators.

Europe adopted GSM as the single standard for second generation mobile phones, mandating common frequency bands through the CEPT and a timetable for its coordinated introduction.[74] This policy translated into a large home base and allowed network equipment and handset manufacturers, and mobile operators to realize economies of scale. In addition, for the first time, roaming across national borders would be possible although, illustrating the limits to policy harmonization, on the basis of licensing competing national operators rather than pan-European operators.

GSM represents the star case of European high-technology policy.[75] Unlike the analog high-definition television standards, examined below, which are an example of defensive standardization where Europe was reacting to developments and initiatives launched by its main competitors, the search for a second generation mobile standard came out of European market needs and in particular the wish to overcome the incompatibility of the first generation analog mobile systems and consequent market fragmentation by building a truly European mobile communications market. The subsequent worldwide success of the GSM standard was undoubtedly linked to first-mover advantages. Europe was first to launch second generation mobile services. Building on its European success, GSM soon became the dominant international digital cellular standard, driven by manufacturers and network operators with global ambitions. With no real market competitor in sight, this was the perfect opportunity for them to expand and achieve a leading international market position. Mobile became the technology made in Europe.

The international success of the GSM standard is attributed not just to European policy but also to respective developments and policy failures in Europe's main competitors. The USA and Japan chose different second generation mobile standards from Europe. For Kano, the size and rapid growth of the Japanese domestic market explains why Japanese operators and manufacturers did not have international ambitions and, in turn, why the Japanese standard remained a purely national standard.[76] In the USA, standardization has traditionally been an industry-driven process. There is no formal standards body that selects one standard but rather the decision is left to the market. This standardization model resulted in multiple incompatible second generation mobile systems in the domestic U.S. market as opposed to the case of Japan and Europe, where a single standard was selected by a formal standards body. In other words, the standardization philosophy in the USA resulted in competition between different systems within the same generation of technology (multi-standard approach), whereas in Europe the practice has been to have competition between operators and manufacturers on the basis of a single pan-European standard (mono-standard approach). The lack of a single standard and consequent market fragmentation in turn slowed down the market for second generation mobile phones in the USA.[77]

The experience with second generation systems in Europe, Japan and the USA led to diverging industrial interests when the time to standardize third generation mobile systems arrived. Discussion on a third generation mobile system started internationally within the International Telecommunication Union in the mid-1980s, before second generation systems became established. Arguably, this can be seen as a reaction to the unprecedented European cooperation on a common digital cellular standard. But whereas GSM was an initiative of the traditional telecommunications operators, the original European vision of a third generation mobile system was developed, quite independently of the GSM community, by manufacturers working in the RACE project. They viewed the so-called Universal Mobile Telecommunications System (UMTS) as "mobile access to broadband ISDN," as part of the transition toward broadband networks and fixed-mobile communications convergence, intended to supersede all second generation mobile systems.[78] This scenario would necessitate a migration from all existing networks to a new system based on ISDN able to support all services.

The early conceptualization of the third generation mobile system as mobile ISDN confirms Werle's argument that Europe for a long time ignored and even resisted the internet.[79] As late as 1995, as examined in chapter 6, the vision of UMTS was not linked to internet standards, again illustrating the different vision of next generation networks in Europe compared to the USA. In the rivalry regarding the future of broadband networking, Europe represented the so-called ISDN camp promoted by (fixed) telecommunications operators, in which technology it had invested a lot in time and financial terms. On the other side, the TCP/IP camp was originally supported by the USA, the birthplace of the internet, and the internet and computer industry segments. This second vision of broadband networking has now become accepted by the market.

ISDN and UMTS can be seen as attempts to support Europe's traditional strength in telecommunications and, though to a lesser extent, in telecommunications manufacturing, both of which historically relied on monopolistic and closed national markets, against competition from the USA and its strong computer industry.

PAN-EUROPEAN TELEVISION:
BETWEEN DEMOCRATIC IDEALS, CULTURAL UNITY
AND INDUSTRIAL COMPETITIVE ADVANTAGE

Whereas the EU's first moves into telecommunications were based on industrial policy considerations in turn linked to the more politically salient information technology sector, the EU's first attempts to move into television were in pursuit of democratic idealistic objectives. These, however, were soon mixed with cultural unity and industrial competitive advantage aims.

Transfrontier Television and the Pursuit of Democratic Ideals

The 1977 World Radio Administrative Conference of the International Telecommunication Union allocated orbital slots for Direct Broadcasting by Satellite (DBS) for Europe. At the time, DBS satellites were expected to conveniently be confined to national boundaries, therefore not posing a challenge to the established national broadcasting markets and regulatory structures. Each such national satellite could carry a maximum of five television channels. Although each European country could launch such a high-powered satellite if it so wished, in reality only the big EU countries were expected to do so.[80] Indeed, Britain, France and West Germany separately developed plans to launch DBS satellites for, initially at least, national technological and industrial competitive advantage rather than for broadcasting policy objectives. These plans were heavily promoted by the respective national governments in efforts to challenge the strength of the USA in satellite technology.[81] Full operation of these satellites was placed around 1985. But already by the early 1980s, it was becoming clear that due to technological progress the transmission area covered by such satellites would extend beyond national borders, making transfrontier broadcasting a reality and at the same time threatening the existing national broadcasting order. At a time when national governments conceptualized satellite broadcasting narrowly on the basis of industrial competitive advantage to rival U.S. supremacy, the European Parliament seized upon the potential for transfrontier broadcasting in an effort to address the legitimacy and democratic deficits of the EU.

The European Parliament, still having simply a consultative role in EU decision-making but strengthened following the first universal suffrage in 1979, was the first EU institution to draw attention to the potential of broadcasting in advancing political integration and social cohesion.[82] In the first half of the 1980s, several reports came out of the European Parliament noting weak public identification with Europe, and highlighting the inadequacy of reporting of EU activities and the need for the media, in particular television, to portray and promote European culture. It was in response to these concerns that the idea for pan-European broadcasting emerged. Yet, from the outset, conflicting approaches were visible. In September 1980, whereas one Parliament report welcomed the new technologies and called for the establishment of a European broadcasting channel to be funded by advertising, another report was cautious, expressed concern about the threat to diversity of opinion posed by the commercialization of television and, to address this, called for the elaboration of EU-wide rules.[83] The suggestion for a European television channel to provide adequate and expert information about the EU was subsequently endorsed by the Parliament's Schall Report in 1981.[84]

A year later, in the Hahn Report, the European Parliament blamed the existing national media structures for the "alarming disappointment" among citizens with the EU, where reporting was at best inadequate and often negative. It highlighted the need for EU citizens to be well informed in order "to be given a share in the political responsibility."[85] It explained:

Europeans will only want [European integration] if there is such a thing as a European identity. A European identity will only develop if Europeans are

adequately informed. At present, information via the mass media is controlled
at national level. [. . .] Therefore, if European unification is to be encouraged,
Europe must penetrate the media.[86]

Once again, the Parliament called for the establishment of a European
television company or channel. The first option was rejected as unrealistic
on grounds of considerable political, managerial, financial and legal difficulties. Thus, the report explored the second option for a European channel. The model would be: same picture, several languages. The channel
"should be European in origin, transmission range, target audience and
subject matter." Following Reithian values, programming would provide information, education and entertainment. It would take account of "the
essence of European culture, namely diversity in unity" and aim at increasing "European awareness." The easiest way to implement the proposed
channel, the report argued, would be to rely on the public service broadcasters, at that time the only broadcasters in the EU. Cooperation with their
European association, the EBU, was deemed as "imperative." To effect its
proposal, the Parliament called for a European broadcasting order to be
based on common "outline rules" to address, among other issues, the protection of young people and advertising.[87]
    It is in these European Parliament reports in the early 1980s that the ori-
gins of pan-European broadcasting and minimum harmonization of rules
can be traced. The issue of divergences in the national treatment of advertising and copyright in particular was also raised in the Debauve and Coditel cases respectively of the European Court of Justice.[88] It was subsequently taken up by the 1984 Green Paper on Television without Frontiers
which, viewing divergent national rules as obstacles to the free flow of television programs and the functioning of the single market, called for their
harmonization.

From Democratic Ideals to Cultural and Industrial
Policy Considerations

The follow-up Commission report "Realities and Tendencies in European
Television" in 1983, drafted by the DG Audiovisual, Information, Communication and Culture (DG X), was broadly in line with the main concerns
expressed by the European Parliament.[89] The central subject in the report
was the question of a European television channel, and here the Commission, like the Parliament, supported close cooperation with the EBU. Satellite broadcasting was considered "a powerful unifying factor," "the most effective means of increasing mutual understanding among the peoples of
Europe, and [. . .] give them a greater sense of belonging to a common cultural and social entity."[90]

The Commission took this first opportunity to go beyond the democratic ideals of the Parliament and outline its vision for a European broadcasting order grounded on cultural and industrial policy considerations. It expressed concern about the threat for non-European audiovisual content to increase disproportionately as a result of technological developments, associated commercial pressures, proliferation of media outlets and extended transmission hours. This would adversely affect on the one hand European cultural identity and on the other the European programming industry. The Commission called for action to alleviate these consequences (the subsequent MEDIA program). It also advocated the adoption of a common European transmission standard in satellite television.

In its subsequent Arfé report in 1984, the European Parliament took on again the question of a European television channel, which it considered "to be of fundamental importance in developing the public's awareness of its own European identity."[91] The Parliament envisaged an active role for the EU. It suggested that it would be the responsibility of a body presided over by an EU delegate and composed of representatives of the national public service broadcasters, the governments and the EU institutions to guarantee the independence of the proposed channel.[92] The Parliament noted that one of the principal problems the European channel would encounter would be competition, in particular from commercial channels, and opined that "[t]he battle between commercial channels and the European channel could very probably turn to the former's favour."[93] Noting that the introduction of private commercial television was already underway in several countries, it concluded that "[a]t this stage it is already backward-looking and anachronistic to say that broadcasting is the vehicle of national sovereignty."[94]

At the time of the Arfé report, there was concern about the emergence of all-news channels, notably the U.S. CNN (Cable News Network, founded in 1980). One of the scenarios being considered by the EU and the EBU was the launch of a generalist European channel to be supplemented with a second all-news channel. The latter channel had attracted the attention of (semi-)private news agencies too, including Visnews which had already approached the EU with precisely such a proposal.[95] There was strong concern within the EU and some individual countries, France in particular, that in the absence of a European-led initiative "the Americans would certainly get in first" and monopolize the news market.[96] Hence, in spite of the fact that it belonged to the "anglo-saxon" news agencies often criticized for "their monopoly of television news," the Parliament found the Visnews proposal of "great interest."[97] In its attempt to pre-empt a U.S. initiative, the Parliament was ready to accept the proposed Visnews channel as "European" and as one that "would complement perfectly" the proposed EBU-led generalist European channel.[98] In other words, the EU was prepared to consider any

"European" all-news channel, 'ie it public (EBU) or private (Visnews), as long as it would block non-European (read U.S.) initiatives.

The Arfé report, similar to the Commission's "Realities & Tendencies" report, went beyond earlier democratic concerns to outline what were to become the main EU television policy lines. More specifically, it envisaged a European television order based on a common general regulatory framework—that would address, among other things, the allocation of transmission time between national, European, and other productions, advertising, copyright and protection of minors—on technical and industrial cooperation in order to unify the transmission standards and enhance the competitiveness of European industry, and finally, in view of the anticipated huge increase in demand for content, on financial aid for the production and distribution of television programs and cinema films. To these three policy lines of the Arfé report, the concurrent Hutton report hinted on a fourth media concentration and urged cooperation with both the EBU and the Council of Europe.[99] The original intention then was not to antagonize but to work closely with the two existing European organizations that had so far taken the lead in broadcasting matters in order that the EU too would become a credible policy actor.

In sum, the European Parliament's original ideas were short-lived. By 1983/4 the balance was tilting away from democratic ideals toward cultural and primarily industrial policy concerns for which the single market and associated economies of scale for manufacturers and program producers were crucial. The EU would fail to win the support of the public but would eventually gain the support of major economic and industrial constituencies and national governments. Similar to the case of information technology and telecommunications analyzed above, it would be enough support to establish EU competence in television.

Defensive Standardization: MAC/HDTV

As noted, the European consumer electronics industry was one of the weakest information technology sectors, further enfeebled by the video-format war. The challenge here came primarily from Japan and later the Asian Tigers, rather than the USA. It is not therefore surprising that when Japan in 1986 presented its new MUSE standard to the International Telecommunication Union for worldwide adoption, Europe opposed it. The new standard would allow better quality high-definition television (HDTV) pictures for satellite analog transmission. The adoption of an international standard was deferred for four years, during which time Europe had to come up with its own rival standard in an effort to try to protect its consumer electronics industry from another Japanese onslaught. The European HDTV standardization efforts were in reaction to the Japanese standard.

The stakes were high with serious implications for the technological leadership race, not just for future television but also for computing and semiconductors. It is for these wide-ranging strategic implications that the USA, having no worthy domestic television manufacturing industry to promote, decided to abandon its initial support for the Japanese standard in an attempt to safeguard the interests of its military and defense establishment, broadcasters and computing industry.[100]

In Europe, it was television manufacturers, notably the Dutch Philips and the French Thomson, that lobbied their respective governments and the European Commission to block the adoption of the Japanese standard. The aim was twofold: overcome the existing fragmentation within the EU market based on the two color television systems (PAL and SECAM) and avoid a market solution that in the case of video formats worked at the expense of European industry.

The European Commission, in particular the Information Technology Task Force—the forerunner of the DG Telecommunications, Information Industry and Innovation (DG XIII)—and the DG Industry (DG III), saw in HDTV a perfect opportunity for a European industrial policy initiative. Support went all the way up to the highest levels. Commission President Delors viewed a European standard as essential not just for promoting the competitiveness of European manufacturers but also for protecting European culture against the Americans.[101] In 1986, national governments launched a project under the intergovernmental Eureka R&D program. For the first time, European intervention targeted specifically consumer electronics rather than the information technology industry. Besides the financial injection of £1 billion there was also regulatory intervention.[102] An EU directive in 1986 mandated the adoption of the European MAC standards for high-powered satellites (DBS). However, the directive expired in 1991 largely unfulfilled. It was overtaken by technological developments, in particular the growth of medium-powered satellites manifested in the 1990 takeover of the official British DBS project (BSB) by Murdoch's Sky using the medium-powered Astra satellite. The interventionist EU policy was also facing growing resistance internally. Finally, it was overtaken by further technological progress, the breakthrough of digital television in the USA, as the next chapter explains.

The EU's HDTV policy is a case of defensive standardization, a response to a perceived Japanese trade threat.[103] It is an example of exclusionary and protectionist industrial policy based on close links between parts of the European Commission and leading European consumer equipment manufacturers and where broadcasters and consumers/viewers were absent.

Pan-European Television Experiments: Collaborating with
Public Service Broadcasters

The calls for European television resulted in two EBU-sponsored trans-frontier ventures: *Eurikon* (1982) and *Europa TV* (1985–1986). The EBU, representing the public service broadcasters, came to enjoy a close working relationship with the European Parliament and the Commission. Coopera-tion with the EBU would strengthen the EU institutionally and establish it as a key European organization in a field in which it enjoyed no legal com-petence. In any case, the EU depended on the EBU and its members for the practical implementation of pan-European broadcasting since public ser-vice broadcasters were at the time the only broadcasters in Western Europe and as such vital to any television plans.[104]

For its part, the EBU stood to benefit from the pan-European television projects in various ways. Since its inception, the EBU has served as "a forum of professional expertise" where its members experiment with new technolo-gies and in general share experiences.[105] It was natural then for the EBU to get involved in DBS, the latest technology at that time. Furthermore, the EBU was familiar with transnational television, having acquired extensive technical and management expertise through its Eurovision program exchange system created in 1954. The EBU also stood to gain institutionally by becoming es-tablished as a credible actor in broadcasting and, importantly, get recognized as such by the European political organizations, the EU and the Council of Europe, especially at a time when the broadcasting market was changing from being public and national to having to accommodate private commercial and transnational broadcasters. Finally, the EBU's members, the public service broadcasters, stood to gain valuable experience with DBS, a new disruptive technology that would challenge the established broadcasting order which they had so far fully controlled. For them, the pan-European television proj-ects were a proactive strategy to gain competitive advantage in this new field and pre-empt competition from commercial broadcasters.[106] Still, there were divisions among them and certain big public service broadcasters, such as the BBC and the French ones, decided not to participate, perceiving the projects to be in conflict with their own national satellite television plans. Besides, the motivations of the participating broadcasters in *Europa TV*, as Collins found out, were anything but European: the German ARD wished to gain experience in new technologies; for Dutch NOS, the venture offered "the opportunity to play on a bigger stage"; for Italian RAI, expanding its activities was a defensive response to pre-empt competitive commercial television; the Portuguese RTP saw it "as a source of low cost programming"; while the Irish RTE participated for "fun."[107]

In other words, the EBU's first transfrontier television ventures (*Eurikon* and *Europa TV*) seen as "European" concealed the narrow interests that the

EBU and the EU as organizations, and each of the participating public service broadcasters were pursuing. Although these ventures were construed as "European," they were anything but European. And despite the idealistic rhetoric of the European Parliament, it soon turned out that the only reason the ventures went ahead was not because of their democratic potential essential for active citizenship and shared political responsibility but because established interests saw in them an opportunity to protect and promote their interests, especially in the changing television environment.

The EBU-sponsored pan-European television channels were effectively an attempt at European public service broadcasting. Small budgets, the absence of major public service broadcasters and the fragmentation of audiences across Europe along linguistic and cultural lines were some of the main reasons behind their failure.[108] These channels—effectively modelled on the first phase of national public service broadcasting which, despite national variations, was paternalistic and the broadcasters, as typical monopolists, were not interested in the market they were serving—were not concerned about audience tastes and preferences.[109]

The EBU experiments also failed in their original substantive aim. The idea that pan-European television would forge a European culture and identity was based on the unproved assumption of strong media effects, what Schlesinger calls the "fallacy of distribution" whereby the consumption of the same cultural product is believed to automatically lead to a common cultural identification.[110] In other words, it was premised upon the passivity of the audience and the concomitant power of the message. The end of the EBU experiments coincided with a more fundamental change in the relationship between the EBU and the EU, a change that was intimately related to the concept and future of public service broadcasting. As explored in subsequent chapters, from the mid-1980s onward, the relationship between commercial broadcasters and the European Commission, notably the DG Competition on the one hand and the EBU and public service broadcasters on the other hand, became adversarial.

In the second half of the 1980s, commercial broadcasters became established market players and transfrontier television became a reality, though not in its original conception as a uniform pan-European service but as an oligopoly controlled by a handful of private commercial players, broadcasting not the same content but content suited to diverse (sub)national tastes. In other words, transnational European television exists at the supply side whereby a handful of European (e.g., Murdoch's Sky pay-TV ventures, Bertelsmann's free-to-air RTL empire) and non-European players (e.g., Viacom's MTV) are dominant. Television markets are Europeanized only in the sense that there exist a few market players with activities in several European countries. This Europeanization, however, is the result of media concentration driven by the economic characteristics of the sector, not the result of a European identity or culture. Localized content that satisfies (sub)national tastes and preferences has become a fundamental precondition for the business success of these transnational channels. This is true for both general interest and thematic channels. Even sports and music, where cultural and linguistic differences seem less significant, have not turned out to travel across national boundaries as easily as had initially been anticipated.[111] Perversely, therefore, satellite television has served to re-nationalize television in Europe.

The Search for Cultural Unity and European Identity

The 1980s witnessed concrete positive action with regard to a European identity. Whereas in the early 1970s it was EU political leaders that raised the question of a European identity primarily concerned with its *external* dimension in the context of changing international circumstances, in the 1980s initiatives came from the EU institutions and the main preoccupation was Europe's *internal* identity. Of course, the two facets of identity (internal and external) are mutually constitutive and reinforcing. The point here is that there was a change of emphasis.

Concerns about insufficient public support for European integration increased during the course of the 1980s. In response to the low, for that period's standards, and, more worryingly, falling turnout in the European Parliament elections from 63 percent in 1979 down to 61 percent in 1984, the new Commission President Jacques Delors formed the Adonnino Committee for a People's Europe. Many of the recommendations in the 1985 Adonnino Report aimed at strengthening the Union's image and identity and included the adoption of a standardized European passport, an EU flag and an anthem.[112] In other words, the Report assigned state-like characteristics to the EU and, accordingly, the Commission became involved in the development of European symbols. The launch of pan-European television channels and the attempt at European public service broadcasting can be seen as part of these efforts to increase popular support and develop EU statehood. The European Parliament and the Commission perceived cultural and political integration as a complement to economic integration in order to make the latter sustainable. This vision required a strong European identity similar to the one underpinning nation-states.

European pro-integrationist forces wished to re-construct at the European level the congruence between polity and culture associated with the nation-state. But, as Collins based on Gellner points out, in the experience of the nation-states, the creation of a cultural community historically preceded the establishment of a political community.[113] European unionists, concerned about weak popular support for European integration, conveniently forgot this. They thought that the process could work equally well in reverse order:

a European cultural community could follow the creation of European political institutions. This was a technologically determinist top-down vision. Pan-European satellite television was *Deus ex machina,* the perfect medium to awaken and affirm dormant feelings of European consciousness and identification. Or, if a European identity did not exist, one could be fostered "from above." Just as nations, to use Anderson's oft-quoted phrase, are "imagined communities" and national identities are constructs that can be instilled through invented traditions, symbols, myths and rituals, official EU policy aimed at manufacturing an imagined community and state-like symbols at European level.[114]

However, traditional national identity forging tools—for instance, common history, language, culture, memories, myths and symbols—suggest that a European identity is but an illusion. For while these elements are present and are shared within nation-states, or at least are perceived as such, they do not exist at European level and attempts to construct a European identity by manufacturing some of these elements from above—such as pan-European television and symbols—have failed. As Smith explains,

> national identifications possess distinct advantages over the idea of a unified European identity. They are vivid, accessible, well established, long popularized, and still widely believed, in broad outline at least. In each of these respects, "Europe" is deficient both as idea and as process. Above all, it lacks a pre-modern past—a "prehistory" which can provide it with emotional sustenance and historical depth.[115]

But does the EU need a strong identity? There is disagreement about whether the EU needs an identity and whether one is possible. There are those who see identity, culture, citizenship and democracy along state national lines (nationalists) and those who do not (postnationalists).[116] Whereas the national state is evidence that supports the claims of the first group of scholars, the second vision has been criticized as not feasible and for lack of empirical evidence.

But although the national state may be the only actual example on which to base claims about identity formation, nationalists by giving too much emphasis to this historical empirical evidence tend to suppress mention of the fact that national identity itself has been challenged for some time now and tend to assume that strong national identifications present a real obstacle to the formation of a European identity. This perspective appeals to a nostalgic and idealistic view of national identity and to a unified national public sphere. It is problematic first, because it fails to recognize that identities are not fixed and rigid but rather porous and malleable and thus the extent to which (national) identities are open to transformation and influences from new contexts is an open question. And second and most importantly, national identities as historically formed face a crisis.

Historically, European nation-states developed on the basis of a relative congruity between bounded territory, functional tasks and a shared identity. This
congruity is no longer assured as the link between territory, governance and
identity is eroded at national level and is not replaced by an equivalent set of
institutions and shared symbols elsewhere.[117]

In other words, the congruity between political and cultural community has
been eroded at the national level. Indeed for Morley, genuine cultural diversity
entails precisely the deconstruction of the normative congruity between polity
and culture and not its replication at a higher European level.[118]

A related issue is that of public sphere, a normative concept that has been
used to guide policy and shape the transformation of the media landscape.[119] For Garnham, for instance, the national state is a necessary condition for the emergence of a public sphere and democratic governance.[120] Yet
others have questioned the extent to which there exists a singular public
sphere at the national level.[121] Nevertheless, allegiance to the national ter-
ritorially bounded public space is still strong and definitely stronger than
allegiance to an imagined European public space. Both Schlesinger and
Shore have concluded that there is a nascent mediated European public
sphere but one that is highly exclusive and elitist.[122]

For the nationalist camp, the difficulty in, or even impossibility of, creating a European public sphere appears to be one of scale and associated
complexity: it cannot be replicated at the European level because of the EU's
sheer size and diversity. But, as multi-lingual, -ethnic, -cultural countries
show (e.g., Belgium, Canada, Switzerland), it is neither size nor diversity
that makes the exercise more difficult. In many respects, the dilemmas that
the EU is facing are similar to those of multicultural societies. Whereas in
the past, most nations were founded on the basis of (artificial) cultural, linguistic and ethnic ties, multicultural societies need to give more emphasis
to a shared political culture as opposed to cultural affinities. Indeed, as will
be seen in the next chapter, in the 1990s in view of the problems encountered with forging a strong European identity and in the context of the
post–Cold War order, the conceptualization of EU identity came to emphasize citizenship rather than cultural unity.

The point made here is that the very notions of identity, culture, citizenship, legitimacy and democracy have been eroded at the national level and,
indeed, it is for this reason that these concepts have become core in social
sciences since the 1970s. These issues are not specifically "national" or
specifically "European." They do not concern a specific level of politico-
socioeconomic organization but rather they are part of the continued crisis
of modernity. Europeanization, itself cause and effect of the wider process
of globalization and the crisis of the nation-state, is at the same time an expression of, a response and a contributor to this crisis.

CONCLUSIONS

Between the late 1970s and the mid-/late 1980s the EU gradually entered the fields of information technology and electronics, telecommunications and television. It was the limitations of the established national Keynesian welfare order in the context of structural change that gave rise to EU governance. The EU assumed an interventionist managerial role, roughly the same role that national states had performed hitherto within their relatively closed national economies. EU state-building efforts were expected to compensate for the diminishing governance capacities—be they in the economic, industrial or cultural sphere—of the national state.

In contrast to the earlier period, the European Commission now was not isolated but had the support of key industrial players. Fostered by strong personalities, such as Davignon, it actively sought to co-opt the established interests in the communication sector rather than antagonize them. The Commission found in them a much-needed strong ally in favor of European-level solutions which would also benefit it institutionally. In turn, the European industry was willing to accept European-level initiatives but ones which it itself helped to shape significantly and did not in any way challenge its interests. A mutually supportive relationship therefore developed between (parts of) the European Commission and the key constituencies in the three sectors of information technology and electronics, telecommunications and television. These interests saw in market integration the answer to their own problems. The objective was not liberalization. Procompetitive thinking became dominant in the late 1980s. This was the period of defensive Europeanization concerned with industrial policy aims. The EU originally accepted monopolies and cooperated with them in order to gain knowledge and legitimacy and become a credible policy actor.

More specifically, persistent economic recession coupled with new theoretical understandings—highlighting the critical contribution of ICT to economic growth and competitiveness and pointing to the role of public policy—increased the political saliency of ICT, a sector where Europe was lagging behind. The EU, an organization concerned with trade and commercial matters, moved center stage. For the first time in 1979, political leaders endorsed the "information society" as the answer to Europe's socioeconomic malaise. In various reincarnations, the information society has remained a key driver of European integration ever since. Policy intervention, now under the new label of technology, rather than industrial, policy gave new momentum to European-level action and helped overcome deepseated controversies, for the short-term at least, concerning the need for and character of industrial policy, controversies which in the 1970s had crippled Commission proposals.

A new sectoral political economy, the result of technological developments, in particular digitalization and the consequent merging of information technology and telecommunications, exacerbated the vulnerability of
European industry, increased its exposure to intensifying international
competition, and vividly illustrated the limits of national parochial measures. In response, industrialists, many of them national champions, turned
to Europe. With the active encouragement of the Commission, new European interest groups (e.g., the European Round Table for industrialists and
Task Force on Information Technologies and Telecommunications) were
formed, advocating European solutions. The result was French-inspired industrial policy intervention, which included EU-sponsored R&D programs
(Esprit and Race) essentially drafted by the industry itself, pan-European
networks (ISDN and GSM) and defensive standardization (HDTV).

Network planning (ISDN and GSM), similar to earlier initiatives covered
in chapter 3, served to strengthen the position of the PTTs, and to a lesser
extent of telecommunications manufacturers, and contributed to European
high-technology policy being telecommunications, rather than information
technology and computer, driven, which in turn led to Europe's delayed acceptance of the internet.

From the start, the advent of transfrontier television gave rise to a heated
and complex debate. The original conceptualization of new television technologies on grounds of their democratic potential was quickly overshadowed by more urgent industrial mixed with cultural concerns. The EBU-
sponsored pan-European television ventures, with the active support of the
European Parliament and the Commission, were a well-intended but ill-
conceived attempt to address the perceived communication and information deficits of the EU. Although they were pursued in the name of Europe
and democratic ideals, these ventures, as noted, were anything but European. They served the institutional interests of the EU and the EBU, and the
narrow interests of the participating public service broadcasters. These ventures were a failed attempt to forge a common European identity by creating a single audiovisual space through the dismantling of national cultural
rather than market barriers. The most concrete action in the field of transnational satellite television had to do with industrial policy. The mandating of
common HDTV standards was a defensive response to a Japanese threat,
aiming to support the European consumer electronics industry.

In this period of defensive Europeanization, Europe was being built looking inward. European integration was relaunched on the basis of the needs
of European industrialists, the majority of whom, especially in the field of
ICT, were not ready to face international competition. The aim was to create a unified economic area through internal market liberalization and temporary external trade protection, offering manufacturers a large home base
and substantial economies of scale, and thus help them transform from na-

tional into European champions. A related aim, pursued principally by EU institutions, was to complement economic with political integration and develop EU statehood through European public service broadcasting and the construction of a European identity.

The mutually supportive relationship between the Commission and the established interests in information technology and electronics, telecommunications and television came under challenge especially in the latter half of the 1980s and early 1990s when the EU policy, now supported by a different set of stakeholders, had clearly become procompetitive. The concurrent pursuit of procompetitive and interventionist technology-push policy measures was no longer sustainable.

NOTES

1. For instance, Fritz Machlup, *The Production and Distribution of Knowledge in the United States* (Princeton, N.J.: Princeton University Press 1962). Daniel Bell, *The Coming of the Post-Industrial Society: A Venture in Social Forecasting* (Harmondsworth: Penguin 1976). Marc Uri Porat, *The Information Economy: Definition and Measurement* (Washington, D.C.: Government Printing Office, 1977).

2. Paschal Preston, *Reshaping Communications: Technology, Information and Social Change* (London: Sage, 2001), 63–64.

3. Simon Nora and Alain Minc, *The Computerization of Society: A Report to the President of France* (Cambridge, MA and London: MIT Press, 1980 [1978]). European Commission, *European Society Faced with the Challenge of New Information Technologies: A Community Response*, COM(79) 650 (Brussels, 26 November 1979), 1.

4. See, for instance, Robert E. Lucas Jr., "On the Mechanics of Economic Development," *Journal of Monetary Economics* 22, no. 1 (1988): 3–42.

5. Michael Porter, *The Competitive Advantage of Nations* (London: Macmillan, 1990).

6. Joseph Schumpeter, *The Theory of Economic Development* (Cambridge, MA.: Harvard University Press, 1961 [1934]).

7. Paul Romer, "The Origins of Endogenous Growth," *Journal of Economic Perspectives* 8, no. 1 (1994): 19.

8. Dieter Ernst and David O'Connor, *Competing in the Electronics Industry—The Experience of Newly Industrializing Economies* (Paris: OECD, 1992), 40.

9. Kenneth Flamm, *Targeting the Computer: Government Support and International Competition* (Washington, D.C.: The Brookings Institution, 1988), 13.

10. Paul Krugman, *Rethinking International Trade* (Cambridge, Mass., and London: MIT Press, 1990), 1–8.

11. Steven McGuire, "Trade Tools: Holding the Fort or Declaring Open House?," in *European Industrial Policy and Competitiveness*, ed. Thomas Lawton (London: Macmillan, 1999), 76–77.

12. Robert Brainard and John Madden, *Science and Technology Policy Outlook* (Paris: OECD, 1985), 68.

13. Ernst and O'Connor, *Competing*, 40.

14. Mark Blyth, *Great Transformations. Economic Ideas and Institutional Change in the Twentieth Century* (New York: Cambridge University Press, 2002), 190–99. Paul Krugman, *Peddling Prosperity: Economic Sense and Nonsense in the Age of Diminished Expectations* (London and New York: Norton, 1994), 245–80.

15. For instance, Laura D'Andrea Tyson, *Who's Bashing Whom? Trade Conflict in High-Technology Industries* (Washington, D.C.: Institute for International Economics, 1992).

16. Lester Thurow, *The Zero-Sum Society* (New York: Basic Books, 1980).

17. I. M. Destler, *American Trade Politics* (4th ed. Washington, D.C.: Institute for International Economics, 2005), 182.

18. Luca Guzzetti, *A Brief History of European Union Research Policy* (Luxembourg: Office for Official Publications of the European Communities, 1995), 87.

19. For its origins see <http://www.kangaroogroup.org/E/032_origin_D.lasso> (21 Oct. 2005).

20. Maria Green Cowles, "Setting the Agenda for a New Europe: The ERT and EC 1992," *Journal of Common Market Studies* 33, no. 4 (1995): 501–26.

21. Keith Richardson [ERT Secretary General, 1988–1998], "Big Business and the European Agenda," *Sussex European Institute Working Paper* No. 35 (Brighton: Sussex European Institute, 2000), 10.

22. UNICE (Union of Industrial and Employers' Confederations of Europe) was set up in 1958.

23. Michael Hodges, "Industrial Policy: Hard Times or Great Expectations?," in *Policy-Making in the European Community*, ed. Helen Wallace, William Wallace and Carole Webb (Chichester: John Wiley, 1983), 279.

24. Belén Balanyá, Ann Doherty, Olivier Hoedeman, Adam Ma'anit and Erik Wesselius, *Europe Inc.* (London: Pluto, 2000), 20.

25. Cowles, "Setting the Agenda," 503, and Wayne Sandholtz and John Zysman, "1992: Recasting the European Bargain," *World Politics* XLII, no. 1 (1989): 95–128.

26. Bastiaan Van Apeldoorn, *Transnational Capitalism and the Struggle over European Integration* (London and New York: Routledge, 2002), 47–48.

27. For a detailed analysis see Van Apeldoorn, *Transnational Capitalism.*

28. "Gyllenhammar's Vigilantes," *Economist*, 28 January 1984, 69.

29. Cowles, "Setting the Agenda," 509–13.

30. For an analysis see Joan Pearce and John Sutton, *Protection and Industrial Policy in Europe* (London: Routledge & Kegan Paul, 1985).

31. Vivien Schmidt, "National Patterns of Governance under Siege: The Impact of European Integration," in *The Transformation of Governance in the European Union*, ed. Beate Kohler-Koch and Rainer Eising (London and New York: Routledge, 1999), 155–72.

32. Thomas Risse, "A European Identity? Europeanization and the Evolution of Nation-State Identities," in *Transforming Europe*, ed. Maria Green Cowles, James Caporaso and Thomas Risse (Ithaca and London: Cornell University Press, 2001), 210–13.

33. For the history of French cultural exceptionalism see Bill Grantham, *Some Big Bourgeois Brothel: Context for France's Culture Wars with Hollywood* (Luton: University of Luton Press, 2000).

34. ERT, *Changing Scales* (Paris: ERT, 1985).

35. Pierre Buigues and Philippe Goybet, "The Community's Industrial Competitiveness and International Trade in Manufactured Products," in *The European Internal Market: Trade and Competition*, ed. Alexis Jacquemin and André Sapir (Oxford: Oxford University Press, 1989), 227–47.

36. Data from European Commission, "Written Question 1539/80 by Mr. Adam to the Commission (20 November 1980). Subject: Community Electronics Industry. Reply Given by Mr. Davignon on Behalf of the Commission (2 March 1981)," *Official Journal* C78/9 (6 April 1981).

37. Claudio Ciborra, "Alliances as Learning Experiments: Cooperation, Competition and Change in High-tech Industries," in *Strategic Partnerships and the World Economy: States, Firms and International Competition*, ed. Lynn Krieger Mytelka (London: Pinter, 1991), 63–66.

38. "No, by Jove," *Economist*, 13 October 1984, 15.

39. Rex Malik, "France's Social Agenda for Le Computer," *Computerworld*, 9 May 1983, ID/1.

40. "No Novelty, Please," *Economist*, 24 November 1984, 103.

41. Rhonda Crane, *The Politics of International Standards: France and the Color TV War* (Norwood, N.J.: Ablex, 1979).

42. Alan Cawson, Kevin Morgan, Douglas Webber, Peter Holmes and Anne Stevens, *Hostile Brothers: Competition and Closure in the European Electronics Industry* (Oxford: Clarendon Press, 1990), 224–27.

43. Jürgen Müller, *The Benefits of Completing the Internal Market for Telecommunications Services/Equipment in the Community. Research on the "Cost of Non-Europe,"* Basic Findings, vol. 10 (Luxembourg: Office for Official Publications of the European Communities, 1988).

44. European Commission, *Towards a Dynamic European Economy: Green Paper on the Development of the Common Market for Telecommunications Services and Equipment*, COM(87) 290 (Brussels, 30 June 1987), 90.

45. Guzzetti, *A Brief History*, 76–77. The "Big Twelve" were Bull, CGE and Thomson from France; AEG, Nixdorf and Siemens from Germany; Olivetti and STET from Italy; Philips from the Netherlands; and GEC, ICL and Plessey from Britain.

46. Council, "Decision 84/130/EEC of 28 February 1984 Concerning a European Programme for Research and Development in Information Technologies (ESPRIT)," *Official Journal* L67/54 (9 March 1984).

47. See, for instance, Wayne Sandholtz, *High-Tech Europe: The Politics of International Cooperation* (Berkeley and Oxford: University of California Press, 1992), 308–10.

48. Lynn Krieger Mytelka, "States, Strategic Alliances and International Oligopolies: The European ESPRIT Programme," in *Strategic Partnerships and the World Economy: States, Firms and International Competition*, ed. Lynn Krieger Mytelka (London: Pinter, 1991), 182–210.

49. John Peterson, *High Technology and the Competition State: An Analysis of the Eureka Initiative* (London: Routledge, 1993).

50. Council, "Decision 85/372/EEC of 25 July 1985 on a Definition Phase for a Community Action in the Field of Telecommunications Technologies—R&D Programme in Advanced Communications Technologies for Europe (RACE)," *Official Journal* L210/24 (7 Aug. 1985).

51. Claude Labarrère, *L' Europe des Postes et des Télécommunications* (Paris: Masson, 1985), 18.

52. Guzzetti, *A Brief History*, 91.

53. Brian T. Hanson, "What Happened to Fortress Europe? External Trade Policy Liberalisation in the European Union," *International Organization* 52, no. 1 (1998): 55–85.

54. European Commission, *Recommendations on Telecommunications*, COM(80) 422 (Brussels, 1 September 1980).

55. European Parliament, *Report Drawn up on Behalf of the Committee on Economic and Monterrey Affairs on the Recommendations from the Commission of the European Communities to the Council on Telecommunications*. Rapporteur: F.H.J Herman, PE71859 (Brussels, 27 April 1981).

56. Godefroy Dang-Nguyen, "The European Telecommunications Policy or the Awakening of a Sleeping Beauty" (paper presented at the European Consortium of Political Research conference, Amsterdam, April 1987), 16.

57. Herbert Ungerer and Nicholas Costello, *Telecommunications in Europe* (rev. ed. Luxembourg: Office for Official Publications of the European Communities, 1990), 130.

58. Interview with European Commission—DG Competition official, Brussels, 18 April 1994.

59. European Commission, *Telecommunications*, COM(83) 329 (Brussels, 9 June 1983).

60. European Commission, *Discussion Paper for the Special Council Meeting of 20-21 September on the Question of Improving the International Competitive Position of European Firms*, COM(83) 547 (Brussels, 14 September 1983).

61. Michel Carpentier, "Toward Smooth Europe-U.S. Telecom Relations," *Transnational Data and Communications Report* (June 1986), 7.

62. European Commission, *Progress Report on the Thinking and Work Done in the Field, and Initial Proposals for an Action Programme*, COM(84) 277 (Brussels, 18 May 1984).

63. GAP, *Proposals for the Coordinated Introduction of Integrated Services Digital Networks in the Community*, mimeo (Brussels: European Commission, 5 June 1985). GAP, *Proposals for the Coordinated Introduction of Broadband Services in the Community*, mimeo (Brussels: European Commission, 16 October 1986).

64. Robin Mansell, Peter Holmes and Kevin Morgan, "European Integration and Telecommunications: Restructuring Markets and Institutions," *Prometheus* 8, no 1 (1990): 50–66.

65. Gerhard Fuchs, "Integrated Services Digital Network: The Politics of European Telecommunications Network Development," *Journal of European Integration* XVI, no. 1 (1992): 63–88.

66. Peter Haas, "Introduction: Epistemic Communities and International Policy Co-ordination," *International Organization* 46, no. 1 (1992): 1–35.

67. For an analysis of how a new technology's growth is based not just on its own potential but also on the opportunities and constraints created by existing technologies, see Harmeet Sawhney, "Wi-Fi Networks and the Rerun of the Cycle," *Info: The Journal of Policy, Regulation and Strategy for Telecommunications, Information and Media* 5, no. 6 (2003): 25–33.

68. Loretta Anania, "The Protean Complex: Are Open Networks Common Markets?" (paper presented at the VIII Annual International Telecommunications Society, Venice, Italy, March 1990).

69. Council, "Recommendation 86/659/EEC of 22 December 1986 on the Co-ordinated Introduction of the Integrated Services Digital Network (ISDN) in the European Community," *Official Journal* L382/36 (31 December 1986).

70. "Turing Copper into Gold," *Public Network Europe* (November 1998): 42–45.

71. Anton Huurdeman, *The Worldwide History of Telecommunications* (New Jersey: John Wiley, 2003), 528.

72. Alan Cox, "The Years from Mid-1998 to Early 2001," in *GSM and UMTS: The Creation of Global Mobile Communication*, ed. Friedhelm Hillebrand (Chichester: John Wiley, 2002), 286–300.

73. Michel Mouly, "System Architecture," in *GSM and UMTS: The Creation of Global Mobile Communication*, ed. Friedhelm Hillebrand (Chichester: John Wiley, 2002), 306.

74. Council, "Recommendation 87/371/EEC on the Co-ordinated Introduction of Public Pan-European Cellular Digital Land-based Mobile Communications in the Community," *Official Journal* L196/81 (17 July 1987). Council, "Directive 87/372/EEC on the Frequency Bands to be Reserved for the Co-ordinated Introduction of Public pan-European Cellular Digital Land-based Mobile Communications in the European Community," *Official Journal* L196/85 (17 July 1987).

75. Johan Lembke, *Competition for Technological Leadership: EU Policy for High Technology* (Cheltenham and Northampton, MA: Edward Elgar, 2002).

76. Sadahiko Kano, "Technical Innovations, Standardization and Regional Comparison—A Case Study in Mobile Communications," *Telecommunications Policy* 24 (2000): 305–21.

77. For the effects of standardization on mobile diffusion see Heli Koski and Tobias Kretschmer, "Entry, Standards and Competition: Firm Strategies and the Diffusion of Mobile Telephony," *Review of Industrial Organization* 26, no. 1 (2005): 89–113.

78. Friedhelm Hillebrand, "The Creation of the UMTS Foundations in ETSI from April 1996 to February 1999," in *GSM and UMTS: The Creation of Global Mobile Communication*, ed. Friedhelm Hillebrand (Chichester: John Wiley, 2002), 187.

79. Raymund Werle, "Internet @ Europe: Overcoming Institutional Fragmentation and Policy Failure," in *Governing Telecommunications and the New Information Society in Europe*, ed. Jacint Jordana (Cheltenham and Northampton, MA: Edward Elgar, 2002), 137–58.

80. European Parliament, *Report on Radio and Television Broadcasting in the European Community on Behalf of the Committee on Youth, Culture, Education, Information and Sport. (The Hahn Report)*, PE Doc 1-1013/81 (Brussels, 23 February 1982), 7.

81. Jill Hills, with Stylianos Papathanassopoulos, *The Democracy Gap: The Politics of Information and Communication Technologies in the United States and Europe* (Westport, Conn.: Greenwood Press, 1991), 93–117.

82. The European Court of Justice, as noted, had already been called upon to intervene in the field of broadcasting. The Parliament, unlike the Court, was acting on its own initiative and approached broadcasting from the point of view of its democratic potential and contribution to integration. The Court was more restricted in its

approach as it had to interpret if and how the EU Treaty applied to the specific case brought before it.

83. European Parliament, *Motion for a Resolution on Radio and Television Broadcasting in the European Community*, EP Doc. 1-409/80 (Brussels, September 1980). European Parliament, *Motion for a Resolution on the Threat to Diversity of Opinion Posed by Commercialisation of New Media*, EP Doc. 1-422/80 (Brussels, September 1980).

84. European Parliament, *Report on the Information Ppolicy of the European Community, of the Commission of the European Communities and of the European Parliament (Schall Report)*, PE DOC 1-596/80 (Brussels, 16 January 1981).

85. European Parliament, *Hahn Report*. All quotes are from page 5.

86. European Parliament, *Hahn Report*, 8.

87. European Parliament, *Hahn Report*. All quotes in this paragraph are from page 6.

88. European Court of Justice, "Judgment of 18 March 1980 in Case 52/79. Procureur du Roi v Marc J.V.C. Debauve and Others," *European Court Reports* (1980), 833. European Court of Justice, "Judgment of 18 March 1980 in Case 62/79. SA Compagnie générale pour la diffusion de la télévision, Coditel, and Others v. Ciné Vog Films and Others," *European Court Reports* (1980), 881.

89. European Commission, *Realities and Tendencies in European Television: Perspectives and Options*, COM (83) 229 (Brussels, 25 May 1983).

90. European Commission, *Realities and Tendencies*, 22.

91. European Parliament, *Report Drawn on Behalf of the Committee on Youth, Culture, Education, Information and Sport on a Policy Commensurate with New Trends in European Television. (Arfé Report)*, EP 1-1541/83, PE 85.902, (Brussels, 16 March 1984), 8.

92. European Parliament, *Arfé Report*, 9.

93. European Parliament, *Arfé Report*, 13.

94. European Parliament, *Arfé Report*, 19.

95. The BBC and Reuters each had a 40 percent stake in Visnews and the remaining 20 percent was owned by broadcasting organizations from Australia, Canada and New Zealand.

96. European Parliament, *Arfé Report*, 33. The report was working on the assumption that, at least for the foreseeable future, there was room for only one European news channel and so the first organization to enter the market would dominate it.

97. European Parliament, *Arfé Report*, 31–32.

98. European Parliament, *Arfé Report*, 32.

99. European Parliament, *Report Drawn on Behalf of the Committee on Youth, Culture, Education, Information and Sport on Broadcast Communication in the European Community (the Threat to Diversity of Opinion Posed by the Commercialization of New Media) (Hutton Report)*, PE 78.983, Doc. 1-1523/83 (Brussels, 15 March 1984). Strictly speaking, media concentration has not turned out to be an actual EU policy line since there are no pan-European media concentration rules, but rather competence rests entirely with national governments and regulatory authorities. However, the EU can intervene using its strong competition powers.

100. Hernan Galperin, *New Television, Old Politics: The Transition to Digital TV in the United States and Britain* (Cambridge: Cambridge University Press, 2004), 71–89.

101. Charles Grant, *Delors: Inside the House That Jacques Built* (London: Nicholas Brealey Publishing, 1994), 156.

102. Xiudian Dai, Alan Cawson and Peter Holmes, "The Rise and Fall of High Definition Television: The Impact of European Technology Policy," *Journal of Common Market Studies* 34, no. 2 (1996): 155.

103. Alan Cawson, "High-Definition Television in Europe," *The Political Quarterly* 66, no. 2 (1995): 160.

104. In 1982, commercial television existed in Britain, Italy, Luxembourg and Finland (the latter not an EU member state yet).

105. Stig Hjarvard, "Pan-European Television News: Towards a European Political Public Sphere?," In *National Identity and Europe*, ed. Phillip Drummond, Richard Patterson and Janet Willis (London: British Film Institute, 1993), 81.

106. Richard Collins, *From Satellite to Single Market* (London and New York: Routledge, 1998), 79.

107. Collins, *From Satellite*, 138.

108. For a detailed analysis of the first EBU-sponsored pan-European channels see Collins, *From Satellite*, 75–205.

109. Michael Tracey, *The Decline and Fall of Public Service Broadcasting* (Oxford: Oxford University Press, 1998), 11–12.

110. Philip Schlesinger, "Wishful Thinking: Cultural Policies, Media and Collective Identities in Europe," *Journal of Communication* 43, no. 2 (1993): 11–13. See also Collins, *From Satellite*, 17.

111. See, for instance, Jean Chalaby, "Transnational Television in Europe: The Role of Pan-European Channels," *European Journal of Communication* 17, no. 2 (2002): 183–203. Keith Roe and Gust De Meyer, "Music Television: MTV-Europe," in *Television Across Europe*, ed. Jan Wieten, Graham Murdock and Peter Dahlgren (London: Sage, 2000), 141–57.

112. European Commission, "Report Submitted to the Milan European Council (Milan, 28–29 June 1985) [Adonnino Committee Report on a Citizens' Europe]," *Bulletin of the European Communities Supplement*, no.7 (1985).

113. Ernest Gellner, *Nations and Nationalism* (Oxford: Blackwell, 1983). Collins, *From Satellite*, 1–13, 206–20.

114. Benedict Anderson, *Imagined Communities. Reflections on the Origin and Spread of Nationalism* (2nd ed. London and New York: Verso, 1991). Eric Hobsbawm and Terence Ranger, eds., *The Invention of Tradition* (Cambridge: Cambridge University Press, 1983).

115. Anthony Smith, "National Identity and the Idea of European Unity," *International Affairs* 68, no. 1 (1992): 62.

116. In addition to the references in the text, for the "nationalist proposition" see indicatively: Chris Shore, "Wither European Citizenship? Eros and Civilization Revisited," *European Journal of Social Theory* 7, no. 1 (2004): 27–44. Philippe Schmitter, *How to Democratize the European Union . . . and Why Bother?* (Lanham, Md.: Rowman & Littlefield, 2000). For the "postnationalist proposition" see indicatively Anthony McGrew, "Democracy beyond Borders?," in *The Global Transformations Reader*, ed. David Held and Anthony McGrew (Cambridge: Polity, 2000), 405–19. Jürgen Habermas, "Citizenship and National Identity: Some Reflections on the Future of Europe," *Praxis International* 12, no. 1 (1992): 1–19.

117. Brigid Laffan, "The Politics of Identity and Political Order in Europe," *Journal of Common Market Studies* 34, no. 1 (1996): 82.

118. David Morley, "Media Fortress Europe: Geographies of Exclusion and the Purification of Cultural Space," *Caradian Journal of Communication* 23, no. 3 (1998), <http://www.cjc-online.ca/viewarticle.php?id=471&layout=html> (19 May 2006).

119. See, for instance, Peter Dahlgren, *Television and the Public Sphere* (London: Sage, 1995). Nicholas Garnham, "The Media and the Public Sphere," in *Communicating Politics*, ed. Peter Golding, Graham Murdock and Philip Schlesinger (Leicester: Leicester University Press, 1986), 45–53. David Ward, *The European Union Democratic Deficit and the Public Sphere: An Evaluation of EU Media Policy* (Amsterdam and Oxford: IOS Press, 2002).

120. See, for instance, Nicholas Garnham, "Comments on John Keane's 'Structural Transformations of the Public Sphere,'" *The Communication Review* 1, no. 1 (1995): 23–25.

121. John Keane, "Structural Transformations of the Public Sphere," *The Communication Review* 1, no. 1 (1995): 1–22. Gerard Delanty, "Beyond the Nation-State: National Identity and Citizenship in a Multicultural Society—A Response to Rex," *Sociological Research Online* 1, no. 3 (1996), <http://www.socresonline.org.uk/socresonline/1/3/1.html> (23 May 2006). Arjun Appadurai, "Disjuncture and Difference in the Global Cultural Economy," in *Global Culture, Nationalism, Globalization and Modernity*, ed. Mike Featherstone (London: Sage, 1990), 295–310.

122. Philip Schlesinger, "Changing Spaces of Political Communication: The Case of the European Union," *Political Communication* 16, no. 3 (1999): 263–79. Chris Shore, *Building Europe: The Cultural Politics of European Integration* (London and New York: Routledge, 2000), 222. See also Colin Sparks and Risto Kunelius, "Problems with a European Public Sphere," *Javnost/The Public* 8, no. 1 (2001): 5–20. Colin Sparks, "Is There a Global Public Sphere?" in *Electronic Empires*, ed. Daya Thussu (London: Arnold, 1998), 108–24.

5

Liberalization and Re-regulation

The High Peak of European Governance? (Mid-/Late 1980s to Late 1990s)

INTRODUCTION

This chapter examines the most intensive phase of European governance of communications covering the period from the mid-/late 1980s to the late 1990s. Although elements can be traced in earlier periods, it is in this phase that procompetitive policies became dominant. A combination of political economy and institutional factors—the latter often neglected in political economy analyses placing emphasis on transnational forces and private actors—contributed to the progressive restructuring of television and telecommunications markets.

This chapter demonstrates how, with market restructuring and the launch of the single market project, the contestation concerning the relationship between state and market clearly penetrated European politics, and how this was reflected in and shaped by institutional parameters.

THE "CONSTRUCTIVE AMBIGUITY" OF THE SINGLE MARKET PROJECT

For Woolcock a central ambiguity ran in the single market project. On the one side, there were those viewing it as a lever to promote liberalization working with international market pressures and hence part of the wider process of globalization. On the other side, there were those viewing it "as a means of retaining control over markets" in response to growing internationalization and economic interdependence, processes that rendered national policy measures inadequate.[1] Under the first scenario, the internal market was about negative integration, the removal of market barriers. Under the second scenario, the internal market was also about positive integration; regulatory intervention would complement the removal of market barriers. This "constructive ambiguity" enabled governments and interests with very different views to support the creation of the single market. In essence, this ambiguity was nothing other than the fundamental contestation about the relationship between state and market. From the mid-/late 1980s to the late 1990s, this contestation most clearly penetrated EU politics.[2] Following Woolcock's argument, the first view conceptualized the state and market as diametrically opposed, whereas the second view perceived the state and market in a co-constitutive relation.

Similar to Woolcock, for van Apeldoorn, the single market contained a conflict between two main contending projects: neomercantilism and neoliberalism.[3] Both projects had their own strong supporters within the industry, the European institutions, and among national governments. Large sections of Europe's industrial capital—still mostly nationally embedded—supported the neomercantilist vision. For them, the main culprit of the ills of the European economy and their woes lay with the presence of small and fragmented national markets and consequent insufficient economies of scale. These problems could be addressed through the building of the single market and the abolition of internal trade barriers. But, crucially, the single market was to be also premised on active EU-level industrial policy—through, for instance, R&D, network planning and standardization, examined in the previous chapter—and on temporary external trade protection. These measures would allow national champions to transform into European champions. This Fortress Europe scenario had strong political currency. Its advocates included Europe's largest firms in information technology and electronics, importantly, sectors perceived to be critical to economic growth. For the neomercantilist faction then, the crisis of the Keynesian welfare state and rising economic interdependence necessitated a move from the positive interventionist to the regulatory state at the national level but also the concomitant transfer of regulatory competence from the national to the European level, particularly in the fields of industrial and trade policies.

The rival neoliberal fraction had a different vision of European integration. Whereas neomercantilists stressed insufficient economies of scale and promoted the technology gap discourse, neoliberals stressed structural weaknesses and promoted the "Eurosclerosis" discourse.[4] For the latter, the economic downturn, the high levels of inflation and unemployment and the loss of international competitiveness were all linked not to market fragmentation but to systemic problems of the European economy, such as labor market rigidity. The Eurosclerosis discourse was part and parcel of the "government failure" discourse which grew out of mounting skepticism in the face of the 1970s crisis about the ability of the state to deal with the tasks it was facing.[5] For neoliberals, similar to the hyperglobalization thesis, the crisis of the positive interventionist state required a move from government to governance, meaning the decline and roll-back, rather than the transformation, of the national state.[6] In this context, European integration should simply be confined to negative integration and not involve the creation or transfer of regulatory responsibilities.

These divisions, the conflict between the neomercantilist and neoliberal visions of European integration, came to a head in the late 1980s/early 1990s but, as will be demonstrated, neither faction won.

RESTRUCTURING TELECOMMUNICATIONS MARKETS

In the mid-1980s, economic arguments and the idea of trade in telecommunications were increasingly gaining ground. A unique confluence of factors facilitated the shift to procompetitive thinking.[7]

First, technological developments, notably digitalization, fundamentally transformed the telecommunications sector and brought in new market players, manufacturers and operators. These developments underscored the economic growth potential of the sector. The contribution of telecommunications to the EU Gross Domestic Product was expected to rise from 3 percent ($98 billion) in 1987 to 7 percent per annum by 2000.[8]

Second, starting in the USA and spreading to Japan and Britain, the established national monopoly paradigm was disintegrating.[9] The progressive liberalization of the U.S. domestic telecommunications market ahead of other countries and a worsening trade deficit with several of its main competitors led the Reagan administration to adopt a two-pronged strategy. At the international level, the USA managed to include liberalization of trade in services in the GATT Uruguay Round officially launched in 1986 while, following the reform of its domestic trade law with the 1988 Omnibus Trade and Competitiveness Act, the USA could resort to "aggressive unilateralism" and threaten its trading partners with sanctions in cases where there was no open market reciprocity.[10] In short, the USA became a strong procompetitive force.

Third, the international liberalization of service industries, in particular those that rely heavily on telecommunications infrastructure and services for their transnational operations such as finance and travel, strengthened calls for liberalization.

Corporate telecommunications users—increasingly dissatisfied with the existing monopolistic telecommunications order, lack of choice and high prices, all more pronounced in the recessionary 1970s, and especially those active in the EU market, feeling seriously disadvantaged vis-à-vis U.S. competitors who were now beginning to reap the benefits of domestic market liberalization in terms of a greater variety of services, of better quality and at lower cost—started organizing themselves to press for the introduction of competition. In 1974, the International Telecommunications Users' Group (Intug) was set up to ensure that "the voice of industry users [is] heard wherever telecommunications policy is made."[11] In the 1980s, the corporate community, working with international organizations like the International Chamber of Commerce and the OECD, came to progressively influence policy debates on liberalization.[12] It was instrumental in drawing attention to the potential economic benefits of advanced communications systems, thereby shifting the perception of telecommunications away from a technical engineering field to one of vital economic importance.

Fourth, the above developments need also to be understood in the context of the breakdown of national Keynesian economic consensus and the shift toward neoliberal economics broadly embraced by all major European countries, including France after the 1983 turn. Significantly then, it was not just economic interests that were pushing for liberalization. European governments, many of them having launched domestic consultations about the reform of their telecommunications sectors, were now more receptive to EU policy action. Britain was the first EU country under the recently elected Thatcher government to initiate liberalization of its domestic telecommunications market in 1982 and privatization of the incumbent operator British Telecom in 1984. But other countries too, like Germany, France and the Netherlands, had initiated debates about reform.[13] Indeed, there are striking similarities between some of the national studies on telecommunications and the subsequent landmark 1987 Green Paper of the European Commission on the development of the common telecommunications market.[14] In turn, the Green Paper provided added support and legitimacy for national reform plans.

Fifth, the revival of European integration with the single market project provided further impetus to procompetitive market restructuring. Institutional factors, finally, contributed to the adoption of a procompetitive EU policy. In the 1980s, important power-shifts took place within the Commission. The end of economic recession and the launch of the single market project challenged the active role that DG Industry and DG Telecommunications had assumed in supporting European industry. In particular, DG Industry and Internal Market, as it subsequently became, got absorbed by the internal market legislation. It was after 1988 that it and DG Telecommunications regained their power, now both under Commissioner Bangemann. In turn, the procompetition bias of the internal market and the strong leadership of Commissioners Sutherland (1985–1988) and Brittan (1988–1992) transformed DG Competition from an isolated, legalistic and bureaucratic Commission department to an aggressive and central policy actor.[15]

Whereas the conceptualization of the Commission as a dynamic corporate actor[16] interested in increasing its institutional power and in expanding its competence is right in that it treats institutions as actors rather than passive institutional frameworks, it should be stressed that the Commission is not a single unitary entity. Its predominantly vertical organization can have fragmenting implications for the formulation and coordination of policies. This has been the case in both television and telecommunications. By virtue of the diverse interests they represent, the action and solutions that various Commission departments promote differ and may even clash.

Besides the Commission, the European Court of Justice in several pro-competitive rulings gave the Commission the strongest possible legal basis to intervene in and gradually liberalize telecommunications markets. Both the Commission and the European Court, based on the competition provisions of the EU Treaty, attacked the restrictive practices of the PTTs and their European association, the CEPT. Similar to the television field, the mutually supportive relationship between (parts of) the Commission and the monopolist PTTs in pursuit of industrial policy objectives was coming under considerable strain.

The End of Mutual Interdependency

The British Telecom (BT) Case

The so-called BT case arose in 1982 when Telespeed Services Ltd., a private telecommunications company in Britain, lodged a complaint with the European Commission's DG Competition alleging that the incumbent BT, still a state-owned monopoly, was abusing its dominant market position by impeding the operation of private messaging agencies. These would collect telex traffic from outside Britain and forward it, using leased lines from BT's network, and take advantage of the lower international tariffs when originating traffic from Britain (telex refilling).

The case was controversial for two reasons. First, it involved a so-called sector of general economic interest—the EU general term for public utilities—and at issue were the role of the state and the definition of public monopolies. Second, at the heart of the case was a conflict between EU and international obligations agreed within the International Telecommunication Union and on which the provision of telecommunications services across borders was based.

The Commission found that BT had abused its dominant position. It explained that its practices "both limit[ed] the development of a new market and the use of new technology."[17] The Commission also maintained that the EU obligations as arising from, in particular, the competition provisions of the EU Treaty may override a member state's international obligations.

It was neither BT nor the British government but a third party, the Italian government, that challenged the Commission's decision before the European Court of Justice. This was an attack on the Commission's newly exercised power to intervene, especially along competition lines, in the historically monopolistic, nationally defined and regulated telecommunications sector. The Court upheld the Commission's decision.[18]

It is not clear if the Commission would have been reluctant to attack BT's practices and the international regulatory framework from which they emanated, had there not been a timely change on the part of the Thatcher government in favor of competition with the enactment of the 1981 British Telecommunications Act. Indeed, the British government intervened as a third party in support of the Commission against the Italian government, who appealed the decision while BT retreated from its restrictive practices before the Commission reached its decision. In other words, the British government itself needed the Commission's decision to legitimize its own procompetition policy and to face opposition from other PTTs and countries.

The BT case, the first competition case in the EU concerning telecommunications, was path breaking. It recognized the application of competition rules to telecommunications organizations. But it also had wider ramifications. It shaped telecommunications policy developments internationally since implicit in the ruling was an attack on the old order of telecommunications regulation under the auspices of the cartel-like International Telecommunication Union. The ruling supporting procompetition arguments questioned the relevance of the International Telecommunication Union regulations and the CCITT recommendations and, at least within the EU, it diminished their importance.[19]

SWIFT v. CEPT

One of the first competitive threats that PTTs had to face was the development of large-scale private networks using leased facilities. The PTTs tried to impede their development by imposing various restrictions on their use, connection to public facilities and equipment and tariffing. The CEPT-SWIFT conflict is indicative of the restrictive practices West European PTTs were prepared to adopt.

The Society for Worldwide Interbank Financial Telecommunications (SWIFT), a non-profit international banking service network formed in 1973, brought together European and American banks. It planned to lease public-switched lines at flat rates. For heavy communication users, flat rates are economically beneficial since no matter how much they use the leased lines they pay one flat fee. In contrast, telecommunications operators push for volume-sensitive tariffs under which the heavier the traffic, as is typical for large corporate users, the higher the revenue and profits for telecommunications operators. The latter was precisely the strategy favored by the PTTs acting through their European association, the CEPT. Volume sensitive tariffs would have increased the cost of using the SWIFT network "by two to four hundred percent for communications among European banks and by one thousand percent for communications between European and North American banks."[20] In 1978, the Commission's DG Competition launched an inquiry into the cartel-like behavior of the PTTs organized through CEPT in the imposition of prohibitive tariffs. In 1981, after the Commission had threatened to bring the case in front of the European Court, a compromise was reached between CEPT and SWIFT allowing for special tariff arrangements.

Similarly in 1990, the CEPT was forced by the DG Competition to abandon a proposed recommendation which would have resulted in a 30 percent surcharge on leased lines where these would be used to carry third-party traffic or be connected to the public telecommunications network.[21]

In response to persistent efforts by the PTTs acting through multilateral organizations to restrict competition, in 1991, the Commission reiterated its position that recommendations of the CEPT and the International Telecommunication Union were subject to EU competition law.[22] Existing draft CCITT proposals of the latter organization on the pricing and other supply conditions for international leased lines came under particular scrutiny. The Commission held that the proposals, which among other things prohibited the least-cost routing of services, could constitute restrictive price agreements and therefore infringe the EU competition provisions. The threat of action forced the PTTs acting through the CCITT to revise the recommendation.

Other Cases—Interpreting Monopoly Rights Narrowly

In addition to the BT case, in a series of landmark cases in the mid-1980s, the European Commission and the European Court applied the EU competition rules to the telecommunications services and equipment market segments. For instance, in several cases concerning terminal equipment, the Commission ruled that the extension of monopoly rights into the markets for cordless telephones, modems and private automatic branch exchanges was abusive and restricted the movement of goods within the common market.[23] These cases gave new momentum to the Commission, especially its Competition Directorate. Crucially, the Commission warned that it intended to use fully its competition powers, in particular the controversial article 90(3)—now article 86—concerning the application of competition rules to public monopolies and utilities. This is the only article that gives the Commission the power to pass legislation to member states directly without formal approval by the representatives of national governments in the Council of Ministers.

In short, taking into account the fact that technological advances made competition possible, at least in niche parts of the market, the DG Competition and the European Court of Justice interpreted restrictively existing monopoly rights preventing their extension into new product (e.g., equipment —modems case) and service (e.g., telex refilling—BT Case) markets, thereby opening the way for the liberalization of customer premises equipment and value-added services. As the next chapter explains, this is similar to the approach the European Court has taken in recent years in relation to public service broadcasting.

Launching Liberalization

The factors analyzed in the preceding section led to a proliberalization coalition comprising parts of the European Commission, potential market entrants, corporate telecommunications users and procompetition Public Telecommunications Operators (PTOs) and national governments. The 1987 Green Paper was the first comprehensive document of the European Commission to deal with the introduction of competition in telecommunications markets and associated regulatory, rather than narrowly industrial, issues.[24] It combined liberalization with harmonization, or the dismantling of market barriers with a basic common set of rules.

The implementation of the 1987 Green Paper and the progressive liberalization of telecommunications markets proved a difficult and contentious exercise. There were divisions between liberalizers and protectionists (neomercantilists), each camp having supporters within the industry, the Commission and among the member states.

The terminal equipment market was the first to be liberalized in 1988. Although this was the easiest to start with, since in effect it codified existing practice, the initiative created political upheaval. At issue was the fact that the Commission had unilaterally issued the directive, prepared by the now aggressive DG Competition, bypassing the European Parliament and the Council of Ministers representing the member states. Still, tacit political agreement was essential for the Commission to take such action.[25]

National governments interpreted the Commission's initiative as a direct attack on their national sovereignty. France, supported by Italy, Belgium, Germany and Greece, challenged the directive before the European Court seeking its annulment. Procompetitive governments, such as Britain, refrained from legal action, proving that the issues at stake were political rather than substantive. The Court broadly upheld the Commission's action.[26]

To effect the building of the single market and hasten implementation of common European standards, the Commission also intervened at the institutional level with the creation in 1988 of the European Telecommunications Standards Institute (ETSI) and the transfer of all standardization activities from the CEPT to it. With the creation of ETSI—an important element in the separation of the regulatory from the operational aspects of telecommunications since, with the introduction of market liberalization, the PTTs needed to relinquish their regulatory powers which they could have used to impede competition—standardization ceased to be the domain solely of national monopolist administrations and became an industry-led process.[27]

The controversy surrounding the opening up of the terminal equipment market was nothing compared to the political storm that the liberalization of telecommunications services generated.

Further reflecting its self-assertiveness and while the legal challenge against it was still pending, the DG Competition issued, again unilaterally, another directive stipulating the liberalization of data and value-added telecommunications services, basically all services other than public voice telephony. This concession was significant. The PTOs would continue to control the lion's share of the services market given that, at the time, public voice generated around 90 percent of their revenues.[28] The directive did not attack monopoly rights on the provision of network infrastructure but required the removal of restrictions on leased lines provided by the PTOs. Finally, it required the separation between the regulatory and operational functions of PTOs in order to enable effective competition in the market. It is important to note that the EU has never taken a formal position with regard to the ownership of PTOs, "which raises unique issues related to the regulation of partially state-owned firms."[29]

All the member states disliked the fact that the Commission resorted for the second time to its strong competition powers, issuing the directive without their formal input. But this time there were also substantive issues at stake. The procompetitive states—Britain, Germany, the Netherlands and Denmark—supported the liberalization of data services that was going to benefit their strong business users' communities.[30] But, France, Italy, Belgium, Greece, Spain and Portugal, prompted by their PTOs, vigorously opposed the opening up of data services. Many of these countries, lagging behind in the modernization of their domestic networks, feared that the proposed action would lead to private, especially American, operators taking over their markets. It was France in particular that, having invested heavily in upgrading its domestic infrastructure, adamantly opposed the liberalization of data transmission. Again, the opposing group of countries challenged the Directive in the European Court.[31]

Before resorting to legal means, France, holding the rotating EU Presidency, tried behind the scenes to force the Commission to withdraw the measure. France was blocking the adoption of the harmonization Open Network Provision framework directive—aimed at fair and equal access to and use of the public telecommunications network, which was crucial if services-based competition was to take off, given that network provision would remain a monopoly—in return for the exemption of data transmission liberalization.

In a defensive move in 1989, twenty-two European PTOs proposed a joint venture to offer international managed data network services—basically a broad package of facilities, value-added services and network management—targeting large corporate users. But in view of the Commission's conditions for its approval prohibiting, in particular, discrimination against private service suppliers and unfair cross-subsidization, the initiative was abandoned "because the commercial and regulatory environment was no longer favourable."[32]

A political compromise was eventually reached and both the liberalization and the harmonization directives were adopted simultaneously.[33] Importantly, under the compromise, and following France's insistence, national governments were allowed to lay down licensing conditions and thereby control the degree and form of liberalization of domestic markets.

For potential competitors and telecommunications users, the open network provision concept and process had been heavily influenced by the PTOs.[34] For instance, target periods for the provision and servicing of leased circuits were deleted from the final text, leaving national regulators and operators entirely responsible for their implementation.[35] Simple resale of data services—where leased lines connect to the public infrastructure thereby representing a greater threat to PTOs—was prohibited up until 1993, with an additional three-year transition period for countries with less developed and small networks. And although the directive called for cost-oriented tariffs it did not specify a cost accounting methodology. Similarly, the consequent directive on voice telephony repeated the call for transparent cost-allocation schemes but again did not provide any definition or methods for their achievement, leaving these issues to be addressed at the national level.[36]

The progress of market restructuring subsequent to these first liberalizing steps was influenced by the broader policy turn toward competitiveness and the information society.

Neomercantilists vs. Neoliberals: The Rise of Competitiveness

The power shifts within the Commission and associated interest coalitions, with the ascendancy of DG Competition, took a fundamental turn in the late 1980s/early 1990s. This is when the tension of the EU policy mix combining active industrial policy with procompetitive measures came to a head. The underlying conflict between "interventionists" (neomercantilists) and "free marketeers" (neoliberals) was finally resolved following compromises from both sides.[37]

More specifically, in the late 1980s, there was dissatisfaction with the EU's subsidized collaborative R&D efforts, especially Esprit, in that they had failed to rejuvenate the European information technology and electronics sectors. There were concerns that the R&D initiatives were effectively subsidizing the industry—more accurately a handful of companies—while having produced few commercial applications. The EU trade deficit in information technology had widened throughout the 1980s, reaching over US$30 billion in 1989. Most of the European industry was barely profitable, with Philips, a leading European manufacturer, in the midst of a financial and management crisis. The penetration of Japanese manufacturers into the EU market culminated in the takeover of the British ICL, one of the original "Big Twelve" firms, by the Japanese Fujitsu and its consequent suspension from Esprit.[38]

These developments made parts of the Commission (notably DG Industry and DG Competition) and some member states led by Britain and Germany increasingly skeptical about the purpose of EU collaborative R&D projects. In its defense, DG Telecommunications, responsible for administering Esprit and having cultivated a clientelistic network with the leading European information technology companies benefiting from these programs, was arguing that the initiatives simply needed more time to produce results.[39] But the problem was bigger. For the EU interventionist industrial policy was coupled with trade protectionist measures, including high tariffs on several consumer electronics products, such as video recorders, and a rise of anti-dumping investigations targeting low-cost competition from South East Asia.[40] There were serious fears that the "1992" project was about the building of a protectionist "Fortress Europe."

In 1990, a draft report on the European electronics industry by DG Telecommunications—that effectively advocated the use of public procurement to stimulate demand for the troubled European information technology industry—provided further evidence to its critics, who accused it of being "more interested in empire building and forging cosy links with industry than in devising effective technology policies."[41] DG Telecommunications was viewed as a "bastion of *dirigisme*," with its long-standing Director General Michel Carpentier the most powerful exponent of French-style interventionism.[42]

DG Telecommunications' plans were thwarted when, in late 1990, the Commission issued a paper, prepared by DG Industry, headed by Bangemann, outlining a new industrial policy strategy.[43] The new strategy signaled a move away from traditional *dirigiste* industry-specific assistance toward a horizontal industrial policy. The DG Telecommunications' long awaited review of the European electronics industry was finally published in 1991 in a significantly damped down version and with the disputes between neomercantilists and neoliberals having clearly influenced its vague and often inconclusive content.[44]

The European Round Table of industrialists (ERT) which—reflecting transformations in the European capital with the rise of more globalized transnational parts—was itself shifting from neomercantilism toward neoliberalism, influenced the move toward a horizontal industrial policy.[45] The new policy was in line with ERT's new key project: competitiveness.[46] As Keith Richardson, then ERT Secretary General, recollects: "what was really at stake was an overall objective commonly described as 'putting competitiveness on to the political agenda.'"[47] In the course of the 1990s, competitiveness came to dominate the European policy discourse.

In the EU, the move from active industrial to competitiveness policy was gradual and heavily contested. Even after the 1990 industrial policy paper, conflicts remained. Renewed recession led to fresh calls for protectionism by France and the industry, which national governments resisted.[48] Tensions resurfaced within the Commission too. Commissioner for industry Bangemann, who although considered a "free-marketeer" had a more flexible approach to anti-trust policy and shared with the interventionist camp the belief that European champions and economies of scale were essential to Europe's competitiveness, attacked DG Competition officials, describing them as "ayatollahs" for their over-legalistic approach to competition issues.[49]

The conflicts were gradually resolved. The 1992 Maastricht Treaty formalized the shift toward the new industrial policy ethos with a new provision that dared not even contain the term "industrial policy."[50] Although the EU's legal competence was expanded, the new provision, which required unanimity, was clearly an attempt to eliminate the prospects for interventionist policies.

Within the Commission, in 1993 DG Telecommunications was further weakened. Following internal reorganization, Bangemann assumed responsibility for both industry and information technology. One of his first initiatives under his new responsibilities was to put his new horizontal industrial policy into practice by stopping DG Telecommunications' plans to act as a sponsor for the European electronics industry in the High-Definition Television (HDTV) race.

As the previous chapter explained, this HDTV example of defensive standardization was conceptually flawed. It supported the interests of Thomson and Philips—both of which were concurrently participating through subsidiaries in U.S. R&D initiatives—while ignoring those of broadcasters, program makers and consumers/viewers. Besides, European HDTV policy was almost immediately overtaken by technological developments, the arrival of medium-powered satellites which allowed operators to circumvent the legally binding European standards (MAC). The advent of digital television in the USA, finally, dealt the fatal blow to the interventionist EU policy. In this light and against strong British opposition, the HDTV policy was officially abandoned in 1993.[51]

The new industrial policy was subsequently confirmed in 1994, in a follow-up paper prepared by Bangemann. To avoid confusion with the "government knows best" industrial policy targeting specific sectors that preceded it, the new strategy has been now named "industrial competitiveness policy."[52] Its aim is to influence the environment in which firms operate, to "support and strengthen the structural determinants of a competitive economy, such as human capital or [. . .] infrastructure."[53] National governments and international organizations, like the EU, are seen as enablers and facilitators rather than active planners, managers or partners, and the focus is on demand-side, not supply-side, measures.[54] The information society and trans-European networks are two core projects under the new industrial competitiveness policy.

In a clear break with past practice, following the debacle of Europe's HDTV policy and in line with the new industrial competitiveness philosophy, the Commission did not prescribe standards for digital television even when the market-led standardization process under the auspices of the Digital Video Broadcasting Group bringing together broadcasters, consumer electronics manufacturers and regulatory authorities—failed to reach agreement on a single conditional access system.[55] Rather than resolving the deadlock between existing analog pay TV operators supporting a proprietary solution (simulcrypt) and new entrants and public service broadcasters supporting an open solution (multicrypt) by mandating either of them, the Commission left the regulation of conditional access to member states on the basis of the principles of fairness, reasonableness and non-discrimination.[56] The digital television EU regulatory framework marked the end of the old industrial policy of top-down initiatives and compulsory standards that had characterized HDTV in the 1980s. The Commission is no longer planning new technologies but rather enabling their market-led introduction and growth through minimal regulation.

THE (RE)EMERGENCE OF THE INFORMATION SOCIETY: MOVING TOWARD FULL LIBERALIZATION

In December 1993, the European Commission under Delors published a "White Paper on Growth, Competitiveness, Employment," once again putting forward the information society as Europe's response to these challenges.[57] But although the information society and the process of globalization—the latter figuring more and more prominently on the EU political agenda in the post–Cold War order—were portrayed as inevitable, as objective external forces, a closer look reveals the interests behind this particular construction of the external environment.

The reappearance of the notion of information society on the EU agenda was largely in reaction to developments in the USA under the recently elected Clinton-Gore administration, in particular the resurgence of strategic trade policy and the adoption and subsequent popularization of the information superhighway metaphor placed at the heart of economic planning. But, whereas in the USA, the consequent National Information Infrastructure initiative had the internet at its core, in the EU, in contrast, it was telecommunications policy concerns that dominated the information society agenda in the first half of the 1990s. This is not surprising. In the EU, incumbent telecommunications operators still held the monopoly over the provision of most market segments, and in particular public infrastructure and voice telephony. Besides, the relative strength of Europe's telecommunications industry and the relative weakness of its computing and internet sectors can further explain this difference in the initial conceptualization of the information society between the USA and the EU.

In addition to the urgency of accelerating toward the information society, the Delors White Paper stressed the critical importance of pan-European infrastructure for improving Europe's competitiveness. Trans-European networks in telecommunications, transport and energy, incorporated in the 1992 Maastricht Treaty, were long-standing objectives of European industrialists.[58] Effectively, by pushing for new infrastructural projects, the European Round Table of industrialists was creating new markets for its members—Europe's major manufacturers—while at the same time urging a reorientation of public financial resources, crucial in recessionary times, to that area. Now, as earlier in the 1980s, technology and European networks were identified as priorities and seen as preconditions for European economic growth and modernization.

Similarly, the report of the Bangemann group in May 1994 underlined the importance of moving toward the information society.[59] Its emphasis on infrastructure and telecommunications is not surprising since the group was dominated by well-known information technology and electronics industrialists—including Alcatel, IBM-Europe, ICL, Olivetti, Philips and Siemens—many of them members of the European Round Table of industrialists. Broadcasters were notable by their absence, although two media conglomerates were represented (Canal+ from France and CLT from Luxembourg). The Bangemann report stressed the pivotal role that the private, not public, sector would play in the implementation of the information society. A fully liberalized telecommunications market was predicted to unleash substantial private revenues to meet the high infrastructure investment costs. The report finally called for the adoption of a common regulatory framework but one that entailed the transfer of regulatory responsibilities from the national to the European level with the creation of a pan-European regulatory authority and one that neglected broadcasting regulatory concerns. With the focus moving to the information society and competitiveness, telecommunications as an infrastructure attracted more attention, whereas television and the media were sidelined.

Developments were fast. In July 1994, the Bangemann report was incorporated into the information society action plan.[60] With full political support, the information society was placed at the heart of the European project destined to shape economic and political integration in the years to come. The information society became the new mobilizing theme following the completion of the single market.[61] The Commission moved quickly to draw up plans for the complete liberalization of telecommunications markets and the associated regulatory framework.[62]

Concomitantly, in February 1995, the Competitiveness Advisory Group (CAG), modelled on the U.S. Competitiveness Council, was formed under the newly appointed Santer Commission with the mandate "to advise on economic policy priorities and guidelines with the aim of stimulating competitiveness."[63] Unsurprisingly, since it was set up upon the European Round Table of industrialists' suggestion, the Group's membership included Round Table members as representatives of specific corporations.[64] In effect, the Group was the European Round Table of industrialists' "institutional link to the European Commission."[65] The Group did not define competitiveness but instead adopted "a pragmatic approach" according to which competitiveness "should be seen as a way of thinking through the factors of economic performance with a view to acting on them."[66] In its first report to the Commission later that year, the Group called, among other things, for the full opening up of the telecommunications sector and priority to a pan-European infrastructure.[67]

The TransAtlantic Business Dialogue (TABD)—formed in 1995 and bringing together top business leaders, many European Round Table of industrialists members, and high level government officials—repeated the same call. It was the late U.S. Secretary of Commerce Ronald Brown who conceived the idea for a transatlantic business forum in 1994 in an effort to promote transatlantic trade and investment. Due to the fear that in the post–Cold War era the USA would aim to foster its economic links with East Asia at the expense of Europe, the idea quickly won the active support of the European Commissioners for Trade (Brittan) and Industry (Bangemann), and leading European industrialists.[68]

In 1996, and with the World Trade Organization (WTO) negotiations for the liberalization of basic telecommunications well underway, full competition in EU telecommunications markets (by 1998) was finally endorsed.[69] Indeed, the EU reinforced calls for liberalization within the WTO.[70]

Toward an Uncommon Telecommunications Market

The ten-year period from 1988 to 1998 leading to full liberalization was very intensive in terms of regulatory reform. The reform package comprising liberalization and harmonization measures—the latter concerning the adoption of common rules for a single telecommunications market dealing, among other things, with interconnection, licensing and universal service—led to the so-called 1998 regulatory framework summarized in table 5.1.

But the adoption of the regulatory package was just the beginning. National governments and competent regulatory authorities remained primarily responsible for putting the reforms into practice. As Majone explains, the Commission is biased in favor of regulatory policies precisely because, unlike directly (re)distributive measures, the actual implementation and cost of such initiatives have to borne by the member states.[71] By implication

Table 5.1. Main Measures in the EU 1998 Telecommunications Regulatory Framework*

Liberalization measures[1]	Harmonization measures[2]
1988: Equipment directive (last amended in 1994)	1986: Mutual recognition of equipment directive (last amended in 1999)
1990: Competition in telecommunications services	1990: Establishment of the internal market for telecommunications services through the implementation of Open Network Provision (ONP framework) (last amended in 1997)
1994: Satellite directive	1992: Application of ONP to leased lines (last amended in 1997)
1995: Abolition of restrictions on cable TV networks for the provision of already liberalized services	1997: Common framework for general authorization and individual licenses
1996: Mobile and Personal Communications directive	1997: Common framework for interconnection (last amended in 1998)
1996: Implementation of full competition in telecommunications	1998: Voice telephony and universal services
1999: Cable ownership directive	

* The 1998 telecommunications regulatory package is available at <http://europa.eu.int/information_society/topics/telecoms/regulatory/98_regpack/index_en.htm> (2 June 2006).
[1]Liberalization has been introduced on the basis of article 86 (ex 90) through Commission Directives without formal approval by national governments.
[2]Harmonization measures are Council and European Parliament Directives based on article 95 (ex 100).

then, the EU policy has contributed to the strengthening and expansion of member states' regulatory responsibilities. The emergence of the EU regulatory state is part and parcel of the rise of the national regulatory state.

The European Commission has used both formal and informal mechanisms to promote the implementation of EU rules. Mechanisms have included peer pressure in various committees bringing together national and Commission officials, often in combination with "name and shame" tactics through, for example, the publication of reports comparing the status of national implementation.[72] Throughout the implementation stage, the Commission remains in close contact with national authorities to assist them and assess progress. If such informal channels fail, the Commission may resort to formal infringement proceedings by bringing a case in front of the European Court of Justice.

In general, countries that had already proceeded with market restructuring domestically had fewer problems complying with the EU regulatory framework. This has been particularly the case of Britain that, having initiated liberalization in the early 1980s, has led Europe in regulatory innovation. But overall, delays and significant variations in implementation have been the norm in relation to both liberalization and harmonization measures.

With regard to liberalization, the degree and form of competition in different market segments varies significantly between countries. Britain, for example, has been a notable exception compared to its EU partners in favoring facilities-based competition (competition between infrastructure providers) rather than service-based competition (competition between service providers using the facilities of the incumbent telecommunications operator).[73] In 1992, Britain used cable television as an alternative telecommunications infrastructure when it allowed cable operators to offer telecommunications services over their networks. The varying degrees of competition and, in particular, its almost complete absence in the local access market were to become an urgent priority in the late 1990s in view of the commercialization of the internet.

In the area of harmonization, the picture resembled a "regulatory patchwork."[74] To start with, there were issues with national telecommunications regulatory authorities. For instance, just after the 1998 liberalization deadline, there were concerns about the sufficiency of powers and resources available to some national regulators (e.g., in Belgium, Greece, Italy), questions about their political independence—especially in cases where the incumbent PTO was still majority owned by the state, as in Belgium and France—and differences in regulatory style with the regulators in Denmark, France, the Netherlands and Sweden being reactive rather than proactive.[75]

Part of the problem of insufficient harmonization lies with the EU regulatory framework itself. The principle of subsidiarity, endorsed by the 1992

Maastricht Treaty, according to /ḥ:ich policy issues should be decided at the lowest political level possible, puts limits on EU regulation. In addition, the real need to accommodate diverse interests during policy-making often leads to vague provisions or, in other cases, agreement may not be possible at all. It is indicative that regulatory issues central to promoting competition—such as cost methodologies and cost accounting that are necessary for cost-oriented tariffs and interconnection and may reveal cross-subsidies that distort competition—were left out of the EU regulatory framework altogether. In an effort to encourage harmonization in these cases, the Commission relied on soft non-binding measures, such as benchmarks.[76]

Certain technical areas, such as radio spectrum planning, have remained the responsibility of national governments working through the European Conference of Postal and Telecommunications administrations (CEPT). The latter was reformed in 1992 from a cartel-like body of monopolist PTTs to the coordinating body of telecommunications regulators covering practically, with the accession of the ex-communist bloc, the entire geographical area of Europe.[77] Several working groups and project teams, comprising representatives from national administrations, support its work. This practice uses the technical expertise that lies primarily in the national administrations, thereby ensuring the political support of national governments.

Another example illustrating the lack of harmonization is licensing. Timeframes, requirements, selection procedures, all differed among member states. Through licensing national regulators can influence market entry conditions and developments. In the absence of a common selection procedure, for instance, third generation mobile licenses were awarded at the turn of the millennium through various methods. Some countries, including Britain and Germany, used auctions, whereas others, like Finland and Spain, used comparative selection procedures.

The absence of a pan-European licensing regime and mutual recognition of licenses has meant that network and service provision remains the responsibility of individual national authorities. Even in cases where an operator has established activities in more than one country, to a large extent, it is still the interconnection of separate national networks that makes cross-border services possible. This is best illustrated in mobile telephony. A common second generation standard (GSM) has not resulted in a truly common market in network operation and services. Instead, there are several national European markets. Indeed, this has proved very lucrative for mobile operators, who by "treat[ing] their customers not as European customers but as national customers paying excessive charges when travelling to foreign countries" have benefited from high roaming charges.[78]

In sum, directives, the main legislative instrument in the field of telecommunications, state the overall objectives with which member states have to comply but leave them sufficient leeway as to the choice of form and methods to achieve them. This confirms the duality of regulation at EU and national levels. During the process of transposition of EU directives into national legislation, policies are mediated through the political, economic, social and institutional characteristics of each member state. This process of "domestication" has resulted in variations among national regulatory responses.[79] The lack of consistency in how rules are applied in different member states contributed to calls for a European regulator.

The 1994 Bangemann report was the first official document that placed the creation of a pan-European communications regulator (like the U.S. Federal Communications Commission) on the agenda. At a time when few countries had established independent regulatory authorities, the idea appealed to operators with transnational expansion aspirations and corporate users with cross-border activities. But unsurprisingly, national governments and the few national regulatory bodies that had been set up perceived the proposal as a direct attack on their powers and strongly opposed it.[80]

In 1997, just before the official deadline for full liberalization, upon the initiative of the Director General of the British regulatory authority Oftel in cooperation with his Dutch and Danish counterparts, the national regulators for telecommunications established their own forum, the Independent Regulators' Group (IRG), which gradually expanded to include over thirty regulators from wider Europe.[81] This was a defensive move to fend off calls for a pan-European regulator but also an effort by more advanced national regulatory authorities to support newer regulators and share practices. The IRG acts as an informal discussion forum where national regulators share experiences and information, address issues of common interest and concern and develop common practices.

The persistent lack of consistency in the implementation of the EU rules was one of the key issues in the review of the 1998 regulatory framework, examined in the next chapter.

RESTRUCTURING TELEVISION MARKETS

Similar to telecommunications, several factors contributed to the restructuring of television markets and some of them, like institutional and ideological factors, were common in both cases.[82] Technological developments—notably the advent of cable and satellite distribution and transfrontier broadcasting—challenged the established state-controlled monopolistic/duopolistic public service broadcasting and the technological rationale for government control, namely spectrum scarcity.[83] These developments brought in new commercial private operators, manufacturers and

Advertisers applauded the potential for more commercially funded media outlets, especially in Europe where advertising was heavily regulated (e.g., in Germany) and even prohibited (e.g., in Belgium and Denmark, the BBC in Britain).[84] For the USA, the proliferation of channels and extended broadcast hours was highly beneficial not just for domestic program producers but also for domestic economic interests since the growth of advertising would create demand for other U.S. goods and services.

However, for existing commercial media players the prospect for new media outlets implied competition for advertising revenue. It was partly the fear of losing that revenue that pushed private press interests, together with powerful financial backers, to move into commercial broadcasting. In turn, this cross-media expansion has highly politicized media ownership and concentration in Europe. It is not therefore surprising that national governments have resisted EU intervention in this politically sensitive area.

A combination of dissatisfaction with and lack of confidence in the public service broadcasting system perceived as politically biased led various newly-elected European governments in the early 1980s to endorse liberalization as a means to gain influence in broadcast media which had hitherto excluded them. Political affiliation played no role. It was the Conservative government under Thatcher in Britain that opened up the television market using all technological platforms—terrestrial, cable and satellite—but it was the Socialist government under Mitterrand in France. In Germany, cable television gave the opportunity to the federal government of Chancellor Kohl to construe it as infrastructure and thus gain legitimacy to intervene in broadcasting, a domain under the strong control of the individual states (Länder).

The search for industrial competitive advantage was another strong reason behind the national cable television and DBS plans of the big EU countries—Britain, Germany and France. In the case of France, the national

s a buffer to Luxembourg's commerrse" for American content.[85]

ore the publication of the main EU
g market reform was well underway
aly, Britain, France and Germany—
lanned for the second half of the
of broadcasting was a national deci-

gether potential commercial market
s, publishing interests, content pro-
ts supported the move from a public
nnel television order.

Television without Frontiers

The milestone in EU television policy is the 1984 Green Paper on Television without Frontiers.[86] It is with this Green Paper that the balance between cultural and economic/industrial aspects of television decisively shifted in favor of the latter. Whereas the 1983 Report *Realities and Tendencies* had been drafted by the DG Audiovisual and tended to emphasize cultural issues, the Green Paper was drafted by the DG internal market and reflected similar concerns.

The Green Paper was full of economic arguments and extensive comparative data and information about broadcasting legislation in the member states. The aim was to highlight the diversity of and incompatibility between national rules. For the Green Paper, this fragmentation was inappropriate in the age of transfrontier broadcasting and hampered the creation of the single market and free flow of television signals. The Green Paper also expressed industrial policy concerns regarding television standards (the European MAC standards) and the European programming sector. With regard to the latter, the Commission noted that most films shown in the EU came from the USA and urged the creation of a common market for television production that would allow European firms to improve their competitiveness and thus counter the dominance of American media.

In effect, despite references to general cultural and political aims, the Green Paper pursued primarily economic objectives. Handicapped by the failure of the founding EU Treaty to give it specific competence in broadcasting, the Commission went to great lengths to justify and legitimize the need for EU intervention. It made repeated references to the earlier European Court of Justice judgments that had defined broadcasting as a telecommunications service and it also stressed technological developments, notably the cross-border nature of satellite broadcasting. Finally, in another attempt to increase its legitimacy and be perceived as an expert and knowledgeable policy actor, it relied heavily on market data provided by the advertising industry itself. For the Commission, the growth of advertising would support the internal market and promote cross-border trade.

At the time the Green Paper was being drafted, there were very few pan-European interest groups. Commercial broadcasters were in their infancy and had not yet formed their own European association, preferring to work at the national level and lobby either as individual companies or through their national governments. The EBU, the umbrella organization of public service broadcasters, had established contacts with the DG Audiovisual, but that was a weak department within the Commission and not the leading DG in the preparation of the Green Paper. It was just the advertising industry that not only had a pan-European body representing its interests—the European Association of Advertising Agencies—but, importantly, had already established a close relationship with the DG Internal Market responsible for writing the Green Paper going back to the mid-1970s when the Commission was working on the advertising standards legislation.[87] In effect, the Green Paper treated television as an economic sector like any other and presented the positions of the advertising lobby while excluding all other interests.

The Green Paper generated strong reactions. On the one side, the advertising industry and the Commission had the support of private commercial broadcasters, cable and satellite operators and procompetition member states, especially Britain, Germany and Luxembourg. On the other side, public service broadcasters, the European production industry and countries with a low production capacity or restricted language area, such as Denmark, were concerned about the adverse effects of a European broadcasting space on cultural identity.[88] The conflict between the two camps was about the very nature of broadcasting (is it an economic and/or a cultural activity?) and the need, if any, for supranational intervention, especially of the economic EU kind, in this politically sensitive field traditionally under strong national control.

For the EBU, the definition of broadcasting as a mere economic activity was a direct attack on what it stood for, public service broadcasting. This view was shared by its members, the public service broadcasters. The EBU reluctantly accepted the need for a basic European broadcasting regulatory framework but one which itself in cooperation with the Council of Europe, and not an economic organization like the EU, would design.[89] The German Länder responsible for broadcasting and cultural matters vigorously resisted EU competence, perceiving it as an infringement upon their regulatory powers. France was primarily concerned about the rise of imported U.S. programs following the liberalization of its domestic broadcasting market and was therefore interested in support measures, including funding, for Europe's programming industry.

Differing approaches and conflicting interests were being simultaneously pursued and debated at the European level. Those resisting EU intervention (including the German Länder, Belgium, Denmark and the Netherlands), sought to press their interests on the EU's institutional rival, the Council of Europe, that became increasingly active in broadcasting matters in the 1980s.[90] In parallel to the EU's draft Television without Frontiers Directive, the Council of Europe was preparing its own separate policy document on the same subject, what became the European Convention on Transfrontier Television.[91]

The approaches of the two organizations were contrasting. On the one hand, the Council of Europe was stressing the social, cultural and democratic functions of broadcasting, while on the other, the Commission was concerned with economic and industrial aspects and the creation of the single market. In the end, this institutional rivalry was to the detriment of a strong European regulatory framework, a solution supported by France. The binding EU directive had to be watered down in order to be aligned with the Council of Europe's non-binding Convention in order to avoid any conflict between the two policy instruments.

After a lengthy and contentious process and years of political wrangling, the EU Television without Frontiers Directive was adopted in October 1989.[92] By that time, the majority of EU member states had introduced pro-competitive broadcasting policies, with the notable exceptions of Ireland, the Netherlands and, outside the EU, Austria, Sweden and Norway.

The directive represents a victory of liberal economic over cultural arguments. Its basic tenet is the free flow of television programs—like other goods and services—throughout the internal market subject to minimal harmonization rules concerning advertising, sponsorship and protection of minors. The directive established that a broadcaster is subject to the rules of the country of establishment rather than the country of destination. This means that a member state cannot restrict the reception or retransmission of television signals originating in another member state. In effect, the television directive expanded the two core principles of the single market—harmonization of minimum requirements and mutual recognition of national rules that, as discussed in chapter 3, originated in the 1970s—to television services.

From Cultural "Unity" to "Diversity" and "Exceptionalism"

By the time the Commission presented its proposal for a directive in 1986, in an attempt to appease strong opposition, the proliberal elements of the 1984 Green Paper had been toned down with the insertion of protectionist elements, notably quotas for European content.[93] The latter was one of the most contentious issues.

France, supported by other countries with struggling domestic film industries such as Italy and Spain, led the pro-quota camp. Quotas were seen as a bulwark against the rising tide of U.S. program imports and a means to protect European cultural identity. In effect, similar to the information technology sector, France was trying to export to the EU its national broadcasting policy that included strong domestic content requirements.[94] The recipe was the same. Domestic and European market liberalization coupled with external trade protection would allow European content producers, such as the French Canal+, to transform from national into European champions strong enough to take on world markets.

Britain and Germany, but also countries with a low production capacity or restricted language, such as Denmark, concerned that they would not be able to fulfil the quota requirements given the small size of their domestic market, led the opposing camp. Luxembourg—home of the most commercial satellite television network, CLT, and of Société Européenne des Satellites (SES), Europe's first private satellite operator formed in 1985 operating the Astra satellites—was another strong opponent of the quotas. The powerful U.S. producer lobby, the Motion Picture Association of America (MPAA), fearing adverse trade implications, strongly criticized the quota proposal as a protectionist trade restrictive measure, and the U.S. administration threatened unilateral retaliatory action against the EU to force it to abandon it.[95]

Under the compromise reached in 1989, the quota provisions were significantly watered down. Whereas the original proposal stipulated a 30 percent, rising to 60 percent within three years, quota for European programs, following British opposition, under the adopted television directive broadcasters are required to reserve "where practicable and by appropriate means" a majority of their transmission time for European content, excluding the time allocated for news, sports events, games, advertising and teletext services. In addition, broadcasters have to reserve either 10 percent of their transmission time or programming budget for European independent productions. Governments are free to introduce stricter limits. Moreover, upon the insistence of Germany, the quota provisions are not legally binding but simply represent a political commitment. This means that the Commission can monitor implementation but cannot initiate infringement proceedings in cases of non-compliance. As a trade-off, France got the EU to agree to support measures for the European production industry, through the Eureka Audiovisual and the MEDIA programs. And failing to get its proposal for direct funding of audiovisual production under the EU, France succeeded in pursuing this objective within the Council of Europe with the establishment of Euroimages in 1988 to support European co-productions. The resources allocated to these programs were too small to make any substantial contribution to the overall competitiveness of the European industry. Indicatively, MEDIA I (1991–1996) had a budget of 200 million ECU (US$274 million). Nevertheless, such redistributive action assisted the Commission in gaining new competence and strengthening its institutional power.

The debate on quotas in the mid-1980s marked a shift of emphasis away from "cultural unity," implying one European identity and concerned with the dissemination of information for active citizenship, to "cultural diversity" promoted by the *"dirigistes,"* notably France, stressing national diversity and calling for active regulatory intervention and external trade protection.[96] Increasingly, cultural arguments became interwoven with economic and industrial considerations, in a way affirming the dual character of the audiovisual sector. The sector has fundamental democratic, social and cultural functions to fulfil but also has a growing economic importance.

Just as the anti-Americanization theme was used internally as an argument in favor of mandatory European content quotas, similarly, externally, for the first time during the GATT Uruguay Round, anti-Americanization was presented as a "European" concern to support efforts to exclude cultural goods and services from the trade negotiations.[97] In 1993, the highly political conflict concerning the audiovisual dossier risked derailing the entire Round. On the one side, the USA and its strong MPAA trade lobby, treating broadcasting as if it were any other economic sector, were pushing for full liberalization. The stakes were high. Film is a huge U.S. export industry that realized US$3.7 billion sales to Europe alone in 1992, second in sales to Europe only to aerospace.[98] On the other side, the EU was against liberalization and tried to gain a "cultural exception" in the agreement. In effect, French cultural exceptionalism was exported and fought as European cultural exceptionalism.[99] Interestingly, to the extent that the EU as an international actor claims to protect a "European" identity it shows that, in a sense, national identities have come to accept and incorporate an EU identity.[100] In the end, the EU and the USA agreed to disagree and left the issue of audiovisual products on the negotiating table.[101] European support measures and quotas have been left intact for the time being.

Within the EU, the debate on quotas and support measures has continued. The pro- and against-quota coalitions largely remained the same in the subsequent revision of the television directive launched in 1994.[102] The against-quota camp was further strengthened with the enlargement of the EU in 1995 and the accession of Austria, Sweden and Finland. Even the newly appointed Commission President Santer, who before assuming this post had just renewed as Prime Minister of Luxembourg the license for CLT, was enlisted in the opposition camp, when, in 1995, he criticized Europe's audiovisual policy, stating that quotas "represent 'an artificial and protectionist formula.'"[103] During the review of the television directive, there was an attempt by the *dirigiste* camp led by France to make the provisions binding and even expand them to new services. But again this attempt was unsuccessful on both counts. The second aim in particular never really stood a chance in view of the rising information society agenda emphasizing light-touch regulation. The review completed in 1997 served another defeat to the pro-quota camp. The proliberal stance of the directive has remained intact.

Overall, the 1997 revision of the television directive was minimal, aiming principally at clarification and better implementation.[104] The only significant amendment concerns a provision to ensure that events of major importance for society (listed events) are available on free-to-air channels via live or deferred coverage. With the growth of subscription television, the fear was that large parts of the society would be excluded from accessing events of national importance, in particular sports. The listed events provision is a rare positive broadcasting regulatory action that the European Parliament, strengthened under newly acquired codecision powers, managed to introduce. Still, this requirement concerns effectively the application of competition rules to content—targeting anti-competitive behaviour and preventing monopoly rights over socially important content—rather than mandated access to content for its democratic, social and cultural significance. The underlying rationale, therefore, is typical of the EU intervention in the broadcasting field based on economic and competition considerations, over which it enjoys strong competence, while avoiding addressing content issues in their own right.[105]

The television directive, as amended, also provides for the mutual recognition of the listed events of one member state by the other member states so that they cannot be circumvented by broadcasters acquiring the rights for these events but broadcasting from another country.[106] This is a derogation of the country of origin principle whereby public interest objectives—public access to events of national importance—take precedence over single market objectives.

The Information Society Hype Takes Over Broadcasting

The rise of the information society agenda from the early 1990s onward had implications for broadcasting policy. The audiovisual Green Paper in 1994, published as part of the review of the television directive, though it did not contain any significant new proposals, signaled a shift away from a "European audiovisual space" toward a "European information area," that is, a technologically driven communicative space.[107] Responding to the American and Japanese strategies of "digital highways" and the technological convergence between broadcasting, computing and telecommunications, the Green Paper emphasized the economic and industrial significance of the audiovisual sector. The explosion of demand for content instigated by technological developments and the increase in channels and broadcast hours was juxtaposed to rising production costs, lack of economies of scale, small and fragmented national markets, weak intra-EU distribution and circulation, and a widening EU trade deficit, especially in films. At issue was the loss of competitiveness of the European production industry and the absence of big transnational companies.[108] The Green Paper urged the industry to take advantage of the expansion opportunities emerging in Central and Eastern Europe following the collapse of communism.

The Green Paper contained a fundamental contradiction. Cultural diversity sat uneasily with the emphasis on economies of scale needed to increase international competitiveness:

concentrating on "market niches" may be a way of safeguarding and developing diversity, but it is no substitute for a wider strategy aimed at building up attractive programme catalogues for broader segments of the European and world markets.[109]

The suggestion was that the promotion of intra-European trade, essential for the creation of European champions, required that audiovisual products lose their national, cultural, ethnic and other specificity in order that they travel more easily across borders. Instead of serving diverse publics and societies, if the industry was to become internationally competitive, it had to produce low common denominator content for an undefined transnational audience.

Many of the arguments in the audiovisual Green Paper were later that year reiterated in the Bangemann report. The solution put forward to address the problem of small and fragmented markets was to break down barriers—especially regulatory ones traditionally dominant in the television sector—and create a pan-European market subject to minimum Europe-wide rules, primarily horizontal competition rules but also, among other things, rules for media ownership and intellectual property rights. The Bangemann report stressed external pluralism. The proliferation of media outlets, the result of technological advances, was expected to automatically promote cultural diversity and opportunities for expression.

In general, the EU's approach to pluralism and media concentration, perhaps not surprisingly since it has lacked legitimacy to address them as issues in their own right, has tended to emphasize open market structures which concern diversity of media outlets and not diversity of content reflecting a wide range of social, political and cultural values, opinions, information and interests. From the start, the 1992 Green Paper, prepared by the DG Internal Market, framed media concentration as a single market issue.[110] The European Parliament and the DG Audiovisual supported a common pan-European regulatory framework for media ownership and content. But the rise of the competitiveness discourse alongside the information society hype served to reinforce economic and industrial policy arguments at the expense of the politically controversial questions about pluralism and culture. Still, in 1996, four years after the Green Paper on pluralism and media concentration—evidence in itself of the controversies surrounding the issue—the DG Internal Market produced a draft for a directive on "Media Pluralism" which met strong opposition from commercial broadcasters—who argued that the main barriers to a single market were cultural and linguistic rather than regulatory—national governments —who opposed the Commission's interference with such a highly political issue—but also the Commissioners for external trade (Brittan), telecommunications (Bangemann) and audiovisual (Oreja).[111] A new proposal in

1997 was again rejected. Although it no longer dealt with media pluralism, but, as its new title suggested, with media ownership and its main objective was the liberalization of national media markets in order to facilitate the creation of big European companies able to compete with the U.S. giants, this second proposal again faced strong opposition from commercial broadcasters and national governments. This time, in an effort to appease opposition, the Commission had inserted a so-called flexibility clause that would have effectively allowed for continued diversity among national rules and as such it would have defeated the purpose of the exercise.

As a result, the EU regulatory framework does not address media ownership and pluralism in their own right. These issues remain the responsibility of members states. The EU can intervene on the basis of general competition rules but competition concerns are not the same as those about pluralism, and pluralism is not simply a question of market share. In effect, the EU has primarily utilized telecommunications-type regulation in regard to television, dealing primarily with technological and infrastructure related issues.[112] In this sense, the EU television regulatory framework is partial and incomplete.

In summary, the EU debate regarding the audiovisual sector and culture has been preoccupied with the increasingly questionable issue, in view of the results achieved and within the context of progressive international liberalization, of trade protection rather than the more fundamental question of the contribution of broadcasting to democracy and active citizenship.[113] Similar to the information and communication technology sector, the issue at stake has been trade flows. The EU broadcasting policy is, therefore, primarily a matter of economic and commercial advantage.

The political saliency of the information society, the dominant competitiveness discourse and the attendant emphasis on technological and economic/industrial considerations have further sidelined social, cultural and political issues and instead prioritized the rights of consumers over the rights of citizens. Greater choice in the information society refers to greater consumer choice, more paid for personalized consumption of customized content and services.[114] This presents a paradox. For if, as Schlesinger notes, audiovisual culture is perceived as a market-driven means to promote consumption, it will accentuate existing differences among the European publics at the expense of existing commonalities and the fostering of an eventual political community and culture.[115]

The End of Mutual Interdependency

Similar to telecommunications, procompetitive market restructuring transformed the relationship between the EU and incumbent market players—public service broadcasters and their European association, the

EBU—from one of mutual interdependency to adversarial. At the heart of this tension was the very concept of public service broadcasting in a liberalized market.[116]

The Eurovision Cases

Whereas market positions in telecommunications have been more clearly delineated and as a result competition law intervention tends to be based on the presence of strong market power aiming at the prohibition of abuse of dominant positions, the existence of highly oligopolistic market structures in the media sector means that intervention has tended to target anticompetitive behavior. Moreover, the Eurovision cases need to be understood within the context of two main aims governing the application of competition law in the media sector: access to critical premium content, such as sports, and the creation of a level playing field between public and private broadcasters.[117]

The Eurovision cases arose in December 1987 when the Commission, responding to a complaint by Screensport, a transnational satellite and cable sports channel controlled by W. H. Smith Ltd., launched an investigation into the EBU's Eurovision system. Under this scheme, the EBU may collectively acquire the television rights to international sports events on behalf of its active members, that is public service broadcasters, who then share the rights and the associated cost between them. The complaint concerned the refusal of the EBU to grant sublicenses for the retransmission of sports events.

In response, the EBU adopted a sublicensing scheme granting non-EBU private commercial broadcasters contractual access to Eurovision broadcast rights. Twice, in 1993 and in 2000, the Commission, incorporating non-economic considerations in its competition law analysis, ruled that even though the Eurovision system of joint negotiation, acquisition and sharing of television rights represented a restriction on competition it was permissible in view of its advantages and thus granted an exemption from the EU competition rules.[118] In particular, the Commission noted that the system resulted in reduced transaction costs in the negotiation of broadcast rights, benefited in particular small broadcasting organizations from smaller countries that might not be able to gain access to the rights concerned otherwise, increased viewer choice as it enabled EBU members to provide a wider range of programs and facilitated cross-border broadcasting and thus contributed to the development of a single European market. By approving the Eurovision scheme, the Commission allowed the restriction of competition in pursuit of the public interest.

The European Court of First Instance, upon appeals lodged by private commercial television channels, subsequently annulled both Commission decisions. In 1996, the European Court annulled the Commission's decision on legal substance grounds, ruling that the Commission had failed to assess whether the EBU membership rules were "objective and sufficiently determinate so as to enable them to be applied uniformly and in a non-discriminatory manner vis-à-vis all potential active members."[119] The annulment related in part to the fact that in 1984 the EBU admitted as a member the French private channel Canal+ while in 1986 the French channel TF1 remained an active member even though it had been privatized.[120] Two of the complainants—M6 (France) and Antena 3 (Spain)—had applied for and been refused EBU membership on the ground that they did not fulfil the required conditions. The Court also found that, although the Commission had taken into consideration the fulfilment of public mission, it had failed to establish that its pursuit required exclusivity of rights to transmit sports events.

The second time, in 2002, the European Court of First Instance did not find the joint purchase of televised transmission rights for an event itself a restriction on competition but noted that "the exercise of those rights in a specific legal and economic context may none the less lead to such a restriction."[121] In other words, at issue was not the Eurovision system as such but the sublicensing scheme. In particular, the Court held that the EBU's rules did not allow non-members to broadcast live sports events, even when the EBU members would not use them, while the sublicensing scheme giving non-members the right to deferred coverage was subject to several restrictions, in particular as regarded editing and embargo times. The Court therefore ruled that the Commission's conclusion that the new rules did not eliminate competition was a "manifest error of assessment."

In sum, twice the Commission granted an exemption to the EBU's Eurovision system as justified in the public interest, and twice the European Court of First Instance subsequently annulled both decisions. The Eurovision cases show that while the Commission has been able to accommodate noncompetition considerations in its analysis, the European Court has been unable to do so. In general, the Court bases its rulings on narrow competition law principles and analysis as stemming from the EU Treaty it is called upon to interpret. Unsurprisingly, therefore, private commercial interests faced with unfavorable Commission decisions call upon the European Court, the regulator of last resort.

State Aid: Funding of Public Service Broadcasting

From the early 1990s onward, commercial broadcasters have been trying to limit competition from public service broadcasters by lodging complaints with the European Commission's DG Competition about the funding of public service broadcasting. These cases come under the regulation of state aid. State aid cases pit the Commission against national governments and their investigation is therefore politically sensitive.

In 1992, the Spanish commercial broadcaster *Gestevisión Telecinco* was the first to file a complaint with the European Commission alleging that regional channels and the public broadcaster RTVE were recipients of illegal state aid and this distorted the common market. Similarly, the following year, commercial broadcasters in France and Portugal submitted complaints attacking the financing schemes of public service broadcasting in their countries. In all these cases, commercial interests questioned the dual funding scheme of public service broadcasters, combining state funds and commercial—such as advertising—revenues. Of particular concern to commercial broadcasters was the competition public service broadcasters represented for advertising revenues.

Because of the political sensitivity of the issue, the Commission delayed the investigations. In 1996, it decided on part of the complaints concerning the Portuguese public television, ruling that public financing in that case did not constitute state aid insofar as it was compensation for obligations imposed by the state and which private broadcasters were not required to fulfil such as national coverage and the provision of certain types of content such as regional, religious, cultural and educational.[122] Delays in the first case led the Spanish commercial broadcaster to submit an action to the Court of First Instance, which in June 1996 condemned the Commission for failure to act.[123]

The pressure on the Commission to conclude these cases increased, with more complaints being lodged and the advent of digital television. With regard to the latter, in 1997 and 1998, commercial broadcasters questioned the use of public funds by public service broadcasters to finance thematic channels which would be in direct competition with the commercial broadcasters' own offerings. More specifically, the German association of private broadcasters (VPRT) filed a complaint against the public service broadcasters ARD and ZDF, who used licence fee revenues to fund a children's channel (*Kinderkanal*) and a political discussion and documentary channel (*Phoenix*), alleging that their financing constituted illegal state aid and therefore distorted competition. In Britain, BSkyB lodged a complaint with the Commission arguing that the use of licence fee revenues to finance BBC's 24-hour news channel was illegal state aid conferring on the BBC an unfair advantage. Like the two German thematic channels mentioned here, the BBC news channel did not accept advertising. In 1999, the Commission approved the public funding of all three thematic channels.[124]

The rise of competition cases against public service broadcasters triggered two responses.

The Amsterdam Protocol and European Citizenship

First, the so-called Amsterdam protocol was adopted in 1997 in order to circumscribe EU-level competence and protect public service broadcasters from attacks by commercial interests.[125] It acknowledges the importance of public service broadcasting and establishes that its remit, organization and funding remain the responsibility of member states. The Amsterdam protocol on public service broadcasting needs also to be understood as part of the reconceptualization of European culture and identity beginning in the early 1990s and the new EU approach to public services.

More specifically, the conceptualization of European culture and identity —that, as analyzed, was originally modelled on unity based on the experience of the nation-state and in the mid-1980s came to emphasize diversity internally and exceptionalism externally—was to change again in the early 1990s. The EU search for culture and identity now shifted toward a post-national, de-territorialized civic conceptualization. Economic recession and high unemployment, growing concerns about the EU's democratic deficit and remoteness from ordinary people and, finally, the end of the Cold War, which accentuated diversity especially along the traditional nation-state identity building tools— that is, ethno-cultural-linguistic-historical elements—on which a European identity was hitherto expected to be built, all contributed to this reassessment. A civic European identity grounded on political and civic rights will neither be built, nor challenge historically shaped notions of national identity.[126] Rather, it will be a post-national identity and as such, the expectation is, easier to forge. The aim is to shape a "European" people by uncoupling nationality from citizenship. Put differently, the objective is to pursue European citizenship instead of European patriotism, or European nationalism not based on emotion. But it is for precisely this rationality and neglect of emotional attachments to the notions of citizenship and identity that this view has been criticized.[127]

The civic reorientation was endorsed by the 1992 Maastricht Treaty, which introduced, after thirty-five years, for the first and at the same time in EU treaty texts, the notions of "citizenship," "national identity" and "culture." Paradoxically, the notion of European citizenship is derivative of national citizenship. This is then a symbolic rather than substantive gesture since it has not created new rights—except so-called mobility rights and minimal political rights like voting in European Parliament elections—but has simply confirmed existing rights. In its current form, as a broad and weakly defined concept, European citizenship is unlikely to foster a sense of belonging among Europeans, even if a supranational citizenship based on civic rights was feasible. EU competence over culture is quite remarkable, but any action has to be unanimously agreed upon by national governments, again making the importance of this provision symbolic rather than substantive.

European civic citizenship was further elaborated in the 1997 Amsterdam Treaty which, while upholding the primacy of competition rules in principle, explicitly recognized the importance of services of general economic interest—public services—and placed them for the first time among the shared values of the EU.[128] In doing so, it signalled a *volte-face* on public services. In the run-up to the creation of the single market, public services were generally considered barriers to market integration. But in the early 1990s, as the deadline for the internal market was nearing, it became clear that a truly neoliberal scenario grounded on market-making measures alone would not suffice but had instead to be complemented with market-shaping and market-correcting rules. Since the 1997 Amsterdam Treaty, public services are perceived as an integral part of the European model of society, characterized by the coexistence of publicly funded and commercial services, and as key contributors to social cohesion, equality and welfare. The new approach to public services was the result of lengthy political battles in which France played a leading role, having effectively, once more, exported a domestic political conflict over the implications of liberalization for public utilities to the European arena.[129] The new approach was also a response to the accountability crisis that became so manifest during the national ratification of the Maastricht Treaty. And finally, the new approach has to be seen in the context of the rising in the post–Cold War globalizing world order discourse of the "European way of life." The concept is left vague but implicit are nuances about a social Europe defined by the welfare state and basic provision of affordable public services to all.[130]

The EU Charter of Fundamental Rights in 2000 further confirmed the new perception of public services. It established citizens' right of access to services of general economic interest, integrated article 10 of the European Convention of Human Rights on freedom of expression and information, and stipulated respect for media freedom and pluralism. Although the Charter's legal standing is uncertain,

> [t]hese new provisions are important elements in the development of the process of European integration: from the economic sphere towards broader issues relating to the European model of society, [and] to the concept of European citizenship.[131]

Had the Constitutional Treaty, signed by EU political leaders in 2004, been nationally ratified, these provisions would have been strengthened.

Guidelines on State Aid Rules

The second response to the rising number of competition cases against public service broadcasters concerned the clarification of the application of state aid rules to public service broadcasting.

In September 1998, responding to complaints about delays and failure to act, the Commission's DG Competition tried unsuccessfully to adopt guidelines on state aid to public service broadcasters. The aim was to move away from the case-by-case investigation of complaints and create a framework that would enhance legal certainty. In the discussion paper, the DG Competition sought to delimit public service broadcasting to specific program types, stating that public service broadcasters would not be allowed to use public funding to acquire major sports rights, when not defined as events of major importance to society, and entertainment programs, that is categories that commercial broadcasters can cater to.[132]

The discussion paper provoked a powerful reaction from national governments, public service broadcasters and their supporters. They interpreted it as an attempt by the Commission to define the public service remit which would have been in direct contradiction to the recently adopted Amsterdam protocol. In the end, it was withdrawn. The subsequent Communication on state aid to public service broadcasters abandoned the most controversial proposal of the discussion paper that would have confined public service broadcasting to certain content.[133] All other provisions, such as financial transparency and accounting separation, were restated.[134]

Television Is National

Regulation of broadcasting remains the primary responsibility of national governments and competent regulatory authorities. The EU television regulatory framework is significantly less comprehensive compared to the EU telecommunications regulatory framework, which itself, as analyzed, leaves too much discretion to national regulators. The EU framework does not deal with the heart and soul of television: content regulation and media (cross-)ownership.

The principal significance of the television directive, the main EU policy instrument, is to allow trans-border television on the basis of a minimal regulatory framework. Not surprisingly, since it introduces very few provisions, its impact on national broadcasting systems has been relatively negligible. The few provisions that exist are ambiguous, making enforcement difficult and non-compliance easy.

To start with, national states have paid lip service to the quotas on European works and independent productions. The Commission's monitoring reports, based on data—often unverified—provided by the member states and even the broadcasters themselves, present a generally satisfactory picture of national compliance, particularly by public service broadcasters, although certain channels—new and thematic channels, channels targeting non-European diasporas broadcasting in non-European languages (e.g., Zee TV) and subsidiaries of non-EU companies (e.g., Cartoon Network)—

consistently fail to meet them.[135] As Levy observes, "even amongst their supporters, quotas [are] valued increasingly in terms of the symbolic rather than the real."[136]

Given that hardly any intra-European circulation of television programs takes place, except some in same language countries and regions, the notion of "European" television quotas turns out to be a misnomer since it effectively concerns quotas on domestic programming. And given the resistance of European viewers to non-domestic European content, to which broadcasters, even new ones, progressively respond by increasing domestic programs, the same result would have been achieved without any legislation but as a "function of market demand and competition."[137]

Regardless of the support measures, the EU's trade deficit has deteriorated. In 2000, despite increased European exports, trade in TV rights with the USA reached US$ 5 billion, an increase of 17.5 percent over the previous year, out of a total audiovisual deficit evaluated at US$10 billion, a 14 percent rise over 1999.[138] A substantial part of this deficit was due to the trade in feature films, TV fiction and cartoons.

Besides quotas, many television channels fail to observe the directive's quantitative restrictions on advertising. This is perhaps not surprising taking into account the proliferation of television channels depending on advertising revenue. The number of channels with national coverage in the EU doubled between 1990 and 1996 to reach 250, and then increased from 660 in 2001 to over 800 in 2003.[139] To address implementation problems, the Commission itself has started to monitor compliance with the advertising rules in roughly three countries per year.[140]

As always, although the actual implementation of directives lies with the member states, the European Commission is responsible for monitoring. As part of the compromise reached during the 1997 review of the directive and as a trade-off for not making the quotas compulsory, the anti-quota countries, notably Britain and Germany, agreed to set up a committee to improve compliance.[141] The so-called Contact Committee comprises representatives of the broadcasting authorities of the member states and is chaired by the Commission. Its role is to facilitate the effective implementation of the directive regarding in particular issues of jurisdiction, listed events and reports on quotas. It acts as a forum for the sharing of experiences, the exchange of information and the discussion of relevant developments in the sector. It establishes regular institutionalized contact among the national regulatory authorities for broadcasting and between them and the Commission.

Whereas the Contact Committee is part of the EU structures, the European Platform of Regulatory Authorities (EPRA) operates outside them, though the European Commission contributes to its budget. Set up in 1995, EPRA is a voluntary discussion forum where broadcasting regulators

from around forty countries in ' rope exchange information and share experiences. Its output is informal and unlike its telecommunications coun-
terpart, the IRG, it does not produce agreements or best-practice models.[142]

POST–COLD WAR ORDER
AND OTHER EUROPEAN ORGANIZATIONS

The advent of new technologies and the procompetitive restructuring of television markets especially from the mid-1980s onward saw the EU, emphasizing economic and industrial issues, assume a leading role in the European media policy arena relative to other European organizations. This
was to change in the post–Cold War order.

In the 1980s, the EBU, representing public service broadcasters, became
absorbed by an identity crisis intimately linked to the concept and future of
public service broadcasting. Its policy agenda was reactive. It had to respond
to two important challenges: the explosion of commercial broadcasting and
the actions against it by the EU competition authorities.[143] It was the
Marino Charter in 1990 that resolved the conflict about the organization's
future. The EBU was to remain an association of public service broadcasters
—and thus not represent the entire industry—barring the anomaly of a couple of commercial broadcasters already admitted by historical accident. Interestingly, the Marino Charter came a year after European commercial
broadcasters had set up their own association. The founding members of
the Association of Commercial Television in 1989 were Fininvest (Italy),
Sat-1 (Germany), CLT-RTL (Luxembourg), ITV (Britain) and TF1 (France),
the last three of which were also EBU members.[144] In 1992, following the
Marino Charter and the EU competition investigations, the EBU membership requirements were strengthened.[145] The EBU now serves as a political
platform of public service broadcasters in their relationships with other international organizations, in particular the EU.

In the past, the Council of Europe's principal role, by virtue of its wider
membership, was to act as a link between the EU and the rest of Western
Europe. Even that role had started to wane when Sweden, Finland and Austria decided to join the EU, a process concluded in 1995.[146]

The geopolitical changes in Central and Eastern European countries in
the late 1980s/early 1990s and their subsequent accession, prior to the EU,
to the EBU and the Council of Europe brought about a refocusing and
strengthening of both these organizations' policy activities. Especially in the
immediate aftermath of the collapse of communism, these two organizations, emphasizing democratic and socio-cultural values, regained importance in the European media policy sphere, challenging the dominant economic agenda promoted by the EU.[147] Besides, the sectoral expertise of the

EBU and the loose intergovernmental framework of the Council of Europe made these organizations less threatening to the newly acquired independence of ex-communist countries.

The EBU has actively assisted the emerging democracies with the introduction and consolidation of public service broadcasting and has, among other things, adopted a Model Law on Public Service Broadcasting.[148] Similarly, the Council of Europe has been actively involved in assisting the transition of ex-communist countries from state controlled to independent and pluralistic media, the cornerstone of democracy, through a wide range of activities including legal advice, training, seminars and workshops. The main objective has been to foster freedom of expression and information in line with the respective Council of Europe standards.

Subsequent to the political change in Central and Eastern Europe, the policy output of the Council of Europe has increased. For instance, whereas the EU tried to use competition rules to delimit public service broadcasting and later, instead of a definition, clarified with the Amsterdam Protocol that its remit, mission and funding are the responsibility of national states, the Council of Europe, at the Prague European Ministerial Conference in 1994, established the major principles of public service broadcasting.[149] These include the provision of a reference point for all members of the public, contribution to social cohesion and integration of all members of society, pluralistic and original programming, impartial and independent news, independence of political and economic interference and direct accountability to the public. Further, the Council of Europe has dealt with the independence of public service broadcasting, and the independence and functions of national regulatory authorities.[150]

Overall, the Council of Europe has addressed a wider and politically sensitive set of media issues. Compared to the EU, the Council of Europe's output is more substantive and prescriptive. It has managed to be so partly because it is a weaker organization and its policy measures are not binding but rather, in contrast to the EU, have a normative character and offer guidance. And whereas the Council of Europe's work on broadcasting focuses on media freedom and human rights, the EU's work is not guided by any specific viewpoint but rather adopts a horizontal approach:

> Under the Treaties, the Community has no independent mandate to shape the area of the media. Rather, the legal bases are "horizontal," in other words they are designed to achieve general objectives of the Community, especially the completion of the internal market.[151]

The Council of Europe through the adoption of non-binding policy instruments seeks to trigger domestic adjustment indirectly by framing domestic beliefs and expectations. As noted in chapter 1, for Knill and Lehmkuhl, this indirect form of influence is the weakest Europeanization mechanism.[152] It may, however, prepare the ground for subsequent policy reform and may promote support and legitimacy for further policy initiatives. This "framing" mechanism is also encountered in relatively newer EU governance non-law-making instruments aiming to share national experiences, disseminate best practice and develop benchmarks, such as the open method of coordination and groupings of national regulators.

TOWARD A CONVERGENT REGULATORY REGIME

It should be clear by now that, mirroring the situation at the national level and despite their potential technological convergence, the European telecommunications and television markets and regulatory frameworks have been construed as distinct from one another.

Just before the 1998 deadline for complete liberalization of telecommunications markets, the European Commission approached the notion of the information society from the perspective of technological convergence between telecommunications, computing and broadcasting.[153] The Green Paper on convergence was the initiative of Commissioner Bangemann based on a KPMG report. The aim was to expand telecommunications-type regulation into broadcasting. More specifically, the argument put forward by the Commission, notably the DG Information Society—the other directly concerned DG (DG Audiovisual) was sidelined—was that technological convergence effectively negated the distinct features of the previously separate sectors and as such existing sector-specific rules would need to be abolished and all sectors should come under the same, light, regulatory framework.

The most contentious issue, as became evident during the public consultation, was content regulation and the specificity of the broadcasting sector.[154] On the one hand, the internet and publishing communities were concerned that unless a minimalist regulatory approach to technological convergence was adopted, they risked having to comply with heavy and prescriptive broadcast-type content regulation. On the other hand, public service broadcasters in particular and their regulators maintained that the view that technological convergence equals regulatory convergence failed to recognize the continuing importance of public service obligations. Under the regulatory model favored by the Green Paper on convergence, which implied minimal internet-type content regulation based on self-regulatory measures and content classification, public service broadcasting would have little, if any, purpose. In the end, in response particularly to the strong reaction of public service broadcasters, this model was rejected. The principal conclusion of the public consultation was homogenous treatment of all transport network infrastructure and associated services, irrespective of the types of services carried, complemented by content regulation on the basis of the specific characteristics and public policy objectives of given services (i.e., public service broadcasting subject to heavier regulation compared to the internet).[155] As the next chapter explains, this consensus was confirmed in the wide-ranging Communications Review in 1999, which set out proposals for the regulation of electronic communications.

The EU attempted to use technological convergence to redefine markets and regulation by prioritizing competition over sector-specific rules and, related to this, international over national regulatory structures. This model would have strengthened the EU institutionally and, arguably, had the potential to enhance harmonization since it did not foresee a role for national sector-specific rules. This attempt failed. The consensus reached—horizontal regulation of infrastructure at the European level and sector-specific regulation at the (sub)national level—illustrates the limits to the EU's regulatory role and to a common regulatory framework in the era of technological convergence. But, and this is the crucial point, the discretion afforded is necessary for the fulfilment of public policy objectives and ultimately the legitimacy of the EU.

CONCLUSION

This chapter examined the most intensive period in market restructuring, regulatory reform, and Europeanization of communication policies covering the mid-/late 1980s until the late 1990s. A few observations can be made.

First, a confluence of political economy factors contributed to the progressive liberalization of telecommunications and television markets. Importantly, as analyzed, institutional factors were instrumental in mediating broader structural pressures and shaping market restructuring. But whereas in telecommunications the EU supported international liberalization during the GATT Uruguay Round and helped diffuse and amplify global procompetition pressures, in contrast, in the audiovisual sector the EU resisted and acted as a bulwark against international liberalization pressures. In both cases, the EU as an external actor was aiming to advance and defend the "European" interest.

The European Commission on several occasions acted as a "policy entrepreneur" taking advantage of "policy windows" to actively promote further integration in an attempt to serve its institutional self-interests.[156] Another institutional actor, the European Court of Justice, granted the EU the strongest possible legitimacy to intervene and thus facilitated the procompetitive turn of EU communication policy. However, inter- and intra-institutional tensions were common. For instance, whereas parts of the Commission representing producers' interests—DG Industry and DG Telecommunications—were favoring a policy mix of intervention and protectionism, other parts, notably DG Competition, were supporting open markets. The pursuit of procompetitive policy objectives disrupted the close links between the Commission and the incumbent market players (PTTs and public service broadcasters) and their European associations (the CEPT and the EBU) established during the previous European governance period.

The chapter also examined the role of alternative institutional policy arenas. With regard to transfrontier television, conflicting approaches and interests were being simultaneously fought at the EU and the Council of Europe. Later, in the early 1990s, whereas the EU was resigned to a broadly proliberal economic media policy approach, the dissolution of the communist bloc sparked an intense interest in the democratic, social and cultural aspects of the media. The Council of Europe and the EBU, emphasizing precisely these values, gained new prominence in the European media policy arena.

A second observation is that it was in this period from mid-/late 1980s to late 1990s that the tension between neomercantilist and neoliberal forces became most visible. There were tensions in the fields of both telecommunications and television, and in relation to both manufacturing/technological and content/ cultural issues. Neomercantilists, or *dirigistes* or protectionists, emphasized the importance of economies of scale for the nurturing of European champions and to this end advocated intervention and external trade protection. Neoliberals, or free-marketeers, on the other hand, emphasized structural weaknesses and the need for Europe to integrate into the emerging global economy. In effect, the conflict was about the relationship between state and market and the associated balance between positive integration (market-shaping and market-correcting rules) and negative integration (market-making rules). Each camp had its own supporters among national governments, the industry and parts of the European institutions.

The conflict between the two factions was gradually resolved in the 1990s. But, importantly, as documented in this chapter, neither of the two rival projects won in the end. Compromises on both sides were inevitable for European integration to progress. The new industrial competitiveness policy promoted by the neoliberal faction defeated strong calls for active industrial support measures and external trade protection. Still, the end result did not conform to a truly neoliberal scenario either. As the example of digital television illustrated, although there no longer was direct intervention in the form of mandated technical standards but rather greater reliance on market forces operating through the industry Digital Video Broadcasting Group, the EU assumed an enabling role in the introduction and diffusion of this new technology through the adoption of a light regulatory framework.

Similarly, in the area of culture, efforts to make the European content provisions stronger and binding were defeated. But again this was not a clear victory for the neoliberal camp. Quotas were incorporated in the EU television directive, even if significantly diluted. In addition, limited distributive measures (e.g., MEDIA program) aiming at strengthening the EU production industry were adopted, and a new, even if weak, regulatory body, the Contact Committee, has been established within the EU institutional structures to improve compliance.

Competitiveness came to denote a new approach to industrial policy which, although less sector-specific, accentuated emphasis on advanced communications infrastructure, which once again came to be seen as the savior of the European economy. The endorsement of the information society at the highest political level and the subsequent debate on the technological convergence between telecommunications and the media served to move the policy debate further away from controversial television and cultural concerns.

But again, socio-cultural considerations are not completely absent. For instance, whereas at the beginning EU actions in relation to public service broadcasting were reactive in response to an agenda set by its rivals, progressively the EU has come to recognize its importance (1997 Amsterdam Protocol). So-called services of general economic interest and citizens' access to them are seen as fundamental elements of the "European model of society" and are part of the move away from a European identity premised on the traditional national-state identity, forging tools toward a European identity based on civic citizenship, all the more significant in the post–Cold War order, and in the enlarged, highly diverse EU.

However, and this brings us to the third observation, while their recognition is important, there is a fundamental difference in the treatment of market-making and market-shaping measures within the EU. Whereas market-making measures are legally binding and, crucially, can be enforced through the EU's strong competition powers, the non-binding character of market-shaping and market-correcting measures renders their importance symbolic rather than substantive. The implementation of market-shaping rules rests with member states while the EU lacks legal enforcement powers. It uses comparative implementation reports and benchmarks, which operate at the cognitive level and rely on peer-pressure and processes of socialization and learning. Soft non-binding EU measures, complemented by the prescriptive normative output of the Council of Europe, important though they are, cannot afford an adequate degree of protection and promotion of public service objectives. In effect, while, contra a truly neoliberal scenario, public service objectives have been explicitly recognized, they are subordinated to market-making measures.

Finally, a fourth observation related to the last point, is that, overall, EU policies have been a more significant liberalization rather than harmonization force. Even the more prescriptive, compared to television, 1998 EU regulatory framework for telecommunications left national governments and regulators with too much discretion during implementation. The result is that the European market remains fragmented, characterized by an array of diverse national rules. Partly in response to the need to increase harmonization and fend off the idea of a pan-European regulator and partly because national regulators as a relatively new constituency did not have a European voice, this period witnessed the origin of soft policy coordination through the creation of groupings of national regulators in both broadcasting (European Platform of Regulatory Authorities in broadcasting, EPRA) and telecommunications (Independent Regulators' Group) outside the EU structures, but also inside them with the establishment of the Contact Committee. Reliance on soft measures and institutions increased significantly in the next period of European governance.

Despite its inadequacies, conflicts and contradictions, this period was the most intense phase of European governance yet in regulatory reform terms. This might well have been the highest peak of Europeanization.

NOTES

1. Stephen Woolcock, "Competition among Rules in the Single European Market," in *International Regulatory Competition and Coordination*, ed. William Bratton, Joseph McCahery, Sol Picciotto and Colin Scott (Oxford: Clarendon Press, 1996), 289.

2. Liesbet Hooghe and Gary Marks, "The Making of a Polity: The Struggle Over European Integration," *European Integration Online Paper* 1, no. 4 (1997), <http://eiop.or.at/eiop/texte/1997-004.htm> (20 Dec. 2005).

3. A third project, supranational social democracy associated with Delors' Commission and aiming at a strong social and political union, was significantly weaker. Bastiaan van Apeldoorn, *Transnational Capitalism and the Struggle over European Integration* (London and New York: Routledge, 2002). For the third project see also George Ross, *Jacques Delors and European Integration* (Cambridge: Polity, 1995).

4. Bastiaan van Apeldoorn, "The Political Economy of Regional Integration: Transnational Social Forces in the Making of Europe's Socioeconomic Order," in *Political Economy and the Changing Global Order*, ed. Richard Stubbs and Geoffrey Underhill (2nd ed. Don Mills, Ont., and New York: Oxford University Press, 2000), 237.

5. Andrew Gamble, "Economic Governance," in *Debating Governance*, ed. Jon Pierre (Oxford and New York: Oxford University Press, 2000), 126.

6. For the hyperglobalization thesis stressing the powerlessness of national states in today's globalizing world see Kenichi Ohmae, *The End of the Nation-State* (London: HarperCollins, 1995).

7. For an overview see Volker Schneider, "The Institutional Transformation of Telecommunications Between Europeanization and Globalization," in *Governing Telecommunications and the New Information Society in Europe*, ed. Jacint Jordana (Cheltenham: Edward Elgar, 2002), 27–46. John Braithwaite and Peter Drahos, *Global Business Regulation* (Cambridge: Cambridge University Press, 2000), 322–59.

8. "European Telecommunications; O What a Tangled Web We Weave," *Economist*, 28 October 1989, 113.

9. Jill Hills, *Deregulating Telecoms—Competition and Control in the United States, Japan and Britain* (London: Frances Pinter, 1986).

10. Jagdish Bhagwati and Hugh Patrick, eds., *Aggressive Unilateralism* (London: Harvester Wheatsheaf, 1991). Jill Hills, "A Global Industrial Policy. U.S. Hegemony and GATT: The Liberalization of Telecommunications," *Review of International Political Economy* 1, no. 2 (1994): 257–79.

11. Ernst Weiss [former chairman of Intug], "25th Anniversary Reminiscences," <http://www.intug.net/background/ernst_reminiscences.html> (21 May 2006).

12. Interview, American Express Europe, senior executive responsible for international regulatory affairs, Brighton, 6 January 1994. European Council of American Chambers of Commerce, *Comments on the European Community Action Programme on Telecommunications* (Brussels: EC-AmCham, 1985). ERT, *Clearing the Lines* (Paris: ERT, 1986). UNICE, *A Telecommunications Policy for Europe* (Brussels: UNICE, 1986). OECD, *Trends of Change in Telecommunications Policy* (Paris: OECD, 1987), 146–58. George McKendrick, "The INTUG view on the EEC Green Paper," *Telecommunications Policy* 11, no 4 (1987): 325–29.

13. For Britain and France see Mark Thatcher, *The Politics of Telecommunications* (Oxford: Oxford University Press, 1999).

14. Günther Knieps, "Deregulation in Europe: Telecommunications and Transportation," in *Deregulation or Reregulation?: Regulatory Reform in Europe and in the United States*, ed. Giandomenico Majone (Pinter: London, 1990), 72–100.

15. Stephen Wilks, "The Metamorphosis of European Competition Policy," *RUSEL Working Paper* 9 (Exeter: University of Exeter, 1992). Lee McGowan and Stephen Wilks, "The First Supranational Policy in the European Union: Competition Policy," *The European Journal of Political Research* 28, (1995): 141–69. Keith Middlemas, *Orchestrating Europe. The Informal Politics of European Union 1973–1995* (London: Fontana Press, 1995), 249–51 and 500–529.

16. Volker Schneider, Godefroy Dang-Nguyen and Raymund Werle, "Corporate Actor Networks in European Policy-Making: Harmonizing Telecommunications Policy," *Journal of Common Market Studies* 32, no. 4 (1994): 473–98.

17. Commission, "Decision 82/861/EEC of 10 December 1982 Relating to a Proceeding under Article 86 of the EEC Treaty (IV/29.877—British Telecommunications)," *Official Journal* L360/36, (21 December 1982), paragraph 34.

18. European Court of Justice, "Judgment of 20 March 1985. Case 41/83. Italian Republic v. Commission of the European Communities,"*European Court Reports* (1985): 873.

19. The International Telegraph and Telephone Consultative Committee (CCITT) was one of the permanent organs of the ITU responsible for technical, operational and tariff issues. Its members were the telecommunications administrations (i.e., state-owned monopolist PTTs) of the ITU member countries and any private operating agencies recognized by a member country. The CCITT was the international equivalent of the European CEPT.

20. Joseph Markoski, "Telecommunications Regulations as Barriers to the Transborder Flow of Information," *Cornell International Law Journal* 14 (1981): 299.

21. *European Commission Press Release*, IP/90/188 (6 March 1990).

22. European Commission, "Guidelines on the Application of EEC Competition Rules in the Telecommunications Sector," *Official Journal* C233/2 (6 September 1991): paragraphs 46–47.

23. EC, *Bulletin of the European Communities*, no. 3 (1985): point 2.1.43. European Commission, *Sixteenth Report on Competition Policy* (Luxembourg: Office for Official Publications of the European Communities, 1986), 199–201.

24. European Commission, *Towards a Dynamic European Economy: Green Paper on the Development of the Common Market for Telecommunications Services and Equipment*, COM(87) 290 (Brussels, 30 June 1987).

25. Susanne Schmidt, "Commission Activism: Subsuming Telecommunications and Electricity under European Competition Law," *Journal of European Public Policy* 5, no. 1 (1998): 169–84.

26. European Court of Justice, "Judgment of the Court of 19 March 1991. French Republic v. Commission of the European Communities. Competition in the Markets in Telecommunications Terminals Equipment. Case C-202/88," *European Court Reports* (1991): I-1223.

27. Stanley Besen, "The European Telecommunications Standards Institute: A Preliminary Analysis," *Telecommunications Policy* 14, no. 6 (1990): 521–30.

28. Interview, European Commission official working for DG Competition, Brussels, 18 April 1994.

29. For an analysis see Johannes Bauer, "Regulation and State Ownership: Conflicts and Complementarities in EU Telecommunications," *Annals of Public and Co-operative Economics* 76, no. 2 (2005): 151–77.

30. *Economist*, "European Telecommunications."

31. European Court of Justice, "Judgment of the Court of 17 November 1992. Kingdom of Spain, Kingdom of Belgium and Italian Republic v Commission of the European Communities. Competition in the Markets for Telecommunications Services. Joined Cases C-271/90, C-281/90 and C-289/90," *European Court Reports* (1992): I-5833.

32. *European Commission Press Release*, IP/89/948 (14 December 1989).

33. Hugo Dixon, "Untangling Europe's Telecommunications Networks," *Financial Times*, 11 December 1989, 5.

34. Marc Austin, "Europe's ONP Bargain, What's in It for the User?," *Telecommunications Policy* 18, no. 2 (1994): 97–113.

35. Jennifer Schenker, "Direction of ONP Evaluated," *Communications Week International*, 11 May 1992, 8.

36. European Parliament and Council, "Directive 95/62/EC of 13 December 1995 on the Application of Open Network Provision (ONP) to Voice Telephony," *Official Journal* L321/6 (30 December 1995).

37. "Europe's Industrial Tug-of-war," *Economist*, 25 January 1992, 79. For an outspoken U.S. critique of the Commission's industrial policy in general and the close links established first between DG Industry and Commissioner Davignon and then between DG Telecommunications and big European firms in electronics and IT see George Ross, "Sliding into Industrial Policy: Inside the European Commission," *French Politics & Society* 11, no. 1 (1993): 20–44.

38. "European Information Technology Survey," *Financial Times*, 11 March 1991.

39. Guy De Jonquieres "The European Market: Giving Direction to the Single Market," *Financial Times*, 22 October 1990, 14.

40. Laura D'Andrea Tyson, *Who's Bashing Whom? Trade Conflict in High-Technology Industries* (Washington, D.C.: Institute for International Economics, 1992), 220–37.

41. de Jonquieres, "The European market."

42. "Europe's Computer Industry: The Planners Strike Back," *Economist*, 16 February 1991, 91.

43. European Commission, *Industrial Policy in an Open and Competitive Environment: Guidelines for a Community Approach*, COM(90) 556 (Brussels, 16 November 1990).

44. European Commission, *The European Electronics and Information Technology Industry: State of Play, Issues at Stake and Proposals for Action*, SEC(91) 565 (Brussels, 3 April 1991).

45. For an account of this shift within the ERT see van Apeldoorn, *Transnational Capitalism*, 130–42.

46. ERT, *Reshaping Europe* (Brussels: ERT, 1991). ERT, *Beating the Crisis: A Charter for Europe's Industrial Future* (Brussels: ERT, 1993).

47. Keith Richardson, "Big Business and the European Agenda," *Sussex European Institute Working Paper* No. 35, (Brighton: Sussex European Institute, 2000), 25.

48. William Dawkins and David Buchan, "Electronics Giants Seek Protection," *Financial Times*, 23 April 1991, 3. Council, "Resolution of 18 November 1991 Concerning Electronics, Information and Communication Technologies," *Official Journal* C325/2 (14 December 1991).

49. "Europe's Flexible Friend: Martin Bangemann, European Commission Vicepresident, Talks to Andrew Hill," *Financial Times*, 30 November 1992, 32.

50. EC, "Treaty of the European Union," *Official Journal* C191 (29 July 1992), article 130.

51. Andrew Hill and Andrew Adonis, "Turn on the Bigger Picture," *Financial Times*, 16 June 1993, 19.

52. OECD, *New Directions for Industrial Policy: Policy Brief No. 3* (Paris: OECD, 1998), 2. European Commission, *An Industrial Competitiveness Policy for the European Union*, COM(94) 319 (Brussels, 14 September 1994).

53. Susan Strange, "Foreword," in *European Industrial Policy and Competitiveness*, ed. Thomas Lawton (London: Macmillan, 1999), xiii.

54. Gamble, "Economic Governance," 114.

55. Conditional access is an encryption technology used to prevent unauthorized reception of digital television services. For a detailed account see David Levy, *Europe's Digital Revolution* (London and New York: Routledge, 1999), 63–79.

56. European Parliament and Council, "Directive 95/47/EC of 24 October 1995 on the Use of Standards for the Transmission of Television Signals," *Official Journal* L281/51, 23 November 1995.

57. European Commission, *White Paper on Growth, Competitiveness, Employment—The challenges and ways forward into the 21st century*, COM(93) 700 (Brussels, 5 December 1993).

58. ERT, *Missing Links* (ERT: Brussels, 1984). ERT, *Missing Networks* (ERT: Brussels, 1991). ERT, *Beating the Crisis*.

59. European Commission, *Europe and the Global Information Society: Recommendations to the European Council* [Bangemann Report], (Brussels, 26 May 1994).

60. European Commission, *Europe's Way to the Information Society: An Action Plan*, COM (94) 347 (Brussels, 19 July 1994).

61. Maria Michalis, "Broadband Communications in the European Union: Myths and Realities," in *European Economic and Political Issues*, ed. Frank Columbus (New York: Nova, 2002), 8–9.

62. European Commission, *Green Paper on the Liberalisation of Telecommunications Infrastructure and Cable Television Networks: Part One. Principles and Timetable*, COM(94) 440 (Brussels, 25 October 1994). *Part Two. A Common Approach to the Provision of Infrastructure for Telecommunications in the European Union*, COM(94) 682 (Brussels, 25 January 1995).

63. European Commission—Competitiveness Advisory Group, <http://europa .eu.int/comm/cdp/cag/mission_en.htm> (7 March 2005).

64. ERT, *Beating*, 27.

65. George Draffan, *The Corporate Consensus: A Guide to the Institutions of Global Power. Part 2: Profiles in Corporate Power* (2002), <http://www.endgame.org/corpcon2 .html#UnionofIndustrial> (4 June 2006).

66. Alexis Jacquemin and Lucio Pench, "What Competitiveness for Europe? An Introduction," in *Europe Competing in the Global Economy*, ed. Alexis Jacquemin and Lucio Pench (Cheltenham: Edward Elgar, 1997), 12–13.

67. Alexis Jacquemin and Lucio Pench, eds., *Europe Competing in the Global Economy* (Cheltenham: Edward Elgar, 1997), 62.

68. Maria Green Cowles, "The Transatlantic Business Dialogue and Domestic Business-Government Relations," in *Transforming Europe: Europeanization and Domestic Change*, ed. Maria Green Cowles, James Caporaso and Thomas Risse (Ithaca and London: Cornell University Press, 2001), 168.

69. European Commission, "Directive 96/19/EC of 13 March 1996 Amending Directive 90/388/EEC with Regard to the Implementation of Full Competition in the Telecommunications Markets," *Official Journal* L74/13 (22 March 1996).

The General Agreement on Trade in Services (GATS) concluded during the Uruguay Round covered value-added telecommunications services only. Negotiations on basic telecommunications services were launched after the conclusion of the Uruguay Round (December 1993), on 30 April 1994. Agreement was reached in February 1997.

70. For details see Peter Humphreys and Seamus Simpson, *Globalisation, Convergence and European Telecommunications Regulation* (Cheltenham and Northampton, MA: Edward Elgar, 2005), 143–70.

71. Giandomenico Majone, "The European Commission as Regulator," in *Regulating Europe*, ed. Giandomenico Majone (London: Routledge, 1996), 60–79.

72. The first implementation report was issued in May 1997, just before the complete liberalization deadline. Regular updates have been published ever since. See <http://europa.eu.int/information_society/policy/ecomm/implementation_enforcement/annualreports/previousyears/index_en.htm> (3 June 2006).

73. Maria Michalis, "Local Competition and the Role of Regulation: The EU Debate and Britain's Experience," *Telecommunications Policy* 25, nos. 10/11 (2001): 759–76.

74. Andrienne Héritier, "The Accommodation of Diversity in European Policy-making and Its Outcomes: Regulatory Policy as a Patchwork," *Journal of European Public Policy* 3, no. 2 (1996): 149–67.

75. European Commission, *Fourth Report on the Implementation of the Telecommunications Regulatory Package* (Brussels: European Commission, 1998), 15.

76. European Commission, "Recommendation 98/511/EC of 29 July 1998 Amending Recommendation 98/195/EC on Interconnection in a Liberalised Telecommunications Market. Part 1—Interconnection Pricing," *Official Journal* L228/30 (15 August 1998). European Commission, "Commission Recommendation 98/322/EC of 8 April 1998 on Interconnection in a Liberalised Telecommunication Market. Part 2: Accounting Separation and Cost Accounting," *Official Journal* L141/41 (13 May 1998).

77. Former state-owned telecommunications operators are now organized outside the CEPT and have formed their own organization, European Public Telecommunications Network Operators' association (ETNO).

78. Anders Henten, Henning Olesen, Dan Saugstrup and Su-En Tan, "Mobile Communications: Europe, Japan and South Korea in a Comparative Perspective," *Info: The Journal of Policy, Regulation and Strategy for Telecommunications, Information and Media* 6, no. 3 (2004): 198. Roaming charges have recently come under attack. *European Commission Press Release*, IP/06/978, (12 July 2006).

79. Helen Wallace, "Europeanisation and Globalisation: Complementary or Contradictory Trends?" *New Political Economy* 5, no. 3 (2000), 369. For national variations see Humphreys and Simpson, *Globalisation*.

80. Maria Michalis, "Institutional Arrangements of Regional Regulatory Regimes: Telecommunications Regulation in the Europe and the Limits to Policy Convergence," in *Global Economy and Digital Society*, ed. Erik Bohlin, Stanford Levin, Nakil Sung and Chang-Ho Yoon (Amsterdam: Elsevier, 2004), 290.

81. Interview, head of European national regulatory authority for telecommunications and IRG/ERG member, Berlin, 28 October 2003.

82. For details see indicatively Peter Humphreys, *Mass Media and Media Policy in Western Europe* (Manchester: Manchester University Press, 1996), 159–228.

83. Richard Collins, *Satellite Television in Western Europe* (London: John Libbey, 1992).

84. For the role of commercial lobbies in the endorsement of commercial television in Britain in the early 1950s see H. H. Wilson, *Pressure Group: The Campaign for Commercial Television* (London: Secker & Warburg, 1961).

85. Matthew William Fraser, "Television," in *The European Union and National Industrial Policy*, ed. Hussein Kassim and Anand Menon (London and New York: Routledge, 1996), 211.

86. European Commission, *Television without Frontiers: Green Paper on the Establishment of the Common Market for Broadcasting Especially by Satellite and Cable*, COM(84) 300 (Brussels, 14 June 1984). For a detailed analysis of the developments leading to the television directive see Richard Collins, *Broadcasting and Audio-visual Policy in the Single European Market* (London: John Libbey, 1994), 53–80. Daniel Krebber, *Europeanisation of Regulatory Television Policy* (Baden-Baden: Nomos Verlagsgesellschaft, 2002), 79–125.

87. Armand Mattelart and Michael Palmer, "Advertising in Europe: Promises, Pressures and Pitfalls," *Media, Culture and Society* 13, no. 4 (1991): 537–39.

88. Michel Dupagne, "EC Policymaking: The Case of the 'Television Without Frontiers' Directive," *Gazette* 49 (1992): 101.

89. Humphreys, *Mass Media*, 270.

90. For instance, Council of Europe—Parliamentary Assembly, *Recommendation (1981) 926 on Questions Raised by Cable Television and by Direct Satellite Broadcasts* (Strasbourg, 7 October 1981). Council of Europe—Committee of Ministers, *Recommendation (84) 3 on Principles on Television Advertising* (Strasbourg, 23 February 1984). Council of Europe—Committee of Ministers, *Recommendation (86) 2 on Principles Relating to Copyright Law Questions in the Field of Television by Satellite and Cable* (Strasbourg, 14 February 1986).

91. For details see Krebber, *Europeanisation*, 104–7.

92. Council, "Directive 89/552/EEC of 3 October 1989 on the Coordination of Certain Provisions Laid Down by Law, Regulation or Administrative Action in Member States Concerning the Pursuit of Television Broadcasting Activities," *Official Journal* L298/23 (17 October 1989).

93. European Commission, *Proposal for a Council Directive on the Coordination of Certain Provisions Laid Down by Law, Regulation or Administrative Action in Member States Concerning the Pursuit of Broadcasting Activities*, COM(86) 146 (Brussels, 19 March 1986).

94. Fraser, "Television," 219.

95. Monika Guttman, "GATT: The Sequel," *U.S. News and World Report*, 27 December 1993/3 January 1994, 14.

96. Collins, *Broadcasting*, 26.

97. Philip Schlesinger, "From Cultural Defence to Political Culture: Media, Politics and Collective Identity in the European Union," *Media, Culture and Society* 19, no. 3 (1997): 369–91.

98. Roger Cohen, "Culture Dispute with Paris Now Snags World Accord," *New York Times*, 8 December 1993, A1.

99. Michael Palmer, "GATT and Culture: A View from France," in *Trading Culture: GATT, European Cultural Policies and the Transatlantic Market*, ed. Annemoon van Hemel, Hans Mommaas and Cas Smithuijsen (Amsterdam: Boekman Foundation, 1996), 27–38.

100. Charlotte Bretherton and John Vogler, *The European Union as a Global Actor* (London and New York: Routledge, 1999), 235.

101. David Puttnam, *The Undeclared War: The Struggle for Control of the World's Film Industry* (London: HarperCollins, 1997), 340–43.

102. "The Council Retains the Flexible Broadcasting Quota System," *Agence Europe*, 13 June 1996.

103. "Santer Explains Views on Quotas for European Television Programmes," *Agence Europe*, 31 January 1995.

104. European Commission, "Directive 97/36/EC Amending Council Directive 89/552/EEC on the Coordination of Certain Provisions Laid Down by Law, Regulation or Administrative Action in Member States Concerning the Pursuit of Television Broadcasting Activities," *Official Journal* L202 (30 July 1997).

105. Maria Michalis, "The Debate over Universal Service in the European Union. Plus ça Change, Plus c'est la Même Chose," *Convergence: The Journal of Research into New Media Technologies* 8, no. 2 (2002): 86.

106. The mutual recognition principle was upheld in "Regina v. Independent Television Commission, ex parte. TVDanmark 1 Limited, UK House of Lords, 25 July 2001," *Common Market Law Reports* (2001): 545.

107. European Commission, *Green Paper on Strategy Options to Strengthen the European Programme Industry in the Context of the Audiovisual Policy of the European Union*, COM(94) 96 (Brussels, 6 April 1994), 17.

108. See also Antonio-Pedro Vasconcelos, *Report by the Think Tank on the Audiovisual Policy in the European* Union (Brussels: European Commission, 1994).

109. European Commission, *Green Paper on Strategy*, 20. For the contradiction between cultural specificity and the internal market see also Caroline Pauwels and Jean-Claude Burgelman, "Policy Challenges to the Creation of European Information Society: A Critical Analysis," in *The European Information Society: A Reality Check*, ed. Jan Servaes (Bristol: Intellect, 2003), 59–85.

110. European Commission, *Green Paper: Pluralism and Media Concentration in the Internet Market*, COM(92) 480 (Brussels, 16 December 1992). For an analysis of alternative policy frames see Alison Harcourt, "EU Media Ownership Regulation: Conflict over the Definition of Alternatives," *Journal of Common Market Studies* 36, no. 3 (1998): 369–89. Gillian Doyle, *Media Ownership* (London: Sage, 2002), 154–70. Maria Michalis, "EU Broadcasting and Telecoms: Towards a Convergent Regulatory Regime?" *European Journal of Communication* 14, no. 2 (1999): 155–58.

111. Chris Johnstone, "Commission Trio United over Media Ownership," *European Voice*, 27 February 1997.

112. Michalis, "EU Broadcasting," 147–71.

113. Shalini Venturelli, *Liberalizing the European Media* (Oxford and New York: Clarendon Press, 1998), 187–231.

114. Graham Murdock, "Rights and Representations: Public Discourse and Cultural Citizenship," in *Television and Common Knowledge*, ed. Jostein Gripsrud (London: Routledge, 1999), 7–17.

115. Schlesinger, "From Cultural."

116. Another important EU competition area is the control since 1989 of mergers through which the Commission has influenced market restructuring by often prohibiting mergers in the media sector on the ground that they would have created or strengthened dominant market positions. This section does not examine mergers.

Rather, its aim is to analyze the changing relationship between the EU and the EBU and public service broadcasters, and to shed light on the treatment of public services by the EU that is at the heart of the state-market relationship. For a discussion of merger cases see Levy, *Europe's Digital*, 86–95.

117. Herbert Ungerer [head of the media division of DG Competition], "Switchover of Catch-up? Applying the Modernised EC Competition Regime in the New Media Sectors" (speech delivered at the Law Society's European Group, Brussels, 5 April 2005).

118. European Commission, "Decision 93/403/EEC of 11 June 1993 Relating a Proceeding Pursuant to Article 85 of the EEC Treaty (IV/32.150—EBU/Eurovision System)," *Official Journal* L179/23, (22 July 1993). European Commission, "Decision 2000/400/EC of 10 May 2000 Relating to a Proceeding Pursuant to Article 81 of the EC Treaty (Case IV/32.150—Eurovision)," *Official Journal* L151/18 (24 June 2000).

119. European Court of First Instance, "Judgment of 11 July 1996 in Joined Cases T-528/93, T-542/93, T-543/93 and T-546/93 *Métropole télévision SA (M6) and Others v. Commission*," *European Court Reports* (1996): II-649.

120. The EBU has subsequently changed its rules and Canal+ is no longer a member of the Eurovision system.

121. European Court of First Instance, "Judgment of 8 October 2002 in Joined Cases T-185/00, T-216/00, T-299/00 and T-300/00 *M6 and Others* v. *Commission*," *European Court Reports* (2002): II-3805, para. 64.

122. *European Commission Press Release, IP/96/886* (2 October 1996).

123. European Court of First Instance, "Judgment of 15 September 1998 in Case T-95/96 Gestevisión Telecinco SA v Commission," *European Court Reports* (1998): II-3407.

124. *European Commission Press Release, IP/99/132*, (24 February 1999) and IP/99/706 (29 September 1999). The BBC case is discussed in the next chapter. For the German cases see also David Ward, "State Aid or Band Aid? An Evaluation of the European Commission's Approach to Public Service Broadcasting," *Media, Culture & Society* 25 (2003): 234–37.

125. The Amsterdam Treaty was signed in June 1997 and entered into force in May 1999, <http://www.eurotreaties.com/amsterdamtreaty.pdf> (20 July 2006).

126. See indicatively Dimitris Chryssochoou, "Civic Competence and the Challenge to EU Polity-building," *Journal of European Public Policy* 9, no. 5 (2002): 756–73.

127, Chris Shore, "Wither European Citizenship? Eros and Civilization Revisited," *European Journal of Social Theory* 7, no. 1 (2004): 27–44. See also Schlesinger, "From Cultural," 385–88.

128. Amsterdam Treaty, article 7D.

129. Andrienne Héritier, "Market Integration and Social Cohesion: The Politics of Public Services in European Regulation," *Journal of European Public Policy* 8, no. 5 (2001): 825–52.

130. Jürgen Habermas, "Why Europe Needs a Constitution," *New Left Review* 11 (September/October 2001): 8. Lionel Jospin "L' avenir de L' Europe élargie" (speech to the Foreign Press Association, Paris, 28 May 2001), <http://www.monde-diplomatique.fr/cahier/europe/jospin> (12 July 2005).

131. European Commission, *Green Paper on Services of General Interest*, COM(2003) 270 (Brussels, 21 May 2003).

132. European Commission, *DG IV Discussion Paper on the Application of Articles 90, Paragraph 2, 92 and 93 of the EC Treaty in the Broadcasting Sector* (Brussels: DG Competition, 1998).

133. European Commission, "Communication from the Commission on the Application of State Aid Rules to Public Service Broadcasting," *Official Journal* C320/5 (15 November 2001).

134. The provisions concerning financial transparency and accounting separation had already been endorsed by the DG Audiovisual. European Commission, *Audiovisual Policy: Next Steps*, COM(98) 446 (Brussels, 14 July 1998).

135. Similar to telecommunications, the Commission publishes regular implementation reports, available at <http://ec.europa.eu/comm/avpolicy/reg/tvwf/implementation/index_en.htm> (18 June 2006).

136. Levy, *Europe's Digital*, 48.

137. Bill Grantham, *Some Big Bourgeois Brothel: Context for France's Culture Wars with Hollywood* (Luton: University of Luton Press, 2000), 162. See also Els De Bens and Hedwig de Smaele, "The Inflow of American Television Fiction on European Broadcasting Channels Revisited," *European Journal of Communication* 16, no. 1 (2001): 51–76.

138. European Commission, *Fourth Report on the Application of Directive 89/552/EEC "Television without Frontiers,"* COM(2002) 778 (Brussels, 6 January 2003), 5.

139. European Commission, *Fourth Report*, 4. European Commission, *Second Report on the Application of Directive 89/552/EEC "Television without frontiers,"* COM(1997) 523 (Brussels, 24 October 1997).

140. Interview, Independent Television Commission [UK], official responsible for advertising, London, 18 July 2003.

141. "20 November Culture Council," *European Voice* (23 November 1995).

142. Interview, EPRA secretariat, Düsseldorf (9 September 2003).

143. See Collins, *From Satellite*, 46 and 40–49 for details about the debate leading up to the Marino Charter.

144. Matteo Maggiore, *Audiovisual Production in the Single Market* (Luxembourg: Office for Official Publications of the European Communities, 1990), 110.

145. EBU, *Statutes of the EBU 1992* (Geneva: EBU, 1992), art. 3.

146. Bernd Möwes, *Fifty Years of Media Policy in the Council of Europe—A Review* (Strasbourg: Council of Europe, 2000), Summary point 7, <http://www.coe.int/T/E/human_rights/media/4_Documentary_Resources/MCM%282000%29003_en.asp#TopOfPage> (23 March 2006). Up until 1990, the Council of Europe remained an exclusive west European organization of twenty-three countries. Following the disintegration of communist regimes, it gradually expanded toward Central and Eastern Europe. In April 2006 it brought together forty-six countries of which twenty-one were from Central and Eastern Europe. See "The Council of Europe's Member States," <http://www.coe.int/T/E/Com/About_Coe/Member_states/default.asp> (25 March 2006).

147. Interview, Dr. Karol Jakubowicz, Chairman of the Council of Europe's Steering Committee on the Mass Media, London, 9 October 2005.

148. EBU, *Model Public Service Broadcasting Law* (EBU: Geneva, 1998, updated in 2003), <http://www.ebu.ch/CMSimages/en/leg_p_model_law_psb1_tcm6-14334.pdf> (11 June 2006).

149. Council of Europe, *Resolution No. 1: Future of Public Service Broadcasting of the 4th Council of Europe Ministerial Conference on Mass Media Policy, Prague 1994*, <http://www.ebu.ch/CMSimages/en/leg_ref_coe_mcm_resolution_psb_07_081294_tcm6-4274.pdf> (11 June 2006).

150. Council of Europe—Committee of Ministers, *Recommendation R(96)10 on the Guarantee of the Independence of Public Service Broadcasting* (Strasbourg, 11 September 1996). Council of Europe—Committee of Ministers, *Recommendation R(2000) 23 on the Independence and Functions of Regulatory Authorities for the Broadcasting Sector* (Strasbourg, 20 December 2000).

151. Viviane Reding [European Commissioner for Education and Culture], "The Challenges Facing a Future: European Regulatory System for Media and Communications" (speech/02/490, delivered at Medientage, Munich, 17 October 2002).

152. Christoph Knill and Dirk Lehmkuhl, "The National Impact of European Union Regulatory Policy: Three Europeanization Mechanisms," *European Journal of Political Research* 41, no. 2 (2002): 255–80.

153. European Commission, *Green Paper on the Convergence of the Telecommunications, Media and Information Technology Sectors, and the Implications for Regulation: Towards an Information Society Approach*, COM(97) 623 (Brussels, 3 December 1997).

154. Jill Hills and Maria Michalis, "Restructuring Regulation: Technological Convergence and European Telecommunications and Broadcasting Markets," *Review of International Political Economy* 7, no. 3 (2000): 434–64.

155. European Commission, *The Convergence of the Telecommunications, Media and Information Technology Sectors, and the Implications for Regulation: Results of the Public Consultation on the Green Paper COM(97)623*, COM(1999) 108 (Brussels, 10 March 1999).

156. John Kingdon, *Agendas, Alternatives, and Public Policies* (Boston: Little, Brown, 1984).

6

Competitiveness, Knowledge Economy and Technological Convergence

Toward Policy Coordination (Late 1990s to Early 2007)

INTRODUCTION

The last and current phase of European governance, starting in the late 1990s, has emerged in the context of the post–Cold War order, increasing globalization, renewed concerns about Europe falling behind its main competitors, growing technological convergence and the rising importance of the internet.

This chapter documents the endorsement of competitiveness and the knowledge economy as the new strategic EU goals and the associated prominence of the electronic communications sector. It argues that specific segments within the electronic communications sector have used the dominant orthodoxy of competitiveness in an attempt to promote their own interests.

Some of the efforts to accelerate the move toward the knowledge economy, the new term for the information society, relate to the revision of the EU regulatory frameworks for telecommunications (completed in 2002 and currently again under review) and for television (still underway). The chapter critically assesses the new regulatory package for electronic communications that, in an attempt to enhance harmonization, combines stronger reliance on competition rules with greater use of soft modes of governance, in particular non-binding measures and transnational regulatory committees.

The move toward a less prescriptive and horizontal (technology-neutral) regulatory framework has been relatively easy in the case of electronic communications, in particular in relation to transport network infrastructure. However, initiatives toward a horizontal regulatory approach with regard to television and attempts to incorporate the sector into the regulation of a broader set of economic activities have encountered strong opposition. A horizontal regulatory model to cover audiovisual content services is currently being debated as part of the second review of the television directive. The review illustrates the persistent difficulties that the EU encounters in the formulation of a comprehensive regulatory framework for the converging information and communications sectors.

Still, in the emerging multi-platform digital communications environment, the strongest horizontal policy tool, general competition rules—and in what interests us in particular, the EU state aid rules—play an increasingly prominent role. Despite recognition that public service broadcasting is a member state competence, commercial interests continue to contest the funding and expansion of public service broadcasters into new areas. It appears that the Commission's approach in recent cases concerning the expansion of public service broadcasters into online and neighboring activities departs from its earlier position on expansion within the traditional broadcasting field.

Finally, by means of selected examples, this chapter examines three main challenges that the EU faces in the regulation of electronic communications. The case of application program interfaces in digital interactive television draws attention to the problematic distinction between the regulation of infrastructure and associated services at the EU level and the regulation of content at the national level. The case of third generation mobile standards points to how the broader process of globalization and the international aspirations of European market players may shape the process of Europeanization. Both these examples demonstrate the new enabling, as opposed to the former interventionist, role of the European Commission. Finally, the case of the third generation extension frequency band assesses how new principles underpinning the new electronic regulatory framework and international trade liberalization may limit Europeanization.

MIND THE GAPS: COMPETITIVENESS, PRODUCTIVITY AND THE RISE OF THE KNOWLEDGE ECONOMY

Whereas in the first part of the 1990s the internet was notable for its absence from the EU policy agenda, in the second part it came to figure more and more prominently on that agenda. Still, the first initiatives aimed at addressing associated risks rather than capturing potential benefits were reactions to U.S. policy proposals for the governance of the internet.[1] Eventually, a confluence of factors in the late 1990s—convergence in communication technologies, the commercialization of the internet, associated technological euphoria and the widening productivity and competitiveness gap with the USA—combined to decisively shift the emphasis of the EU policy to the internet. This time the aim was to seize its growth potential in a catch-up race with the USA.

In the latter part of the 1990s, several studies established a link between Information and Communication Technology (ICT), especially the internet, and strong economic performance. Although most of the data concerned the USA and its productivity miracle for most of the decade, comparative studies concluded that, despite differences in economic growth, other countries too benefited from investment in ICT, and the studies warned that failure to accelerate the transition toward an information society and deploy broadband communications would adversely impact economic and productivity gains.[2]

Insufficient ICT spending and use was accepted as the root cause of the gap between U.S. and European productivity and growth. The following quotes are indicative.

> The central message [. . .] is that a key determinant of Europe's recent underperformance in productivity growth is insufficient innovative activity as well as under-investment in, and weak diffusion of, information and communication technologies.[3]
>
> [T]he superior performance of the USA in ICT-producing manufacturing and intensive ICT-using service industries is the principal source of the diverging productivity trends in favour of the USA.[4]

In short, the technology gap was the key explanatory variable for the economic gap with the USA. Yet other studies suggested caution over the interpretation of the data. In particular they drew attention to the inconclusive evidence as to whether the perceived gains were confined to the firm or sectoral level, or whether they concerned entire national economies.[5] The OECD challenged the very notion that ICT was the single most important contributor to U.S. productivity, while for Gordon the reason for U.S. growth, perceived to be cyclical, was simply economic recovery.[6]

Despite diverging interpretations, "[a]t the end of 1999, it became clear that Europe needed focus and a sense of urgency to catch up in the information society."[7] In December 1999, the EU launched the "*e*Europe—An information society for all" initiative aiming to bring every European online.[8] As evidence in itself of the malleability of the concept, whereas in the first half of the 1990s the "information society" was used to advance the full liberalization of the telecommunications market (preceding chapter), in the late 1990s the "information society" became associated with the internet and broadband communications.

At the Lisbon summit in March 2000, just months before the technology bubble was to deflate, EU leaders committed to transforming Europe into the "most competitive and dynamic knowledge-based economy in the world, capable of sustainable economic growth with more and better jobs and greater social cohesion" by 2010.[9] The *e*Europe plan—renamed i2010 in June 2005—is at the heart of the so-called Lisbon agenda. Importantly, it entails neither EU legislation nor expenditure. Rather, in accordance with the open method of coordination endorsed at Lisbon, the *e*Europe initiative is based on definition of common targets and indicators; the drawing up of national plans; and periodic monitoring, benchmarking and dissemination of best practice. There is no common European policy, but rather national policies are coordinated within a general European framework. Implementation is voluntary based on agreement and backed up by "social mechanisms of reputational enforcement," notably encouragement, peer pressure and name-and-shame tactics.[10]

In 2000, a hard law measure was adopted to complement the soft *e*Europe policy initiative. The Regulation mandating local loop unbundling aims at promoting competition in local telecommunications networks—the local loop—by requiring incumbent operators to make their access network available to competitors, who are then able to install new equipment—typically Digital Subscriber Line (DSL)—and upgrade it to offer broadband services to end users.[11] This was an unprecedented step in the field of telecommunications. A Regulation is the strongest EU legislative instrument. It is binding and directly applicable, which means that is does not require transposition into national legislation which may delay the measure. The Regulation was further evidence of the urgency to catch up in the information society race and stimulate the rollout of broadband internet.

In November 2004, despite the burst of the internet bubble and consequent recession, the High Level Group chaired by Wim Kok, in its report "Facing the Challenge," confirmed the key role of the knowledge economy and the *e*Europe plan and recommended, among other things, that broadband internet penetration reach at least 50 percent by 2010.[12] For the Kok report, Europe's competitive advantage must lie with the knowledge economy, and here the USA is its main competitor:

> The U.S. threatens to consolidate its leadership. The U.S. accounts for 74% of top 300 IT companies and 46% of top 300 firms ranked by R&D spending.[13]

The report also noted that the European information technology sector represented 6 percent of European GDP compared with 7.3 percent in the USA, while European investment consistently lagged behind the USA by around 1.6 percent of GDP.[14]

In sum, at the turn of the millennium, competitiveness reached the highest political level, which culminated in its endorsement as the new strategic goal at the Lisbon summit in 2000. A new Council formation, the EU Competitiveness Council, was created in June 2002, bringing together the former Industry, Internal Market and Research Councils with the aim to increase the synergy among these three areas and assess all initiatives against the top priority of competitiveness.

The dominant orthodoxy of competitiveness is based on the assumption that there is a direct link between ICT and productivity and economic growth. Our aim is not to grapple with this relationship that has preoccupied economists and politicians for centuries with no consensus in sight. Rather, we wish to point out that not only does the contribution of ICT to economic growth remain controversial, but also there is not even an agreed definition of "productivity" and "competitiveness." Which interests then promote the competitiveness debate and why? It is here argued that the competitiveness agenda has been hijacked by specific interests in the electronic communications sector who stand to benefit from the policy rhetoric linking ICT to competitiveness.

Productivity

Broadly speaking, there are two types of productivity. What most studies, especially in the USA, refer to is labor productivity, that is, the output per worker. A second more accurate but complex measure is multi-factor productivity, which captures the efficiency with which capital and labor inputs are used.[15]

Labor productivity in the USA grew at an annual average rate of 2 percent in the second half of the 1990s, whereas it slowed in most European countries.[16] Still, the U.S. growth rate was roughly the same as in France and Britain, although faster compared to Germany and Italy.[17] However, multi-factor productivity tells a different story. In the USA, it grew only 1.2 percent in the second part of the 1990s, from an average of 0.8 percent in the first part of the decade. In Britain and Germany its growth was similar, whereas in France it increased faster, at 1.4 percent.[18] In other words, gains in multi-factor productivity in the USA—that is, the most accurate measure of productivity—have been substantially less impressive compared to those in labor productivity, and, crucially, very similar to respective gains in the major European countries. And yet, various studies in the 1990s, referred to in the preceding section, were painting an alarming picture that Europe's productivity gap with the USA was widening.

Moreover, comparisons are typically based on contradictory government statistics. Differences in the way countries measure output and labor productivity produce a distorted picture. For instance, the productivity miracle of the USA in the latter 1990s, as just explained, was effectively about labor productivity, which in turn increased because spending on equipment, notably information technology, increased. In the USA, spending on information technology is considered an investment. In sharp contrast, in most European countries, the practice is for such spending to count not as investment but as a business expense and thus it is excluded from final output.[19] This basic difference in statistics can partly explain why labor productivity in the USA has grown faster while, crucially, it is precisely the principal role attributed to information technology investment, and in turn low interest rates and access to easy money, that bring into question the sustainability of its accelerated growth rate. In short, "[m]easurement issues have contributed to the transatlantic productivity gap."[20] Official statistics are far from reliable in giving an account of productivity and need to be treated with caution.

Higher information technology spending does not automatically result in growth, in multi-factor productivity gains. Paul Strassmann, a consistent skeptic of the contribution of information technology to productivity improvements, argues that investment in better machines and equipment will increase labor productivity, but for benefits to the economy as a whole one needs to also take into account the additional capital spending that this investment implies, not to mention the increasingly rapid depreciation cycles of information technology products and the fact that each wave of investment is bigger than the last. He warns that productivity gains in the USA have to be set against the rising bureaucratization of domestic organizations which, of course, has created demand for more information processing but "increased amounts of unnecessary work [do] not create wealth, whether done faster than before or not."[21] He also maintains, similar to Krugman's argument on competitiveness examined below, that productivity gains are firm, not sector, specific and it is therefore wrong to make generalizations.

In sum, measuring productivity and defining its determinants remains as controversial as ever. The lack of convincing or consistent evidence establishing a clear correlation between information technology spending and productivity gains led Robert Solow to famously declare that computers are everywhere but in the productivity statistics. This is commonly known as the productivity paradox.

Competitiveness

Krugman has argued that concerns about competitiveness are empirically unfounded and has attempted to explain why, in spite of this, there is an obsession with competitiveness. Part of the difficulty is that competitiveness applies to two levels: the level of the corporation and the level of a national economy. The first one is relatively unproblematic; it is "no more than the ability of a business to sell products of the requisite quality at a price which the customer is prepared to pay."[22] It is competitiveness at the level of a national economy that is problematic both to define and to measure. It is this latter concept of competitiveness that Krugman questions, and he argues that it is at best meaningless, at worse dangerous.

Meaningless because, according to the definition provided by the U.S. Economic Advisors Council and equally to that adopted by the EU, competitiveness has at its core the improvement of living standards.[23] For Krugman, the problem is that the growth of living standards is closely related to that of domestic productivity. Hence "'competitiveness' turn[s] out to be a funny way of saying 'productivity.'"[24]

Dangerous because when competitiveness is applied to national economies it implies that countries compete with each other the way firms do and assumes that countries, like corporations, are rivals. It portrays economic growth and international trade as a zero-sum game whereby one country's gains are another country's losses and as such carries the risk of fuelling trade conflicts and increasing calls for protection.

So why is competitiveness such a popular notion? Krugman identifies three reasons.[25] First, competitive images among nations are easy to understand and associate with. Second, the notion that a country's economic problems have to do with external, as opposed to domestic, factors gives the impression that these problems are somehow easier to address. And finally, competitiveness is a useful political construct in that in can legitimize unpopular policies or avoid them.

Whereas Krugman distinguishes between competitiveness at the level of the firm and competitiveness at the level of a national economy, Jacquemin and Pench offer a typology of competitiveness on the basis of variables.[26] "Performance variables"—such as productivity, market shares and profitability—relate to "*ex post*" competitiveness. They concern results and simply describe the state of competitiveness. In contrast, "factor variables" draw attention to the conditions of competitiveness, that is, key structural and institutional determinants including tax, labor law and physical infrastructure. This "*ex ante*" competitiveness cuts across various public policies and, in turn, public policies can greatly influence factor variables. It is this *ex ante* competitiveness that is important to policy-makers. It is related to the restructuring of the capitalist state, in particular the shift from the state producer to the state regulator and increasingly enabler. *Ex ante* competitiveness can justify action supporting open markets and investment in communications infrastructure.

Similar to productivity, different definitions of competitiveness result in different measurements. Lawton explains that the USA and the EU measure *ex post* competitiveness. In contrast, the World Economic Forum (WEF) measures *ex ante* competitiveness, the factors and conditions believed to be conducive to competitiveness. According to the Forum, the EU as a whole fares well but generally lags behind the USA and Japan due to high taxation and rigid labor markets.[27] Importantly, individual EU countries such as Finland, Sweden and Denmark regularly figure in the Forum top ten list of the world's most competitive countries.[28] Hence, Lawton reaches the same conclusion as Krugman:

> [The WEF conceptualization of competitiveness] serves to cast doubt on the argument that Europe as a whole has a competitive problem. It leads one to wonder the extent to which the ongoing debate on Europe's lagging competitiveness is largely a political construct designed to legitimise the introduction of unpopular policy instruments.[29]

In the EU, the rhetoric of competitiveness has proved useful. It has helped define "Europe" against its "competitors," the Other, in both economic and cultural terms. The competitiveness obsession favors integrationist forces since it frames issues as European and calls for European solutions.[30] The assumption is that indeed there is such a thing as a "European" economy and, although the EU has struggled to define it, it has often been linked to the national identity of corporations.[31] The conflation in policy discourse of the competitiveness of a firm and the competitiveness of a national economy allows the latter to be used for the pursuit of the former, and that is not necessarily for the benefit of a national economy and society but rather for the private benefit of individual companies.

THE 1999 COMMUNICATION REVIEW

Open and competitive ICT markets are at the heart of the Lisbon strategy and its objectives of promoting economic growth, competitiveness and social cohesion. In July 2000, the Commission proposed a new regulatory package for electronic communications. The reform of the EU regulatory framework began with the 1997 Green Paper on convergence—which resolved the issue of transmission and content regulation—and the subsequent 1999 communications review. Before moving to the new regulatory package, in order to understand the compromises reached, we will first examine the most controversial issue in the 1999 communications review, the power of the Commission over national regulators and the associated degree of national regulatory discretion.

Proposals and Reactions

The 1999 communications review formally abandoned the idea of a pan-European regulator. Although there was support for greater EU involvement in the areas of competition, harmonization for the creation of a common market, interconnection and enforcement, it was felt that existing but adapted EU structures could address these issues.[32] The Commission proposed a two-pronged strategy.[33]

First, it put forward provisions aiming at strengthening the powers, independence and transparency of national regulators, who were pivotal in safeguarding the integrity of the single market. Second, the Commission proposed the establishment of three bodies in order to improve existing EU institutional structures. First, a new Communications Committee, made up of national representatives, would be a comitology committee working within the Commission.[34] Second, and most controversially, in reaction to the creation in 1997 of the informal Independent Regulators' Group and in an effort to increase regulatory consistency across member states, the Commission called for the establishment of its own coordinating body of national regulators. The proposed High Level Communications Group, comprising representatives of all relevant national regulatory bodies and the Commission, would bring national regulators under the Commission's structures and control. The last proposal was for an advisory Radio Spectrum Policy Expert Group composed of national representatives.

The response of policy stakeholders to the Commission's institutional plans was not surprising.[35] They all confirmed that there was no support for a pan-European regulator and concurred with the Commission that greater consistency in regulatory responses was needed. Industry players and consumer associations stressed that the planned committees should consult closely with them.

Overall, there was support for the Communications Committee, but national governments and regulators, in particular, expressed strong concerns about the role of the High Level Communications Group. For instance, the Dutch government, worried that national regulators with representation in the Group could bypass them, argued that governments too should be represented and that the Group's mandate should have a strictly advisory and monitoring role. Similarly, the existing national regulators' grouping (IRG) and individual regulators strongly opposed the creation of a rival body. The proposed Group, they argued, would end up being a large and diffuse body with representatives from all relevant national authorities and, therefore, unsuitable to address detailed regulatory issues. More importantly, they warned, the Group would be susceptible to political interference since government departments would be entitled to participate to the extent that they retained regulatory responsibilities. The suggestion was that the IRG was best placed to assume the role of close cooperation with the Commission. The IRG maintained that national regulators themselves should deal with practical regulatory matters as well as draft and enforce complementary non-binding guidelines. In the face of such strong opposition, the

Commission abandoned the proposal for a High Level Communications Group. Under the compromise reached, a European Regulators' Group was established, examined below.

Besides the High Level Communications Group, another contentious proposal was the so-called Commission veto-right.[36] There was wide agreement among telecommunications operators and corporate users that, given the new flexible powers that national regulators would be equipped with under the envisaged regulatory framework, "some centrifugal counterbalance which pulls things together [was needed] so that the Commission can prevent chaos."[37] Sharing this view and at the same time promoting its own institutional interests, the Commission advocated a "transparency mechanism" according to which national regulators would have to submit major draft regulatory measures to the Commission and other national regulators for consideration and, crucially, the Commission would have the right to veto them. The European Parliament supported the Commission's greater involvement in national regulatory responses but as anticipated, national governments and regulators emphatically opposed a Commission "veto-right."[38] Eventually, the national governments unanimously rejected the "veto right," thereby reducing the Commission's role in national regulatory decisions.

In the face of the persistent implementation deficit and the incompleteness of the internal market, both the question of a pan-European regulator and the Commission's power over national regulatory decisions have resurfaced in the review of the 2002 electronic communications framework launched in 2006.

The 2002 Regulatory Framework

The revised EU regulatory framework for electronic communications was formally adopted in April 2002. As table 6.1 shows, it combines binding hard-law (directives and regulation) with non-binding soft-law policy measures such as guidelines and recommendations and various transnational regulatory committees, explained below.

Main Principles and Elements

The 2002 EU regulatory framework for electronic communications endorsed the core principles set out in the 1999 communications review. Accordingly, it separates the regulation of transmission from the regulation of content. Broadcast content and electronic commerce services are outside its scope. In line with the principle of technological neutrality, the revised framework adopts a horizontal approach in relation to transmission, under which all transport network infrastructure (e.g., fixed, mobile, cable TV)

Table 6.1. Main Measures in the EU 2002 Electronic Communications Regulatory Framework*

Liberalization measures	Harmonization measures	Accompanying measures
2000: Regulation on unbundled access to the local loop	2002: Framework directive	2002: Commission guidelines on market analysis and the assessment of significant market power
2002: Commission directive on competition in the market for electronic communications networks and services	2002: Authorization directive	2003: Commission recommendation on relevant product and service markets
	2002: Access and interconnection directive	2003: Commission recommendation on notifications, time limits and consultations provided for in article 7 of the framework directive
	2002: Universal service and users' rights directive	2005: Commission recommendation on accounting separation and cost accounting
	2002: Data protection and privacy directive	
	2002: Radio spectrum decision	

*The 2002 regulatory framework is available at <http://europa.eu.int/information_society/policy/ecomm/info_centre/documentation/index_en.htm > (24 January 2007).

and associated services (e.g., conditional access systems) are treated the same irrespective of the services being carried.

The new regulatory framework regulates markets, not technologies. It correlates the degree of regulation and the degree of competition in a market.[39] In markets with effective competition, specific rules should be rolled back and competition law alone should apply. Only in markets where competition is not established should regulators intervene. Thus, competition law is the norm and sector-specific regulation is the exception. But even in the latter exceptional cases, competition law analysis is required to: (1) define the relevant market, (2) assess the market power of operators and (3) decide on regulatory intervention to address problems.

The point of departure then is the definition of markets. To this end, the Commission has issued a recommendation listing eighteen retail and wholesale market segments that could exceptionally be considered to justify specific regulation, such as price controls, cost orientation, account-ing separation and mandatory provision of certain network elements.[40] The eighteen markets identified by the Commission fulfill three main crite-ria: they exhibit high entry barriers, there is no effective competition and competition law alone does not suffice to restore it. National regulators have to use these eighteen market segments as a starting point. They may decide to intervene in other markets but only if, and with the Commission's approval, these satisfy all three criteria just mentioned.[41] Equally, following a market review, national regulators may conclude that a market identified by the Commission is competitive and as such does not require specific regulation.

The second stage is for national regulators to define which operators hold significant market power within each market. Under the new framework, this last concept is no longer based on a 25 percent market share but on the notion of market dominance under competition law.[42] An operator is dom-inant if, individually or jointly with others, it enjoys "a position of eco-nomic strength affording it the power to behave to an appreciable extent in-dependently of competitors customers and ultimately consumers."[43] Based on the Commission's practice and the relevant jurisprudence of the Euro-pean Court, single dominance concerns normally arise in the case of un-dertakings with market shares of over 40 percent. Other criteria that regula-tors have to take into account include the overall size of the undertaking, control of infrastructure not easily duplicated, technological advantages, absence of countervailing buying power, access to financial resources, economies of scale and scope, vertical integration, highly developed distri-bution sales network, absence of potential competition and barriers to expansion.[44]

The third and final stage is for national regulators to decide whether to impose obligations (so called remedies) on operators with significant mar-ket power in a relevant market. If no undertaking is found to have signifi-cant market power, regulation can be rolled back.

Under the compromise reached following the rejection of the original veto-right proposal, the Commission has certain powers over market defi-nitions and the designation of operators with significant market power but none over the imposition of associated obligations. More specifically, ac-cording to the notification procedure under article 7 of the Framework di-rective, national regulators have to submit to the Commission and the other national regulators draft measures concerning the definition of relevant markets, the designation of operators with significant market power and any regulatory requirements that they intend to impose and only where these affect trade between member states.[45] The Commission and other na-tional regulators have one month within which to make comments and the national regulator concerned is required to take "the utmost account" of them. If the Commission has serious reservations about a proposed measure concerning the definition of a market which differs from those defined in its recommendation or the designation of operators with significant market power, and it considers that such a measure would create a barrier to the single market, then it may within a further period of two more months issue a "serious doubts letter" requiring the national regulator in question to withdraw the notified measure. The notification procedure under article 7 of the Framework directive is the most recent expression of the mutual notification principle that goes back to the mid-1960s (chapter 3).

As of June 2006, out of a total of over 410 notifications, the Commission had used its "veto" in only a handful of cases.[46] In some cases the Commission's objections led to significant changes to the proposed national regulatory measures, while in others they were ignored.[47]

Markets as Constructs and Competitiveness as an Argument against Regulation

The Commission's recommendation on relevant markets—setting out the markets that may warrant regulatory intervention and, equally, the markets that do not—was highly contested. The definition of markets is crucial. The narrower the relevant market, the more likely it is to identify market dominance triggering sector-specific regulation.

The definition of the nascent broadband market was among the most controversial ones. As mentioned, the promotion of competition in access networks as a means to accelerate the rollout of broadband internet services was a top political priority and led to the unprecedented step of a Regulation on local loop unbundling. However, competition was not forthcoming. Practical difficulties with the implementation of local loop unbundling, coupled with the financial crisis of the telecommunications and internet sectors following the burst of the technology bubble, meant that there was a real risk incumbent operators would end up re-monopolizing the local market, and, crucially, the emerging broadband and internet access segments. It is indicative that, in June 2002, one and a half years after the introduction of the Regulation, 80 to 90 percent of almost six million DSL connections in the EU were offered by incumbent telecommunications operators.[48] They were the main and, in countries with no cable television infrastructure the sole, investors in and providers of broadband communications. The Regulation required dominant operators to provide access to their local loop on the basis of full unbundling (competitors lease the access network from the incumbent and upgrade it to provide broadband services to end users) and shared access (the incumbent provides basic telephony and competitors offer broadband services using their own DSL technology). At issue now was a third form of access called bitstream, which had originally been proposed but rejected from the final Regulation. This form of access allows competitors to interconnect with the incumbent's broadband network and is therefore a fast and economical way to provide broadband access to consumers.

During the consultation on relevant markets in 2002, two camps were formed. On the one side, incumbent operators and their association ETNO (European Telecommunications Network Operators' association) opposed regulation of the nascent broadband market, arguing that intervention would stifle innovation and market growth and remove investment incentives. For ETNO, new markets and technologies did not require regulation. Incumbent operators were against both the identification of a distinct market for bitstream access and its inclusion as part of a broader market for "unbundled local access."[49] They urged policy-makers to focus their attention on competition across, rather than within, technological platforms and argued for a broad definition of the broadband access market, one that would include all relevant access technologies and not just DSL, in which they were dominant. If this wider definition was accepted, it was likely that national regulators would conclude that the market was competitive and as such there was no need for regulation. If national regulators concluded that the market was insufficiently competitive, incumbent operators stood a good chance to be found as not possessing significant market power and so again would be left unregulated. Equipment manufacturers, fearing they too would stand to lose if investment were to freeze, joined incumbent operators in their "high-level lobbying" efforts.[50]

On the opposite side, new market entrants and their association ECTA (European Competitive Telecommunications Association) called for a distinct market for "wholesale bitstream access" and not for it to be identified as a segment under a broader market since national regulators were not legally required to examine, and in turn regulate, any subsegments. For precisely the same reason, the grouping of national regulators, IRG, supported a distinct market for wholesale bitstream access. INTUG too, representing corporate users, supported this camp. A separate market, similarly to established practice in voice and data network interconnection, would allow broadband interconnection (bitstream access) under regulated terms.

The divisions within the industry mirrored similar divisions within the Commission.[51] At stake was which department should assume primary responsibility for the telecommunications sector. Commissioner for competition Mario Monti was against the very idea of listing relevant markets for fear that that would impede the application of competition law. He was also concerned that the DG Information Society, in line with past practice, was prepared to adopt the argument of dominant fixed operators calling for a broad definition of the broadband market, which most likely would leave them unregulated.

The adopted Recommendation on relevant markets identifies "wholesale unbundled access" and "wholesale broadband market" (bitstream access) as two distinct markets, in line with the wishes of the second camp.

The view of ETNO, representing primarily former state-owned telecommunications operators, that regulation of the nascent broadband market would adversely affect innovation and competitiveness, is a well-rehearsed argument in the history of communication policy and one that has been repeated by several interests in both telecommunications and the digital television sectors, as will be seen.

In 2005, ETNO urged the EU and national regulators to rethink regulation.[52] The existing regulatory model, it argued, containing obligations such as mandated access and resale—under which competitors get access to incumbents' networks—was designed to kick-start competition in previously monopolistic telecommunications markets. New technologies require new regulation. With the move toward next generation networks (such as optic fiber and IP networks), ETNO explains, a regulatory approach concerned with reducing the market share of incumbents is no longer sustainable since it provides no incentives for innovation and investment. These require the relaxation of existing obligations. Effectively, incumbent operators argue that they are prepared to invest in new technologies provided monopolies are re-established, at least temporarily, and competitors are not allowed to benefit from such investment. ETNO emphasizes the high political and economic stakes:

> The role of telecommunications operators goes far beyond the mere provision of networks and services. Through their investment in tomorrow's networks and infrastructures, ETNO members directly contribute to Europe's growth.[53]

The most recent expression of this argument comes from Germany, where Deutsche Telekom, the largest operator in the EU, plans to invest US$3.5 billion to roll out a new broadband network provided it is exempted from regulation—including the obligation to share it with rivals—for an initial period of five years. Failure to invest, Deutsche Telekom warned, would mean that the country's infrastructure would fall behind, putting 5,000 jobs—on top of a planned 32,000 cuts—at stake.[54] The plan has provoked a powerful reaction from Telekom's rivals and the European Commission which, following repeated warnings, eventually in February 2007 launched infringement proceedings against Germany.[55] The Commission has confirmed its opposition to so-called regulatory holidays (an initial period of no regulation to encourage investment in new network infrastructure) in the review of the 2002 electronic communications regulatory framework launched in June 2006.

New Regulatory Committees

The 2002 regulatory framework relies on a number of committees and working groups in order to align national regulatory responses and induce greater harmonization. Table 6.2 summarizes the main ones. These are examined in turn.

Radio Spectrum Policy Group

Due to its cross-border nature, the radio spectrum is an ideal domain for European-level regulation.[56] The industry strongly supported the proposal in the 1999 communications review for an EU policy experts' group

Table 6.2. Main EU Regulatory Committees under the 2002 Regulatory Framework

Radio Spectrum Policy Group (RSPG)
  Coordination body
  Participants: European Commission (Secretariat) and high level policy experts from
    member states (ministries and regulatory authorities). Chair: elected from and by
    members.
  Observers: EU candidate (Croatia and Turkey) and European Economic Area
    countries (Iceland, Liechtenstein, Norway, Switzerland), the European Parliament,
    the European Conference of Postal and Telecommunications administrations
    (CEPT) and the European Telecommunications Standards Institute (ETSI)
  Role: Advisory. Aims to coordinate use of radio spectrum

European Regulators' Group (ERG)
  Coordination body
  Participants: European Commission (Secretariat) and Heads of EU national regulatory
    authorities. Chair: elected from and by members.
  Observers: EU candidate and European Economic Area countries
  Role: Advisory. Aims to promote consistency in regulation across the EU

Communications Committee (CoCom)
  Comitology committee
  Participants: European Commission (Chair and Secretariat) and member states'
    representatives (ministries and regulatory authorities).
  Observers: same as for the ERG
  Role: advisory and regulatory concerning the implementation of harmonization
    directives (table 6.1 above)

Radio Spectrum Committee (RSC)
  Comitology committee
  Participants and Observers: same as for the Communications Committee
  Role: advisory and regulatory concerning technical implementation issues related to
    radio spectrum; develops common external radio spectrum policy

Source: Adapted from http://europa.eu.int/information_society/policy/ecomm/committees_working_
  groups/index_en.htm (4 January 2007).

having a forward-looking strategic orientation.[57] However, there was fierce opposition from national governments. Indeed, radio spectrum was one of the first elements that member states removed from the proposed transparency mechanism, in effect keeping radio spectrum as a national policy domain.

The Radio Spectrum Policy Group (RSPG) was established in 2002.[58] It advises the Commission on strategic radio spectrum matters and to this end it may adopt so-called Opinions. Based on the Group's advice, the Commission may consider whether there is a need for European action and request the comitology Radio Spectrum Committee (see below) to adopt technical implementing measures and the Europe-wide body of telecommunications regulators, CEPT, to provide specific technical expertise. In contrast to the "problem-solving" perspective of these two last bodies that address practical, operational and technical issues, the

> RSPG aims at considering the wider policy context, taking into account in an EU perspective long-term factors such as political priorities, societal needs, future technological developments and market evolution.[59]

The RSPG has ushered in a new era of cooperation between the European Commission and member states over radio spectrum policy and strategic matters. It is a unique forum comprising high-ranking national experts and a high level Commission representative with no voting rights. Similarly to the European Regulators' Group, the RSPG adopts an annual work program indicating the issues it will deal with and on which it may adopt Opinions. It carries out consultations and public hearings where interested parties can comment on its plans.[60]

European Regulators' Group

The creation of the European Regulators' Group (ERG) in 2002 was the result of the compromise following the rejection of the proposed High Level Communications Group. However, the consensus on the need to create a group of national telecommunications regulators within the EU structures was quickly overshadowed by the politically controversial question about its membership. Of particular concern, especially to established regulatory bodies, was the lack of definition of "independent regulatory authority" in the Commission decision establishing the ERG except to note, in line with the World Trade Organization's requirements, that the authority had to be separate from any electronic communications supplier.[61]

Membership in the ERG and independence of national regulatory authorities became two very contentious issues. Concerns about the "independence" of some national regulatory bodies had already been voiced during the 1999 communications review by, among other entities, the European Commission and the U.S. government.[62] Although such concerns were not new, the updated EU electronic communications framework granting national regulators new flexible powers in the areas of market definitions, competition tests and the need or not for regulatory intervention, brought into sharper focus their independence and accountability. Not all authorities in the existing fifteen member states, let alone in the imminent (May 2004) enlarged EU of twenty-five member states, could be characterized as independent, while in some countries national ministries were responsible for certain regulatory tasks under the EU framework and so this could be interpreted as a call for ministries to participate, which would politicize the process.[63] It was for this lack of clarification about what an independent regulator was that, at least initially, the informal regulators' group IRG carried on alongside the ERG. Rather than consolidating the two groups into one, the IRG would continue to function outside the EU structures as a safety net against possible intrusions by national governments, ministries and the European Commission, which could compromise the independence of national regulators.

It was in 2004, just over two years after ERG's creation, that the issue of membership was resolved with a new Commission Decision which clarified that the ERG would comprise the heads of independent regulatory authorities with primary responsibility for overseeing the day-to-day operation of the electronic communications market.[64] It added that there would be only one member per country and it listed the recognized regulatory body for each, as notified by the member states, in its Annex.

The ERG is "a body for reflection, debate and advice for the Commission in the electronic communications field."[65] Its main objective is to facilitate the exchange of views and experiences, and encourage cooperation and coordination between national regulators in order to enhance harmonization and promote consistent interpretation and application of the EU regulatory framework.

The ERG regularly carries out consultations on its proposed work program and draft decisions.[66] The European Commission is represented at all meetings and provides the Secretariat but has no vote. Most of the detailed work is done by working groups and ad hoc project teams. The ERG deals with detailed practical matters. It adopts positions (upon its own initiative) and opinions (upon request by the Commission or a third party) by consensus or, if that is not feasible, by a two-thirds majority.[67]

One of the most important achievements of the ERG is the common position on remedies, agreed upon in April 2004.[68] While allowing for flexibility to accommodate national circumstances, it offers guidance and aims at promoting consistent application of remedies across the EU. This is a particularly important policy document since, as noted, the European Commission has no veto powers over remedies.

Comitology Committees

The Communications Committee (CoCom) is a standard comitology committee that has replaced the Open Network Provision and the Licensing Committees under the former 1998 regulatory framework. Being a comitology committee, CoCom assists the European Commission in carrying out its delegated executive implementation powers. It also acts as a platform for sharing information on market developments and regulatory activities in individual countries. In turn, this exchange contributes to the establishment of best practice models.

The Radio Spectrum Committee (RSC) is another comitology committee.[69] It assists the Commission in the development and adoption of technical implementation measures aimed at ensuring harmonized conditions for the availability and efficient use of radio spectrum, and facilitates the exchange of information concerning radio spectrum use.

Implementation of the 2002 Regulatory Framework

The 2002 EU regulatory framework for electronic communications is a key contributor to achieving the Lisbon goal of competitiveness. From the start, the Commission took a rigorous approach regarding its implementation. In October 2003, two months after the deadline for incorporation of the EU framework into national legislation, the Commission opened infringement proceedings against eight member states for failure to notify about transposition measures.[70] As of December 2006, the Commission had initiated over 100 infringement proceedings against twenty-three member states, that is, all except Denmark and Ireland.[71] In 2005, the European Court of Justice ruled against Belgium, Greece, France and Luxembourg for failing to fulfill their obligations under the new regulatory framework.

According to the latest (eleventh) implementation report, the Commission was overall satisfied that most of the necessary work had been completed, although several member states had concluded only a part of the market reviews.[72] There was evidence of intensifying competition which, in turn, had resulted in innovation, investment and consumer benefits, notably lower prices. With regard to market developments, in October 2005 the EU average of mobile and internet penetration was 93 and 47 percent respectively. Broadband penetration reached 11.5 percent, up from 7.4 percent the previous year, with new market entrants overall controlling half the market. But of course there were significant divergences between countries,

ranging from a 25 percent incumbent market share in Britain to 100 percent in Cyprus.[73] Network-based competition was still weak, with just 8.3
percent of EU subscribers benefiting from it. This reflected the stronghold
of incumbent operators in the local access market. In countries with high
cable TV penetration, notably Britain and Denmark, competition was much
stronger. The Commission identified three major bottlenecks: local loop
unbundling, cost-oriented interconnection and cost accounting.

Regarding the independence of national regulatory authorities, concerns
persisted about the separation of ownership and regulatory functions (in
Belgium, Cyprus, Hungary, Slovakia and Slovenia), their political independence (in Poland, Malta, Slovakia and Slovenia), and limitations on their
powers (as in Ireland, Malta and the Netherlands).

The Rise of Policy Coordination Mechanisms: An Assessment

Whereas the 1998 regulatory package aimed at assisting the progressive
opening up of telecommunications markets, the 2002 regulatory package is
designed to cater for a fully liberalized and technologically convergent market environment. As such, it contains the fundamentals and avoids being
prescriptive. Prescriptive harmonization under the former framework
turned out to be too complicated, undesirable and above all unrealistic. Besides, the imminent enlargement of the EU in May 2004 toward Central
and Eastern Europe and the consequent increase in diversity militated
against rigid regulatory measures.

The 2002 framework aims to harmonize regulation across the EU
through greater reliance on competition rules, the establishment of basic
principles and general objectives and new procedures institutionalizing the
relationship between the European Commission and national regulators.
Even though it did not get the increased powers it sought, the Commission
has been strengthened by the mere fact that the new framework views regulatory intervention as the exception and relies heavily on competition law,
an area where the Commission enjoys strong competence. This is a case
where less is more. Greater emphasis on competition, as opposed to sector-
specific, rules is a backward way to achieve harmonization.[74]

Still, the 2002 regulatory package grants national regulators new flexible
powers in the fields of market definitions, competition reviews and the imposition or not of regulatory measures. On the one hand, this flexibility risks diluting harmonization since the new framework allows for the accommodation
of, and thus accepts, national diversity. But on the other hand, it permits national policy-makers to tailor regulation to the specific circumstances of their
countries, and effective national regulation can help increase the credibility
and acceptability of the EU. Indeed, the consensus following the 1999 review

was that regulation should be carried out as close to the market as possible, and national regulators are best placed to achieve this.

The new framework has left the duality between the EU and national levels intact. The Commission seeks to enhance regulatory consistency across member states by defining markets at the European level and then overseeing, by means of formal and informal mechanisms, national regulators regulating them on the basis of common guidelines.

More specifically, the notification procedure of draft regulatory measures and the European Regulators' Group (ERG), bringing together the national regulators of the member states, are the two principal formal means to increase regulatory consistency. Both mechanisms establish, for the first time, institutionalized procedures for consultation and cooperation among national regulators and between them and the Commission. The Commission is now formally involved in the implementation of the EU regulatory framework at the national level. It interacts with and, to an extent, regulates national regulators. Equally, the national regulators' involvement in the elaboration of the EU framework has been formalized. They are now in a stronger position to influence regulation at the European level. However, the ERG's ability to foster harmonization on the ground is questionable since it cannot take legally binding decisions but primarily assumes a coordinating role. The ERG is an example of "policy-making without legislating."[75] The aim is that best practice models and common positions adopted by the ERG will be "self-binding" through peer-pressure.[76]

In addition to the formal mechanisms just mentioned, the Commission relies on an array of soft non-binding measures in order to promote harmonization and efficient implementation of the EU rules, such as recommendations, guidelines, benchmarking of best practice and regular monitoring through comparative implementation reports (table 6.1). Of course, if all else fails, the Commission may still decide to resort to its strong competition powers and take action against a national regulatory authority's definition of markets or determination of operators with significant market power, or launch a formal infringement procedure before the European Court.

In short, the EU has moved away from legislation-driven harmonization to harmonization through soft governance mechanisms and transnational regulatory committees. This reassessment of governance instruments under the 2002 regulatory package reflects wider trends.

First, the readjustment of policy instruments at the European level mirrors a parallel readjustment within member states where there is a growing tendency to rely on self-regulation of the industry and co-regulation, that is, formal cooperation between self-regulating bodies and public authorities.[77] In turn, this is part of the broader trend of the transformation of statehood and the concomitant shifts from government to governance and from a positive interventionist toward a regulatory state, analyzed in chapter 1.

Second, ever since the 1992 deadline for the internal market, the EU has been forced, in the face of criticisms and inefficiencies, to rethink both the process of EU policy-making and its implementation by member states. With regard to policy-making, there is now greater emphasis on consultations, streamlining and simplification of legislation, while to improve implementation, the Commission increasingly uses new mechanisms such as the open method of coordination, mentioned above, benchmarks and scoreboards. This new mode of governance is in accordance with the ideas put forward in the 2001 White Paper on European Governance and the "better regulation" initiative that aims to ensure that the industry is not overburdened with regulation and which, among other things, calls for regulatory impact assessments, less reliance on formal legislation and greater use of alternative regulatory mechanisms.[78] Unsurprisingly, business interests had long advocated these principles.[79] But in the late 1990s and early 2000s a renewed drive for "better regulation" came from some member states, notably Britain, which has been at the forefront of regulatory innovation, and the formal adoption of economic competitiveness as the key EU strategic goal at the Lisbon summit in March 2000, the underlying assumption being that regulatory intervention may adversely affect the ultimate goal of international competitiveness.[80] "Better regulation" has subsequently become a key tenet of the redefined "growth and jobs" Lisbon agenda.[81]

In recent years, the EU has come to rely on soft-law arrangements in several fields.[82] Soft, unlike binding and restrictive, measures have allowed the Commission to intervene in such politically sensitive and nationally protected areas as macroeconomic policies, where the open method of coordination was inaugurated in 1992 with the Maastricht Treaty and the so-called Broad Economic Policy Guidelines.

Although soft governance mechanisms indicate political consensus, the uncertainty surrounding their legal status, coupled with the lack of sanctions for non-implementation, undermines their potential to enhance harmonization. Informal governance measures and regulatory committees may induce convergence in national regulatory responses indirectly through, for instance, processes of socialization and mutual policy learning. As Wallace remarks, soft governance instruments

are geared towards changes in attitudes and behaviour—implicit convergence rather than explicit, co-ordination rather than common templates. [. . .] To express this in institutional shorthand, a kind of OECD (Organization for Economic Co-operation and Development) technique is being imported into the EU arena.[83]

Hence, though they frame and shape the discretion enjoyed by national regulators, it is likely that informal governance arrangements will promote policy coordination rather than strict policy convergence, which includes common policy objectives, content, instruments, style and ultimately outcomes.[84] Of course, this is not a problem in itself but in the context of the functioning of the internal market it may well be.

Besides, the fact that policy transfer increasingly takes place through specialist interaction in various regulatory committees and networks aggravates transparency and legitimacy problems and does not promote input legitimacy and deliberative democracy.[85] In particular, the heavy reliance of soft policy coordination processes on technical and expert knowledge risks stripping policies from their political, institutional, economic and social context. These newer informal techniques of governance, for example best practice models, promote a functionalist discourse and depoliticize policy choices. The underlying assumption is that all actors face identical external constraints and challenges, and actors' behavior will voluntarily alter under such similarly understood conditions.[86] In short, there are serious questions not only about the effectiveness but also, and more importantly, about the democratic potential and legitimacy of newer informal governance modes.

The first set of problems—policy effectiveness and potential to promote harmonization—is at the center of the review of the 2002 regulatory framework for electronic communications launched in June 2006.[87] The Commission is expected to present formal legislative proposals in October 2007. The revised recommendation on relevant markets will have immediate effect, whereas national implementation of the new framework is planned for around 2010.

More specifically, although the notification procedure has improved harmonization in the areas of market definitions and assessment of market power, for the Commission, the level of regulatory consistency across the EU remains unsatisfactory.[88] The Commission alleges that in many cases regulatory action at the national level is inefficient or seriously delayed in addressing the problem(s) at hand, and that often national regulators have addressed similar issues in strikingly different ways. The reluctance of the national regulator in Germany, mentioned above, to allow competitors to access Deutsche Telekom's planned broadband network, in which company the government holds a 32 percent stake, is a case in point. The business community, the European consumers' organization and new market entrants but also incumbent operators with cross-border activities, all share the Commission's strong dissatisfaction with widely diverging national regulatory practices and inadequate enforcement.[89]

In response, the Commission has proposed the creation of a European Federal Communications Commission, a pan-European regulatory agency that would not replace national regulators but rather would have powers over so-called remedies, that is, regulatory measures that address market failures. Another proposal is that the Commission's powers be extended to cover remedies so that it can ask for a proposed national regulatory measure to be replaced with a more effective one or that a measure be adopted within a specific timeframe.[90] The Commission's own impact assessment report supports the less far-reaching second option, that is, veto powers on selective areas such as access, interconnection and interoperability of services. It is worth remembering that both proposals—pan-European regulator and Commission veto of remedies—were rejected during the 1999 review.

In October 2006 the ERG, the transnational committee of regulators, in a defensive response to prevent the creation of a pan-European regulatory agency, proposed to step up its benchmarking activities. Arguing that rapid dissemination of best practice is "the correct route" to enhance consistency, the ERG went on to single out priority areas for targeted harmonization, in particular broadband access; services with a pan-European potential, including next generation services such as Voice over Internet Protocol; and services with a significant cross-border dimension, such as international roaming.[91] In yet another effort to increase its potential as a mechanism for policy coordination, the ERG announced the establishment of a permanent secretariat in Brussels. It seems that the ERG is transforming from being a source of expertise to becoming an agent for increased harmonization. The interesting point here is that, in this case, "the shadow of hierarchy," the threat of new EU legislative powers and institutional structures (Commission veto of remedies and a pan-European regulatory authority) resulted in the improvement of existing soft governance mechanisms. This development confirms Héritier's conclusion regarding the Florence Energy Forum and underlines the interrelationship between old hierarchical and newer soft modes of governance.[92]

In February 2007, in a joint statement with Information Society and Media Commissioner Viviane Reding, the ERG declared the intention of national regulators to increase cooperation with the European Commission. Both parties agreed to examine various options, including an enhanced role for the ERG in the European regulatory and legislative processes, the strengthening of the Commission's powers and "the transformation of the ERG into a 'federal system' of National Regulators."[93]

In addition to a pan-European regulator, the Commission has also called for the creation of a European agency for managing aspects of the radio spectrum in order to assist the shift of spectrum management away from the traditional rigid administrative model toward a market-oriented system, examined below. Nevertheless, the Commission's impact assessment report favors better coordination through the existing committee mechanisms rather than the formation of a new institution.[94]

Another contentious issue in the review of the 2002 regulatory framework for electronic communications is the proposal to reduce the markets identified for potential regulatory intervention from eighteen to twelve.[95] In particular, the Commission suggests that regulation should concentrate on the wholesale side, where competition is still inadequate. It considers that retail competition has grown faster and, accordingly, proposes the removal of five retail markets.[96] Regarding the wholesale side, the Commission is seeking comments on whether the markets for access and call origination on public mobile telephone networks (market 15) and for broadcasting transmission services (market 18) should be removed. The Commission also plans to remove the wholesale market for international roaming (market 17) upon the adoption of the EU regulation on roaming.[97]

The regulation of roaming, the fees mobile phone operators charge customers who use their phones in another EU country, has been a highly controversial issue. Unsurprisingly, the mobile phone industry—that has only recently been the subject of regulatory intervention and has significantly suffered following the high prices paid at third generation mobile auctions —strongly resists such regulation and argues that this proposal contradicts the Commission's call for regulatory action to concentrate on the wholesale level and is potentially "damaging" for the competitiveness of the industry and, by extension, of the EU.[98] To ward off the threat of regulation, the industry has acted to reduce roaming fees, but for both residential and, in particular, corporate users these reductions are inadequate.[99] It seems that the question is not whether but rather how to regulate international roaming. The political agreement reached at the informal Telecommunications Council meeting in Hannover in March 2007 makes it likely for the proposed EU law to be approved in June and enter into force about a month later.

Finally, another issue associated with the revision of the recommendation on relevant markets is the proposal to simplify the notification requirements for markets which had been found competitive in the first review and introduce a simplified procedure for minor changes to a previous notification. These proposals will reduce the administrative burden at European and national levels.

HORIZONTAL INITIATIVES
AND THE REGULATION OF BROADCASTING

The move toward horizontal regulation, evident in the 2002 electronic communications framework, is part of the "better regulation" initiative aiming to simplify and streamline EU legislation. Horizontal regulatory measures are not sector-specific but cross-sectoral, covering a group of similar economic activities. They typically establish main principles rather than prescriptive rules. In the early 2000s, two major wide-ranging horizontal regulatory initiatives touched on the sectors of telecommunications and television. The first concerned services of general (economic) interest, the EU term for public services. The second had wider scope, covering all economic activities involving services. Concurrently, there has been a move toward a horizontal regulatory approach within the audiovisual sector. As part of the second review of the television directive, the EU has tried to move toward horizontal regulation of audiovisual, not just television, content in the digital multimedia era. In addition, general competition rules, and in what interests us state aid rules, have become increasingly important, strengthening the shift away from sector-specific toward sector-neutral regulation. All these developments are examined in turn.

Services of General (Economic) Interest

Following the explicit recognition of the importance of so-called services of general economic interest in the second part of the 1990s, discussed in the previous chapter, in May 2003 the Commission published a Green Paper launching a wide-ranging debate on the definition and objectives of such services.[100] The Commission was seeking support to pursue a horizontal regulatory approach in relation to all services of general interest.

Again, the Green Paper and the subsequent communication made strong and repeated references to the link between services of general interest and a "European model of society" especially in the context of globalization and international trade agreements.[101] Services of general interest "are part of the values shared by all European societies," they "increas[e] quality of life for all citizens," they are "a factor for competitiveness and greater cohesion," "a pillar for European citizenship," and they "help individuals to make effective use of their fundamental rights."[102]

Although the consultation was about services of general interest (e.g., social services, public education) it was important for services of general economic interest too—including telecommunications and television—because part of the exercise was to clarify these two concepts. Nevertheless, the result was greater confusion.

The Commission avoided the term "public service" because that was often associated with the ownership or status of the service provider. For the Commission, the issue was of substance, not ownership, that is, the actual services being provided. By implication, public service obligations—for instance, universal service in telecommunications and public service broadcasting—may be entrusted to either public or private entities. The Commission explained that the term "services of general interest" is broader than the term "services of general economic interest" and covers both market and non-market services which the public authorities class as being of general interest and subject to specific public service obligations. [. . . Services of general economic interest are] services of an economic nature which the Member States or the Community subject to specific public service obligations by virtue of a general interest criterion. [They cover . . .] in particular certain services provided by the big network industries such as transport, postal services, energy and communications.[103]

Putting aside the definitional problems, the Commission tried to analyze services of general interest on the basis of common values and objectives, including universal service (accessibility), continuity (uninterrupted provision), quality of service, affordability and consumer protection. It invited comments as to whether other sector-specific obligations that were in the general interest could be added to a common set of public service obligations, such as network access and interconnectivity, and media pluralism. The latter, however, similar to the 1994 Bangemann report, was interpreted to mean open market structures and proliferation of media outlets rather than diversity of content reflecting a wide range of social, political and cultural values, opinions, information and interests.

Both public service broadcasters and commercial interests opposed the horizontal regulatory treatment of services of general (economic) interest, albeit for different reasons.[104] Public service broadcasters argued for the exclusion of the audiovisual sector from any horizontal regulatory proposals on the ground that its specificity—that is, its important democratic, social and cultural characteristics—warranted against its treatment as an ordinary sector.[105] They were concerned that under horizontal rules, internal market considerations would take precedence over media and cultural policy objectives and, in turn, national competence in these fields would be undermined.

Whereas public service broadcasters feared that a horizontal framework would undermine the specificity of the audiovisual sector, commercial broadcasters were concerned that a horizontal framework would strengthen its specificity and that, in turn, would hinder the application of competition rules, the only horizontal regulatory framework that commercial broadcasters supported. The Association of Commercial Television broadcasters (ACT) warned:

Calls for greater "recognition" of the "role" played by [services of general economic interest] in delivering "high-quality" services play into the hands of those seeking protection or special treatment from competition law and would seriously undermine the prospects of a dynamic and open services market in Europe. [. . .] the end result of such a recognition could be carte blanche for companies to escape from meaningful scrutiny, and for new distortions to arise.[106]

Similarly, ETNO, the European association representing primarily incumbent telecommunications operators, concerned that the inclusion of telecommunications into a broader regulatory framework would result in more regulation, argued against a horizontal framework.[107]

Overall, the consultation revealed a broad agreement on the essential importance of services of general (economic) interest but opinion significantly diverged on the relationship between such services and market principles. The consensus was that there was no added-value in a horizontal regulatory framework and that the EU should not be given additional powers in that area.

The Services Directive

The second major initiative toward horizontal regulation was a proposal in 2004, prepared by the DG Internal Market, for a directive to cover the entire services sector.[108] Whereas most trade in goods had been liberalized, the same was not true for trade in services, an increasingly important sector for European competitiveness accounting for over 70 percent of jobs. The aim of the proposed directive was to simplify legislation, and eliminate barriers to the freedom of establishment for service providers and the free movement of services across the EU. To effect this, the Commission proposed the blanket application of the "country of origin" principle, under which the recipient country may not restrict services offered by providers established in another member state and has no power over them.

The services directive proposal was one of the most contentious pieces of EU legislation ever encountered. Conflicts concerned primarily the scope of the directive, in particular the extent to which, if at all, public services ("services of general (economic) interest") would be covered; the risk for a competitive race to the bottom, in which service operators would prefer to establish in EU countries with less onerous regulatory frameworks; and associated fears for job losses and low quality standards. We will concentrate on the issues relevant to the audiovisual sector.

The Commission recognized that some services of general economic interest, due to their specific nature, had derogations from the country of origin principle. Indeed, it argued for the exclusion of the telecommunications sector, among other services, from the proposed measure. But with regard to television, the proposed directive would apply in parallel to the sector-specific Television without Frontiers directive. It was not clear, however, which directive would take precedence in the case of a conflict between them. For if the proposed services directive was to take precedence, that would effectively annul sector-specific regulation of the television sector and, by doing so, would reject the associated democratic, social and cultural policy aims. Importantly, the indiscriminate application of the country of origin principle would, in the absence of any substantive harmonization of rules, undermine the competence of member states in politically sensitive areas, such as safeguards for media pluralism and ownership, which had deliberately been left out of the television directive.[109] If, on the other hand, sector-specific regulation was to take precedence, then the purpose of the inclusion of the audiovisual sector in the planned horizontal directive covering all services would be defeated.

For these reasons, the EBU, representing public service broadcasters, and the European Parliament called for the exemption of the audiovisual sector from the scope of the directive and, instead, reliance on the existing sector-specific framework of the television directive.[110] As explained, the latter carefully balances the economic and cultural dimensions of television by endorsing the country of origin principle for specific areas subject to minimum harmonization.

In May 2006, national governments endorsed the revised Commission proposal for a services directive that built on the European Parliament's compromise.[111] In what interests us, the amended proposal specifically excludes telecommunications and audiovisual services. Hence, like the first one, this second attempt to bring these two sectors under a broader horizontal framework and forego any sector-specific rules was defeated.

Toward Horizontal Content Regulation: The Second Review of the Television without Frontiers Directive

In May 2002, the Culture and Audiovisual Affairs Council called for an in-depth review of the television directive, with several national ministers stressing the importance of protecting minors using the internet and video games.[112] Taking into account technological progress, in particular the growth of electronic delivery of content and the emergence of new interactive services, and changes in the structure of the audiovisual market, notably the proliferation of television channels from 50 in 1989 when the directive was first adopted to over 2,000 channels in 2003, the European Parliament supported the review.[113]

Accordingly, the second revision of the television directive was launched in 2003 with the aim to adapt its provisions to the new media environment. In December that year, following the first round of consultations, the Commission proposed a two-step strategy.[114] In the short term, following strong pressure from the advertising industry and commercial broadcasters, in an interpretative communication the Commission found new advertising techniques, such as split-screen and interactive advertising, compatible with the existing regulatory framework provided that they respected the fundamental principles laid down in it, namely clear separation between editorial content and advertising, the integrity of audiovisual works and the viewers' right to protection against excessive advertising.[115] The Commission also announced an update to the Recommendation on the Protection of Minors and Human Dignity to address issues related to online media, including media literacy and the right of reply to the online environment.[116] For the medium term, the consultation revealed that several issues required further debate and could ultimately lead to a revision of the television directive.

The second round of consultations, during 2004–2005, concentrated on six areas: content regulation linked to the scope of the directive, rights to information, cultural diversity and promotion of European and independent audiovisual production, advertising, protection of minors and human dignity and media pluralism.[117]

Similar to the first review completed in 1997, the current review has been highly controversial. At stake is the regulation of audiovisual content, both of traditional television broadcasting and of new interactive audiovisual services. Past battles concerning in particular the balance between liberalization and regulation, and the impact of technological convergence on regulation, are being re-fought. It is indicative that it took more than two years of extensive deliberations for the Commission to finally present in December 2005 its proposal for an amended directive. Following a first reading at the European Parliament and the Council representing national governments, the Commission presented a revised proposal in March 2007. If adopted, national implementation is likely to take place toward the end of the decade.

Toward an Audiovisual Media Services without Frontiers Directive?

The most controversial issue in the current review, especially the second round of consultations, has been the scope of the directive and associated regulatory obligations. More specifically, at issue is whether the directive should continue to cover television content only, and its provisions therefore should be simply updated and clarified, or whether, in the face of technological and market developments, its scope should instead expand beyond television to embrace all audiovisual content services. This second maximum revision scenario may seem premature, but it has to be borne in mind that any new legislative measures will need to be suitable for the post-2007 media environment, by which time it is expected that many new media services will have reached "an importance and an impact similar to television broadcasting services."[118]

On one side, public service broadcasters, their European association the EBU, viewers and listeners' groups and some countries like France and Greece support the pro-expansion camp. For them, the revised directive needs to at least be based on the principles of the existing television directive.[119] These principles include not just internal market objectives but in addition various cultural, social and public interest objectives, such as free access to major events, the promotion of European and independent audiovisual works, protection of minors and public order and protection of consumers. The European Parliament and the EBU have seized the opportunity to argue further that the existing principles should be complemented by new general interest objectives such as cultural diversity, media pluralism, freedom of expression and access to information.[120] The European Parliament, concerned about the growing concentration of media ownership and the implications for pluralism and democracy, has also called for EU-wide rules and specific limits on media ownership, and urged the Commission to monitor media concentration and launch a consultation on this issue. Indeed, in January 2007 the Commission published a working document on media pluralism in which it explains that this notion refers to access to diverse information necessary for full social and political participation, and is thus broader than media ownership.[121] The document reviews the work of other organizations, notably the Council of Europe, promoting media pluralism and contains a survey of media ownership and respective legislation across the EU. The Commission plans to adopt in 2008 indicators for measuring media pluralism which, though not binding, could provide a common framework and assist related European and national efforts.

The main argument put forward by the camp in favor of widening the scope of the directive to cover all audiovisual services is that the aims of content regulation do not change simply because technologies and the consumer devices used to access content change.[122] Audiovisual content will be increasingly available on and accessed through mobile phones and computers rather than traditional television sets. It is for this reason, the argument goes, that some of the rules that apply to traditional television broadcasters need to extend and apply to the new digital broadband media environment. For this camp regulation is not determined by the technology, network or platform used and who provides the service but rather by the content itself. Under this horizontal, platform- and technology-neutral regulatory model, content regulation is based on a graduated approach that takes into account the importance of a service for the formation of public opinion and the degree of user choice and control. News content, for example, will be regulated more strictly on all platforms than entertainment services. Graduated regulation can take different forms, including co- and self-regulatory arrangements which can apply to different categories of services. For the EBU and public service broadcasters the extension of content regulation beyond traditional television services based on a graduated approach is a matter of modernization and survival. Without content regulation, public service broadcasting will cease to exist.

On the other side, commercial broadcasters, publishers, some regulators, telecommunications operators, internet service providers, new media interests and business organizations (like the Confederation of British Industry) argue not only against a widening of the scope of the directive, which may result in traditionally prescriptive television-type regulation being extended to new media and internet content, but also for greater relaxation of the existing rules. Taking advantage of the political saliency of broadband and the information society, this camp argues that any expansion of the scope of the directive will create uncertainty, discourage innovation and inhibit market growth. For ETNO, for instance, representing mainly former state-owned telecommunications operators, such a scenario would adversely affect the development of the emerging broadband market, putting Europe's economic future at serious risk.[123] For others, mainly U.S. internet companies such as Google, the proposed rules for online content would restrict free speech.[124]

Overall, those opposing the extension of the scope of the directive beyond traditional television content put forward three arguments. First, they maintain that there is no need for such an extension since "on demand" services are already regulated as "information society services" under the electronic commerce directive.[125] The latter covers a wide variety of electronic communication and online services upon individual request, such as online newspapers, specialized news services and online provision of financial services. It lays down a light touch regulatory framework, effectively freeing information society services from regulation, allowing for their free movement within the EU. Only for public policy reasons, including the protection of consumers and minors, can a member state restrict the provision of and access to such on-demand services. In response, the pro-expansion camp maintains that the electronic commerce directive is grounded on purely economic, not cultural, social and democratic principles and, therefore, the proposed audiovisual media directive complements rather than contradicts it.[126] Second, for the against-expansion camp, the television directive is primarily an internal market measure and should remain as such. It points out the absence of a legitimacy base for EU-wide rules on culture and content and emphasizes that, under the subsidiarity principle, both come under the sole competence of member states. In the words of the Association of Commercial Television broadcasters "the focus has shifted from the original purpose of the directive, to facilitate an internal market in broadcast services through minimum harmonisation, towards a tool which regulates content per se."[127] Third, the against-expansion camp maintains that alternative regulatory mechanisms (carried out by private actors alone or in cooperation with public authorities, such as self- and co-regulation repsesctively) and individual control and responsibility (for example, through content filters and content rating systems) afford adequate protection for online content. Indeed, failing to outright prevent the expansion of the scope in the proposed directive, the against-expansion camp attempts to minimize its impact by calling for greater reliance on alternative forms of regulation.[128] Britain, where these forms are well established, has been a strong proponent of alternative regulation and has insisted that the envisaged EU legislation clarify that member states are allowed to use co- and self-regulatory arrangements, if they so wish, in order to implement general public interest goals.

Under the draft directive presented in December 2005, the European Commission proposed to expand its scope to cover all audiovisual media services.[129] The draft directive did not cover radio, private communication such as emails, and in general services whose principal purpose was not to provide audiovisual content. The proposed directive planned to base content regulation on a distinction between "linear" and "non-linear" services. The distinction is based on user choice and control, and impact on society.[130] Linear audiovisual services cover scheduled services for which the user does not control the timing of transmission, essentially television broadcasting. Non-linear services refer to non-scheduled on-demand media services.

The Commission proposed that a basic set of mostly negative rules— including the separation of advertising from editorial content, protection of minors, prohibition of incitement to hatred, controls on alcohol and tobacco advertising—apply to all audiovisual services, both scheduled and on-demand. In addition to this set of basic requirements for all audiovisual content, scheduled services would also be subject to further controls (positive regulatory requirements) similar to those that already applied to television broadcasters, such as free-at-the-point-of-use access to major events and quotas on European and independently-produced programming.

For the pro-expansion camp, the distinction between linear/non-linear services is in line with a graduated approach to content regulation. Crucially, for the EBU the basic set of regulatory principles that would apply to non-linear services under the proposed directive is also a matter of consistency between the internal market and external trade policy and, we might add, in line with the UNESCO convention on cultural diversity of 2005 in which Europe played a leading role and which upholds public policy and strengthens the case for "cultural exception." The absence of regulation, the EBU explains, would make difficult to justify the exclusion of audiovisual services from international trade liberalization commitments (WTO GATS).[131]

The against-expansion camp emphatically opposes the linear/non-linear distinction as artificial and thus unworkable. Britain, the most vigorous opponent, has launched a scathing and very public attack against the Commission's plans.[132] It leads the against-expansion camp with the support, among other countries, of the Netherlands, Hungary, Estonia and Slovakia. For Britain, "the identification of some media services as 'television-like,' may lead some to conclude that eventually 'like-services,' should be regulated in a 'like-manner.'"[133] Fearing that the wording in the 2005 Commission proposal was too wide and vague and could therefore be interpreted to include various internet type services, including mobile multimedia and online games, Britain commissioned its own regulatory impact assessment study, which concluded that the envisaged onerous regulatory framework would force the new media industry, which is strategic for Europe's growth and competitiveness, to move overseas.[134] Consequently, the new media environment requires no regulation. In the words of the British Minister for Creative Industries and Tourism:

> We need more liberalisation. I am totally in favour of regulation so long as it is self-regulation and it should only be state regulation when self-regulation cannot work, by and large because I think the experts are better at regulating themselves.[135]

Ironically, at a time when civil society groups were claiming that the domestic British consultation had been biased in favor of large economic commercial interests, such as telecommunications and internet service providers, for the British government and new media interests the Commission's proposal and consultation process, even the Liverpool audiovisual conference, aptly titled "Between Culture and Commerce" and organized by the British presidency of the EU in the second half of 2005, had all been biased in favor of traditional broadcasters, largely overlooking the views of the emerging new media industry, such as the telecommunications and software industries and game developers.[136] For the British government and new media interests, the proposed directive aims

> to protect those with established market positions from threats by new market entrants operating under different business models.[137]

This is the first time that such an allegation has been voiced against the Commission. As seen in previous chapters, it has been the public service broadcasting/culture camp who claim that the EU communication policy output neglects their needs and promotes the interests of telecommunications/internet operators and manufacturers. It appears that the internal reorganization of the Commission in 2005—when Commissioner Reding moved from the DG Education and Culture to head the much more powerful DG Information Society with an expanded remit that now included the media portfolio and was renamed DG Information Society and Media —may have provided more opportunities for the (public service) broadcasting camp to influence the policy debate. Still, the responses to the Commission's consultations do not reveal any bias. It is just that whereas before content and cultural issues were being discussed primarily in non-EU arenas, notably the Council of Europe, now such issues have gained greater prominence in the EU policy debate. The evidence is still circumstantial, but the post–Cold War context, the accession of a large number of ex-communist countries to the EU interested in the role of the media in promoting democracy and the internal re-organization of the Commission all seem to have strengthened ongoing efforts by the Commission—intensified following the rejection of the Constitutional Treaty in May and June 2005 in referenda in France and the Netherlands respectively—to bring the EU closer to the people and to give it a social, cultural and democratic, not just an economic, dimension.[138]

Besides fears that it could result in the regulation of new services, the against-expansion camp also maintains that the distinction is artificial and most likely to be obsolete by the end of the decade, when the new directive is expected to come into force.

In December 2006, the European Parliament adopted the report of the committee on culture and education—the leading but not a significant committee in the Parliament—putting forward several amendments.[139] The Parliament's position closely resembles the general approach of the Council, representing the national governments, endorsed in November 2006.[140] Based on these amendments, the Commission's revised proposal of March 2007 tightens the scope of the directive to audiovisual media services provided under the editorial responsibility of a media service provider, the principal purpose of which is the provision of "programmes" consisting of moving images to the general public over electronic communications networks, for instance on-demand content such as films, sports events and entertainment shows. It covers primarily economic activities, thereby excluding private websites (blogs) and communication (emails), websites for the sharing and exchange of user-generated content (e.g., YouTube) and services where audiovisual content is merely incidental to the service (e.g., online games, gambling sites, search engines).[141] The proposed directive explicitly excludes the electronic press, audio transmission and radio services. Britain remains dissatisfied with the new proposal and is concerned that the Commission is only required to produce an impact assessment report upon publication of its initial legislative proposal and believes that another impact assessment study on the revised proposal is required, hoping that this will recommend greater deregulation.[142]

Under the revised proposal of March 2007, the two-tier approach to regulation remains intact, with scheduled services to be regulated more than on-demand services. The proposal, similar to the original television directive, tries to strike a balance between the economic internal market principle of country of origin regulation on the basis of minimal harmonization and certain general public objectives "such as cultural diversity, the right to information, the importance of media pluralism, the protection of minors and consumer protection and action to enhance public awareness and media skills."[143] It encourages member states to implement the provisions of the directive through co- and self-regulatory arrangements, the first ever EU legislative proposal to do so.

Other Provisions

Jurisdiction

One of the justifications for considering the inclusion of online services in the revised television directive was to strengthen the country of origin principle, the cornerstone of all internal market legislation, according to which providers active in more than one EU country are only subject to the law of the EU country of establishment. It was perceived that the electronic commerce directive, with the exceptions it allowed for public interest concerns, had weakened the country of origin principle and had resulted in additional national rules and greater fragmentation. But ironically, the proposed audiovisual media services directive served to open the debate on the very question of jurisdiction.

Various member states—in particular small ones with large same language neighbors—concerned that the internal market had weakened their regulatory control over the domestic audiovisual environment, seized the opportunity and the momentum that the concurrent services directive, mentioned above, had created, to question the country of origin principle. Indeed, they have been instrumental in diluting it, against the strong opposition of, in particular, the Commission and business interests.

Questions have been raised on occasion about the country of origin principle. Two examples are worth mentioning here. The first concerns the strategic establishment of commercial television stations in one member state in order to avoid stricter regulatory obligations in another. For instance, the Dutch Media Commission had ruled that the commercial channels RTL4 and RTL5, transmitted by a broadcaster based in Luxembourg, were not subject to the broadcasting rules of Luxembourg but rather, in view of the existence of production facilities in the Netherlands, fell under the jurisdiction of the Dutch authorities and had therefore to comply with the more restrictive Dutch broadcasting rules, in particular the ones concerning advertising and sponsorship. In 2003, however, the Dutch Council of State ruled that the strategic and commercial decisions were taken in Luxembourg and thus the two broadcasters fell under the jurisdiction of that country. Another case concerns broadcasters based in Britain, and thus subject to her advertising rules, broadcasting to Sweden and advertising to children, which is not allowed under Swedish legislation.

The second example relates to advertising windows, where broadcasters using a channel intended for viewers in their country of origin reach viewers in other countries that share the same language and replace the original advertising screens by ones specifically targeting the viewers of these other countries. The main argument against this practice is that it undermines the financial viability of the domestic broadcasters in these third countries. In March 2004, at the request of the Irish Presidency of the EU, the European Audiovisual Observatory published a report on transfrontier television in Europe.[144] It concluded that, although the impact of non-national transfrontier television channels varied widely in terms of audience share, its impact on small markets was significant. The report estimated that non-domestic channels had captured 46 percent of total audience in Ireland, and more than 30 percent in Austria and Sweden. These three countries argued that advertising windows should be designated as derogations from the country of origin principle and that instead the country of reception rules should apply. The issue of advertising windows was also raised by the EBU. Nevertheless, the Commission has not proposed a derogation for advertising windows.

The Commission's initial proposal left the country of origin principle intact to assist the free movement of services and the freedom of establishment within the internal market but provided for an exception in cases of "abuse or fraudulent conduct," allowing a member state to adopt proportionate measures against a media service provider established in another member state if it directed all or most of its activity to the first member state.[145] The Commission would then check the compatibility of the proposed measures with EU law.

Unsurprisingly, the industry that has benefited from having to comply with one, instead of potentially twenty-seven, national regulatory regimes strongly supports the country of origin principle.[146] Britain, where more than half of European broadcasters are based precisely in order to take advantage of the more liberalized regulatory framework, argues against the dilution of the country of origin principle since not only the British economy would stand to suffer, but also any proposed cooperation scheme risks, significantly increasing the regulatory burden of domestic regulator Ofcom, which would have to ensure that transnational broadcasters under its jurisdiction complied with requests from other member states.[147]

Following such strong concerns and a declaration signed by thirteen member states in May 2004 to this effect, the Commission could not but take them into account. Still, the Commission's revised proposal is based on the recommendations of the Council and the European Parliament that aim to minimize the weakening of the country of origin principle.

More specifically, the proposal of March 2007 states that the offending broadcaster must have "manifestly, seriously and gravely" infringed the stricter rules of the targeted member state on at least two occasions during the previous year. Against the wishes of Sweden but upon the insistence of

Britain, the proposal establishes a non-binding cooperation procedure whereby the aggrieved member state requests the transmitting member state to ask the broadcaster in question to comply with stricter rules of general public interest. The transmitting member state has to inform the first member state of the results of this procedure within two months. If this informal mechanism fails, there is a fall back binding procedure whereby the aggrieved member state notifies the European Commission and the transmitting member state of the measures it intends to take and ultimately the Commission has three months to check their compatibility with EU law and decide whether the measures can be legitimately taken under the directive.[148]

Advertising

Advertising rules are relaxed. Indeed, that was one of the main objectives of the revision of the directive. Commercial broadcasters, individually (e.g., ITV and RTL) but also through their European association (ACT), advertising associations (e.g., World Federation of Advertisers) and some national regulators (e.g., ITC/Ofcom) have long been pushing for the modernization, meaning relaxation, of advertising rules.[149] Besides the need for advertising revenue, the main arguments put forward are that technological advances render the prescriptive regulatory framework obsolete, users' control and choice have increased and self-regulation can work better.

Under the Commission proposal of March 2007, the daily three-hour advertising limit has been deleted though the hourly limit is retained at twelve minutes, with many of the prescriptive rules abolished altogether, such as detailed rules on insertion of advertising. However, these liberalization measures are at odds with proposals to further restrict the advertising rules in certain types of programs, including news and children's programs, which may only be interrupted for advertising once every thirty minutes, against the original Commission proposal for thirty-five minutes. Commercial public service broadcasters are concerned that the anticipated reduced advertising revenues will undermine investment in children's programming.

Product placement is allowed at the discretion of individual member states and subject to some restrictions; for instance, the viewers must be informed, product placement for tobacco products is banned and it cannot take place in news, current affairs and children's programs.

Cultural Diversity and Promotion of European and Independent Audiovisual Production

Regarding the promotion of European works and independent productions, the general consensus was to respect the delicate political compromise in place. Hence, against the wishes of producers, scriptwriters and distributors, the quota provisions are unchanged and maintain their flexibility. Some interests, including the German public service broadcasters, called for all types of content to count toward their fulfilment. Supporting this position, the British government stressed that European programs such as sports, games and news significantly contributed to European employment.[150] The European Film Companies Alliance, however, was against the extension of the types of programs that count toward their fulfilment, arguing that "a broadcaster can comply with the [EU] Directive without showing a single European film."[151] Commercial broadcasters remained opposed to content quotas, viewing them as "disproportionate intervention in broadcasters' scheduling freedom."[152]

Many of the ex-communist countries with a low production capacity or restricted language area questioned the quota provisions. Content creation costs significant amounts of money. Small domestic markets, especially in light of the minimal intra-European trade in programs, translate into small returns on investment. The fulfilment of quotas, therefore, represents a significant economic burden on small countries.

Similarly to the 1997 review, France seized the opportunity to call for the extension of quotas to on-demand services. The EBU suggested caution but warned that it would be "unfair if support for European works had to be borne solely by so-called traditional broadcasting organizations."[153] The BBC too considered "inappropriate" and "immature" the extension of the quota provision to the new media environment.[154]

According to the proposal for a directive of March 2007, all audiovisual services, linear and not, should promote "where practicable and by appropriate means" the production and distribution of European works.[155]

Calls for a European list of events of major importance for (European) society, as suggested mostly by public service broadcasters and the EBU, were rejected. This can be interpreted as both an indication of the absence of a European culture as well as successful lobbying by commercial interests. The draft directive introduces a new right of access to short news reports of events of high importance to society.

Institutional Aspects

Regarding institutional aspects, the Contact Committee, set up with the 1997 revision of the television directive to monitor its implementation and developments in the sector, was overall regarded as a useful arrangement. There was however widespread criticism about the lack of transparency regarding its work.[156] In response, in October 2004 the Contact Committee's rules of procedure were amended in order to end established practice and make its proceedings public.[157]

Independent regulation remains an issue in both telecommunications and broadcasting. In theory, the Contact Committee comprises representatives of the national regulatory authorities for broadcasting and is chaired by the Commission, which has on occasion invited the heads of the national regulatory authorities on an ad hoc basis.[158] In reality, however, the Contact Committee has been mostly composed of government representatives and not members of independent media regulatory authorities.[159] The former British commercial television regulator (ITC), for instance, called for specific provisions aimed at strengthening national regulatory authorities in the same way that the electronic communications framework had done. There was broad support for greater information and experience exchanges among national regulators. The European Platform of Regulatory Authorities, operating outside the EU context, was perceived as a useful forum that brought together a much wider group of national regulators, including those from the accession countries, the Balkans and Israel. But it was felt that some regulatory issues were specific to the EU and they therefore "warrant[ed] more attention than they [could] be afforded at EPRA meetings."[160]

For the first time, the draft directive calls for national regulators to be independent of national governments and service providers, to work transparently and impartially and to contribute to pluralism. It also calls for information exchanges among national regulators and the Commission as necessary for the implementation of the directive.

State Aid and Public Service Broadcasting

The EU has no explicit powers over public service broadcasting and, as explained, the Amsterdam protocol clarifies that responsibility for its remit, organization and funding rests with the member states. Nevertheless, the EU may intervene on the basis of competition law, another case of horizontal regulation. The aim of this section is to assess the impact of the EU's competition powers, in this case the state aid rules, upon public service broadcasting, a "typical product of the Welfare State" at the core of the state—market relation.[161]

As seen in the preceding chapter, in the 1990s it was commercial broadcasters complaining about public service broadcasters' expansion in the conventional broadcasting field. But in the twenty-first century, complaints against public service broadcasters come also from market players outside the traditional broadcasting sector and increasingly concern new, such as online and neighboring, activities. This is the result of technological convergence. Whereas previously competition was confined among players active in a specific market (e.g., between public and commercial broadcasters) now, with electronic distribution of content, all the players from the previously distinct media markets compete with one another (e.g., broadcasters, publishers, telecommunications operators) and with new players (e.g., new media companies). With technological convergence, the market has grown but, importantly, so has competition. Commercial interests perceive the expansion of public service broadcasters into new areas as threatening since these new activities are in direct competition with the commercial players' offerings.

This section outlines the EU state aid regime and moves on to examine the above developments.

EU State Aid Regime: Main Points

In investigating state aid cases, the Commission needs to do two things: First, establish if the public funding in question constitutes state aid, and second, if yes, establish whether it is contrary to the internal market and EU competition rules and thus inadmissible. In other words, state aid, if found, is not automatically unlawful.

Regarding the first step, it was not until 2003 that the so-called Altmark judgment resolved the legal uncertainty surrounding whether state funding for public services constitutes state aid.[162] More specifically, for the first time, the European Court established criteria to rule whether compensation for the cost of providing services in the general economic interest constitutes state aid. If all criteria are satisfied, then compensation for the costs incurred in the fulfillment of public service obligations does not qualify as state aid since it does not confer any real advantage on the recipient and is thus allowed under the EU Treaty. The four criteria are: (1) clear public service obligations; (2) preestablished parameters for determining the compensation in an objective and transparent manner; (3) no over-compensation; and (4) either a tendering procedure or determination of compensation in line with the costs of a "typical, well-run" company.

Once it finds that public funding constitutes state aid, the Commission then needs to rule whether it is admissible. To do so in cases concerning public service broadcasters, the Commission must establish three things. First, the activities of the public service broadcaster in question must constitute public service activities and the corresponding tasks are clearly defined (definition). Second, the public service broadcaster has been officially entrusted with these public service tasks and supervisory arrangements are in place (entrustment and monitoring). And, finally, the financial compensation granted is proportional to the net cost of the public service activities (proportionality).[163] Where all these three principles are fulfilled, trade between member states is not affected and as such the state aid in question is allowed to take place.

In 2003, for instance, the European Commission ruled on three cases, some pending since the 1990s, concerning the mixed funding schemes of public service broadcasters in Portugal (RTP), Italy (RAI) and France (France 2 and France 3).[164] In all three cases, the Commission found that the funding measures investigated did not cumulatively meet the four conditions established by the Altmark ruling. In particular, they failed to satisfy the second and fourth conditions, namely the compensation had neither been established in advance nor calculated on the basis of an analysis of the costs of a well run and adequately provided broadcaster. As such, the Commission concluded that the funding measures concerned were state aid which was, however, admissible since the principles of definition, entrustment and effective monitoring and proportionality were all met.

State Aid in the Conventional Broadcasting Field

As discussed in the preceding chapter, in the 1990s commercial broadcasters contested, among other things, the use of the license fee by public service broadcasters to finance special interest channels. I will briefly refer to two cases, the BBC's twenty-four-hour news channel and the BBC's nine new digital channels, because, as will be subsequently seen, the Commission has in recent cases changed its approach.

In approving the use of licence fee revenues to finance BBC's twenty-four-hour news channel in 1999, the Commission noted that there was no evident market failure since, before the launch of *BBC News 24*, several commercial news-dedicated channels already existed, such as Sky News, CNN, and Euronews.[165] Crucially, however, the Commission did not perceive the criterion of market failure as significant, an approach that it would abandon in subsequent decisions. Rather, it noted that the BBC's twenty-four-hour news service would meet the democratic and social needs of society, in accordance with the Amsterdam Protocol, by covering a wide range of events and providing in-depth analysis. It also noted that *BBC News 24* had enriched viewers' choice and had thus enhanced media pluralism. The Commission recognized that

> [t]he public service nature of a service cannot be judged on the basis of the distribution platform. Once the UK Government has defined a certain service as being a public service [. . .], such service remains a public service regardless of the delivery platform, as long as its programme concept and its funding arrangements remain unchanged.[166]

Again, in subsequent cases, the Commission has departed from this technology neutral view with regard to the public service remit.

One of the arguments put forward by BSkyB (controlled by Rupert Murdoch's News Corporation and offering the rival Sky News) contesting the classification of *BBC News 24* as a public service was that it was not available to the whole British population but only to 10 percent of households that were cable television subscribers. The Commission accepted state funding for public services even if these made use of emerging technologies and consequently were not initially available to the whole population.

Finally, the Commission recognized that pre-existing commercial competitors suffered a reduction in their market shares and revenues. Nevertheless, it concluded that these market distortions were not excessive and had to be tolerated on the ground that they were necessary for the fulfilment of specific public service obligations. In other words, the provision of free (at the point of use) services defined as public services by a member state entering areas where there was no manifest market failure and competing with commercial players, thereby undermining the latter's revenue opportunities, was not considered a strong enough reason to force the Commission to disapprove public funding of the service. The Commission explained that as long as it was not impossible for competitors to continue to do business and potential competitors were not precluded from entering the market, a certain effect on trade should be tolerated as a consequence of ensuring the provision of a public service remit.

In the new digital BBC services case in 2002, the Commission assessed the funding from the licence fee of nine new thematic digital radio and television channels. Similarly to the technology neutral approach in the *BBC News 24* case, the Commission recognized that "public service broadcasters can develop and diversify their activities in the digital age, as long as they are addressing the same democratic, social and cultural needs of the society."[167] Referring to the Amsterdam Protocol and the 1999 Council Resolution, which proclaims that public service broadcasters need to develop and expand their activities in the digital environment, the Commission advocated a dynamic and evolutionary public service remit that took into account technological developments.[168] It agreed that the new digital channels could be considered "as sound and television programmes of information, education and entertainment provided by digital means" and thus they constituted part of the BBC's public service remit.[169]

The Commission also observed that the new digital services stimulated cultural diversity by providing wide-ranging coverage of sporting and other leisure interests, educational programs and a high standard of original programs for children and young people. The fact that each proposed channel was specialized and covered only part of the content requirements set by the British authorities was considered irrelevant. Taking into account "the explicit wider policy goal of the UK government to promote digital take-up leading to switchover by the whole population," the Commission considered the accessibility limitations justified.[170] In doing so, it acknowledged the important role that public service broadcasters play in promoting the take-up of new services.

Again, although it noted that state funding would favor the BBC over its competitors and as such distort trade, the Commission found that the new digital channels formed part of the BBC's public service mission to be financed out of the licence fee and that the funding did not exceed what was required for the fulfilment of its remit.

Although the Commission did not open proceedings since it concluded that the public funding in question did not qualify as state aid, it made two important observations. The first concerned the entrustment of the public service mission. The Commission found that the new digital services had not been precisely and clearly defined in the legal documents setting out the BBC's public service obligations. It explained that such a definition, as well as the conditions under which such services have to be performed, "[are] important for non-public service operators, so that they can plan their activities."[171] This was repeated in the *BBC Digital Curriculum* decision, as will be seen. The second observation concerned the monitoring of the public service mission. The Commission underlined that the official entrustment of a public service broadcaster with public service obligations had to be accompanied by a mechanism ensuring effective supervision of the fulfilment of these obligations. It added that "the role of such a body would seem to be effective only if the authority is independent from the entrusted undertaking" thereby indirectly attacking the self–governance structure of the BBC.[172]

State Aid in New Activities

In February 2004, the Commission launched an investigation into the state financing of the Dutch public service broadcasters, where it has concluded that the public funding granted exceeds the cost of their public service obligations.[173] In addition, the Commission is currently looking into allegations that the public service broadcasters use these excess public funds to expand into commercial areas, thereby enjoying an unfair advantage over competitors. Importantly, although it recognizes that the Dutch government allows public service broadcasters to fulfil their public service tasks over a variety of media, the Commission "believes that some 'new media' activities, such as SMS-services that are performed by the public broadcasters are commercial activities" outside their remit and as such they should not be funded by the state.[174]

Indeed, and though the case is still open, it seems that the Commission tries to define public service broadcasting by the back door by demarcating which activities are commercial especially in the non-traditional broadcast environment. This would contravene the Amsterdam Protocol, according to which the public service mandate rests with national governments, and also the interpretation of state aid law so far. Furthermore, it suggests the endorsement of a restrictive definition of public service broadcasting, which is precisely what commercial interests have been arguing for.

In another case in May 2004, the Commission delivered its first partially negative decision concerning the funding of public service broadcasters. More specifically, while accepting the broad remit that the Danish government had entrusted its public service broadcaster—TV2/Danmark—with, the Commission found that the broadcaster was being over-compensated.[175] Again, over-compensation raised allegations that TV2 used state support to fund its commercial activities, including commercial internet sites and sales of programs, thereby distorting competition.

The Commission did not question the public service remit as defined by the Danish authorities. Regarding TV2's online activities, the Commission accepted that the site "limited to informing the user about its public service television programmes" fell within the public service remit.[176] However, in addition, TV2 operated a commercial internet site. The Commission agreed with the Danish authorities that that site was a purely commercial activity since

> it offers interactive products on individual demand like games or chat rooms, which do not differ from similar commercial products. Since such services do not address the democratic, social and cultural needs of society they cannot constitute services of general economic interests.[177]

In this case, the Commission noted that the Danish government itself had ruled that the activities in question fell outside the scope of the broadcaster's public service remit. Still, the Commission's decision implicitly accepts that the online activities of public service broadcasters can only go as far as the market does not. The risk is that public service broadcasters may be marginalized in the online media environment and their activities confined to information about conventional broadcast services.

More recently, other cases have raised new questions regarding online activities. In March 2005, the European Commission requested clarifications from the governments of Germany, Ireland and the Netherlands about the role and financing of public service broadcasters.[178] Having looked into allegations from several commercial competitors, the Commission has preliminary concluded that the funding systems in place are not in accordance with the EU treaty rules and that they therefore distort competition. In addition to issues concerning the non-implementation of the 2001 Communication on state aid to public service broadcasting (clear definition of public service mandate, separation of accounts between public service and commercial activities, proportionate funding, commercial activities in line with market principles and independent monitoring), the complaints against the public service broadcasters in Germany and the Netherlands have also raised new issues regarding specifically online activities. The Commission clarifies that it does not question that such activities can be part of the public service remit. Rather, it is their scope and financing that is at issue.

> In both cases, the Commission has concerns that, whereas online information services may be included, online activities such as e-commerce and mobile telephone services may not be regarded as a "service of general economic interest."[179]

Although according to the Amsterdam Protocol the definition of the public service broadcasting remit rests with the member states, the Commission has a role to assess it for "manifest error." This would happen if the remit "included activities that could not reasonably be considered to meet—in the wording of the [Amsterdam] Protocol—the *'democratic, social and cultural needs of each society.'*"[180]

State Aid in Neighboring Markets

In October 2003, the Commission approved public funding for the *BBC Curriculum*, providing interactive learning materials free to schools and students.[181] The cost of this new online service (£150 million over five years) would be covered by the licence fee.

The Commission recognized that the public service remit was a matter for the British government and noted that the latter had already approved the Digital Curriculum as an ancillary service part of the BBC's remit. Nevertheless, similarly to its earlier decision on *BBC News 24*, it expressed concern that it was incumbent upon the BBC itself to propose for its remit to include new services even though, but only subsequently, the British government would need to approve them.

The Commission observed that the term "ancillary service" was "open-ended" since there was no clear definition of the services the BBC could provide under this category.[182] Moreover, it found problematic the notion that the Digital Curriculum was proposed as an "ancillary service" because it did not have a close association with the BBC's television and radio activities. The Commission reasoned that the proposed service concerned a new area of activity in the market for electronic learning materials and that therefore there was no continuity within the existing licence fee funding system. Importantly, in this market there already existed commercial operators. Departing from its approach in the *BBC News 24* case, the Commission pointed out that

> [t]he use of public funding to enter markets that are already developed and where the commercial players have had little or no exposure to the BBC as a

competitor cannot be considered as maintaining the status quo regarding the nature of the [licence fee funding] scheme. [. . .] although the proposed service builds on the educational traditions of the BBC and may be seen by some to be a logical and natural extension of the BBC's activities, the Digital Curriculum is a digression from the various markets within which the BBC has been active.[183]

From the above it appears that, although it acknowledged that the inclusion of non-television and -radio services to the BBC's remit was a matter for British legislation, the Commission did not share the opinion of the British authorities that the proposed online service constituted part of the BBC educational public service remit.

Based on the above analysis, the Commission concluded that the funding of the Digital Curriculum from licence fee revenues did not qualify as existing but rather constituted new state aid. The rules for new state aid are stricter. In particular, new state aid requires prior notification to and approval by the Commission, which may decide to call it back in its entirety

In approving the service, the Commission referred in some detail to the conditions attached by the British government in response to strong domestic opposition from commercial interests, notably educational publishers and information technology suppliers.[184] The Commission drew attention to the condition requiring the BBC service to be "distinctive from and complementary to services provided by the commercial sector."[185] It also referred to the condition obliging the BBC to publish in detail, at least fifteen months before launching the service, the activities it planned to undertake in the initial five-year public funding period. The aim of this condition was that competitors of the BBC would know in advance the parameters of the BBC's service and could on that basis plan and market their activities. Although it established that the proposed service would potentially distort competition and affect trade between member states, taking into account the conditions put in place by the competent national authorities to reduce such effects, the Commission approved Digital Curriculum as a service of general economic interest.

The BBC Digital Curriculum decision broke entirely with the approach adopted in previous Commission decisions. The Commission's opinion in this case is that the BBC's educational public service remit is confined to the conventional broadcast technology. It is indicative that for the first time, in this decision the Commission made no reference to the Amsterdam Protocol that gives responsibility to member states to decide on the mission, organization and funding of public service broadcasting. The Commission's decision implicitly accepts a negative definition of public service broadcasting, at least in relation to new media. Public service broadcasters can assume the activities the market fails to offer at all or at the socially desirable level. The presence or absence of commercial players in these new areas of activity has constituted a determining factor in the Commission's analysis.

Analysis—Whither Public Service Broadcasting?

The beginning of a new approach regarding public service broadcasters' new media activities, and in particular the determining role that technology and the (potential) activities of competitors have in this new reasoning, are discussed in an article published in the newsletter of the European Commission's Directorate for Competition. While accepting that member states retain responsibility over public service broadcasting, the authors (two DG Competition officials) express concerns over the wide discretion that member states enjoy and in particular about the risk of "mission creep," meaning the gradual expansion of the methods and goals of public service remit, especially in cases where public service broadcasting is defined broadly, and the consequent rise of the cost of fulfilling it.[186] At a time when public finances are already under strain, any increase in cost has typically resulted in public service broadcasters relying more on commercial revenues, thus representing a bigger commercial threat.

The authors of the article maintain that although television programs and internet services may use the same content, there are differences. Conventional free-to-air television was about the same content being transmitted to all viewers through a small number of channels (one-to-many communication). In contrast, the internet is about many-to-many communication, it offers interactivity, and users can choose the content they wish to access. In this context, they explain,

> [m]ost of the original considerations to regulate broadcasting, such as frequency scarcity, need to preserve pluralism, reach of whole population are not necessarily valid for new media services.[187]

The article effectively calls into question the future relevance of public service broadcasting by, ironically, implying in its analysis the distinction between linear and non-linear services, that is, the two most widely contested concepts due to be incorporated in the revised television directive.

The weakness of this argument lies in its technological determinism. It assumes that the cultural, political and social rationales for regulating broadcasting all emanated from, and were therefore subordinate to, the basic technological rationale: spectrum scarcity. Hence, the argument goes, once spectrum scarcity is removed, the need for sector-specific regulation and public service broadcasting is removed as well. This argument fails to appreciate that the non-technological rationales for broadcasting regulation do not change because the technological constraints are no longer relevant.

For even if spectrum scarcity that traditionally restricted market entry to broadcasting has been lifted, the fact remains that the market cannot be perfectly competitive.[188] Technological developments make the fulfilment of the cultural, political and social objectives harder but not obsolete.

In recent years, commercial interests have increased their efforts to influence policy developments. For instance, in May 2003, several Europe-wide associations of private commercial media submitted a memorandum expounding their views on broadcasting and competition to the Convention responsible for drafting the EU Constitution. While acknowledging the societal and democratic functions of broadcasting, they stressed the "growing similarity" between public and commercial broadcasters with regard to content, social and market functions, and analyzed the "privileges" of public broadcasters, including public funding and special regulatory treatment. They argued that these privileges "can lead to considerable distortions of competition to the detriment of private broadcasters and other media players," particularly when public broadcasters expand into the online sector and e-commerce, television production and cross-border digital satellite television.[189]

More recently, in March 2004, in response to the Commission decisions favorable for the public service broadcasters in state aid investigations and the growing competitive threat they represent in the age of digital television and the internet, commercial broadcasters and publishers adopted a White Paper titled "Safeguarding the Future of the European Audiovisual Market." In it, they condemned years of "unfair" competition from public service broadcasters and "under-regulation (meaning competition law regulation)" of the sector, which in turn have

> undermined the competitiveness of the television and radio industries as well as adversely affecting the related sectors of multi-channel television, TV programme production, press and internet content.[190]

For commercial interests the starting point is that public service broadcasters "distort markets by their very existence."[191] Indicative of the fact that they define public service broadcasting on the basis of its funding alone is that the White Paper dropped the term "public service broadcasters" and instead used the term "publicly funded broadcasters," thereby implying that the only difference between private and public broadcasters has to do with funding and not mission, content or terms of access. It is also indicative that they referred to public funding as "State Aid," implying that such funding automatically qualifies as state aid under EU law and comes therefore under the strong competence of the European Commission.

Commercial interests expressed concern about the "massive amounts of State Aid" granted, which totalled €15 billion in 2001, making public service broadcasting the third most subsidized industry in Europe, ahead of agriculture and behind transport and manufacturing.[192] The total state aid represented more than one-fourth of the total revenues in the nearly € 60 billion European broadcasting market. They called on member states and the Commission for immediate action to initiate a process of migration toward a single funded model for public broadcasters, elimination of all commercial revenues and the full application of competition rules.

Furthermore, commercial broadcasters and publishers complained about distortions in the advertising market, vague programming remits and unchecked expansion of public broadcasters into new media markets. They were also concerned about the absence of independent national regulation where a number of publicly funded broadcasters, such as the BBC, regulated themselves, and they condemned the, until recently, prolonged inaction of the European Commission and accused it of failure to apply the methodology required by the Altmark ruling. In particular, they interpreted the fourth criterion of the ruling as a call for state aid to be benchmarked against a reasonably efficient private operator, and if public service broadcasters were not as efficient as private broadcasters, then they should not benefit from public funds. This is similar to the commercial broadcasters' earlier position calling, in line with the current vogue in regulatory practice, for a

> comparison and exchange of best practice between national definitions of public service remit. [. . .] the Commission could establish clearly which functions of a media company cannot be regarded as public service.[193]

In short, commercial broadcasters and publishers contend that the Commission should demarcate the concept of public service. In effect, they call for a return to the approach of the September 1998 discussion document, which attempted, unsuccessfully, to identify types of programs which could be considered as public service and could therefore benefit from public funding, and those that could not.

Although the Commission attempts to reassure member states and public service broadcasters that state aid investigations "do not question the prerogative of the Member States to organise and finance public service broadcasting, as recognised in the Amsterdam Treaty protocol," the real danger is that this may well happen.[194] The Commission has clarified that its task is "to assess whether there is an appropriate balance between the requirements of public service broadcasting and fair competition."[195] Provided there exists a clear definition of the public service broadcasting mandate (be it narrow or broad) to "allow other operators to plan their activities" and provided that the available funding is proportionate to the costs of these tasks, then the European Commission will have no reason to rule against the member states concerned.[196] Indeed, it has so far ruled only once against a public service broadcaster, in the TV2/Danmark case, where it endorsed the decision of the Danish national government.

Even so, it appears that the principles laid down in the Amsterdam Protocol are being squeezed "into the rigid structure" of the competition law articles of the EU Treaty and associated European Court jurisprudence.[197] This diminishes the flexibility of the Commission to take into consideration non-economic factors in its analysis. State aid cases will tend to be examined on the basis of narrow competition rules and judged against mechanistic criteria, such as the Altmark case test.

In response to complaints from commercial interests, the Commission may insist that member states further clarify the public service remit. The risk is that, in contradiction to the 1999 Council Resolution on public service broadcasting, a prescriptive role will curb the development and modernization of public service broadcasting, boxing it into a few areas. A detailed remit would also be in contradiction to the move, evident in the EU regulatory package for electronic communications, away from a prescriptive toward a goal-oriented regulatory framework so that, instead of being in constant need for review, it is flexible to respond to market and technological change. Finally, there is a danger that a detailed remit may undermine one of the core principles of public service broadcasting, its independence. State authorities, in an attempt to fend off potential complaints by commercial interests, or indeed in a thinly concealed attempt to intervene in public service broadcasting, could use this as an excuse to prescribe in detail the content/services that public broadcasters could offer.

Despite the emergence of new distribution platforms and technological possibilities, the attacks on public service broadcasting are effectively based on the same old arguments. On the one side, commercial interests maintain that public service broadcasting should be confined to non-commercial areas, areas where the profit opportunities are not sufficiently attractive to be served by the market. This will result in the marginalization of public service broadcasting; European public service broadcasting will turn into American Public Broadcasting Service (PBS).[198] On the other side, public service broadcasters, their association the EBU, together with the Council of Europe, the European Parliament and viewers and listeners' groups, call for a technologically and platform neutral definition of public service broadcasting.[199] They argue that its principles and objectives do not change with technological progress. On the contrary, these become even more important. In particular, public service broadcasting, by providing reliable information and a high proportion of original content that, moreover, resonates with the issues and references familiar to the destined audience, and by catering for all segments of society, not just those that are commercially attractive, can facilitate social cohesion.[200] For public service broadcasters the issue is how to increase access to content, whereas for commercial interests the issue is how to limit access and, in turn, charge a high enough price to reflect this artificial scarcity. Public service broadcasting addresses users as citizens, rather than consumers, enabling them to make informed decisions about their social and political lives.

Unless public service broadcasting is allowed to evolve and modernize, it will be confined to the old analog mono-media world, which is about to become extinct. The challenge is to transfer the dual system of public and private market players from the field of analog broadcasting to the field of broadband digital media.

CHALLENGES AHEAD

This last section draws attention to three main challenges that lie ahead in the regulation of electronic communications in the EU context. First, it examines how the artificial distinction between the regulation of infrastructure and associated services at the EU level and the regulation of content at the national level presents problems in the technologically converging communications environment. Second, it looks at the standardization of third generation mobile systems to illustrate how, in this case, the broader process of globalization shaped the process of Europeanization. Third, it investigates how the principle of technological neutrality endorsed by the 2002 electronic communications regulatory framework challenges harmonization, and ultimately, the single market.

Digital Interactive Television: The Artificial Distinction between Content and Infrastructure

As stated, the 2002 EU regulatory framework covers all electronic communications networks and associated services and facilities, such as conditional access systems and application programming interfaces (API), but excludes broadcast content.[201] The issue of common standards and interoperability in digital television was extensively discussed during the consultations on the Green Paper on convergence (1997) and the revised regulatory framework for electronic communications. In contrast to the high-definition television case, the Commission refrained at the time from imposing standards for conditional access systems and application programming interfaces.

When digital television was launched in Europe in 1996, there was no European API standard, and the market for interactive services developed on the basis of proprietary non-interoperable systems. The 2002 Framework directive requires member states to encourage the use of open standards for

APIs or, alternatively, the sufficient availability of information on proprietary standards in order to enable third-party providers to offer services.[202] The directive acknowledges that lack of interoperability may adversely affect the free flow of information, media pluralism and cultural diversity by limiting freedom of choice for users. In March 2004, the Commission launched a public consultation to examine whether interoperability had been adequately achieved and whether there was need to impose a common API standard.

The consultation on standardization and interoperability of digital interactive television services is important because it was the first one dealing with these issues under the 2002 electronic communications regulatory framework and may well provide indications for future responses to related matters.

Consultation

In the consultation paper, the Commission opposed mandating a single API standard for four main reasons.[203] First, it argued that while the compulsory implementation of a single standard could ensure technical interoperability of equipment and services, it could not on its own ensure interoperability at the consumer level since content and service providers would still need to negotiate on a commercial basis access to the networks and associated facilities. Second, it explained that digitalization had changed fundamentally the broadcasting landscape so that the old solution in the analog mono-platform environment of achieving interoperability via a single receiver standard was no longer sustainable. Third, the Commission challenged another rationale for mandating standards prominent in the analog terrestrial television era, that of industrial policy. It held that, even with the implementation of a single system, national markets could no longer provide enough economies of scale. Instead, manufacturers had to rely on global markets. Finally, given the diverging market conditions and development of digital television across the EU, the Commission maintained that, in any case, it was unlikely that implementation of a single standard could be achieved.

The response of industry players to the Commission's consultation was not surprising.[204] Similarly to the earlier debate on conditional access systems, two main groups can be identified.

First, the consultation revealed continued concern of free-to-air public service broadcasters about the gatekeeping role of vertically integrated pay-TV operators controlling proprietary APIs. Public service broadcasters and their association, the EBU, joined forces with supporters of the open Multimedia Home Platform (MHP) standard developed by the Digital Video Broadcasting Group, advocating the imposition of open standards on all platforms and not just on the free-to-air one as suggested by the Commission. The BBC acknowledged the significant role that vertically integrated platform operators (such as BSkyB) using proprietary standards had assumed in the early development of the market but argued that proprietary standards now could slow down, rather than promote, innovation at the public's expense.

For equipment manufacturer Philips, the compulsory implementation of a single standard would reduce uncertainty for the consumer electronics industry. It held that manufacturers would benefit from economies of scale, which in turn would translate into lower prices for consumers, improved prospects of take-up of digital television and acceleration of the switchover to digital transmission. Philips explained that proprietary standards were embedded elements of the vertical business models of pay-TV operators who dominated the market, and thus market forces alone would take a long time to achieve interoperability.

This camp, similar to the opposing camp as will be seen, was quick to establish a strong connection between their position and the Lisbon strategy by emphasizing the significance of open standards in providing information society services on TV screens—particularly important in the context of Europe where penetration of computers is relatively low—thereby making the information society accessible to all.

For the pro-open standards group, interoperability at the level of the consumer—the extent to which citizens can access the full range of services available in the market—had not been achieved and therefore regulatory intervention was justified. Technical solutions such as re-authoring of content, they argued, could not deliver such interoperability, were expensive and handed powerful vertically integrated market players control over the distribution platform and access to it by third parties, which meant that ultimately they decided what services and content consumers could access. Open standards would improve the free flow of information and help promote pluralism and cultural diversity.

On the other side, established digital pay-TV operators using proprietary APIs (e.g., BSkyB, Canal+) and having achieved substantial market shares, together with software and information technology companies (e.g., Microsoft), argued against the imposition of (open) standards. To press their case in view of the forthcoming Commission review on interoperability, in October 2003, this camp formed an issue-based group, the Digital Interoperability Forum (DIF).[205]

In its response, the DIF adopted the usual argument against EU intervention in media markets, holding that these were fragmented not because there was lack of interoperability but because of diverse economic, cultural and technological conditions.[206] There was therefore no point in using a compulsory standard to create pan-European television. Moreover, they argued, Britain, with the most rapid degree of digital television penetration, had proved that the existence of incompatible APIs had not impeded market growth.

For the pro-proprietary standards camp, lack of interoperability was about increasing consumer choice: "[effective choice must also include] the differentiation of interactive services and capabilities of equipment."[207] For this camp market forces, not regulatory intervention, determined interoperability. Weak consumer demand was the major problem. To illustrate this, the DIF raised gambling and video games as examples where reauthoring of content/services had taken place. However, the examples provided suggest that, in the absence of any regulatory obligations, the willingness of operators of proprietary APIs to promote interoperability is directly related to the commercial and revenue potential of the services/content in question.

Finally, the DIF too was quick to appeal to the Lisbon agenda. It suggested that there was a trade-off between investment and innovation on the one hand, and proprietary standards and lack of regulation on the other. Competitiveness and innovation were considered more important values compared to interoperability and public service objectives, such as media pluralism and diversity. "A prescriptive regulatory regime will stifle innovation in the name of interoperability" warned DIF, adding that "disproportionate regulatory intervention, or even the threat of such action, could inhibit the investments and innovation needed to sustain current growth in digital and interactive TV."[208]

Following the public consultation, in August 2004 the consensus reached was that the Commission should merely encourage but not mandate open standards. This approach was confirmed in February 2006.[209] The Commission proposed a range of promotional actions to support the deployment of interactive digital services using the open MHP system. These include the creation of a member states' group on MHP implementation to facilitate sharing of experiences and possibly policy transfer, confirmation that national governments can offer subsidies for interactive television receiver equipment provided they conform to state aid rules and monitoring of access to proprietary technologies. In short, the Commission now promotes and encourages but no longer mandates the adoption of standards.

The Commission noted that:

General interests like cultural diversity and media pluralism are central to the European social model, while economic success is essential to ensure that the Union retains competitiveness.[210]

The problem is that the EU regulatory framework is premised upon the distinction between the regulation of content and transmission. The former, which includes issues of cultural diversity, media pluralism and ownership, is the sole responsibility of member states, while the latter is a shared competence between the European Commission and member states. But this distinction, the result of a political compromise, is artificial. The very notion of technological convergence implies that these two layers (transmission and content) cannot be clearly demarcated.[211] It is precisely because the two meet at the regulation of the application program interface that the debate has been so intense. The regulation of so-called digital gateways, such as conditional access systems and APIs, has implications for access to content. The issue is that ostensibly technical decisions, such as those involving the adoption of standards, are left in the hands of the market. But these decisions are not purely technical and, crucially, affect provision of, and access to content and services. In other words, and this is the important issue, private decisions (e.g., on standards and gateways) have serious implications for public policy issues (access to what content and services).

3G Standards: Globalization Limits Europeanization

Different second generation mobile technologies in Europe, Japan and the USA resulted in diverging industrial interests in relation to third generation (3G) mobile systems.[212] Europe wished to repeat the huge success of GSM, Japan wanted to adopt a more outward strategy and for the USA the absence of a single standard (GSM case) could halt European dominance in the cellular mobile market. In response, in 1995 the International Telecommunication Union announced that a single global third generation mobile standard was not possible. Rather, the development of a family of standards was a more realistic approach albeit with adequate common elements to facilitate international roaming. The 3G standardization race began in earnest.

In Europe, the success of GSM brought about a corresponding change in the 3G vision, Universal Mobile Telecommunications System (UMTS). During the first phase of standardization up until the first half of the 1990s, the 3G mobile system was the domain of manufacturers in general working within the Race program (chapter 4). But the interests of GSM operators and manufacturers had grown too strong to be ignored. The consensus was that UMTS would be evolutionary and based on GSM, not revolutionary as originally envisaged, requiring the migration of all existing systems to a new network. The overriding aim was to capitalize on the vast GSM footprint and thereby strengthen Europe's international lead in cellular mobile technology.[213]

The 1995 EU enlargement brought in Sweden's Ericsson and Finland's Nokia, the world's leading mobile network equipment and handset manufacturers respectively, both of which had gained significant advantages from the success of GSM. In early 1995, in response to discussions with the telecommunications industry and in particular Ericsson, the European Commission got actively involved in the establishment of the UMTS Task Force, an ad hoc advisory group of manufacturers, network operators and European regulatory authorities charged with developing Europe's strategy toward UMTS. The Task Force recommended the creation of a high level forum to contribute, on the basis of industry-wide consensus, to smooth the transition to UMTS. To this effect, the UMTS Forum was established in December 1996, with the members major manufacturers and operators. It worked closely with the GSM Association, representing the interests of the GSM community, thereby increasing the input of telecommunications operators. In contrast to the earlier engineering-led phase, the standardization process was now becoming market-led. Still, the Forum was originally dominated by telecommunications rather than computing interests, to meaning that the internet was not yet part of the UMTS vision. This was to change toward the end of the decade.[214]

In June 1996, realizing the strategic importance of UMTS, the European Telecommunications Standards Institute's Special Mobile Group plenary got properly involved and established close cooperation with the UMTS Forum.[215] Previously, ETSI was overloaded with GSM issues and effectively work on UMTS was the task of a single subcommittee.

From the outset, it was clear that the two leading European manufacturers, Ericsson and Nokia, had global, as opposed to parochial European, aspirations. In particular, they were aware of the importance of the Asian markets and the need to keep abreast of developments in Japan, where the process of standardizing third generation mobile systems had gone the furthest and which moreover was a strategic market in the emerging Asia Pacific region.

In January 1997, the Japanese adopted Wideband CDMA (W-CDMA) as their proposal for a standard. At the Asia Telecom Trade show in June 1997, the two European companies—Ericsson and Nokia—announced their support for W-CDMA as a joint European-Asian standard.[216] Japan's NTT Do-CoMo, the first operator to propose a third generation system, established cooperation with non-domestic firms, including Nokia and Ericsson, for the development of handsets and infrastructure respectively. From early on, it became clear that the development of a 3G standard would be based on multi-regional cooperation.

At the same time, while expecting ETSI to play a central role, the Commission clarified that it supported international cooperation in the fields of frequency allocation and standardization and called for a broad consensus "both within and *outside* the Community."[217] Similarly, the UMTS Forum published a report in 1997 emphasizing the global dimension of 3G mobile communications and favoring an outward-oriented strategy.[218]

The same year, Gunnar Sandegren of Ericsson and vice president of ETSI's Special Mobile Group (SMG) committee—with the support of France

Télécom, Alcatel and Siemens, among other companies—called for cooperation between ETSI and Japanese standardization bodies to be formalized.[219] To this end, a European delegation travelled to Japan in May 1997. As the SMG chairman noted, it was clear during the discussions that European firms active in Japan (notably Ericsson and Nokia) had already prepared the ground, which was why formal cooperation was easy to establish.[220] This cooperation was of fundamental significance. First, it pre-empted an alliance between Japan and the USA, which would have isolated Europe. Second, it meant that European manufacturers would be able to enter the Japanese market, a key market in the broader region. And third, a UMTS solution that included both Europe and Japan stood a better chance to become a global standard.

But although both sides were favorable to forging cooperation, there were internal disagreements within the European side, in particular between companies that had already achieved leading positions on the international market and had global aspirations actively pursued on the basis of an outward-oriented strategy, notably Ericsson and Nokia, and those that, although active in the wider telecommunications equipment market, had not as yet become strong players in mobile communications and were less internationally oriented, notably German Siemens and French Alcatel. In other words, the competitive position of the firm in international markets shaped its strategy.

A year after Japan had selected W-CDMA as its proposal for a standard, in January 1998, after two voting rounds that had produced no result, the internal disagreement concerning the European standard that had resulted in a standoff was finally resolved.[221] The two sides reached an agreement by consensus on the radio access system for the European standard. Ericsson and Nokia, pursuing an international strategy and having already established cooperation with Japan on that standard, were supporting W-CDMA. Japan too supported this option and made clear its intention to go ahead with the implementation of the standard in the Asia Pacific region even without Europe. One of the main arguments of this outward-oriented camp was that this proposal had the highest chances to become a global standard, and it warned that any other proposal would impede the European industry's global expansion. The other camp, sponsored primarily by Alcatel and Siemens with the backing of North American manufacturers Motorola and Nortel, were supporting Time Division-CDMA. The compromise was the result of intense negotiations in particular among Nokia, Ericsson and Siemens. The solution, resolving the impasse that had placed at risk the entire standardization effort and could have led to complete loss of competitive advantage for the European industry, was to combine the two competing technologies into one common Universal Terrestrial Radio Access standard, which gained approval by the ETSI.

In sum, in the second phase (1996–98), the European strategy on a third generation mobile standard had not only widened in terms of participation with the creation of the UMTS Forum that, together with the GSM association, brought in operators, but had also become interregional.[222]

Globalizing the Standardization Process

From 1998 onward, the standardization process became globalized. Building on the interregional cooperation established in the previous period, in 1998 the UMTS Globalization Group (UGG) was formed as an ad hoc group by the ETSI Board, with the aim to attract global partners in order to ensure worldwide implementation of a GSM-based UMTS standard.[223] There were strong conflicts within the Group concerning future strategy. Hillebrand, then Special Mobile Group chairman, identified three factions: the "Greater ETSI faction," the "Fixed-Mobile Convergence faction" and the "GSM-UMTS faction."[224]

The "Greater ETSI faction" was effectively protecting the institutional interests of ETSI. The formation of an alternative global partnership group and the transfer of ETSI's mobile work to it, one of its best achievements, were perceived as a huge setback to the organization and Europe in general. This camp, supported by ETSI's bureaucracy, tried to keep future work on UMTS within ETSI by internationalizing the organization. Indeed, proposals were put forward to open ETSI to non-European partners, but its General Assembly agreed to grant such partners not full but instead associate membership which, at that time, conferred no voting rights. As such, this solution was not acceptable to the non-Europeans. The attempt therefore to keep work on UMTS within ETSI failed.

The "Fixed-Mobile Convergence faction" was dominated by fixed operators such as British Telecom. Like the first faction, it opposed the creation of a separate partnership project. Given that the spectacular growth of mobile communications had the potential to adversely affect fixed telecommunications business and revenues, this group, in contrast to the first one, tried to influence the actual UMTS vision. It argued that the main priority should be fixed-mobile convergence and that all the work should come under the responsibility of one group within ETSI under the leadership of fixed operators.

Finally, the "GSM-UMTS faction" represented the interests of the GSM/UMTS communities. For them, international cooperation would safeguard the GSM system, securing the integrity of the two systems while promoting the success of mobile communications. This group supported the formation of an international collaboration initiative and the transfer of all GSM and UMTS standardization work to it. It was this last faction that won in the end.

The Third Generation Partnership Project (3GPP) was set up in December 1998 as a collective international standardization initiative for W-CDMA.[225] Its founding organizations were ETSI, the Association of Radio Industries and Businesses and the Telecommunication Technology Committee from Japan, the U.S. T1 Standards Committee and the Telecommunications Technology Association from South Korea. The aim was to harmonize all the W-CDMA proposals and ensure backward compatibility to the GSM standard but not to cdma2000, the rival standard popular in North America and many countries in Asia, thereby increasing the chances for W-CDMA to become the leading 3G technology.

The creation of this project triggered the formation in January 1999 of a counter Partnership Project, 3GPP2, backed by Qualcomm from the USA, that possesses essential patents for the CDMA technology, one of the primary second generation mobile technologies and key to the proposed third generation standards, making the blockage of a standard by not making available essential patents highly likely. 3GPP2 pushed for cdma2000 and related technologies as the alternative global 3G standard. The main difference between the two initiatives in terms of membership was ETSI's involvement in the first project backing only W-CDMA. Japan and South Korea were involved in both projects since they had decided to launch both competing systems in domestic markets, thereby improving the chances of domestic manufacturers in world markets. Both partnerships were innovative. They broke with the hitherto national or at best regional standardization efforts and ushered in a new era of standardization initiatives based on international collaboration.

The conflict between cdma2000 and W-CDMA almost caused a trade war between the USA and the EU. Besides the intellectual property conflict, the U.S. administration reacted strongly to the imminent adoption by the EU of a decision on UMTS ahead of the ITU preliminary ruling for a standard.[226] Following company lobbying, notably by Qualcomm, in December 1998 the U.S. Secretary of Commerce and the U.S. Trade Representative wrote to Bangemann, European Commissioner for Information Society and Industry, to stress that mandating a single standard in Europe might threaten access of U.S. telecommunications equipment companies to European markets and be contrary to the WTO agreement on technical barriers to trade.[227] They emphasized the importance of the standardization principles agreed by the transatlantic grouping of business leaders, TABD, in October 1998, one of which called for reciprocal acceptance of standards developed by other regions.[228] The U.S. administration threatened unilateral retaliatory action against the EU to force it to drop its proposal. Bangemann explained that standardization was an industry-led process in which the European Commission could not intervene and clarified that non-UMTS standards were not excluded since member states were required to grant at least one UMTS license in order to enable roaming.[229]

Besides the transatlantic grouping of business leaders, leading mobile operators too decided to intervene in the standardization process that, despite initial expectations, had so far been dominated by standardization bodies and manufacturers. In 1998, major mobile operators with international footprints, such as Vodafone and Telefonica Moviles, together with others wishing to strengthen their international market positions (including Bell Atlantic Mobile, China Mobile and NTT DoCoMo) formed the Operators' Harmonization Group. Its creation was in response to the conflicts that had divided the manufacturers' camp and threatened the development of third generation mobile technology. The aim of the Group was to promote agreement on key elements of the different standards in order to enable global 3G service provision. They put pressure on standards bodies and manufacturers, and they reached a harmonization agreement in June 1999.[230]

Partly in response to U.S. pressure and partly because it could be in contravention of its obligations under the WTO technical barriers to trade agreement, the EU did not mandate the adoption of a single standard. Nevertheless, all the third generation licenses that have been awarded in Europe are based on UMTS. The international ambitions of European manufacturers and operators shaped standardization, and in particular they were instrumental in internationalizing the process.

Radio Spectrum: Technological Neutrality Limits Europeanization

EU intervention in radio spectrum management has been minimal. Based on the harmonization work of the CEPT—the Europe-wide grouping comprising national technical experts—it has been confined to standards and frequency coordination on a case-by-case basis.[231] This limited regulatory intervention, under which all EU member states have been required to use the same frequency bands for the same service (e.g., GSM), has contributed to technical spectrum efficiency, the creation of a single market in goods and services offering equipment manufacturers and operators significant economies of scale and the provision of cross-border services. During the late 1980s/early 1990s, this narrow harmonization of frequency bands and respective uses was a key part of industrial policy initiatives aimed at promoting European champions.

However, recently even this limited consensus on designation of common spectrum uses has come under attack from two main fronts. First, both EU and WTO rules increasingly put limits on mandating specific standards and/or technology for a given frequency, promoting instead the principle of technological neutrality and minimum harmonization to prevent harmful interference.[232] Second, the growing trend toward the marketization of radio spectrum management, through for instance auctions, further questions the traditional consensus. Greater use of market forces in radio spectrum management is about moving away from the traditional command-and-control approach, under which the regulator would determine the technology and use of specific frequency bands and who could access them, toward a less prescriptive approach where such key decisions are left to the market players themselves. In short, it is no longer the regulator but rather the market that determines who uses the spectrum and how.[233] Market-based mechanisms emphasize greater flexibility and less central harmonization. In this context, intervention—be it at EU or national level—becomes simply enabling.

Spectrum Liberalization: 3G Extension Frequency Band

The ITU World Radiocommunications Conference in 2000, at the peak of the technological euphoria, decided to allocate additional spectrum to third generation mobile (3G) services in order to accommodate the anticipated rapid take-off of this new technology. However, the launch and take-up of 3G services in Europe has been slow, while new wireless technologies rival to 3G, such as WiMax, have come along that need to deploy the same frequencies that were reserved as additional spectrum for 3G mobile services back in 2000.[234] Following the ITU conference, in response to mandates by the European Commission, the CEPT has designated the entire additional frequency band as identified by the ITU for use by 3G services.[235]

However, there have been divisions between countries and within the industry about the use of this 3G extension band.[236] This is a clear example where competing uses for the same frequency create conflicts of interests.

On the one side, Britain leads the pro-flexibility and technological neutrality camp, arguing that the additional frequency band should not be used exclusively by the 3G family of technologies but rather by any technically compatible technologies. This camp is supported by, among other countries, Denmark, Germany, the Netherlands, Poland and Sweden. Industry stakeholders include market players wishing to use wireless broadband access technologies such as WiMax that are potential competitors to 3G services (e.g., WiMax Forum), various fixed telecommunications operators from and outside Europe who have seen their revenues and profits being attacked by cellular mobile operators (e.g., AT&T and BT) and themselves wish to use alternative wireless technologies to minimize the competitive threat and at the same time constrain the growth of their competitors, and several manufacturers from the computing/internet sector where these alternative wireless technologies have originated (e.g., Dell, Intel).

For the pro-flexibility and technological neutrality camp, regulators should not pick winners by restricting access to the band in question to one particular technology, but rather the market should be left to decide which technology is best. Opening the band to other technologies will increase competition, widen choice of services and lower prices for consumers. This camp warns that Europe would lose out significantly if it is not involved in the development and use of alternative wireless technologies, technologies which can deliver new applications around IP access.

The main members of the opposite pro-harmonization camp in favor of reserving the band for 3G technologies exclusively are, unsurprisingly, operators and manufacturers with vested interests in terrestrial cellular mobile technologies, in particular GSM Europe, the UMTS Forum, Orange, Ericsson, Siemens, Nokia and Qualcomm, which holds key patents in 3G mobile technologies and stands to benefit from their market success. Finland, France and Spain, among other countries, support this camp.

The pro-harmonization camp argues that a flexible and technologically neutral approach will fragment the market and result in confusion, higher prices, interoperability difficulties and limited roaming possibilities and thereby adversely affect consumer welfare. Importantly, this camp holds that exclusive use of the band in question can help the European industry replicate the success of GSM technology in the case of 3G. Terrestrial cellular mobile is portrayed as a predominantly European technology, perhaps the single area in the field of information and communication technology in which Europe has a competitive advantage. For this camp, the opening of the given frequency band to non-3G technologies—crucially, technologies lacking strong participation of European companies—would serve to weaken the European high-technology industry, with adverse effects on the European economy. Understandably it sees in competing technologies (e.g., WiMax) a serious threat that could make their investment, not least the huge amounts paid for 3G licenses, redundant. This camp concludes that the degree of competition within the 3G technology group is sufficiently strong and can deliver substantial benefits to consumers in terms of prices, choice and seamless service provision. In other words, the pro-harmonization camp favor the traditional EU model of competition that, as the case of GSM illustrates, restricts competition through regulatory intervention within the same group of technologies. It is against competition between alternative technologies (e.g., 3G—WiMax), the competition model traditionally favored in the USA.

The case of the 3G extension frequency band is about whether regulators should specify the technologies that can access specific frequencies and the associated degree of harmonization. At issue is the state-market relationship and whether regulatory intervention is necessary.

CONCLUSIONS

At the Lisbon European Council of March 2000, EU political leaders endorsed competitiveness as a top policy priority and committed themselves

to the ambitious goal of transforming Europe into the world's most competitive and dynamic knowledge-based economy. The knowledge economy
has moved at the forefront of economic development planning. At the heart
of this strategy is Information and Communication Technology (ICT).

A key explanatory variable put forward for the competitiveness and productivity gaps between Europe and the USA in particular is the technology
gap, that is, insufficient spending in and use of ICT. But although the very
concepts of competitiveness and productivity are contested and the link between them and ICT is as intriguing today as it has ever been, various parts of
the electronic communications sector make often competing claims to competitiveness and the knowledge economy in an attempt to promote their own
interests. This chapter has alluded to two main competitiveness models advanced by differing economic, political and institutional interests and
grounded on contested assumptions about the state-market relationship.

On the one side, the Schumpeterian model, that has dominated (inter)national policy circles especially from the second half of the 1990s onward, emphasizes innovation and associated monopoly rents and is therefore inconsistent with open markets. For this model, regulatory
intervention, especially of a sector-specific kind, is restrictive. Public policy
has only a general enabling role to play. This role refers in particular to the
nurturing of an investment- and innovation-friendly environment which,
for this model, means no regulation and the at least temporary support of
oligopolies, even monopolies, as necessary incentives for innovation.

As this chapter analyzed, various interests advocate the Schumpeterian
model of competitiveness. Incumbent telecommunications operators, be
they fixed or mobile, are prepared to undertake the high investments
needed to roll out advanced broadband infrastructure—and in doing so
manifest their commitment and indispensable contribution to the Lisbon
goal of fostering Europe's competitiveness, and in turn assisting in the delivery of political promises made at the height of the technological euphoria concerning the advent of the knowledge economy—only if left unregulated and effectively allowed to monopolize new emerging markets, at least
for the short term.

Similarly, private, commercial, vertically integrated broadcasters warn
against regulatory intervention in the field of interactive digital television
services, as even the threat of it would put at risk Europe's competitiveness.
No regulation in this case has resulted in multiple non-interoperable proprietary standards for application program interfaces and, crucially, has
served to keep the European digital television market fragmented. Innovation and competitiveness are construed as more important values than media pluralism and diversity. In turn, the example of application program interfaces illustrates the problematic division of work between the EU and
member states whereby the former regulates infrastructure and associated

services and the latter regulates content. The regulation of associated services and facilities, so called digital gateways, is challenging precisely because it cuts across this division. The artificial distinction between infrastructure and content regulation depicts the difficulties in and limits to the formulation of a comprehensive EU regulatory framework for the regulation of the converging communication sectors.

Equally, the debate on radio spectrum and the 3G extension frequency band is essentially about competitiveness and the role, if any, of European and national public policy in shaping competitiveness through decisions on access to and terms of use of scarce resources. The pro-flexibility and technological neutrality camp, with strong supporters in the WiMax industry, advocates the Schumpeterian model that emphasizes innovation and implies competition between technologies.

But the pro-harmonization camp in radio spectrum management, with strong supporters within the established second generation and the nascent 3G industry, advocates a different model of competitiveness. For this camp, competitiveness is conditioned upon a big market, large economies of scale and competition within the same group of technologies, all of which may result in lower consumer prices and fast penetration of new technologies. Again this scenario implies an oligopoly but, unlike the Schumpeterian model, by emphasizing economies of scale and the creation of a big market through binding harmonized rules, this model is consistent with a more active public policy. This second alternative model of competitiveness can be seen as a leftover of the active industrial policy ethos of the 1980s and the associated neomercantilist vision of European integration. Indeed, it has large appeal among the interests that this ethos benefited in the first place. The case of radio spectrum and the 3G extension frequency band also depicts the potential conflict between harmonization, a core internal market principle, and international trade liberalization and technological neutrality, the latter a core tenet in the 2002 electronic communications regulatory framework of the EU.

The debate on competitiveness and the arguments of various sections of the electronic communications industry also need to be understood within the broader context of globalization and the position of the different sections in the international political economy. The case of 3G mobile standards demonstrated how the broader process of globalization may impact the process of Europeanization and, more specifically, how the competitiveness of internationally oriented economic actors can shape market developments and challenge established institutional structures. European manufacturers and operators with global strategies were interested less in the narrower European market and more in international markets, particularly those in East Asia in view of their huge growth potential. Cooperation with the Japanese and support for the W-CDMA standard was an attempt to translate the success and significant worldwide footprint of GSM into 3G. Ericsson and Nokia were instrumental in forging this cooperation. Crucially for outward-oriented economic players, unless they facilitate their international ambitions, European institutions and structures are limiting. Indeed, the need to expand to foreign markets challenged existing European structures, that is, the standardization body, ETSI. In the end, European standardization policy and its institutional framework were opened up and became internationalized with the formation of an international collaborative initiative (3GPP). In line with the Schumpeterian competitiveness model, the Commission, breaking with past practice, did not mandate standards but instead acted as an enabler, facilitating and fostering the growth ambitions of European industry.

The orthodoxy of competitiveness has impacted the character of European governance. The Schumpeterian model of competitiveness that sees prescriptive sectoral rules as restrictive and as business-, investment-, and innovation-unfriendly, together with the "better regulation" initiative, have contributed to the shift toward light-touch horizontal regulation and greater reliance on soft policy measures.

But whereas the horizontal model, that is technology- and platform-neutral regulation, has been relatively uncontroversial in relation to electronic communications infrastructure and associated services, it remains highly contentious in relation to the regulation of content. The attempt at the beginning of the 1990s to incorporate the regulation of the audiovisual sector into that of the broader category of services of general economic interest was defeated for fear that that would have negated (public service broadcasters) or strengthened (commercial broadcasters) the sector specificity of the audiovisual sector. In the early 2000s, a second attempt to subsume the audiovisual sector under a broader regulatory framework for services in general was also rejected.

The issue of horizontal content regulation has resurfaced in the current review of the television directive. The arguments in the debate mirror arguments raised in the late 1990s during the consultation on the Green Paper on convergence. On the one hand, technological convergence is used by public service broadcasters in particular as an argument to confirm the importance of regulation in the fulfilment of certain public service objectives, and by implication public service content, and to extend certain content rules horizontally to other platforms. On the other hand, commercial broadcasters and publishers, telecommunications operators, internet-related interests and some governments, notably Britain, use technological convergence as an argument for reduced regulatory oversight for all the communications sectors that are coming together, and in particular as an argument to forego, or at least considerably reduce, content regulation especially of the prescriptive type applied to terrestrial broadcasting. In effect, this latter group of interests appeals to the Schumpeterian model of competitiveness that perceives regulation as stymieing innovation and, in turn, economic growth. These interests maintain that the scope of the television directive, and arguably that of public service broadcasting too, should be left intact, confined to traditional television broadcasting.

Under horizontal regulation come also the general competition rules and the strong competence of the Commission in this area. The debate on public service broadcasting has entered a new stage. The very concept, evolution and modernization of public service broadcasting are being disputed. The debate is as lively and controversial as ever. Commercial interests have resorted to the EU's state aid regime to contest the expansion of public service broadcasters not only in the conventional broadcasting field but increasingly in online and neighboring activities. Although, with the exception of the TV2/Danmark case, the Commission has ruled in favor of public service broadcasters, there is growing pressure from commercial interests for the adoption of a negative definition of public service broadcasting which will confine it to areas that are not commercially attractive (market failure argument), a scenario that would seriously limit its role in the emerging new media. Indeed, as the *BBC Digital Curriculum* decision shows, in contrast to the practice so far, the presence or absence of commercial players has become a crucial factor in the definition of public service broadcasting in the nascent multi-platform digital communications landscape.

Finally, in addition to the shift toward horizontal regulation, the current phase of Europeanization increasingly relies on informal governance arrangements. The regulatory framework is less prescriptive and harmonization is less hierarchical, driven less by formal legislation and more by soft policy measures such as non-binding guidelines and specialist interaction in groupings of national regulators. Although the effectiveness and legitimacy potential of such new modes of governance are open to question, the important point is that their very existence affirms that EU integration is not simply about liberalization but also about re-regulation, not just about economic goals but also about social, cultural and democratic objectives. The prominence of the latter objectives has increased in the post–Cold War context, with the subsequent accession of many ex-communist countries into the EU and growing public discontent with European economic integration. But their pursuit through primarily informal governance arrangements makes their recognition symbolic rather than substantive. The political saliency of competitiveness is not likely to change this.

NOTES

1. European Commission, *Illegal and Harmful Content on the Internet*, COM(96) 487 (Brussels, 16 October 1996). European Commission, *Communications on Globalisation and the Information Society*, COM(98) 50 (Brussels, 4 February 1998).

2. Paul Schreyer, "The Contribution of Information and Communication Technology to Output Growth: A Study of the G7 Countries," *OECD STI Working Paper*, no. 2000/2 (Paris: OECD 2000). Alessandra Colecchia and Paul Schreyer, "ICT Investment and Economic Growth in the 1990s: Is the United States a Unique Case? A Comparative Study of Nine OECD Countries," *OECD STI Working Paper*, no. 2001/7 (Paris: OECD, 2001). Charles Ferguson, *The United States Broadband Problem: Analysis and Recommendations* (Washington, D.C.: Brookings Institution, 2002).

3. European Commission, *Productivity: The Key to Competitiveness of European Economies and Enterprises*, COM(2002) 262 (Brussels, 21 May 2002), 4–5.

4. European Commission, *The EU Economy: 2003 Review*, COM(2003) 729 (Brussels, 26 November 2003), 7.

5. OECD, *OECD Economic Outlook No. 67* (Paris: OECD, 2000), 208–9.

6. OECD, *The New Economy: Beyond the Hype* (Paris: OECD, 2001). Robert Gordon, "Does the 'New Economy' Measure up to the Great Inventions of the Past?," *Journal of Economic Perspectives* 14, no. 4 (2000): 49–74.

7. Erkki Liikanen [European Commissioner for Information Society], "The Future of the eEurope Action Plan," (speech/02/81, delivered at the Informal Telecommunications Council, Vitoria, 22 February 2002).

8. European Commission, *eEurope. An Information Society for All* (Brussels: European Commission, 1999).

9. EU, *Presidency Conclusions. Lisbon European Council. 23 and 24 March 2000*, (2000), paragraph 5, emphasis deleted, <http://www.consilium.europa.eu/ueDocs/cms_Data/docs/pressData/en/ec/00100-r1.en0.htm> (28 June 2006).

10. Giandomenico Majone, "The European Commission: The Limits of Centralization and the Perils of Parliamentarization," *Governance: An International Journal of Policy, Administration and Institutions* 15, no. 3 (2002): 387.

11. European Parliament and Council, "Regulation 2887/2000/EC of 18 December 2000 on Unbundled Access to the Local Loop," *Official Journal* L336/4, (30 December 2000). For a discussion see Maria Michalis, "Local Competition and the Role of Regulation: The EU Debate and Britain's Experience," *Telecommunications Policy* 15, nos. 10/11 (2001): 759–76.

12. European Commission, *Facing the Challenge. The Lisbon Strategy for Growth and Employment. Report from the High Level Group Chaired by Wim Kok* (Brussels: European Commission, 2004), 22.

13. European Commission, *Facing,* 12.

14. European Commission, *Facing,* 20.

15. "A Productivity Primer," *Economist*, 6 November 2004, 93.

16. Steve Lohr, "Computer Age Gains Respect of Economists," *New York Times*, 14 April 1999, A1.

17. "A Productivity Primer," *Economist*.

18. Steve Lohr, "Computer Age."

19. "A productivity Primer," *Economist*. See also: "Software Investment: Now They See It," *Economist*, 18 February 2006, 29.

20. "Lex: Productivity Growth," *Financial Times*, 3 October 2004, <http://www.ft.com> (4 October 2004).

21. Paul Strassmann, "Facts and Fantasies about Productivity," in *Information Productivity* (1997), <http://www.strassmann.com/pubs/fnf/factnfantasy.shtml> (24 June 2006).

22. Jürgen Strube [President of UNICE], "EU Competitiveness: More Enterprise, less State," *Financial Times*, 5 October 2003, <http://www.ft.com> (6 October 2003).

23. European Commission, *European Competitiveness Report*, SEC (2001) 1705 (Brussels, 29 October 2001), 9.

24. Paul Krugman, "Competitiveness: A Dangerous Obsession," *Foreign Affairs* 73, no. 2 (1994): 32.

25. Krugman, "Competitiveness," 39–41.

26. Alexis Jacquemin and Lucio Pench, "What Competitiveness for Europe? An Introduction," in *Europe Competing in the Global Economy*, ed. Alexis Jacquemin and Lucio Pench (Cheltenham: Edward Elgar, 1997), 14.

27. Thomas Lawton, "Introduction: Concepts Defined and Scenes Set," in *European Industrial Policy and Competitiveness*, ed. Thomas Lawton (London: Macmillan, 1999), 6.

28. See for instance the 2004–2006 WEF global competitiveness reports, <http://www.weforum.org/site/homepublic.nsf/Content/Global+Competitiveness+Programme%5CGlobal+Competitiveness+Report> (28 June 2006).

29. Lawton, "Introduction," 6.

30. Ben Rosamond, "Imagining the European Economy: 'Competitiveness' and the Social Construction of 'Europe' as an Economic Space," *New Political Economy* 7, no. 2 (2002): 157–77.

31. Susan Strange, "Who Are the EU? Ambiguities in the Concept of Competitiveness," *Journal of Common Market Studies* 36, no. 1 (1998): 101–14.

32. Eurostrategies and Cullen, *The Possible Value Added of a European Regulatory Authority for Telecommunications*, Report for the European Commission (1999).

33. European Commission, *Towards a New Framework for Electronic Communications Infrastructure and Associated Services. The 1999 Communications Review*, COM(1999) 539 (Brussels, 10 November 1999), 51–54.

34. Comitology committees are implementation committees chaired by the Commission. They comprise national policy experts and address measures of a technical nature. Effectively they allow national representatives to oversee the exercise by the European Commission of delegated implementation powers.

35. All responses referred to here are available at *Comments on the 1999 Communications Review*, <http://europa.eu.int/ISPO/infosoc/telecompolicy/review99/comments/comments.html> (1 July 2006).

36. European Commission, *Proposal for a Directive of the European Parliament and of the Council on a Common Regulatory Framework for Electronic Communications Networks and Services*, COM(2000) 393 (Brussels, 12 July 2000), article 6.

37. Iain Osbourne, "Consolidation of European Telecom Regulatory Boards. A Round Table Discussion on Broadband," 18 June 2001, <http://www.totaltele.com> (11 April 2004). See also Intug comments.

38. European Parliament, "Position of the European Parliament of 1 March 2001 on the Proposal for a European Parliament and Council Directive on a Common Regulatory Framework for Electronic Communications Networks and Services. A5-0053/2001," *Official Journal* C277/91 (1 October 2001).

39. European Parliament and Council, "Directive 2002/21/EC of 7 March 2002 on a Common Regulatory Framework for Electronic Communications Networks and Services (Framework Directive)," *Official Journal* L108/33, (24 April 2002).

40. European Commission, "Commission Recommendation 2003/312/EC of 11 February 2003 on Relevant Product and Services Markets Within the Electronics Communications Sectors Susceptible to ex ante Regulation in Accordance with Directive 2002/21/EC of the European Parliament and of the Council on a Common Regulatory Framework for Electronic Communication Networks and Services," *Official Journal* L114/45, (8 May 2003). The retail markets are: (1) Access to the public telephone network at a fixed location for residential customers, (2) Access to the public telephone network at a fixed location for non-residential customers, (3) Publicly available local and/or national telephone services provided at a fixed location for residential customers, (4) Publicly available international telephone services provided at a fixed location for residential customers, (5) Publicly available local and/or national telephone services provided at a fixed location for non-residential customers, (6) Publicly available international telephone services provided at a fixed location for non-residential customers. And the wholesale markets are: (7) The minimum set of leased lines, (8) Call origination on the public telephone network provided at a fixed location, (9) Call termination on individual public telephone network provided at a fixed location, (10) Transit services in the fixed public telephone network, (11) Wholesale unbundled access (including shared access), (12) Wholesale broadband access, (13) Wholesale terminating segments of leased lines, (14) Wholesale trunk segments of leased lines, (15) Access and call origination on public mobile telephone networks, (16) Voice call termination on individual mobile networks, (17) The wholesale national market for international roaming on public mobile networks, (18) Broadcasting transmission services, to deliver broadcast content to end users.

41. For instance, Ofcom in Britain has divided the market for international telephone services further on a destination basis.

42. European Commission, "Commission Guidelines on Market Analysis and the Assessment of Significant Market Power under the Community Regulatory Framework for Electronic Communications Networks and Services," *Official Journal* C165/6, (11 July 2002).

43. European Parliament and Council, "Directive 2002/21/EC," article 14(2).

44. European Commission, "Commission Guidelines on Market Analysis," paragraphs 75, 78.

45. European Commission, "Commission Recommendation 2003/561/EC of 23 July 2003 on Notifications, Time Limits and Consultations Provided for in Article 7 of Directive 2002/21/EC of the European Parliament and of the Council on a Common Regulatory Framework for Electronic Communications Networks and Services," *Official Journal* L190/13 (30 July 2003).

46. *European Commission Memo*, MEMO/06/257 (29 June 2006).

47. See the cases of mobile termination in Luxembourg (case LU/2005/231) and Finland (FI/2003/321) respectively. European Commission, "Article 7 procedures," <http://ec.europa.eu/information_society/policy/ecomm/article_7/index_en.htm> (5 Feb. 2007).

48. ECTA, *ECTA DSL Scorecard—June 2002*, <http://www.ectaportal.com/regulatory/dsl_jun02.xls> (20 August 2002).

49. EU, *Comments on Draft Commission Recommendation on Relevant Markets* (2002). All responses are available at <http://europa.eu.int/information_society/topics/telecoms/regulatory/publiconsult/documents/comments_on_draft_rec_relevant_prod_service_mkts.htm> (25 June 2006).

50. Michelle Donegan, "Big Brass Get Heavy with the Regulators," *Communications Week International*, 16 December 2002, 12.

51. "European Officials Clash over Pace of Unbundling," 20 February 2003, <http://www.totaltele.com> (22 February 2003).

52. ETNO, "E-Communications Driving European Competitiveness. ETNO's Vision for the Future," 2005, 10, <http://www.etno.be> (20 March 2005).

53. ETNO, "E-Communications," 6.

54. Gerrit Wiesmann, "DT Rivals up in Arms at Broadband Exemption," *Financial Times*, 13 November 2005, 21.

55. *European Commission Press Release*, IP/07/237 (26 February 2007).

56. Jeanne-Mey Sun and Jacques Pelkmans, "Why Liberalisation Needs Centralisation: Subsidiarity and EU Telecoms," *World Economy* 18, no. 5 (1995): 635–64.

57. See comments on the 1999 Communications review by DVB Group, EBU, Ericsson, GSM Europe, Nokia, Vodafone AirTouch.

58. European Commission, "Commission Decision 2002/622/EC of 2 July 2002 establishing a Radio Spectrum Policy Group," *Official Journal* L198/49 (27 July 2002).

59. RSPG, "RSPG 04-56. Proposal for Strengthening Further the Future Working of the RSPG," 5 November 2004, <http://rspg.groups.eu.int/doc/documents/meeting/rspg5/rspg04_56_prop_strengh_work_rspg.doc> (22 April 2005).

60. See RSPG, <http://rspg.groups.eu.int/> (26 June 2006).

61. European Commission, "Commission Decision 2002/627/EC of 29 July 2002 Establishing the European Regulators Group for Electronic Communications Networks and Services," *Official Journal* L200/38 (30 July 2002), article 3(2).

62. European Commission, *Fifth Report on the Implementation of the Telecommunications Regulatory Package*, COM(1999) 537 (Brussels, 10 November 1999), and U.S. government response to 1999 Review.

63. Interview with head of national regulatory authority, member of ERG/IRG, 28 October 2003, Berlin. As of 2007, with the accession of Bulgaria and Romania, the EU has twenty-seven members.

64. European Commission, "Commission Decision 2004/641/EC of 14 September 2004 Amending Decision 2002/627/EC Establishing the European Regulators Groups for Electronic Communications Networks and Services," *Official Journal* L293/30 (19 September 2004).

65. European Commission, "Commission Decision 2002/627/EC," preamble 7.

66. See ERG, <http://erg.eu.int/index_en.htm> (26 June 2006).

67. ERG, *ERG (03) 07. Rules of Procedure for ERG*, April 2004, <http://erg.eu.int/doc/work_progr_2003/erg_03_07_rules_of_procedure_clean.pdf> (1 July 2006).

68. It has subsequently been amended. See ERG, *ERG (06) 33. Revised ERG Common Position on the Approach Remedies in the ECNS Regulatory Framework* (May 2006), <http://erg.eu.int/doc/meeting/erg_06_33_remedies_common_position_june_06.pdf> (29 June 2006).

69. European Parliament and the Council, "Decision 676/2002/EC of 7 March 2002 on a Regulatory Framework for Radio Spectrum Policy in the European Community (Radio Spectrum Decision)," *Official Journal* L108/1 (24 April 2002).

70. *European Commission Press Release*, IP/03/1356, 8 October 2003.

71. European Commission, *Eleventh Report on the Implementation of the Telecommunications Regulatory Package*, SEC(2006) 193 (Brussels, 20 February 2006), 41 (vol. 1), and *European Commission Memo*, MEMO/06/487 (13 December 2006).

72. European Commission, *Eleventh Report*, 50 (vol. 1).

73. European Commission, *Eleventh Report*, 36 (vol. 1).

74. Interview with high level OECD official, London, 10 October 2005.

75. Andrienne Héritier, "New Modes of Governance in Europe: Policy-Making without Legislating?," *Max Planck Project Group: Common Goods: Law, Politics and Economics*, 2001/14, <http://papers.ssrn.com/abstract=299431> (2 July 2006).

76. Annegret Groebel, "European Regulator Group (ERG)," (2002), <http://www.regtp.de/en/international/start/in_11-02-00-00-00_m/> (12 April 2005).

77. For instance, Oftel, *The Benefits of Self- and Co-regulation to Consumers and Industry. Statement Issued by the Director General of Telecommunications* (London: Oftel, 2001).

78. European Commission, *European Governance. A White Paper*, COM(2001) 428 (Brussels, 25 July 2001). European Commission, *Action Plan: Simplifying and Improving the Regulatory Environment*, COM(2002) 278 (Brussels, 5 June 2002).

79. See indicatively UNICE, *Releasing Europe's Potential through Targeted Regulatory Reform. The Unice Regulatory Report* (Brussels: Unice, 1995).

80. Better Regulation Task Force, *Regulation—Less Is More: Reducing Burdens, Improving Outcomes* (London: BTRF, 2005).

81. European Commission, *Better Regulation for Growth and Jobs in the European Union*, COM(2005) 97 (Brussels, 16 March 2005).

82. Michelle Cini, "The Soft Law Approach: Commission Rule-Making in the EU's State-aid Regime," *Journal of European public Policy* 8, no. 2 (2001): 192–207. Andrea Lenschow, "Transformation of European Environmental Governance," in *The Transformation of Governance in the European Union*, ed. Beate Kohler-Koch and Rainer Eising (London and New York: Routledge, 1999), 39–60.

83. Helen Wallace, "The Changing Politics of the European Union: An Overview," *Journal of Common Market Studies* 39, no. 4 (2001): 588, 591.

84. Colin Bennett, "Review Article: What Is Policy Convergence and What Causes It?," *British Journal of Political Science* 21 (1991): 215–33.

85. European Parliament, *Report on the Commission White Paper on European Governance*, Rapporteur: Sylvia-Yvonne Kaufmann. A5-0399/2001 (Brussels, 15 November 2001). Caroline de la Porte and Patrizia Nanz, "The OMC—A Deliberative-democratic Mode of Governance? The Cases of Employment and Pensions," *Journal of European Public Policy* 11, no. 2 (2004): 267–88. For deliberative democracy see Erik Oddvar Eriksen and John Erik Fossum, eds., *Democracy in the European Union: Integration through Deliberation?* (London: Routledge, 2000).

86. Brigid Laffan and Colin Shaw, "Classifying and Mapping OMC in Different Policy Areas," 2005, 11, <http://www.eu-newgov.org/database/DELIV/D02D09_Classifying_and_Mapping_OMC.pdf> (7 Feb. 2007).

87. European Commission, *Communication on the Review of the EU Regulatory Framework for Electronic Communications Networks and Services*, COM(2006) 334

(Brussels, 29 June 2006), And *Staff Working Document on the Review of the EU Regulatory Framework for Electronic Communications Networks and Services*, SEC (2006) 816 (Brussels, 29 June 2006).

88. Viviane Reding [European Commissioner for Information Society and Media], "Towards a True Internal Market for Europe's Telecom Industry and Consumers —The Regulatory Challenges Ahead" (speech/07/86, delivered at the 20th Plenary of the European Regulators' Group, Brussels, 15 February 2007).

89. See indicatively the contributions of Unice, BEUC, ECTA and BT to EU, *Responses to the Consultation on the Review of the 2002 Regulatory Framework for Electronic Communications*, October 2006, <http://ec.europa.eu/information_society/policy/ ecomm/info_centre/documentation/public_consult/review_2/index_en.htm> (15 March 2007).

90. European Commission, *Communication on the Review of the EU Regulatory Framework for Electronic Communications Networks and Services: Impact Assessment*, SEC(2006) 817 (Brussels, 28 June 2006), 19–21.

91. ERG, *ERG (06) 67. Harmonisation—The Proposed ERG Approach*, October 2006, <http://erg.eu.int/doc/publications/consult_erg_approach_harmonisation/erg_06_ 67_harmonisation_approach.pdf> (3 Feb. 2007). ERG, *ERG (06) 68. Effective Harmonisation within the European Electronic Communications Sector*, October 2006, <http://erg.eu.int/doc/publications/consult_effective_harmonisation/erg_06_68_ effective_harmonisation.pdf> (3 Feb. 2007).

92. Andrienne Héritier, "New Modes of Governance in Europe: Increasing Political Capacity and Policy Effectiveness?," in *The State of the European Union, 6: Law, Politics, and Society*, ed. Tanja Börzel and Rachel Cichowski (2003), 105–26.

93. *European Commission Memo*, MEMO/07/87 (27 February 2007).

94. European Commission, *Impact Assessment*, SEC(2006) 817, 13–19.

95. European Commission, *Draft Commission Recommendation on Relevant Product and Service Markets within the Electronic Communications Sector Susceptible to ex ante Regulation in Accordance with Directive 2002/21/EC on a Common Regulatory Framework for Electronic Communication Networks and Services*, SEC(2006) 837 (Brussels, 28 June 2006).

96. The markets are publicly available local and/or national telephone services provided at a fixed location for residential and non-residential customers (markets 3 and 5), publicly available international telephone services provided at a fixed location for residential and non-residential customers (markets 4 and 6), and available international telephone services provided at a fixed location for non-residential and the minimum set of leased lines (market 7). It further proposes to merge the retail markets for access to the public telephone network at a fixed location for residential and non-residential users (markets 1 and 2).

97. European Commission, *Proposal for a Regulation on Roaming on Public Mobile Networks within the Community and Amending Directive 2002/21/EC on a Common Regulatory Framework for Electronic Communication Networks and Services*, COM(2006) 382 (Brussels, 12 July 2006).

98. See the GSM Association's contribution to: EU, *Second Phase Consultation on International Roaming*, March 2006, <http://ec.europa.eu/information_society/activities/ roaming/roaming_regulation/consultation/index_en.htm> (15 March 2007).

99. See respectively BEUC's and Intug's comments on EU, *Second Phase Consultation on International Roaming*, March 2006, <http://ec.europa.eu/information_

society/activities/roaming/roaming_regulation/consultation/index_en.htm> (15 March 2007).

100. European Commission, *Green Paper on Services of General Interest*, COM(2003) 270 (Brussels, 21 May 2003).

101. European Commission, *White Paper on Services of General Interest*, COM(2004) 374 (Brussels, 12 May 2004).

102. European Commission, *Green Paper*, 3.

103. European Commission, *Green Paper*, 6–7.

104. EU, *Comments on Green Paper on Services of General Interest* (2003). All comments are available at <http://ec.europa.eu/services_general_interest/comments/public_en.htm> (10 July 2006).

105. EU, *Comments on Green*, EBU and ARD/ZDF submissions.

106. EU, *Comments on Green*, ACT, 1–2.

107. EU, *Comments on Green*, ETNO.

108. European Commission, *Proposal for a Directive of the European Parliament and of the Council on Services in the Internal Market*, COM(2004) 2 (Brussels, 13 January 2004).

109. EBU, *EBU Position Paper on the Commission Proposal for a Directive on Services in the Internal Market* (Geneva: EBU, 2004), 10.

110. EBU, *EBU Position Paper*, 2. European Parliament, *Position of the European Parliament Adopted at First Reading on 16 February 2006 with a View to the Adoption of Directive 2006/.../EC of the European Parliament and Council on Services in the Internal Market*, PE 369.610 (Brussels, 16 February 2006).

111. European Commission, *Amended Proposal for a Directive of the European Parliament and of the Council on Services in the Internal Market*, COM(2006) 160 (Brussels, 4 April 2006).

112. *European Report*, "Culture/ Audiovisual Council," 25 May 2002.

113. European Parliament, *Resolution on Television without Frontiers (2003/2033(INI))*, P5_TA(2003)0381 (Brussels, 4 September 2003).

114. EU, *Comments on TVWF Review 2003*, <http://ec.europa.eu/comm/avpolicy/reg/tvwf/modernisation/consultation_2003/contributions/index_en.htm> (1 July 2006). European Commission, *Communication on the Future of European Regulatory Audiovisual Policy*, COM(2003) 784 (Brussels, 15 December 2003).

115. European Commission, *Interpretative Communication on Certain Aspects of the Provisions on Televised Advertising in the "Television without Frontiers" Directive*, C(2004) 1450 (Brussels, 23 April 2004).

116. European Commission, *Commission Proposal for a Recommendation on the Protection of Minors and Human Dignity and the Right of Reply in Relation to the Competitiveness of the European Audiovisual and Information Services Industry*, COM(2004) 341 (Brussels, 30 April 2004).

117. See the European Commission, *Issues Papers for the TVWF Review 2005*, <http://ec.europa.eu/comm/avpolicy/reg/tvwf/modernisation/consultation_2005/index_en.htm> (1 July 2006). EU, *Comments on TVWF Review 2005*, <http://ec.europa.eu/comm/avpolicy/reg/tvwf/modernisation/consultation_2005/contributions/index_en.htm> (1 July 2006).

118. European Commission, *Communication on the Future*, 14.

119. For instance, see EU, *Comments on TVWF Review 2003*, by the German broadcasters ARD/ZDF.

120. European Parliament, *Resolution on Television*. EU, *Comments on TVWF Review 2003*, EBU.

121. European Commission, *Media Pluralism in the Member States of the European Union*, SEC(2007) 32 (Brussels, 16 January 2007).

122. For instance, see EU, *Comments on TVWF Review 2003*, by the BBC and the EBU. Also EU, *Comments on TVWF Review 2005*, by ARD/ZDF, EBU, and Nordic public service broadcasters.

123. EU, *Comments on TVWF Review 2003*, ETNO. Also comments by GSM Europe.

124. Andrew Murray-Watson, "Google Challenges EU Plan to Regulate the Internet," *Telegraph*, 29 January 2006, <www.telegraph.co.uk> (1 Feb. 2006).

125. An information society service is "any service normally provided for remuneration, at a distance, by electronic means and at the individual request of a recipient of services." This definition does not cover in particular radio and television broadcasting services (including near-video-on-demand) and teletext. European Parliament and the Council, "Directive 2000/31/EC of 8 June 2000 on Certain Legal Aspects of Information Society Services, in Particular Electronic Commerce, in the Internal Market," *Official Journal* L178/1 (17 July 2000).

126. EU, *Comments TVWF 2005*, EBU.

127. EU, *Comments TVWF 2005*, ACT, 2.

128. For instance, Ofcom, *Online Protection: A Survey of Consumer, Industry and Regulatory Mechanisms and Systems* (London: Ofcom, 2006).

129. European Commission, "Proposal for a Directive Amending Council Directive 89/552/EEC on the Coordination of Certain Provisions Laid Down by Law, Regulation or Administrative Action in Member States Concerning the Pursuit of Television Broadcasting Activities," COM(2005) 646 (Brussels, 13 December 2005).

130. European Commission, "Proposal," recital 28.

131. EBU, *Draft Audiovisual Media Services Directive: Initial EBU Contribution to the First Reading* (Geneva: EBU, 2006), 4. For an analysis see Ivan Bernier, "Content Regulation in the Audio-visual Sector and the WTO," in *The WTO and Global Convergence in Telecommunications and Audio-Visual Services*, ed. Damien Geradin and David Luff (Cambridge: Cambridge University Press), 215–42.

132. For a useful summary of the British position see House of Lords—European Union Committee, *Television without Frontiers? Report with Evidence* (London: Stationery Office, 2007).

133. House of Lords, *Television*, paragraph 82, emphasis deleted.

134. RAND Europe, *Assessing Indirect Impacts of the EC Proposals for Video Regulation. Prepared for Ofcom* (Cambridge: RAND Europe, 2006).

135. House of Lords, *Television*, Mr. Shaun Woodward, oral evidence question 157.

136. Campaign for Press and Broadcasting Freedom [UK], *Television Without Frontiers*, 10 October 2006, <http://keywords.dsvr.co.uk/freepress/body.phtml?category=&id=1512> (9 Nov. 2006). House of Lords, *Television*, paragraphs 170–83. DCMS/EU, *Liverpool Audiovisual Conference. Between Culture and Commerce. 20–22 September 2005* (London: DCMS, 2005), <http://ec.europa.eu/comm/avpolicy/docs/reg/modernisation/liverpool_2005/uk-conference-report-en.pdf> (1 July 2006).

137. House of Lords, *Television*, paragraph 81, emphasis deleted.

138. See indicatively European Commission, *The Commission's Contribution to the Period of Reflection and Beyond: Plan-D for Democracy, Dialogue and Debate*, COM(2005) 494 (Brussels,13 October 2005).

139. European Parliament, *Legislative Resolution on the Proposal for a Directive Amending Council Directive 89/552/EEC on the Coordination of Certain Provisions Laid Down by Law, Regulation or Administrative Action in Member States Concerning the Pursuit of Television Broadcasting Activities*, P6_TA-PROV(2006)0559 (Strasbourg, 13 December 2006). European Parliament, *Report on the Proposal for a Directive Amending Council Directive 89/552/EEC on the Coordination of Certain Provisions Laid Down by Law, Regulation or Administrative Action in Member States Concerning the Pursuit of Television Broadcasting Activities*, Rapporteur: Ruth Hieronymi. A6-0399/2006 (Brussels, 22 November 2006).

140. Council, *Proposal for a Directive Amending Council Directive 89/552/EEC on the Coordination of Certain Provisions Laid Down by Law, Regulation or Administrative Action in Member States Concerning the Pursuit of Television Broadcasting Activities (Television without Frontiers) General Approach*, 14464/06 (Brussels, 31 October and 7 November 2006).

141. European Commission, *Draft Audiovisual Media Services Directive. Consolidated Text*, 9 March 2007, <http://ec.europa.eu/comm/avpolicy/docs/reg/modernisation/proposal_2005/avmsd_cons_amend_0307_en.pdf> (10 March 2007).

142. House of Lords, *Television*, paragraph 183.

143. European Commission, "Proposal [2007]," recital 6.

144. European Audiovisual Observatory, *Transfrontier Television in the European Union. Market Impact and Selected Legal Aspects* (Strasbourg: EAO, 2004), <http://www.obs.coe.int/> (1 June 2005).

145. European Commission, "Proposal [2005]," articles 2.7–2.10.

146. Satellite and Cable Broadcasters' Group, EU, *Comments on TVWF Review 2003*.

147. House of Lords, *Television*, paragraphs 36–37, 100.

148. European Commission, *Draft Audiovisual*, articles 2a, 3.

149. See their submissions to the 2003 consultation.

150. See *Comments on TVWF Review 2003*, by UK Government, ARD-ZDF and ACT.

151. EU, *Comments on TVWF Review 2003*, EFCA, 1.

152. EU, *Comments on TVWF Review 2003*, ACT, 5.

153. EU, *Comments on TVWF Review 2005*, EBU, 7.

154. EU, *Comments on TVWF Review 2005*, BBC.

155. European Commission, "Proposal [2007," article 3f.

156. See EU, *Comments on TVWF Review 2003*, by RTE, ACT, EBU, ARD/ZDF.

157. EU Contact Committee of the TVWF Directive. "Rules of Procedure of the Contact Committee," 2004, <http://ec.europa.eu/comm/avpolicy/docs/reg/tvwf/contact_comm/doccctvsf97-2_rulesofpr-rev041021.pdf> (12 June 2006).

158. European Commission, "Conclusions. High-level Group of Regulatory Authorities in the Field of Broadcasting—Incitement to Hatred in Broadcasts Coming from Outside of the European Union" (17 March 2005), <http://ec.europa.eu/comm/avpolicy/docs/library/legal/conclusions_regulateurs/conclusions_regulateurs_fin_en.pdf> (1 July 2006).

159. European Parliament, *Report on the Risks of Violation, in the EU and Especially in Italy, of Freedom of Expression and Information*, Rapporteur: Johanna Boogerd-Quaak, A5-0230/2004 (Brussels, 5 April 2004), 9.

160. EU, *Comments on TVWF Review 2003*, ITC, 7.

161. Council of Europe, *Explanatory Memorandum: Report on Public Service Broadcasting*, Rapporteur: Paschal Mooney (Strasbourg, 12 January 2004), paragraph 68.

162. European Court of Justice, "Judgment of 24 July 2003 in Case C-280/00, Altmark Trans GmbH and Regierungspräsidium Magdeburg v Nahverkehrsgesellschaft Altmark GmbH," *European Court Reports* (2003): I-7747.

163. European Commission, "Communication on the Application of State Aid Rules to Public Service Broadcasting," *Official Journal* C320/5 (15 November 2001).

164. European Commission, "Commission Decision 2005/406/EC of 15 October 2003 on ad hoc Measures Implemented by Portugal for RTP," *Official Journal* L142/1 (6 June 2005). European Commission, "Commission Decision 2004/339/EC of 15 October 2003 on the Measures Implemented by Italy for RAI SpA," *Official Journal* L119/1 (23 April 2004). European Commission, "Commission Decision 2004/838/EC of 10 December 2003 on State Aid Implemented by France for France 2 and France 3," *Official Journal* L361/21 (8 December 2004).

165. European Commission, *State Aid No. NN 88/98—United Kingdom, Financing of a 24-hour Advertising-free News Channel out of the Licence Fee by the BBC*, SG(99) D/10201 (Brussels, 14 December 1999).

166. European Commission, *State Aid No. NN 88/98*, paragraph 57.

167. European Commission, *State Aid No. N 631/2001—United Kingdom BBC Licence Fee*, C(2002) 1886 (Brussels, 22 May 2002), paragraph 27.

168. EU, "Resolution of the Council and of the Representatives of the Governments of the Member States Meeting within the Council of 25 January 1999, Concerning Public Service Broadcasting," *Official Journal* C30/1 (5 February 1999).

169. European Commission, *State Aid No. N 631/2001*, paragraph 29.

170. European Commission, *State Aid No. N 631/2001*, paragraph 30.

171. European Commission, *State Aid No. N 631/2001*, paragraph 36.

172. European Commission, *State Aid No. N 631/2001*, paragraph 37.

173. *European Commission Press Release*, IP/06/822 (22 June 2006).

174. *European Commission Press Release*, IP/04/146 (3 February 2004).

175. *European Commission Press Release*, IP/04/666 (19 May 2004). European Commission, *Decision on Measures No. C 2/2003 (ex NN 22/02) Implemented by Denmark for TV2/DANMARK*, C(2004)1814 (Brussels, 19 May 2004).

176. European Commission, *Decision on Measures*, point 91.

177. European Commission, *Decision on Measures*, point 92.

178. *European Commission Press Release*, IP/05/250 (3 March 2005).

179. *European Commission Memo*, MEMO/05/73 (3 March 2005) and MEMO/06/273 (7 July 2006).

180. European Commission, "Communication on the Application," paragraph 36, original emphasis.

181. European Commission, *State Aid No. N 37/2003—United Kingdom BBC Digital Curriculum* (Brussels, 1 October 2003).

182. The Independent Review Panel on the Future Funding of the BBC chaired by Gavyn Davies shared this view: "Too often, the BBC in effect behaves as if public

service broadcasting is everything the BBC chooses to put out." DCMS, *The Future Funding of the BBC: Report of the Independent Review Pane, Chairman Gavyn Davies* (London: DCMS, 1999), 139.

183. European Commission, *State Aid No. N 37/2003*, paragraph 36.

184. Dominic Timms, "Learning to Fight Back," *Guardian*, 13 January 2003, 50.

185. European Commission, *State Aid No. N 37/2003*, paragraph 41.

186. Stefaan Depypere and Nynke Tigchelaar, "The Commission's State Aid Policy on Activities of Public Service Broadcasters in Neighbouring Markets," *EU Competition Policy Newsletter*, no. 2 (2004): 19.

187. Depypere and Tigchelaar, "The Commission's," 20. This view is shared by the OECD. OECD, *Policy and Regulatory Issues for Network-Based Content Services*, DSTI/ICCP/IE(96) 9/REV1 (Paris: OECD, 1997), 6.

188. Richard Collins, "The Contemporary Broadcasting Market and the Role of the Public Service Broadcaster. A View from the UK" (paper presented at the meeting on the future of broadcasting at YLE, Helsinki, 20 March 2002). Nicholas Garnham, "The Broadcasting Market," *The Political Quarterly* 65, no. 1 (1994): 11–19. For a comprehensive analysis see DCMS, *The Future*, 202–8.

189. ACT, ICRT, ENPA, EPC and AER, "Broadcasting and Competition Rules in the Future EU Constitution—A View from the Private Media Sector" (paper submitted to the European Convention, 2003), 4, <http://www.icrt.org/pos_papers/2003/030502_BO.pdf> (1 July 2006).

190. ACT, AER, and EPC, *Safeguarding the Future of the European Audiovisual Market. A White Paper on the Financing and Regulation of Publicly Funded Broadcasters* (2004), 1, 3, <http://www.epceurope.org/presscentre/archive/safeguarding_audiovisual_market_300304.pdf> (1 July 2006). The Association of Commercial Television in Europe, ACT, represents the interests of around twenty leading private sector television companies in the EU, including the Spanish Antena 3 and Telecinco, the British BSkyB and ITV, the French Cana+ and M6, the German Premiere, the pan-European RTL Group based in Luxembourg, the Italian Mediaset and the Swedish TV4. The AER is a pan-European trade body representing approximately 4,500 private commercial radio stations. The European Publishers' Council is a high level group of nearly thirty Chairmen and CEOs of European media corporations active in various media markets, including newspapers, magazines and online databases, and private television and radio.

191. ACT, AER, and EPC, *Safeguarding*, 4.

192. ACT, AER, and EPC, *Safeguarding*, 14–15.

193. EU, *Comments on Green*, ACT, 5.

194. *European Commission Press Release*, IP/05/250 (3 March 2005).

195. *European Commission Memo*, MEMO/05/73 (3 March 2005), emphasis deleted.

196. *European Commission Memo*, MEMO/05/73 (3 March 2005).

197. Michael Wagner, "Liberalization and Public Service Broadcasting. Competition Regulation, State Aid and the Impact of Liberalization" (1999), 5, <http://www.ebu.ch/CMSimages/en/leg_p_psb_liberalization_mw_tcm6-4356.pdf> (4 July 2006).

198. Council of Europe, *Explanatory Memorandum*, paragraph 3.

199. European Parliament, *Resolution on the Risks of Violation, in the EU and Especially in Italy, of Freedom of Expression and Information*, P5_TA(2004)0373 (Brussels,

22 April 2004). See EU Dutch Presidency, "The Key Role of Public Service Broadcasting in the 21st Century" (conference proceedings, Amsterdam, 2–3 September 2004), <http://www.omroep.nl/eu2004/> (1 July 2006). EBU, "The Lisbon Strategy and the Specific Role of Public Service Broadcasting," *EBU Diffusion*, no. 1 (2005): 24–26. Council of Europe—Committee of Ministers, *Recommendation (2007) 3 on the Remit of Public Service Media in the Information Society* (Strasbourg, 31 January 2007).

200. Council of Europe, *Explanatory Memorandum*, paragraph 91.

201. Application Programming Interface is the equivalent to a computer operating system and controls even the most basic application.

202. European Parliament and Council, "Directive 2002/21/EC," article 18.

203. European Commission, *Commission Staff Working Paper on the Interoperability of Digital Interactive Television Services*, SEC(2004) 346 (Brussels,18 March 2004), 11–12.

204. EU, *Responses to the 2004 Digital Interoperability Consultation*, <http://europa.eu.int/information_society/policy/ecomm/info_centre/documentation/public_consult/interoperability_idtv/index_en.htm> (1 July 2006).

205. Digital Interoperability Forum <http://www.difgroup.com/> (26 June 2006). Sky Digital, controlled by BSkyB—dominant market player in Britain operating the satellite digital television platform—was instrumental in its creation.

206. See the debate on media pluralism and ownership in chapter 5.

207. EU, *Responses to the 2004 Digital*, DIF submission, point 63. See also Microsoft's submission.

208. DIF submission, point 20. DIF, "Welcome to the Digital Interoperability Forum," <http://www.difgroup.com> (26 June 2006).

209. European Commission, *Communication on Reviewing the Interoperability of Digital Interactive Television Services Pursuant to Communications COM(2004) 541 of 30 July 2004*, COM(2006) 37 (Brussels, 2 February 2006).

210. European Commission, *Communication on Interoperability of Digital Interactive Television Services*, COM(2004) 541 (Brussels, 30 July 2004), 6.

211. ITU, *Regulatory Implications of Telecommunications Convergence, Chairman's Report of the Sixth Regulatory Colloquium* (Geneva: ITU, 1997).

212. Bosco Eduardo Fernandes, "The UMTS Task Force," in *GSM and UMTS. The Creation of Global Mobile Communication*, ed. Friedhelm Hillebrand (Chichester: John Wiley, 2002), 147–48.

213. European Commission, *Towards the Personal Communications Environment: Green Paper on a Common Approach to Mobile and Personal Communications in the European Union*, COM(94) 145 (Brussels, 27 April 1994), section III.1.

214. Thomas Beijer, "The UMTS Forum," in *GSM and UMTS. The Creation of Global Mobile Communication*, ed. Friedhelm Hillebrand, (Chichester: John Wiley, 2002), 160–61.

215. Friedhelm Hillebrand, "The Creation of the UMTS Foundations in ETSI from April 1996 to February 1999," in *GSM and UMTS: The Creation of Global Mobile Communication*, ed. Friedhelm Hillebrand (Chichester: John Wiley, 2002), 188.

216. Newsbytes News Network, "Nokia & Ericsson Backing Wideband CDMA," 9 June 1997, <http://www.newsbytes.com> (5 Mar. 2005).

217. European Commission, *Communication on the Further Development of Mobile and Wireless Communications—Challenges and Choices for the European Union*, COM(1997) 217 (Brussels, 29 May 1997), 18, emphasis added.

218. UMTS Forum, *A Regulatory Framework for UMTS*, 1997, <http://www.umts-forum.org/servlet/dycon/ztumts/umts/Live/en/umts/Resources_Reports_01_index> (29 Mar. 2005).

219. Hillebrand, "The Creation," 193.

220. Hillebrand, "The Creation," 207.

221. For details see Hillebrand, "The Creation," and Johan Lembke, *Competition for Technological Leadership. EU Policy for High Technology* (Cheltenham and Northampton, MA: Edward Elgar, 2002), 185–95.

222. I adopt the three periods in European 3G standardization identified by Josef Huber, Dirk Weiler and Hermann Brand, "UMTS, the Mobile Multimedia Vision for IMT-2000: A Focus on Standardization," *IEEE Communications Magazine* (September 2000): 129–36.

223. Huber et al., "UMTS," 131.

224. Hillebrand, "The Creation," 217.

225. 3GPP, <http://www.3gpp.org/About/about.htm> (5 Mar. 2005).

226. European Parliament and Council, "Decision 128/1999/EC of the on the Co-ordinated Introduction of a Third-generation Mobile and Wireless Communications System (UMTS) in the Community," *Official Journal* C17/1 (22 January 1999).

227. Joanne Guth, "Update on the U.S.-EU Third-Generation Mobile Phone Technology Debate: Who's Calling the Shots on Standards?" *International Economic Review* (May/June 1999): 23–2.

228. TABD, "1998 Charlotte Transatlantic Business Dialogue" (1 October 1998), 9, <http://128.121.145.19/tabd/media/1998CharlotteCEOReport.pdf> (31 Mar. 2005).

229. Guth, "Update," 24.

230. PR Newswire, "Wireless Operators Announce Agreement on Globally Harmonized Third-Generation (G3G) Code Division Multiple Access Standard," 8 June 1999, <http://www.prnewswire.co.uk/cgi/news/release?id=51166> (30 Mar. 2005). OHG, "Open Letter to Standard Organizations from Operators Harmonization Group on Global 3G (G3G) CDMA Standard," June 1999, <http://www.3gpp.org/ftp/tsg_ran/TSG_RAN/TSGR_04/Docs/Pdfs/rp-99358.pdf> (31 Mar. 2005).

231. For instance, Council, "Directive 87/372/EEC of 25 June 1987 on the Frequency Bands to be Reserved for the Coordinated Introduction of Public Pan-European Cellular Digital Land-based Mobile Communications in the Community," *Official Journal* L196/85 (17 July 1987). Council, "Directive 91/287/EEC of 3 June 1991 on the Frequency Bands to be Reserved for the Coordinated Introduction of Digital Cordless Telecommunications (DECT) into the Community," *Official Journal* L144/45 (8 June 1991).

232. Martin Cave, *Review of Radio Spectrum Management. An independent Review for Department of Trade and Industry and HM Treasury* (2002), 221, <http://www.ofcom.org.uk/static/archive/ra/spectrum-review/index.htm> (26 June 2006).

233. Cave, *Review*. Ofcom, *Spectrum Framework Review* (London: Ofcom, 2004).

234. Wi-Max (World Inter-operability for Microwave Access) is the long-range wireless broadband technology offering around 2–10Mbits access over wide areas up to 50km. 3G networks are upgrading to offer 2 Mbits.

235. Electronic Communications Committee [CEPT], *ECC Decision (02)06 on the Designation of Frequency Band 2500–2690 MHz for UMTS/IMT-2000*, 2002, <http://www.ero.dk/documentation/docs/doc98/official/Word/DEC0206.DOC> (6 June 2006). ECC, *ECC Decision (05)05 on Harmonised Utilisation of Spectrum for IMT-2000/UMTS Systems Operating Within the Band 2500–2690 MHz*, 2005, <http://www.ero.dk/documentation/docs/doc98/official/pdf/ECCDEC0505.PDF> (6 June 2006).

236. EU, *Consultation on 3G Extension Band*, 2005, <http://forum.europa.eu.int/Public/irc/infso/radiospectrum/home> (21 November 2005). For a summary of the consultation see Radio Spectrum Committee, RSC *Report on the Invitation for Comments to the Use of the Band 2500–2670 MHz. RSCOM05-44rev1* (Brussels: European Commission, 28 October 2005).

7
Conclusions

We set out with the intention of studying the governance of communications at the European level, combining two analytical strands. The historical account of the origins, dynamics and changing character of European governance has pointed to its contested character, a contestation, we have argued, that has less to do with the territorial more-or-less Europe dichotomy and more with socioeconomic conflicts over which interests, sectors and values should be promoted, and the power to influence such choices. This historical contextualization allows us to understand the present phase of governance as the latest phase in a process that goes back to the early days of European-level cooperation in the postwar period.[1]

In this study, the European and the national regulatory states, comprising both formal and, increasingly, informal governance arrangements, are not construed as antithetical or mutually exclusive but rather as co-constitutive and interdependent, both integral elements of the European system of governance which reproduces the fundamental problem of governmentality that prioritizes output over input legitimacy and the "economic" over the "political" sphere; both, in turn, are embedded in broader economic and political changes of Europe in a global context. From this perspective, regulatory issues and governance challenges are neither national nor European alone; rather, they need to be understood as part of wider developments.

Thus, the historical account has run alongside a political economy account in an attempt to open up the theorizing of "Europe" by placing the process and evolution of European governance within the context of broader transformations, looking at technological and economic change, general developments in the political economy of capitalism and the modern state—notably the move from the positive welfare to the regulatory competitive state—ideational and institutional factors. In doing so, some of the themes underlying the analysis provided in this volume have been the relation between states and markets; the view of regulation as a political—not a functional, technocratic—process; changes in the form and instruments of governance over time, across and within sectors; and the forces of and limits to above-the-national-state regulation.

The concluding chapter summarizes the main findings; reviews what European governance has achieved so far; and considers the implications of recent developments, notably the softer regulatory treatment of market-shaping and market correcting measures, for harmonization, legitimacy, and the attainment of public service objectives.

The origin of European governance of communications in the postwar period was situated within the broader process of postwar reconstruction and the debate on, and subsequent launch of, Western European integration in the shadow of U.S. hegemony in the West and the Cold War. In Europe, telecommunications and broadcasting markets and regulation were divided along national lines. The former was the classic example of natural monopoly under the strong control of a state-owned public administration. The latter was generally organized along the public service tradition. In essence, both telecommunications and broadcasting were an essential part and manifestation of the Keynesian welfare state, the state provider that assumed an extensive socioeconomic role.

The formative postwar period of Europeanization, in particular the decade from the late 1940s to the late 1950s, witnessed the creation of the main politico-economic European organizations (Council of Europe and European Economic Community) and professional associations (European Broadcasting Union and European Conference of Postal and Telecommunications administrations) that, although they have evolved through the years, still dominate the European communications policy landscape.

The cross-border nature of telecommunications and aspects of broadcasting from the outset made both sectors favorable candidates for European-level cooperation. Indeed, the history of international regulation of communications, established shortly after respective technological inventions, confirms that. The question and character of European cooperation in telecommunications and broadcasting became entangled in the politics of the postwar reconstruction effort, in turn embedded in the international order of that period. As a result, developments were highly politicized and intergovernmental, not least because both telecommunications and broadcasting were typically under state control. Views differed on the need for and aims of any cooperation arrangements, with implications as to which countries, telecommunications administrations and broadcasting organizations would participate in them.

The governance of broadcasting was highly contentious and, in the end, it built upon pre-war structures. The pressing functional need to regulate the ether coupled with the onset of the Cold War accelerated developments and eventually split the organization of the European broadcasting area in two. European integration had hardly begun, and so broadcasting, unlike telecommunications, was spared the complexities and tensions of that process. The main issue was whether to bring broadcasting under the intergovernmental control of United Nations agencies (International Telecommunication Union—ITU—and possibly UNESCO), a view supported by the USA and Britain, or under the professional control of broadcasting organizations. The compromise reached combined elements of both alternatives. The European Broadcasting Union (EBU) was set up in 1950 as a professional nongovernmental association, but membership was conditioned upon ITU membership, thereby putting national governments in control over who could join. The EBU brought together mainly the broadcasting authorities of Western Europe at a time when a monopoly broadcaster was the norm. On the other side of the Iron Curtain, there existed the International Radio and Television Organization (OIRT) comprising the East European broadcasting institutions. The EBU and the OIRT eventually merged in 1993 in the aftermath of the collapse of communist regimes in Europe.

Governance arrangements in the seemingly technical area of telecommunications were not less contested. The idea of a European postal and telecommunications union was first raised in the Council of Europe shortly after its creation in the late 1940s. It subsequently became embroiled in the broader process of European integration and the tension between functional sector-specific (as per the supranational European Coal and Steel Community or the intergovernmental European Conference of Ministers of Transport) and more general politico-economic integration. Under the latter scenario, there was also the question of whether cooperation should take place under the auspices of the Council of Europe, a loose intergovernmental organization with wide West European membership, or the auspices of the newly established European Economic Community (forerunner of the EU), the more ambitious politico-economic integration with just six member countries, which would have implications for its operation. All these scenarios were rejected and in 1959, as the original idea was launched, the European Conference of Postal and Telecommunications administrations (CEPT) was founded as a Europe-wide professional association of state-owned monopolies, so-called PTTs.

At the time, European governance was loose in character. It was strictly confined to technical, operational and commercial necessities and, crucially, it did not impinge upon the national order of telecommunications and broadcasting. Not only would cooperation stop at, and not penetrate into, national borders, but also any agreements reached were not legally binding.

With the benefit of hindsight, there were two major implications of the resulting European governance structures. First, cooperation in both broadcasting and telecommunications was organized outside the EU structures and as such the EU did not get competence over these sectors. Second, governance, even though limited in scope, became the exclusive domain of (near) monopolist operators—public service broadcasters and PTTs. It is the case that professional associations, like the EBU and the CEPT, that establish close, even though voluntary, cooperation among their members, have the potential to discriminate against non-members. Indeed, this potential for exclusion has often been the subject of competition investigations under the EU structures, as analyzed in chapter 5 (e.g., the Eurovision cases and CEPT's tariff arrangements). Technological developments and procompetitive market restructuring would subsequently further challenge these two professional bodies. The CEPT has transformed from a professional (Western) European association of monopoly postal and telecommunications administrations to a pan-European voluntary intergovernmental organization with responsibility over technical regulatory matters, primarily in radio communications. The EBU, set up in direct response to the Cold War as a professional association of public service broadcasters, has evolved, like its sister Association of Commercial Television broadcast-
_____ization representing and promoting the interests of its
_____national arenas.

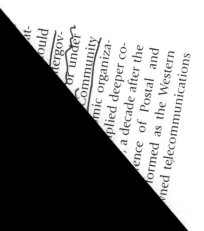

_____overnance of communica-
1960s exposed Western
time of fast technologi-
_nication and when new
_gnificant contribution of
competitiveness. The tur-
_e 1970s and the levelling
_racle accentuated concerns

_logical gap" discourse was
_ European integration. Pre-
_aboration were intergovern-
_he exception rather than the
_essing, where Europe's weak-
_confined to the national level.

The threat from IBM in particular led major West European states to individually resort to protectionist solutions in search of national champions, further fragmenting markets and insulating domestic firms from competitive pressures.

Developments so far have to be understood in the context of the postwar Keynesian national state order characterized by an interventionist managerial state, relatively closed national economies, the predominantly national organization of capital and close government-industry relations. During the international crisis years in the late 1960s and throughout the 1970s, with the established Keynesian order showing clear signs of severe strain, the EU—an organization concerned with economic, trade and commercial issues—started to gradually move into the field of Information and Communication Technology (ICT).

Initially, EU initiatives were reactive to more general international developments rather than part of a comprehensive policy plan. They originated mainly inside the European Commission and, not surprisingly, they largely fell on deaf ears. The EU—a new organization trying to find its feet, handicapped by the lack of competence over industrial or technological affairs, and facing its own politico-institutional crisis—attempted to intervene in three areas, but in all cases initiatives failed because the international context had undermined the weak political commitment to the creation of the single market and because neither governments nor the industry were yet convinced that common action was needed.

First, the Commission, as part of efforts to eliminate trade barriers, promoted the harmonization of technical standards and administrative rules across the Union. It was in response to this exercise that the EU accidentally stumbled upon the sector of telecommunications and as a result of the failure of this harmonization strategy, that originally conceptualized it as uniformity, the two core tenets of the single market project were established: mutual recognition of national rules based on minimal harmonization and mutual notification of proposed national rules.

Second, one can trace in the Commission's effort in this period to assume a general economic and industrial planning role the conflict concerning the balance between free and regulated liberalization and trade. This conflict, which had previously led to the division of Western Europe at "sixes and sevens," has been rehearsed several times throughout the history of European integration. At the time of the 1970 Colonna report, this conflict reflected differing views among member states over the necessity for and character of a European-level industrial policy, views shaped by the competitiveness of domestic industry and its degree of incorporation into the international economy, with France favoring controlled liberalization and Germany, the Netherlands and, subsequently, Britain favoring free liberalization and trade.

Finally, in the first half of the 1970s the EU got involved in network planning and development. Open Systems Interconnection (OSI)—which would allow any-to-any computer communication—was a concerted European effort backed by the industry, national governments and the EU to promote open standards in order to counter IBM's dominance. Euronet, the first European data network endorsed in the mid-1970s, was important because for the first time European-level cooperation in telecommunications moved beyond the PTTs and the exclusive domain of their association, the CEPT, to embrace the EU. However, as explained in chapter 3, these two initiatives in network planning and development mirrored, and at the same time served to strengthen, the interests of PTTs and at a broader level those of the telecommunications industry in the emerging electronic communications environment, and contributed to the disregard of advances in the computing sector, in particular the internet TCP/IP protocols and, ultimately, to the weakness of the European computing and internet industries. Moreover, contrary to original expectations that it would usher in a new era of pan-European cooperation, the Euronet initiative failed to challenge the traditional focus on national network development. In fact, the national character of telecommunications markets was reproduced in the nascent data communications market, entrenching the position of the PTTs.

Other Commission efforts in the field of telecommunications, such as the opening up of public procurement and the harmonization of equipment and services, were strongly resisted by the dominant PTTs and the CEPT and as a result were unsuccessful. In other words, European initiatives that would seem to antagonize established interests had no chance of getting anywhere, whereas initiatives that would support established (monopolistic) interests were acceptable. This would prove to be a valuable lesson and one that would influence subsequent EU policy.

Separately, in 1973, again as part of efforts to deal with the international political economic turmoil and reinvigorate the process of European integration, Europe's political leaders for the first time became concerned with the notion of European external identity. Finally, and quite independently from the actions discussed so far, in response to technological developments and a legal case (1974 Sacchi judgment), the EU had its first encounter with the field of television broadcasting.

In contrast to these ad hoc reactive initiatives of the 1970s, in the subsequent period running up until the mid-/late 1980s the EU managed to enter the fields of ICT, telecommunications and television and to gradually become established as an important policy actor. As analyzed in chapter 4, this change was premised on solid support from Europe's industrial capital that, responding to growing international economic openness and interdependence and this time working closely with the European Commission, aimed at relaunching integration and the single market and at developing a European socioeconomic order that would serve its needs.

The single market was conceived as a temporary shield from growing international competition. Its creation would combine internal market liberalization, active industrial policy at the EU level, and temporary external trade protection in order to give sufficient time to national champions to become European champions ready to take on world markets. A confluence of factors contributed to the reorientation of Europe's ICT industrialists. First, technological change, notably digitalization and new transmission technologies, on the one hand challenged the traditionally national order of telecommunications and on the other altered the economics of the sector. The resulting technological convergence between telecommunications and information technology and the emergence of new products and services presented both opportunities and threats as the new markets were bringing in new competitors, in particular from the field of information technology, a field where U.S. strength was pronounced. The internationalization of telecommunications, a symptom of and a contributor to the wider process of economic globalization, exacerbated the vulnerability of European industry and highlighted the limits of national markets. Quite simply, small protected domestic EU markets could not carry the European ICT industry into the digital era. National parochial responses had failed to rejuvenate Europe's techno-industrial base, while the demise of the Keynesian national welfare paradigm and the emerging neoliberal order made active state support and intervention unattainable. Second, the ICT was not just any industry. Its rising economic significance made high level political support certain. New economic growth and trade theories, analyzed in chapter 4, emphatically pointed to the crucial contribution of technology to economic development and competitiveness. Industrialized countries, in particular, not being able to compete with low-cost economies on labor-intensive industries, needed to concentrate on technology-intensive sectors where competition is based on innovation. These theories singled out technology-intensive industries as strategic industries and provided a forceful justification for active industrial—more acceptably now called technology —policy with an emphasis on sectors that exhibited substantial economies of scale. According to these new understandings, public policy intervention was crucial in countries' efforts to gain and sustain competitive advantage.

Confirming the rising political saliency of ICT, in 1979 Europe's political leaders endorsed the "information society" vision in response to rising U.S. and Japanese competition and in an effort to revive and modernize European economies. In short, European governments identified in ICT, experiencing rapid development, the potential for a dynamic high growth sector which could drive their economies and societies out of the crippling recession, inflation, and unemployment.

In sum, this period of defensive Europeanization covering the late 1970s to mid-/late 1980s was dominated by industrial policy considerations. It was the protectionist faction of the European industrial capital feeling threatened by intensifying competitive pressures, such as Europe's ICT industry, that was most influential in shaping the course of the integration process. This faction attributed its decline to small and fragmented EU markets and insufficient economies of scale, and thus perceived the single market as the answer to its own problems. The technology gap and information society discourses provided useful justification for this vision. Both discourses have remained key themes in European integration ever since.

French-inspired industrial policy goals, and to a degree policy measures too, were exported to the European level in the pursuit of European champions. A mutually supportive relationship was established between (parts of) the European Commission on the one hand and leading European ICT manufacturers, the PTTs and their association, the CEPT, on the other. Initiatives included EU-sponsored R&D collaborative programs (Esprit and Race), network planning (ISDN and GSM), and defensive standardization (analog HDTV). Telecommunications, being the most important field of information technology applications, was going to rescue the European ICT industry. Pan-European telecommunications networks, in particular, were necessary for coordinated investment and for providing a big enough market for Europe's manufacturers. For the PTTs, network modernization was crucial if they were to keep valuable corporate customers and fend off emerging competition. And finally, a common integrated infrastructure was a key element in the building of the single internal market and the relaunch of European integration, and would, as a result, strengthen the institutional interests of the EU.

Besides close links with Europe's major ICT manufacturers and the PTTs, the European Commission also came to enjoy an equally strong relation with public service broadcasters and their European association, the EBU, as part of the idea of pan-European broadcasting. In all cases, the alliance between the Commission and the key constituencies in ICT manufacturing, telecommunications and broadcasting was relatively easy because EU actions sought to support, not antagonize, their interests.

The original aim to use the advent of transfrontier satellite television for democratic ideals, as a means to create a direct link between the EU and its citizens, was quickly overshadowed by cultural and industrial policy considerations. As analyzed in chapter 4, established institutional (EBU and EU) and market actors (Europe's consumer electronics industry and public service broadcasters) saw in pan-European television an opportunity to promote their own interests, especially at a time when the broadcasting market was changing from being public and national to having to accommodate private commercial and transnational broadcasters. The EBU-sponsored pan-European television channels and the attempt at European public service broadcasting need to be understood also as part of concurrent efforts to assign state-like characteristics to the EU, an ambitious plan most actively promoted during the Delors Commission Presidency (1985–1995). Although the attempt to use transfrontier television to forge cultural unity and a strong European identity failed, not least because it was based on false assumptions, as we argued in chapter 4, the related issues of identity, culture, citizenship, legitimacy and democracy should not be understood as specifically EU issues. Rather, these notions emerged at the European level in the context of, and as a means to deal with, the growing crisis of these notions at the national level. In a sense, the period of defensive Europeanization from the late 1970s to the mid-/late 1980s can be read as an attempt to substitute at the European level what was being challenged at the national level, be it culture, identity or economic management and industrial policy capacities.

From the mid-/late 1980s till the late 1990s, procompetitive market restructuring gained ascendancy in Europe. As explained in chapter 5, a unique combination of factors contributed to the gradual liberalization of telecommunications and television markets. A new international political economy (the limitations of the postwar Keynesian order; the liberalization and internationalization of economic activities, especially those that are highly dependant on electronic communications such as finance), a new sectoral political economy (technological change challenging the natural monopoly foundation of communication markets and regulation and introducing new market players; pressure from Europe's trading partners looking for new markets to expand, notably the USA; where market restructuring was already underway, the inadequacy of the narrow confines of national states to serve the needs of ICT capital; strong dissatisfaction of big economic actors with Europe's established monopolistic high-cost communications order) and ideational factors (the rise of neoliberal ideology, new understandings about economic growth, the idea of trade in services pursued in the Uruguay round of GATT) all combined to support the move from monopolistic state controlled to liberalized telecommunications markets, and the move from a public service toward a commercial multi-channel television order. In Europe, institutional parameters mediated these broader structural changes. Three points are worth making here concerning the role of institutional factors.

First, although this study has proved that the EU institutional context has played an important role in mediating and advancing market restructuring in the face of structural change, and that the European Commission in particular has often acted as a policy entrepreneur, the fact that, first, the Commission did not resort to its strong competition powers earlier and, second, telecommunications and broadcasting market reform was already underway in the major EU member states, suggests that the Commission's autonomy is circumscribed by what is considered, at least in some quarters, to be politically acceptable or feasible at that time.

Second, alternative institutional policy spheres shaped the restructuring of television markets. Arguably, the institutional rivalry over the regulation of transfrontier television between the politically weaker Council of Europe emphasizing the social, cultural and democratic aspects, of broadcasting, and the politically stronger EU stressing economic and industrial aspects in the end worked to the detriment of a strong, comprehensive European regulatory framework.

Third, it is worth noting that the mediation of broader structural change through the EU institutional context did not have the same objective in all cases. Thus, whereas the EU acted in tandem with globalizing pressures and reinforced calls for the liberalization of telecommunications during the GATT Uruguay round, in the case of audiovisual services it resisted and acted against them.

With the launch of the single market project and associated market restructuring, EU policy moved inside national borders to touch on domestic political, economic and social structures. The fundamental contestation concerning the relationship between state and market came to clearly penetrate the EU level. During the single market phase, Europe's potential as a political and social project became apparent. The battle between models of capitalism was being played out at the European level.

The two main competing conceptualizations of the internal market—the neomercantilist and the neoliberal vision, each with its own supporters within industry, European institutions and among national governments—eventually clashed in the late 1980s/early 1990s. But as chapter 5 demonstrated in detail, neither vision prevailed. The crisis of the Keynesian welfare national state led, contra the neoliberal vision, to managed liberalization and the rise of the regulatory state at both the national and European levels. But equally, the neomercantilist scenario and associated strong calls for interventionist industrial policy and external trade protection were defeated.

The interventionist industrial policy of the EU was under attack from the more globalized transnational parts of the European capital and their supporters within European institutions and national governments. Ironically, in the case of cellular mobile, the very success of French-inspired industrial policy in the case of GSM would subsequently contribute to alter the preferences of the leading European manufacturers and operators and transform them from inward-looking market players interested narrowly in the European market to outward-looking market players interested in emerging international markets. The neomercantilist project was also undermined by the very fact that the technology-push initiatives had failed to turn around the prospects of the European ICT industry. Finally, it was being challenged by Europe's trading partners, notably the USA, and multilaterally through the GATT Uruguay round.

Competitiveness came to underline the new approach to industrial policy and to signal a shift away from active interventionism toward horizontal initiatives aiming at nurturing macroeconomic conditions conducive to innovation, productivity and economic growth, initiatives that are concerned with general economic competitiveness rather than that of specific sectors or firms. The new industrial competitiveness approach characterizing the regulatory competition state perceives public intervention as enabling, guiding and facilitating. Accordingly, the Commission no longer assumes an actively interventionist role but aims simply to enable the introduction and take-up of new technologies. Thus, whereas in the 1980s, responding to a Japanese trade threat, the EU mandated technical standards for analog high-definition television, in the 1990s it was the industry itself that assumed responsibility for digital television standards, including conditional access systems and application program interfaces, within an overall EU regulatory framework.

The period from the mid-/late 1980s to the late 1990s was the most intense regulatory reform period of Europeanization. However, this should conceal neither the inadequacies, asymmetries and contradictions that the resulting system of European governance exhibits nor the fact that the degree of Europeanization differs across and within sectors.

The Europeanization of telecommunications governance has been relatively easier, though by no means smooth, than that of television. As noted, the EU institutional context in this case amplified international procompetitive pressures and provided the overall momentum for the progressive liberalization of telecommunications markets. Market restructuring went hand in hand with the emergence of a comprehensive body of rules at the EU level, the so-called 1998 regulatory framework. Despite its limitations, the framework was detailed and prescriptive. And for the first time, informal governance techniques, notably benchmarks and identification of best practice, were inaugurated to tackle highly contentious issues not amenable to command-and-control harmonization, such as cost methodologies and interconnection pricing, that are, however, central to advancing efficient and sustainable competition. Effective implementation rested with national governments and competent regulatory authorities. Thus, the rise of the European regulatory state has served not to undermine but instead reinforce, to the national regulatory state.

The European regulatory framework is binding. It sets the overall policy aims and main principles but leaves member states with substantial discretion to work out how to fulfill them. During implementation, EU rules are filtered through the political, economic, social and institutional features of each member state ("domestication"). The resulting lack of consistency in national regulatory responses and the inability of the EU's monitoring and enforcement processes to timely and effectively address this contributed to calls for a central telecommunications regulatory authority, calls supported by transnational economic actors but defeated following strong opposition from national governments and regulators. Instead, the reformed 2002 electronic communications regulatory package has tried to curtail the degree of discretion at the national level.

The Europeanization of broadcasting governance has been limited and much more politicized and contentious. Overall, the EU has primarily utilized telecommunications-type regulation in regard to television, dealing with primarily economic, technological and industrial aspects. It does not cover the heart and soul of television: content regulation and media (cross) ownership. In this sense, the EU television regulatory framework is incomplete. In many ways media markets, not least for cultural and linguistic reasons, are still national and are regulated at the national level. The limited and less institutionalized European governance model of television is both a manifestation and a reinforcing element of its still predominantly national character. It should not be wrongly interpreted as a sign of deregulation. Rather, there has been strong opposition from member states to supranational intervention and as a result no great supply.

The EU television regulatory framework has progressed more via European Commission competition decisions and European Court judgments rather than legislation. This matters for two reasons. First, these two measures are "vertical" and "hard" instruments of public policy in a field—competition—where the EU enjoys its strongest competence and autonomy for action.[2] These binding instruments relate to, in particular, negative integration, that is, market-making policies, and imply coercion. Second, the regulatory style of this governance model is reactive as opposed to proactive, responding to events rather than shaping them. The EU institutions are asked to intervene (actors by invitation) to resolve contested cases and often rule on a relatively small matter which nonetheless may have far-reaching implications.

Public service broadcasting presents an interesting example here. In the absence of a strong regulatory framework and positive rules concerning public services, competition law has had a much bigger role in and impact on it. Ironically, the minimal EU regulatory framework for broadcasting that was meant to protect television as a cultural and nationally regulated area has left public service broadcasting exposed to competition law arguments. This is not to argue that competition law has no role in broadcasting. Rather, the point is that competition concerns and aims are not the same as public service concerns and aims. And although, as illustrated in the cases discussed in this volume, the European Commission has so far managed to incorporate non-economic considerations in its competition law analysis, this may not necessarily be the case in the future, while the European Court of Justice, the regulator of last resort, that is called upon to interpret the application of the predominantly economic provisions of the EU Treaty, has been less able to take into account non-economic considerations. Indeed, in the *BBC Digital Curriculum* state aid case, discussed in chapter 6, the Commission has departed from its earlier approach, and it seems likely that in the emerging multi-platform digital communications landscape the presence or absence of commercial players will be a crucial factor in the definition of public service broadcasting. The market failure argument, that finds growing acceptance, tolerates "distortions" from free market principles such as public funding and consequently public service broadcasting, on the basis of a market logic rather than on the basis of social and cultural policy objectives. The economic sphere, therefore, is prioritized over the political sphere, and non-economic interests and concerns are marginalized.

Failed attempts to foster a single market by breaking down cultural barriers in the name of a latent European culture and the awakening of shared feelings of Europeaness were succeeded in the mid-1980s by legislative measures aimed at abolishing market barriers to create the internal market. Still, the Television without Frontiers directive—the main EU legislative instrument in the field providing for the free flow of television programs throughout the single market subject to minimal harmonization rules concerning advertising, sponsorship and protection of minors—was a post-hoc regulatory initiative, acknowledging the altered situation in the broadcasting field.

In the second half of the 1980s and the early 1990s, the aim of EU broadcasting policy shifted from "cultural unity," associated with the EBU-sponsored pan-European television experiments and the search for one European identity, to "cultural diversity," to be promoted via the twin-pronged strategy of internal market liberalization (television without frontiers directive) and external trade protection (quotas). But the emphasis on cultural diversity sat uneasily with the emphasis on the internal market and economies of scale regarded as essential for the improvement of competitiveness of Europe's content producers and which implied low common denominator content. In addition, and here lies a second contradiction, the EU promoted cultural diversity internally at the same time that it was protecting a "European" cultural identity within the GATT Uruguay round of trade negotiations.

The EU has approached pluralism and media concentration from an internal market perspective, again perceiving small and fragmented markets as holding back European media players and seeing the creation of a pan-European market as vital for their international competitiveness. Thus, overall European broadcasting policy has been, in a significant part, a question of economic and commercial advantage.

This is not to say that social, cultural, democratic and public interest concerns have been absent. For instance, various European initiatives promote the production and distribution of European content, notably through co-productions and other support measures such as quotas. Distributive measures (e.g., MEDIA program), though negligible, are important because they establish the EU as an actor in the field.

Crucially, the post–Cold War order has come to challenge the predominantly economic policy output of the EU. Various factors contributed to this. First, in the early 1990s, with a renewed wave of economic recession and high unemployment, there was a perception that the internal market project had failed to deliver the anticipated benefits. Strong public discontent was evidenced in referenda across member states. It became clear that a truly neoliberal scenario grounded on market-making measures alone would not suffice, a view strengthened with the accession of Austria, Finland and Sweden in 1995. In a complete volte-face, and in response also to the growing perception that the ongoing process of economic globalization was further threatening these values, the EU came to explicitly recognize the significance of social and cultural objectives and public services. The ascendancy of public policy objectives and their conceptualization as integral parts of the "European model of society" implied the end of the neoliberal belief, dominant in the 1980s, that liberalization and regulation (market and state) are antithetical. This reorientation was also in line with the new post-national deterritorialized civic construction of European identity, all the more important for the about to enlarge EU. Besides, the accession of ex-communist countries to the Council of Europe and the EBU, prior to the EU, strengthened these two organizations on the European stage. Both went on to actively assist the emerging democracies by emphasizing democratic and socio-cultural values, thereby further challenging the predominantly economic values of the EU. In was in this context that the 1997 Amsterdam protocol on public service broadcasting was adopted in order to circumscribe EU-level competence by establishing that member states alone are responsible for its definition, finance and organization, and to safeguard public service broadcasters from attacks by commercial interests using economic and competition law arguments. But, although beginning in the early 1990s public policy objectives started to figure prominently on the EU policy agenda, the consensus has been that, in contrast to market-making liberalization measures, they will be treated on the basis of soft-law measures.

Overall, the EU has had difficulties reconciling the democratic and cultural with the economic, industrial and trade aspects of broadcasting. The reemergence of the information society vision in the 1990s, as the answer to renewed economic recession and in reaction to developments in the USA, related to the privatization and commercialization of the internet, strengthened the emphasis on advanced electronic communications infra-structure as a key parameter of competitiveness. The political endorsement of the information society, and the technological convergence between information technology/internet, telecommunications and the media has further moved policy emphasis away from more controversial cultural concerns and moved television toward economic and industrial concerns.

Developments in the last and current phase of European governance of communications covering the period from the late 1990s till early 2007 need to be understood in the context of intensifying globalization, growing technological convergence and renewed concern about Europe's relative economic decline compared to, in particular, the USA in terms of productivity but also more generally on the world stage, despite major initiatives to redress this decline such as the single market project, economic and monetary union and enlargement. This anxiety resulted in a refocusing of Europe's strategy on competitiveness and the knowledge economy, both famously endorsed by the EU political leaders at the Lisbon summit in 2000.

Although industrial policy for competitiveness is associated with a loose set of horizontal sector-neutral measures, we suggested that policy may still be associated with efforts to support specific industries and is not synonymous with nonintervention and free markets and trade. The empirical evidence in chapter 6 demonstrated how, despite continuing controversy surrounding the definition and measurement of productivity and competitiveness, various segments of the electronic communications sector have attempted to capitalize on the dominant orthodoxy of competitiveness and the associated strong correlation between ICT and economic growth in order to promote their own narrow interests. Thus, both private commercial vertically integrated broadcasters and public service broadcasters have appealed to the ultimate goals of competitiveness and knowledge economy but have made competing claims. For the former, the absence of regulation and the existence of fragmented markets on the basis of multiple non-interoperable proprietary standards—an integral part of their business model—are essential for innovation and growth in the field of digital interactive broadcasting. Conversely, for public service broadcasters it is open standards that can accelerate the move toward a knowledge economy and improve competitiveness.

Equally, incumbent telecommunications operators argue that they would be prepared to invest in advanced next generation networks, on which Europe's economic future depends, provided there is no regulatory intervention and that regulatory obligations requiring them to share their investment with competitors are lifted. In other words, for them the at least temporary erection of monopolies in the nascent broadband electronic communications market is justified in the name of competitiveness. This Schumpeterian understanding of competitiveness in the 1990s and early

2000s contrasts with the previous understanding of competitiveness as a matter of economies of scale and a big harmonized home market.

A central element of the Lisbon agenda to improve competitiveness and the associated "better-regulation" initiative has been the review of the EU regulatory frameworks for telecommunications and broadcasting to take into account technological convergence and increasingly open markets. A major feature of the latest phase of European governance of communications has been a shift away from sector-specific toward horizontal rules. This shift has been relatively easy in relation to electronic communications infrastructure but strongly contested in relation to audiovisual services and content. Horizontal rules aim to simplify, streamline and update regulation. But importantly, in the context of the EU this move needs to be understood also as an attempt to limit the regulatory discretion enjoyed at the national level. The greater emphasis on general competition rules that often accompanies horizontal regulation has the potential to promote harmonization while it hands the European Commission a strong input in regulatory matters on the basis of its strong competition powers, which is why it is in the institutional interest of the EU to bring as many sectors and issues as possible under competition rules. The 2002 electronic communications regulatory package that introduced a horizontal (technology neutral) regulatory framework for transport network infrastructure and associated services aims at precisely that. By getting rid of detailed prescriptive rules which, under the 1998 regulatory framework, had bestowed national regulators with considerable discretion, and by limiting the need for regulatory intervention in markets that are not (sufficiently) competitive, the new framework seeks to enhance consistency in national regulatory practices. Under the 2002 electronic communications regulatory framework, the European Commission has identified eighteen markets that are not yet competitive and may therefore exceptionally warrant regulatory intervention. Under the 2006 review of this framework, the Commission has proposed to reduce the number of relevant markets to twelve and to increase its powers over the imposition of regulatory obligations—the only area where the Commission has currently no powers—and finally, has put back on the agenda the question of a central European regulatory authority.

The move toward a more horizontal regulatory approach in relation to broadcasting has been heavily contested. Two efforts to incorporate the regulation of broadcasting into a broader regulatory framework covering several economic sectors (services of general economic interest and the entire services sector) encountered strong objections in the 1990s and early 2000s, albeit for different reasons. Public service broadcasters and their supporters feared that the proposed horizontal regulatory model would result in the treatment of broadcasting like any other ordinary economic activity, thereby negating its important democratic, cultural and social aspects. Conversely, for commercial broadcasters the risk was that a horizontal framework for public services in general would have strengthened the sector specificity of broadcasting, impeding the application of competition rules, the only horizontal regulatory framework that commercial interests accept.

The second review of the Television without Frontiers directive, currently underway, represents the latest attempt toward horizontal regulation, this time in relation to audiovisual content. In its proposal, the Commission suggests the extension of certain, mostly negative, content rules from the traditional broadcasting platform horizontally to other platforms. This view is supported by public service broadcasters, who see this extension as essential for the future and modernization of public service broadcasting. It is, however, strongly opposed by commercial broadcasters and publishers, telecommunications operators and internet-related interests, and some member states led by Britain, who see regulatory intervention as hindering innovation and, in turn, they argue, Europe's growth and competitiveness. Overall, the review of the scope of the Television without Frontiers directive and associated regulatory obligations has sparked a heated debate. Competing conceptualizations of technological convergence and implications for regulatory intervention are being rehearsed again.

It is worth noting here that greater reliance on general competition as opposed to sector-specific rules does not make regulation less controversial. Although at first sight one could assume that a regulatory model premised on economic and competition law principles would be more "objective" and less prone to capture, the analysis in chapter 6 demonstrated that regulation remains contested and political. Indeed, the starting point of the 2002 electronic communications framework—the definition of relevant markets—was one of its most controversial elements, with diverse market players putting forward competing definitions of markets in order to safeguard their interests, proving in the process that markets are not neutral but political constructs and illustrating the distributional character of regulation.

A more horizontal regulatory framework does not imply less regulation either. The proliferation of regulatory committees under the 2002 EU regulatory framework is evidence that the new "lighter" regulatory framework based on competition rules has not reduced the need for and scope of regulation. The analysis of the framework also showed that, at least in the short term, the regulatory burden on national authorities has increased rather than decreased.

A second major feature of the current mode of European governance of communications is the move away from vertical directive-driven and legally binding prescriptive harmonization toward "soft" informal policy coordination arrangements and greater reliance on cooperation between the European Commission and national regulators and among national regulators. To an extent, the historically established fact of weak enforcement, the very limitations and problems of traditional regulatory tools, the unattainable proposition of pursuing harmonization through formal rigid legislation in an enlarged and more diverse EU and the inadequate accountability of the EU can all explain the recent readjustment of governance instruments and the shift away from hierarchical command-and-control legislation and formal enforcement toward flexible, non-binding instruments (such as recommendations, guidelines, declarations, sharing of experiences, benchmarking and dissemination of best practice); light institutional arrangements such as transnational regulatory groupings; and voluntary implementation on the basis of agreement and consensus. It has been argued that the notion of the "regulatory state" needs to be conceptually stretched to account for not only formal but also informal governance techniques.

The two changes in the form of governance mentioned so far—greater reliance on horizontal, in particular general competition, rules and soft policy arrangements—complement each other. Competition rules aim at limiting the discretionary powers available at the national level, while soft policy arrangements aim at shaping the discretion left in order to enhance harmonization. Harmonization now does not denote uniformity but rather a move toward the same direction on the basis of a common conceptualization of problems and on the basis of common principles.

Overall, it has been relatively easy for the EU to adopt procompetitive measures and significantly less so to adopt common policies. Even in the most intense period of Europeanization, as demonstrated in chapter 5, European governance was more about liberalization rather than harmonization. The picture that emerges in both television and telecommunications is one of stubbornly national, albeit liberalized, markets despite the Europeanization of (some) rules. The European market is still fragmented, characterized by an array of diverse national rules. There is no linear progression toward greater Europeanization of regulatory policies, nor is there a single European regulatory mode of governance. The suggestion that EU policies have been a more significant liberalizing rather than harmonizing force confirms Scharpf's strong argument that the EU is biased toward negative integration, that is market-making rules, and has had difficulties in promoting the harmonized re-regulation of domestic markets on the basis of common European rules (positive integration).[3]

In the era of technological convergence, the distinction is no longer between telecommunications and media regulation but more rightly about economic regulation on the one hand and social and cultural regulation on the other. While soft policy arrangements deal with market-correcting and market-shaping measures, proving that the EU does not simply promote liberalization but rather liberalization and re-regulation, and while it may be true that such arrangements represent an attempt to close the regulatory gap between negative and positive integration and to overcome resistance to the formal transfer of powers to the European level in contested public policy areas, the flexible and voluntary nature of these arrangements cannot afford an adequate degree of protection and promotion of public service objectives.[4] The symbolic importance of soft governance may be high, but its substantive importance remains unproven. Soft measures may influence and frame but cannot substantially shape developments and outcomes. Thus, in essence, economic priorities prevail over non-economic considerations and public service objectives. Whereas market-making regulatory output remains strong and relies on hard, legally binding and enforceable policy mechanisms, interventions in social and cultural areas that come under positive integration (market-correcting and -shaping measures) remain legally uncertain and rely on soft, voluntary policy tools. And since they are not afforded the same degree of legal protection, non-economic considerations become tributary to overriding market-creating priorities. The European governance of communications is, therefore, asymmetric. The substantive regulatory output of the EU has remained unchanged, centered on economic and competitiveness areas. Any substantive changes in social welfare-enhancing areas are less likely to originate at the EU level and more likely to originate at the (sub)national level within the constraints of the European and international order.

The non-legally binding character of soft policy measures and the absence of strong enforcement tools make non-observance highly likely. Soft policy arrangements aim at inducing harmonization indirectly through socialization, peer pressure, sharing of experiences and learning. They aim at cognitive convergence and make greater use of communicative and ideational parameters. The proliferation of regulatory committees within and outside the EU structures, is an attempt to address the regulatory and harmonization deficits, though their potential to do so varies significantly, as figure 7.1 shows.

The European model of governance that is emerging resembles what Dehousse has called "regulation by networks" and Majone "regulation by information" to underline that these regulatory committees are mainly concerned with exchanging information and networking with other institutions and that they do not enjoy powers normally associated with regulatory authorities.[5] For instance, as explained in chapter 6, the European Regulators' Group bringing together the national regulators of the member states has primarily an informal coordinating role rather than substantial regulation-making powers. On the one hand, the voluntary character of such arrangements risks increasing diversity in national regulatory responses, but on the other their flexibility allows member states to tailor regulation to the circumstances of their own countries, which in turn may indirectly increase the acceptance and legitimacy of the EU. In a sense, and

EU networks   *Highest*

European Regulators' Group (ERG, 2002)
    Formal EU regulatory committee between the European
    Commission and national telecommunications
    regulators. Created as a forum of expertise and
    gradually transforming into a harmonization agent.
    Focuses on benchmarking, dissemination of best
    practice and peer-pressure.
Radio Spectrum Policy Group (RSPG, 2002)
    Formal EU regulatory committee between the European
    Commission and national high level policy experts.
    Concerned with forward-looking radio spectrum strategic,
    not technical, matters.

                                                              Policy harmonization
Non-EU networks   *potential*

European Conference of Postal and Telecommunications
administrations (CEPT, set up in 1959 as a PTT-forum;
transformed in 1992 into a coordinating body of
telecommunications regulators from nearly 50 European
countries)
    Deals with technical telecommunications regulatory
    matters, primarily in radio communications. Decisions are
    not binding. The European Commission can issue
    "mandates" for the Electronic Communications Committee
    (ECC) of the CEPT to look into technical radio spectrum
    aspects. The Commission's comitology Radio Spectrum
    Committee may adopt ECC recommendations as technical
    implementing measures, making them binding on EU
    member states.
Independent Regulators' Groups (IRG, 1997)
    Informal discussion forum where national
    telecommunications regulators from over 30 European
    countries share experiences and information, address
    issues of common concern and develop common
    practices. Used as a safety net against possible intrusions
    notably by the European Commission.
European Platform of Regulatory Authorities (EPRA, 1995)
    Voluntary discussion forum where broadcasting regulators
    from around 40 European countries exchange information
    and share experiences. Its output is informal and, unlike
    its telecommunications counterpart the IRG, it does not
    produce agreements or best-practice models.   *Lowest*

**Figure 7.1.   European Transnational Regulatory Networks and Potential for Policy
Harmonization**

notwithstanding the EU's strong competition powers, the recent refocusing on soft policy instruments has brought the form, though not the substance, of EU governance closer to that of other European organizations that deal with communications policy issues. For instance, both the OECD and the Council of Europe have for years now relied on soft policy measures but arguably their impact on the ground is questionable. Soft policy coordination, as opposed to strict policy convergence in and of itself is of course not a problem. But in the EU context it may become a problem in the sense that the internal market will continue to be characterized by a mosaic of national rules at the expense of a level playing field.

In short, the imbalance characterizing the European governance of communications concerning the treatment of economic and non-economic (social and cultural) issues raises effectiveness, substantive, democratic and legitimacy concerns. The current phase of European governance of communications is increasingly complex. It has become more pluralistic and more institutionalized but at the same time more dispersed, lacking a clear locus of authority and power and obscuring lines of accountability and transparency. Policy coordination increasingly relies on overlapping networks and expertise with the tendency to de-politicize regulatory issues and present solutions in technical neutral terms on the false assumption that thus construed, solutions can travel uncontested across national borders. Not only has the Europeanization of governance failed to adequately address problems related to, in particular, accountability, transparency and input legitimacy but, it is argued here, it has compounded them by relocating and multiplying them, from the national to the EU and other formal and informal institutional spheres, thereby accentuating the problem of governmentability.

In addition to these governance challenges, the current phase of European governance faces two additional challenges, examined in chapter 6. First, the division between the regulation of infrastructure and associated services at the EU level and the regulation of content at the national level presents problems in the technologically converging communications environment. The division is artificial. The aim was to safeguard member state competence in the politically sensitive areas of content, media ownership and concentration. But this distinction is problematic for two main reasons. First, regulatory issues cannot be clearly characterized as infrastructure only or content only issues. Indeed, in some instances the two are interwoven, as the example of application program interfaces in digital interactive television demonstrated. Second, this distinction continues to leave the EU communications regulatory framework incomplete since it does not deal with content and related issues.

Broader globalization pressures are the second main challenge that the European governance of communications faces. The case of third generation mobile standards illustrated how export-oriented market players— Europe's leading mobile phone manufacturers and, to a lesser extent, operators—managed to challenge and eventually alter European regulatory structures concerning standardization where these were perceived as not conducive to their international aspirations. The case of the radio spectrum showed how new regulatory principles, such as technological neutrality, that are integral elements of the European and international trade liberalization agenda, may condition and put limits on EU-level regulatory intervention, which may in turn adversely affect harmonization within the internal market.

Throughout, this book has argued that the European governance of communications has been embedded within more general changes in international and sectoral political economy. Clearly these changes are not uniquely European. It is just that they have had to be channeled through, and in turn shaped by, the dense institutional web that has characterized (Western) Europe in the postwar period. The analysis of the origins, dynamics and evolution of European governance of communications has stressed its contested character, a contestation about "what kind of Europe?" that is, in turn, linked to views about the relationship between state and market, the role of regulation in the attainment of public service objectives, the balance between economic and social and cultural aims and the tension between free and regulated liberalization and trade. In particular, the EU governance of communications has appeared at times to be a very different kind of project, a neomercantilist in the 1980s becoming neoliberal in the 1990s, acting as a bulwark against globalizing pressures in the case of audiovisual services but working with them in the case of telecommunications. But as explained, it would be a simplification to associate European governance with just one—ideal—vision. On the whole the European governance of communications has been more liberalizing rather than harmonizing, more about market-making rules than market-shaping rules, and this is reflected in and reinforced by the choice of governance instruments. The direction of change is similar (procompetitive market restructuring), but the system of governance allows for, and thus accepts, diversity in outcomes. There are significant variations on the same theme, managed liberalization. The picture that emerges is one of policy coordination rather than convergence, which in itself attests that European governance arrangements have not worked at the expense of national governance arrangements. The European regulatory state is a symptom of and a contributor to the national regulatory state, both embedded within a wider global context. It is this interrelationship between the European/national regulatory state and broader economic and political transformations that will shape the future of communications in Europe and also determine the direction that European governance will take.

NOTES

1. The appendix summarizes the main elements of the evolution of the European governance of communications.

2. Claudio Radaelli, "The Europeanization of Public Policy," in *The Politics of Europeanization*, ed. Kevin Featherstone and Claudio Radaelli (Oxford and New York: Oxford University Press, 2003), 41–43.

3. Fritz W. Scharpf, *Governing in Europe: Effective and Democratic?* (Oxford: Oxford University Press, 1999).

4. For a similar argument see Fritz W. Scharpf, "The European Social Model: Coping with the Challenges of Diversity," *Journal of Common Market Studies* 40, no. 4 (2002): 645–70.

5. Renaud Dehousse, "Regulation by Networks in the European Community: The Role of European Agencies," *Journal of European Public Policy* 4, no. 2 (1997): 246–61. Giandomenico Majone, "The New European Agencies: Regulation by Information," *Journal of European Public Policy* 4, no. 2 (1997): 262–75.

Appendix

EVOLUTION OF EUROPEAN GOVERNANCE OF COMMUNICATIONS

Formative Years (late 1940s–1960s)

Broader context

U.S. hegemony. Cold War. Conflicts over the need for and character of Western European cooperation for postwar reconstruction. Telecommunications and broadcasting under sovereign control of national monopolies and national governments.

Key actors

National governments (European and non-European). State-owned or controlled national monopolies. Council of Europe, EBU, CEPT.

Governance areas and style: Main characteristics

Intergovernmental (Council of Europe) and professional (EBU/OIRT & CEPT cooperation on cross-border commercial technical and operational issues. No challenge to established national communications order. Consensual style. Communication sector's needs often victim of broader international political and diplomatic imperatives (e.g., Cold War).

Governance instruments

Mostly non-binding recommendations.

Implementation

Voluntary. No sanctions. National governments and administrations enjoyed great latitude.

Relationship among European organizations

No direct formal links. Sectors and policy competence clearly demarcated.

Crisis Years (late 1960s–1970s)

Broader context

International political economic turmoil. Crisis of Keynesianism. Theoretical understandings stressing role of ICT in economic growth. Growing competitive threats from USA and later Japan in high technology, especially computing and data processing (e.g., IBM). Technological disparities and gap discourses. Telecommunications and broadcasting under sovereign control of national monopolies and national governments.

Key actors

National governments (mostly European and U.S.). Individual firms (e.g., national champions, IBM). PTTs and CEPT, Council of Europe, EBU, European Commission, European Court of Justice.

Governance areas and style: Main characteristics

Individual national interventionist industrial policies focusing on computing. Promotion of national capital (national champions). Selective intergovernmental cooperation in high technology (e.g., aerospace, space). Failed attempts at European cross-national groupings in computing. EU pursues broad policy objectives but no support from either governments or industry. Three-pronged strategy: harmonization of European technical standards and administrative rules; broad economic and industrial planning role (including science and technology, and opening up of public procurement); common network planning and standards and common network development (e.g., OSI, Euronet). Emphasis on information technology and on countering IBM's dominance. European external identity. Reactive style.

Governance instruments

National protectionist solutions (e.g., nontariff trade barriers, subsidies, managed industry restructuring). European Commission own initiatives. Competition law (European Court of Justice).

Implementation

No support for European common action. Policies are national.

Relationship among European organizations

No direct formal links. Sectors and policy competence clearly demarcated.

Defensive Europeanization (late 1970s–mid-/late 1980s)

Broader context

Increasing internationalization and competitive threats from USA, Japan and Asian Tigers. "Information society": answer to falling productivity and growth. Relaunch of Europe on the basis of the needs of European industrial capital. Neomercantilist vision of European integration. New growth and new trade theories justifying public intervention and emphasizing economies of scale. Digitalization: technological convergence of telecommunications and information technology. U.S. domestic telecommunications liberalization raises alarm in Europe. Gradual entry of private commercial and transnational broadcasters in Europe.

Key actors

European industrialists (ERT). Europe-wide interest groups (e.g., Big 12, ITTF). EU (Commission and Court). Mutually supportive relationship between parts of European Commission and established interests (PTTs/CEPT, public service broadcasters/EBU, major European ICT manufacturers, ailing national champions).

Governance areas and style: Main characteristics

Construction of "Europe," inward-looking phase. European-level industrial policy measures: emphasis on big home market and economies of scale. Promotion of transnational European capital (European champions). Sponsored R&D programs (ESPRIT, RACE). Network planning (ISDN, GSM). Defensive standardization (MAC HDTV). Transfrontier television and pursuit of democratic ideals. Pan-European television experiments. European cultural unity and internal identity based on nation-state experience. Mostly reactive style.

Governance instruments

European single market: internal liberalization, active industrial policy and temporary external trade protection (Fortress Europe scenario). Emphasis on technology-push initiatives.

Implementation

Top-down measures and enforcement.

Relationship among European organizations

Mutually supportive.

Liberalization and Re-regulation: High Peak of European Governance (mid-1980s–late 1990s)

Broader context

Changing international and sectoral political economy leads to progressive procompetitive restructuring of telecommunications and television markets. Main factors: limitations of Keynesian order, economic liberalization and internationalization, technological change, pressure from Europe's trading partners—notably USA—bilaterally and multilaterally within GATT, dissatisfaction of big economic actors with existing monopolistic high-cost national communications order in Europe, rise of neoliberal ideology, international acceptance of trade in services. EU mediates globalizing pressures: reinforcing them in telecommunications, resisting them in audiovisual. End of Cold War. Internal market project: neomercantilist vs. neoliberal vision. Competitiveness industrial policy (against active interventionism). Renewed information society vision as the answer to Europe's economic malaise in reaction to U.S. and internet-related developments and technological convergence.

Key actors

Proliberalization coalition in telecommunications: USA, GATT Uruguay Round, parts of European Commission, European Court of Justice, potential market entrants, corporate telecommunications users, procompetition PTOs and national governments. Proliberalization coalition in broadcasting: potential commercial market entrants, advertisers, big electronics manufacturers, publishing interests, content producers, procompetitive governments (European and U.S.), parts of European Commission, European Court of Justice. Industry fora (e.g., Digital Video Broadcasting group).

Governance areas and style: Main characteristics

Liberalization and re-regulation through harmonized rules. Rise of European regulatory state in parallel to national regulatory state. Cultural diversity internally—cultural exceptionalism externally. European model of society: explicit recognition of importance of public services; civic conceptualization of identity. Hierarchical, coercive style.

Governance instruments

Legally binding and enforceable measures for market-making rules. Largely non-binding measures for public policy objectives. Emphasis on sector-specific rules. Binding and prescriptive measures. Increasing application of EU competition rules and state aid rules. Soft non-binding measures (e.g., benchmarks). European Commission: enabling role with regard to new technologies (e.g., digital television). EBU and Council of Europe (post–Cold War): non-binding prescriptive measures regarding content and cultural issues. Transnational regulatory networks (e.g., EU Contact Committee, EPRA and IRG).

Implementation

Duality of regulation: EU rules—national implementation but too much discretion. Delays and significant variations. Result: "regulatory patchwork." Formal rigid approach backed up with sanctions (e.g., formal infringement proceedings) coupled with informal mechanisms (peer pressure, "name and shame"). Regular monitoring reports by European Commission. Idea of pan-European regulatory authority: rejected.

Relationship among European organizations
Alternative institutional policy arenas (EU vs. Council of Europe). End of mutual interdependency.

Competitiveness, Knowledge Economy, Technological Convergence: Policy Coordination (late 1990s–early 2007)

Broader context
Growing globalization and renewed concern about Europe's relative economic decline compared to the USA in particular and on the world stage in general. Technological convergence, internet and broadband communications. Lisbon strategy: competitiveness and knowledge economy adopted as strategic political goals. "Better regulation initiative." EU enlargement toward Central and Eastern Europe. Interrelationship between Europeanization and globalization. Schumpeterian notion of competitiveness emphasizing innovation and monopoly rents and against market intervention vs. competitiveness conditioned on a big market, harmonized rules and active public policy.

Key actors
Increasing number of public and private actors operating at different levels. European and international organizations (e.g., WTO). Growing reliance on transnational regulatory networks.

Governance areas and style: Main characteristics
Modernization and streamlining of regulation in view of fully liberalized and technologically converging communication markets. Competitiveness vs. public policy objectives. Away from vertical directive-driven and legally binding harmonization toward policy coordination through flexible non-binding instruments, and (non)institutionalized interactions between Commission and groupings of national regulators and among national regulators. Emphasis on regulation by experts and specialist interaction. Market impact assessment (evidence-based regulation). Less rigid hierarchical style.

Governance instruments
Great mix of instruments. Asymmetry in governance between market-making and public policy objectives remains. Emphasis on horizontal (sector-neutral) measures, mainly competition rules. Framework regulation founded on competition law and setting out common objectives. Binding but room for discretion. eEurope/i2010: Non-binding targets and broad goals to be implemented through national plans rather than prescriptive reform. Harmonization through agreed main

principles, and stronger use of voluntary flexible measures (e.g., bench-marking, non-binding recommendations, regulatory committees, dis-semination of best practice, mutual learning, sharing of information, policy transfer).

Implementation

Formal mechanisms exist but emphasis is on implementation by agreement and consensus. Monitoring and encouragement rather than enforcement. First time European Commission is formally involved in national implementation.

Relationship among European organizations

Complementary but asymmetrical.

Bibliography

3GPP [Third Generation Partnership Project]. <http://www.3gpp.org/About/about.htm> (5 March 2005).

Abbate, Janet. *Inventing the Internet*. Cambridge, Mass. and London: The MIT Press, 1999.

ACT [Association of Commercial television In Europe], ICRT [International Communications Round Table], ENPA [European Newspapers Association], EPC [European Publishers Council], and AER [Association of European Radios]. "Broadcasting and Competition Rules in the Future EU Constitution—A View from the Private Media Sector." 2003. Paper submitted to the European Convention. <http://www.icrt.org/pos papers/2003/030502_BO.pdf> (1 July 2006).

ACT [Association of Commercial television in Europe], AER [Association Européenne des Radios], and EPC [European Publishers Council]. *Safeguarding the Future of the European Audiovisual Market: A White Paper on the Financing and Regulation of Publicly Funded Broadcasters*. 2004. <http://www.epceurope.org/presscentre/archive/safeguarding_audiovisual_market_300304.pdf> (1 July 2006).

Agence Europe. 16 September 1983–13 June 1996.

Albert, Michel. *Capitalism against Capitalism*. London: Whurr, 1993.

Alter, Karen J. "Who Are the 'Masters of the Treaty'? European Governments and the European Court of Justice." *International Organization* 52, no. 1 (1998): 121–47.

Anania, Loretta. "The Protean Complex: Are Open Networks Common Markets?" Paper presented at the VIII Annual International Telecommunications Society, Venice, Italy, March 1990.

Anchordoguy, Marie. *Computers Inc.: Japan's Challenge to IBM*. Cambridge, Mass.: Council on East Asian Studies, Harvard University, 1989.

Anderson, Benedict. *Imagined Communities. Reflections on the Origin and Spread of Nationalism*. 2nd ed. London and New York: Verso, 1991.

Appadurai, Arjun. "Disjuncture and Difference in the Global Cultural Economy." Pp. 295–310 in *Global Culture, Nationalism, Globalization and Modernity*, edited by Mike Featherstone. London: Sage, 1990.

Armstrong, Kenneth, and Simon Bulmer. *The Governance of the Single European Market*. Manchester: Manchester University Press, 1998.

Aspinwall, Mark D., and Gerald Schneider. "Same Menu, Separate Tables: The Institutionalist Turn in Political Science and the Study of European Integration." *European Journal of Political Research* 38, no. 1 (2000): 1–36.

Austin, Marc. "Europe's ONP Bargain. What's in It for the User?" *Telecommunications Policy* 18, no. 2 (1994): 97–113.

Bache, Ian, and Stephen George. *Politics in the European Union*. 2nd ed. Oxford and New York: Oxford University Press, 2006.

Bailey, David J. "Governance or the Crisis of Governmentality? Applying Critical State Theory at the European Level." *Journal of European Public Policy* 13, no. 1 (2006): 16–33.

Balanyá, Belén, Ann Doherty, Olivier Hoedeman, Adam Ma'anit and Erik Wesselius. *Europe Inc: Regional & Global Restructuring and the Rise of Corporate Power*. London: Pluto, 2000.

Barber, Russell B. "The European Broadcasting Union." *Journal of Broadcasting* 6, no. 2 (1962): 111–24.

Bartle, Ian. "When Institutions No Longer Matter: Reform of Telecommunications and Institutions in Germany, France and Britain." *Journal of Public Policy* 22, no. 1 (2002): 1–27.

Bauer, Johannes. "Normative Foundations of Electronic Communications Policy in the European Union." Pp. 110–33 in *Governing Telecommunications and the New Information Society in Europe*, edited by Jacint Jordana. Cheltenham and Northampton, Mass.: Edward Elgar, 2002.

———. "Regulation and State Ownership: Conflicts and Complementarities in EU Telecommunications." *Annals of Public and Cooperative Economics* 76, no. 2 (2005): 151–77.

Begg, Iain. "Introduction: Regulation in the European Union." *Journal of European Public Policy* 3, no. 4 (1996): 525–35.

Beijer, Thomas. "The UMTS Forum." Pp. 156–64 in *GSM and UMTS. The Creation of Global Mobile Communication*, edited by Friedhelm Hillebrand. Chichester: John Wiley, 2002.

Bell, Daniel. *The Coming of the Post-Industrial Society: A Venture in Social Forecasting*. Harmondsworth: Penguin 1976.

Bennett, Colin. "Review Article: What Is Policy Convergence and What Causes It?" *British Journal of Political Science* 21 (1991): 215–33.

Bernier, Ivan. "Content Regulation in the Audio-visual Sector and the WTO." Pp. 215–42 in *The WTO and Global Convergence in Telecommunications and Audio-Visual Services*, edited by Damien Geradin and David Luff. Cambridge: Cambridge University Press.

Besen, Stanley. "The European Telecommunications Standards Institute: A Preliminary Analysis." *Telecommunications Policy* 14, no. 6 (1990): 521–30.

Better Regulation Task Force. *Regulation—Less Is More. Reducing Burdens, Improving Outcomes*. London: BTRF, 2005.

Bhagwati, Jagdish, and Hugh Patrick, eds. *Aggressive Unilateralism: America's 301 Trade Policy and the World Trading System*. London: Harvester Wheatsheaf, 1991.

Bieler, Andreas, and Adam David Morton, eds. *Social Forces in the Making of the New Europe: The Restructuring of European Social Relations in the Global Political Economy*. London: Palgrave, 2001.

Blyth, Mark. *Great Transformations. Economic Ideas and Institutional Change in the Twentieth Century*. New York: Cambridge University Press, 2002.

Boddy, William. "The Beginnings of American Television." Pp. 35–61 in *Television. An International History*, edited by Anthony Smith. Oxford: Oxford University Press, 1995.

Boel, Bent. *The European Productivity Agency and Transatlantic Relations 1953–1961*. Copenhagen: Museum Tusculanum Press, 2003.

Borrás, Susana, and Krestin Jacobsson. "The Open Method of Co-ordination and New Governance Patterns in the EU." *Journal of European Public Policy*, Special issue 11, no. 2 (2004): 185–208.

Brack, Hans. *The Evolution of the EBU Through Its Statutes from 1950 to 1976*. Geneva: EBU, 1976.

Brainard, Robert, and John Madden. *Science and Technology Policy Outlook*. Paris: OECD, 1985.

Braithwaite, John, and Peter Drahos. *Global Business Regulation*. Cambridge: Cambridge University Press, 2000.

Brants, Kees, and Els de Bens. "The Status of TV Broadcasting in Europe." Pp. 7–22 in *Television Across Europe: A Comparative Introduction*, edited by Jan Wieten, Graham Murdock and Peter Dahlgren. London: Sage, 2000.

Bretherton, Charlotte, and John Vogler. *The European Union as a Global Actor*. London and New York: Routledge, 1999.

Briggs, Asa. *The History of Broadcasting in the United Kingdom. Volume I. The Birth of Broadcasting*. London: Oxford University Press, 1961.

———. *The History of Broadcasting in the United Kingdom. Volume II. The Golden Age of Wireless*. London: Oxford University Press, 1965.

———. *The History of Broadcasting in the United Kingdom. Volume IV. Sound & Vision*. London: Oxford University Press, 1979.

Buigues, Pierre, and Philippe Goybet. "The Community's Industrial Competitiveness and International Trade in Manufactured Products." Pp. 227–47 in *The European Internal Market: Trade and Competition*, edited by Alexis Jacquemin and André Sapir. Oxford: Oxford University Press, 1989.

Buigues, Pierre, and André Sapir. "Community Industrial Policies." Pp. 21–37 in *Industrial Policy in the European Community: A Necessary Response to Economic Integration?*, edited by Phedon Nicolaides. Dordrecht: Martinus Nijhoff Publishers, 1993.

Bulmer, Simon. "New Institutionalism and the Governance of the Single European Market." *Journal of European Public Policy* 5, no. 3 (1998): 365–86.

Cafruny, Alan, and Magnus Ryner, eds. *A Ruined Fortress?: Neoliberal Hegemony and Transformation in Europe*. Lanham, Md.: Rowman & Littlefield, 2003.

Calabrese, Andrew, and Jean-Claude Burgleman, eds. *Communication, Citizenship, and Social Policy*. Lanham, Md.: Rowman & Littlefield, 1999.

Campaign for Press and Broadcasting Freedom [UK]. *Television Without Frontiers*. 10 October 2006. <http://keywords.dsvr.co.uk/freepress/body.phtml?category=&id=1512> (9 November 2006).

Campbell-Kelly, Martin. *ICL: A Business and Technical History*. Oxford: Clarendon, 1989.

Caporaso, James. "The European Union and Forms of State: Westphalian, Regulatory or Post-Modern?" *Journal of Common Market Studies* 34, no. 1 (1996): 29–52.

Caporaso, James, and John Keeler. "The European Union and Regional Integration Theory." Pp. 29–62 in *The State of the European Union, 3. Building a European Polity?*, edited by Carolyn Rhodes and Sonia Mazey. Boulder, Co.: Lynne Rienner, 1995.

Carpentier, Michel. "Toward Smooth Europe-U.S. Telecom Relations." *Transnational Data and Communications Report* (June 1986): 5–7.

Cave, Martin. *Review of Radio Spectrum Management. An Independent Review for Department of Trade and Industry and HM Treasury*. 2002. <http://www.ofcom.org.uk/static/archive/ra/spectrum-review/index.htm> (26 June 2006).

Cawson, Alan. "High-Definition Television in Europe." *The Political Quarterly* 66, no. 2 (1995): 157–73.

Cawson, Alan, Kevin Morgan, Douglas Webber, Peter Holmes and Anne Stevens. *Hostile Brothers: Competition and Closure in the European Electronics Industry*. Oxford: Clarendon, 1990.

Cerny, Philip. *The Changing Architecture of Politics: Structure, Agency, and the Future of the State*. London: Sage, 1990.

——. "Structuring the Political Arena. Public Goods, States and Governance in a Globalizing World." Pp. 23–35 in *Global Political Economy: Contemporary Theories*, edited by Ronen Palan. London and New York: Routledge, 2000.

Chalaby, Jean. "Transnational Television in Europe: The Role of Pan-European Channels." *European Journal of Communication* 17, no. 2 (2002): 183–203.

Checkel, Jeffrey. "Review Article. The Constructivist Turn in International Relations Theory." *World Politics* 50, no. 2 (1998): 324–48.

Chryssochoou, Dimitris. "Civic Competence and the Challenge to EU Polity-building." *Journal of European Public Policy* 9, no. 5 (2002): 756–73.

Ciborra, Claudio. "Alliances as Learning Experiments: Cooperation, Competition and Change in High-tech Industries." Pp. 51–77 in *Strategic Partnerships and the World Economy: States, Firms and International Competition*, edited by Lynn Krieger Mytelka. London: Pinter, 1991.

Cini, Michelle. "The Soft Law Approach: Commission Rule-making in the EU's State-aid Regime." *Journal of European Public Policy* 8, no. 2 (2001): 192–207.

Cohen, Edward S. "Globalization and the Boundaries of the State: A Framework for Analyzing the Changing Practice of Sovereignty." *Governance: An International Journal of Policy, Administration and Institutions* 14, no. 1 (2001): 75–97.

Colecchia, Alessandra, and Paul Schreyer. "ICT Investment and Economic Growth in the 1990s: Is the United States a Unique Case? A Comparative Study of Nine OECD Countries." *OECD STI Working Paper*, no. 2001/7. Paris: OECD, 2001.

Collins, Richard. *Satellite Television in Western Europe*. London: John Libbey, 1992.

——. *Broadcasting and Audio-visual Policy in the Single European Market*. London: John Libbey, 1994.

——. *From Satellite to Single Market. New Communication Technology and European Public Service Television.* London and New York: Routledge, 1998.

——. "The Contemporary Broadcasting Market and the Role of the Public Service Broadcaster. A View from the UK." Paper presented at the meeting on the future of broadcasting at YLE, Helsinki, 20 March 2002.

Communications Week International, 11 May 1992–16 December 2002.

Coombes, David. *Politics and Bureaucracy in the European Community. A Portrait of the Commission of the E.E.C.* London: George Allen and Unwin, 1970.

Council of Europe. *Statute of the Council of Europe. London 5.V.1949.* <http://conventions.coe.int/Treaty/EN/Treaties/Html/001.htm> (23 March 2006).

——. *European Agreement on the Protection of Television Broadcasts.* 22 June 1960. <http://conventions.coe.int/Treaty/EN/treaties/Html/034.htm> (22 March 2006).

——. *European Agreement for the Prevention of Broadcasts Transmitted from Stations outside National Territories.* 22 January 1965. <http://conventions.coe.int/Treaty/EN/treaties/Html/053.htm> (22 March 2006).

——. *Recommendation 749 on European Broadcasting.* Strasbourg, 23 January 1975.

——. *Resolution No. 1: Future of Public Service Broadcasting of the 4th Council of Europe Ministerial Conference on Mass Media Policy, Prague 1994.* <http://www.ebu.ch/CMSimages/en/leg_ref_coe_mcm_resolution_psb_07_081294_tcm 6-4274.pdf> (11 June 2006).

——. "A Brief History of the Council of Europe." 1998. <http://www.coe.fr/eng/present/history.htm> (23 Oct. 1998).

——. *Explanatory Memorandum. Report on Public Service Broadcasting.* Committee on Culture, Science and Education. Rapporteur: Paschal Mooney. Strasbourg, 12 January 2004.

Council of Europe—Committee of Ministers. *Report of the Committee of Ministers REC 9 (1951). Doc. 2 (Report). To the Consultative Assembly in Pursuance of Article 19 of the Statute. 12 May 1952.* Strasbourg, 12 March 1952.

——. *Resolution (58) 21: Posts and Telecommunications—European Cooperation in this Field. Recommendation 143.* Strasbourg, 18 November 1958.

——. *Resolution (69) 6 on Cinema and the Protection of Youth.* 7 March 1969. <https://wcd.coe.int/com.instranet.InstraServlet?Command=com.instranet.CmdBlob Get&DocId=635222&SecMode=1&Admin=0&Usage=4&InstranetImage=50011> (23 March 2006).

——. *Recommendation (84) 3 on Principles on Television Advertising.* Strasbourg, 23 February 1984.

——. *Recommendation (86) 2 on Principles Relating to Copyright Law Questions in the Field of Television by Satellite and Cable.* Strasbourg, 14 February 1986.

——. *Recommendation R(96)10 on the Guarantee of the Independence of Public Service Broadcasting.* Strasbourg, 11 September 1996.

——. *Recommendation R(2000) 23 on the Independence and Functions of Regulatory Authorities for the Broadcasting Sector.* Strasbourg, 20 December 2000.

——. *Recommendation (2007) 3 on the Remit of Public Service Media in the Information Society.* Strasbourg, 31 January 2007.

Council of Europe—Consultative Assembly. *Recommendation 9 for the Establishment of a Postal Union between the Member States of the Council of Europe.* 5 December

1951. <http://assembly.coe.int/Main.asp?link=/Documents/AdoptedText/ta51/
EREC9.htm> (9 April 2006).

——. *Recommendation 102 on European Co-operation in the Field of Posts and Telecommunications*. Strasbourg, 24 October 1956.

——. *Recommendation 143 on the Institution of a European Conference of Posts and Telecommunications*. Strasbourg, 4 May 1957.

——. *Recommendation 206 on a Proposed European Conference of Ministers of Posts and Telecommunications*. Strasbourg, 15 September 1959.

Council of Europe—Parliamentary Assembly. *Recommendation (1981) 926 on Questions Raised by Cable Television and by Direct Satellite Broadcasts*. Strasbourg, 7 October 1981.

Council [of EU Ministers]. "Décision du 15 avril 1964 créant un Comité de politique économique à moyen terme (64/247/CEE)." *Official Journal* 64/1031, 22 April 1964.

——. "Conseil 69/157/CEE: Second programme de politique économique à moyen terme." *Official Journal* L129, 30 May 1969.

——. "Resolution of 28 May 1969 on the Adaptation to Technical Progress of the Directives for the Elimination of Technical Barriers to Trade Which Result from Disparities between the Provisions Laid Down by Law, Regulation or Administrative Action in Member States." *Official Journal* C76/8, 17 June 1969.

——. Resolution of 15 July 1974 on a Community Policy on Data Processing. *Official Journal* C86/1, 20 July 1974.

——. "Decision 75/200/EEC of 18 March 1975 Adopting an Initial Three-year Plan of Action in the Field of Scientific and Technical Information and Documentation." *Official Journal* L100/18, 21 April 1975.

——. "Directive 77/62/EEC of 21 December 1976 Coordinating Procedures for the Award of Public Supply Contracts." *Official Journal* L13/1, 15 January 1977.

——. "Decision 84/130/EEC of 28 February 1984 Concerning a European Programme for Research and Development in Information Technologies (ESPRIT)." *Official Journal* L67/54, 9 March 1984.

——. "Decision 85/372/EEC of 25 July 1985 on a Definition Phase for a Community Action in the Field of Telecommunications Technologies—R & D Programme in Advanced Communications Technologies for Europe (RACE)." *Official Journal* L210/24, 7 August 1985.

——. "Recommendation 86/659/EEC of 22 December 1986 on the Coordinated Introduction of the Integrated Services Digital Network (ISDN) in the European Community." *Official Journal* L382/36, 31 December 1986.

——. "Recommendation 87/371/EEC on the Co-ordinated Introduction of Public Pan-European Cellular Digital Land-based Mobile Communications in the Community." *Official Journal* L196/81, 17 July 1987.

——. "Directive 87/372/EEC on the Frequency Bands to be Reserved for the Co-ordinated Introduction of Public Pan-European Cellular Digital Land-based Mobile Communications in the European Community." *Official Journal* L196/85, 17 July 1987.

——. "Directive 89/552/EEC of 3 October 1989 on the Coordination of Certain Provisions Laid Down by Law, Regulation or Administrative Action in Member

States Concerning the Pursuit of Television Broadcasting Activities." *Official Journal* L298/23, 17 October 1989.

——. "Directive 91/287/EEC of 3 June 1991 on the Frequency Bands to be Reserved for the Co-ordinated Introduction of Digital Cordless Telecommunications (DECT) into the Community." *Official Journal* L144/45, 8 June 1991.

——. "Resolution of 18 November 1991 Concerning Electronics, Information and Communication Technologies." *Official Journal* C325/2, 14 December 1991.

——. *Proposal for a Directive Amending Council Directive 89/552/EEC on the Coordination of Certain Provisions Laid Down by Law, Regulation or Administrative Action in Member States Concerning the Pursuit of Television Broadcasting Activities (Television without Frontiers) General Approach*, 14464/06. Brussels, 31 October and 7 November 2006.

Cowhey, Peter F. "The International Telecommunications Regime: The Political Roots of Regimes for High Technology." *International Organization* 44, no. 2 (1990): 169–99.

Cowles, Maria Green. "Setting the Agenda for a New Europe: The ERT and EC 1992." *Journal of Common Market Studies* 33, no. 4 (1995): 501–26.

——. "The Transatlantic Business Dialogue and Domestic Business-Government Relations." Pp. 159–79 in *Transforming Europe: Europeanization and Domestic Change*, edited by Maria Green Cowles, James Caporaso and Thomas Risse. Ithaca and London: Cornell University Press, 2001.

Cowles, Maria Green, James Caporaso and Thomas Risse, eds. *Transforming Europe: Europeanization and Domestic Change*. Ithaca and London: Cornell University Press, 2001.

Cox, Alan. "The Years from Mid-1998 to Early 2001." Pp. 286–300 in *GSM and UMTS. The Creation of Global Mobile Communication*, edited by Friedhelm Hillebrand. Chichester: John Wiley & Sons, 2002.

Cox, Robert. "Towards a Post-Hegemonic Conceptualization of World Order: Reflections on the Relevancy of Ibn Khaldun." Pp. 132–59 in *Governance without Government: Order and Change in World Politics*, edited by James N. Rosenau and Ernst-Otto Czempiel. Cambridge: Cambridge University Press, 1992.

Cram, Laura. *Policy-Making in the EU: Conceptual Lenses and the Integration Process*. London and New York: Routledge, 1997.

Crane, Rhonda. *The Politics of International Standards: France and the Color TV War*. Norwood, N.J.: Ablex, 1979.

Crozier, Michel, Samuel P. Huntington and Joji Watanuki. *The Crisis of Democracy*. New York: New York University Press, 1975.

Dahlgren, Peter. *Television and the Public Sphere. Citizenship, Democracy and the Media*. London: Sage, 1995.

Dai, Xiudian, Alan Cawson, and Peter Holmes. "The Rise and Fall of High Definition Television: The Impact of European Technology Policy." *Journal of Common Market Studies* 34, no. 2 (1996): 149–66.

Dang-Nguyen, Godefroy. "The European Telecommunications Policy or the Awakening of a Sleeping Beauty." Paper presented at the European Consortium of Political Research, Amsterdam, April 1987.

Dang-Nguyen, Godefroy, Volker Schneider and Raymund Werle. "Networks in European Policy-making: Europeification of Telecommunications Policy."

Pp. 93–114 in *Making Policy in Europe: The Europeification of National Policy-making*, edited by Svein S. Andersen and Kjell A. Eliassen. London: Sage, 1993.

Dashwood, Alan. "Hastening Slowly: The Community's Path Toward Harmonisation." Pp. 177–208 in *Policy-Making in the European Community*, edited by Helen Wallace, William Wallace and Carole Webb. Chichester: John Wiley, 1983.

DCMS [Department for Culture, Media and Sport, UK]. *The Future Funding of the BBC: Report of the Independent Review Pane, Chairman Gavyn Davies*. London: DCMS, 1999.

DCMS/EU. *Liverpool Audiovisual Conference. Between Culture and Commerce. 20–22 September 2005*. London: DCMS, 2005. <http://ec.europa.eu/comm/avpolicy/docs/reg/modernisation/liverpool_2005/uk-conference-report-en.pdf> (1 July 2006).

De Bens, Els, and Hedwig de Smaele. "The Inflow of American Television Fiction on European Broadcasting Channels Revisited." *European Journal of Communication* 16, no. 1 (2001): 51–76.

de la Porte, Caroline, and Patrizia Nanz. "The OMC—A Deliberative-democratic Mode of Governance? The Cases of Employment and Pensions." *Journal of European Public Policy* 11, no. 2 (2004): 267–88.

Dedman, Martin J. *The Origins and Development of the European Union 1945–95. A History of European Integration*. London and New York: Routledge, 1996.

Dehousse, Renaud. *The European Court of Justice: The Politics of Judicial Integration*. Basingstoke: Macmillan, 1998.

———. "Regulation by Networks in the European Community: The Role of European Agencies." *Journal of European Public Policy* 4, no. 2 (1997): 246–61.

Delanty, Gerard. "Beyond the Nation-State: National Identity and Citizenship in a Multicultural Society—A Response to Rex." *Sociological Research Online* 1, no. 3 (1996). <http://www.socresonline.org.uk/socresonline/1/3/1.html> (23 May 2006).

Depypere, Stefaan, and Nynke Tigchelaar. "The Commission's State Aid Policy on Activities of Public Service Broadcasters in Neighbouring Markets." *EU Competition Policy Newsletter*, no. 2 (summer 2004): 19–22.

Destler, I.M. *American Trade Politics*. 4th ed. Washington, D.C.: Institute for International Economics, 2005.

Diebold, John. "Is the Gap Technological?" *Foreign Affairs*, (1968): 276–91.

Diez, Thomas. "Riding the AM-track through Europe; or, the Pitfalls of a Rationalist Journey Through European Integration." *Millennium: Journal of International Studies* 28, no. 2 (1999): 355–69.

DIF [Digital Interoperability Forum]. "Welcome to the Digital Interoperability Forum." <http://www.difgroup.com> (26 June 2006).

Dinan, Desmond. *Ever Closer Union? An Introduction to the European Community*. Basingstoke: Macmillan: 1994.

Doyle, Gillian. *Media Ownership*. London: Sage, 2002.

Draffan, George. *The Corporate Consensus: A Guide to the Institutions of Global Power. Part 2: Profiles in Corporate Power*. 2002. <http://www.endgame.org/corpcon2.html#UnionofIndustrial> (4 June 2006).

Drake, William J. "The Internet Religious War." *Telecommunications Policy* 17, no. 9 (1993): 643–49.

———. "The Rise and Decline of the International Telecommunications Regime." Pp. 124–177 in *Regulating the Global Information Society*, edited by Christopher Marsden. London and New York: Routledge, 2000.

Dupagne, Michel. "EC Policymaking: The Case of the 'Television Without Frontiers' Directive." *Gazette* 49, (1992): 99–120.

Eberlein, Burkard, and Dieter Kerwer. "New Governance in the European Union: A Theoretical Perspective." *Journal of Common Market Studies* 42, no. 1 (2004): 121–42.

Eberlein, Burkard, and Edgar Grande. "Beyond Delegation: Transnational Regulatory Regimes and the EU Regulatory State." *Journal of European Public Policy* 12, no. 1 (2005): 89–112.

EBU [European Broadcasting Union]. *Statutes of the EBU*. Various years. Geneva: EBU.

———. "25 Years of the European Broadcasting Union. A Retrospect." *EBU Review* XXVI, no. 1 (1975): 10–27.

———. *Model Public Service Broadcasting Law*. Geneva: EBU, 1998, updated in 2003. <http://www.ebu.ch/CMSimages/en/leg_p_model_law_psb1_tcm6-14334.pdf> (11 June 2006).

———. "Before Torquay." *EBU Diffusion* (winter 1999/2000): 12–14.

———. "50 Years of Eurovision." *EBU Dossiers* (May 2004).

———. *EBU Position Paper on the Commission Proposal for a Directive on Services in the Internal Market*. Geneva: EBU, 2004.

———. "The Lisbon Strategy and the Specific Role of Public Service Broadcasting." *EBU Diffusion*, no. 1 (2005): 24–26.

———. *Draft Audiovisual Media Services Directive. Initial EBU Contribution to the First Reading*. Geneva: EBU, 2006.

Economist. 28 January 1984–18 February 2006.

ECSA [European Community Studies Association]. "Does the European Union Represent an *n* of 1?" *ECSA Review* X, no. 3 (1997): 1–5. <http://www.eustudies.org/N1debate.htm> (21 November 2003).

ECSC [European Coal and Steel Community]. *Resolution Adopted by the Ministers of Foreign Affairs of the Member States of the ECSC at Their Meeting at Messina on June 1 and 2, 1955*. <http://www.ena.lu/mce.cfm> (3 Oct. 2005).

ECTA [European Competitive Telecommunications Association]. *ECTA DSL Scorecard—June 2002*. 2002. <http://www.ectaportal.com/regulatory/dsl_jun02.xls> (20 August 2002).

Egan, Michelle. *Constructing a European Market: Standards, Regulation, and Governance*. Oxford and New York: Oxford University Press, 2001.

Eising, Rainer, and Beate Kohler-Koch. "Introduction. Network Governance in the European Union." Pp. 3–13 in *The Transformation of Governance in the European Union*, edited by Beate Kohler-Koch and Rainer Eising. London and New York: Routledge, 1999.

———. "Governance in the European Union." Pp. 267–85 in *The Transformation of Governance in the European Union*, edited by Beate Kohler-Koch and Rainer Eising. London and New York: Routledge, 1999.

Electronic Communications Committee [CEPT]. *ECC Decision (02)06 on the Designation of Frequency Band 2500–2690 MHz for UMTS/IMT-2000*. 2002. <http://www

.ero.dk/documentation/docs/doc98/official/Word/DEC0206.DOC> (6 June 2006).

———. *ECC Decision (05)05 on Harmonised Utilisation of Spectrum for IMT-2000/UMTS Systems Operating within the Band 2500–2690 MHz*. 2005.<http://www.ero.dk/documentation/docs/doc98/official/pdf/ECCDEC0505.PDF> (6 June 2006).

Eliassen, Kjell A., and Marit Sjøvaag, eds. *European Telecommunications Liberalisation*. London and New York: Routledge, 1999.

ERG [European Regulators' Group, EU]. <http://erg.eu.int/index_en.htm> (26 June 2006).

———. *ERG (03) 07. Rules of Procedure for ERG*. April 2004. <http://erg.eu.int/doc/work_progr_2003/erg_03_07_rules_of_procedure_clean.pdf> (1 July 2006).

———. *ERG (06) 33. Revised ERG Common Position on the Approach Remedies in the ECNS Regulatory Framework*. May 2006. <http://erg.eu.int/doc/meeting/erg_06_33_remedies_common_position_june_06.pdf> (29 June 2006).

———. *ERG (06) 67. Harmonisation—The Proposed ERG Approach*. October 2006. <http://erg.eu.int/doc/publications/consult_erg_approach_harmonisation/erg_06_67_harmonisation_approach.pdf> (3 Feb. 2007).

———. *ERG (06) 68. Effective Harmonisation within the European Electronic Communications Sector*. October 2006. < http://erg.eu.int/doc/publications/consult_effective_harmonisation/erg_06_68_effective_harmonisation.pdf> (3 Feb. 2007).

Eriksen, Erik Oddvar, and John Erik Fossum, eds. *Democracy in the European Union: Integration through Deliberation?* London: Routledge, 2000.

Ernst, Dieter, and David O'Connor. *Competing in the Electronics Industry—The Experience of Newly Industrializing Economies*. Paris: OECD, 1992.

ERT [European Round Table of industrialists]. *Missing Links*. Brussels: ERT, 1984.

———. *Changing Scales*. Paris: ERT, 1985.

———. *Clearing the Lines: A Users' View on Business Communications in Europe*. Paris: ERT, 1986.

———. *Reshaping Europe*. Brussels: ERT, 1991.

———. *Missing Networks*. ERT: Brussels, 1991.

———. *Beating the Crisis: A Charter for Europe's Industrial Future*. Brussels: ERT, 1993.

ETNO [European Telecommunications Network Operators' association]. "E-Communications Driving European Competitiveness. ETNO's Vision for the Future." 2005. <http://www.etno.be> (20 March 2005).

EU Contact Committee of the TVWF Directive. "Rules of procedure of the Contact Committee." 2004. <http://ec.europa.eu/comm/avpolicy/docs/reg/tvwf/contact_comm/doccctvsf97-2_rulesofpr-rev041021.pdf> (12 June 2006).

EU Dutch Presidency. "The Key Role of Public Service Broadcasting in the 21st Century." Conference proceedings, Amsterdam, 2–3 September 2004. <http://www.omroep.nl/eu2004/> (1 July 2006).

Eugster, Ernest. *Television Programming across National Boundaries: The EBU and OIRT Experience*. Dedham, Mass.: Artech House, 1983.

European Audiovisual Observatory. *Transfrontier Television in the European Union. Market Impact and Selected Legal Aspects*. Strasbourg: EAO, 2004. <http://www.obs.coe.int/> (1 June 2005).

European Commission. "Article 7 Procedures." <http://ec.europa.eu/information_ society/policy/ecomm/article_7/index_en.htm> (5 Feb. 2007).

———."Recommandation de la Commission 65/428/CEE, du 20 Septembre 1965, aux États membres, relative à la communication préalable à la Commission, à l'état de projets, de certaines dispositions législatives réglementaires et administratives." *Official Journal* 160/2611, 29 September 1965.

———. "General Programme of 28 May 1969 for the Elimination of Technical Barriers to Trade Which Result from Disparities between Provisions Laid Down by Law, Regulation or Administrative Action in Member States." *Official Journal* C76/1. Brussels, 17 June 1969 (in French).

———. *La Politique Industrielle de la Communauté. Mémorandum de la Commission au Conseil.* COM70 (100). Brussels, 18 March 1970.

———. *European Society Faced with the Challenge of New Information Technologies: A Community Response.* COM(79) 650. Brussels, 26 November 1979.

———. *Recommendations on Telecommunications.* COM(80) 422. Brussels, 1 September 1980.

———. "Written Question 1539/80 by Mr. Adam to the Commission (20 November 1980). Subject: Community Electronics Industry. Reply Given by Mr Davignon on Behalf of the Commission (2 March 1981)." *Official Journal* C78/9, 6 April 1981.

———. "Decision 82/861/EEC of 10 December 1982 Relating to a Proceeding under Article 86 of the EEC Treaty (IV/29.877—British Telecommunications)." *Official Journal* L360/36, 21 December 1982.

———. *Realities and Tendencies in European Television: Perspectives and Options.* COM(83) 229. Brussels, 25 May 1983.

———. *Telecommunications.* COM(83) 329. Brussels, 9 June 1983.

———. *Discussion Paper for the Special Council Meeting of 20–21 September on the Question of Improving the International Competitive Position of European Firms.* COM(83) 547. Brussels, 14 September 1983.

———. *Progress Report on the Thinking and Work Done in the Field, and Initial Proposals for an Action Programme.* COM(84) 277. Brussels, 18 May 1984.

———. *Television without Frontiers. Green Paper on the Establishment of the Common Market for Broadcasting Especially by Satellite and Cable.* COM(84) 300. Brussels, 14 June 1984.

———. *Sixteenth Report on Competition Policy.* Luxembourg: Office for Official Publications of the European Communities, 1986.

———. *Proposal for a Council Directive on the Coordination of Certain Provisions Laid Down by Law, Regulation or Administrative Action in Member States Concerning the Pursuit of Broadcasting Activities.* COM(86) 146. Brussels, 19 March 1986.

———. *Towards a Dynamic European Economy. Green Paper on the Development of the Common Market for Telecommunications Services and Equipment.* COM(87) 290. Brussels, 30 June 1987.

———. *Industrial Policy in an Open and Competitive Environment: Guidelines for a Community Approach.* COM(90) 556. Brussels, 16 November 1990.

———. *The European Electronics and Information Technology Industry: State of Play, Issues at Stake and Proposals for Action.* SEC(91) 565. Brussels, 3 April 1991.

———. "Guidelines on the Application of EEC Competition Rules in the Telecommunications Sector." *Official Journal* C233/2, 6 September 1991.

———. *Green Paper. Pluralism and Media Concentration in the Internal Market.* COM(92) 480. Brussels, 16 December 1992.

———. Decision 93/403/EEC of 11 June 1993 Relating a Proceeding Pursuant to Article 85 of the EEC Treaty (IV/32.150—EBU/Eurovision System). *Official Journal* L179/23, 22 July 1993.

———. *White Paper on Growth, Competitiveness, Employment—The Challenges and Ways Forward into the 21st Century.* COM(93) 700. Brussels, 5 December 1993.

———. *Green Paper on Strategy Options to Strengthen the European Programme Industry in the Context of the Audiovisual Policy of the European Union.* COM(94) 96. Brussels, 6 April 1994.

———. *Towards the Personal Communications Environment: Green Paper on a Common Approach to Mobile and Personal Communications in the European Union.* COM(94) 145. Brussels, 27 April 1994.

———. *Europe and the Global Information Society: Recommendations to the European Council* [Bangemann Report]. Brussels, 26 May 1994.

———. *Europe's Way to the Information Society. An Action Plan.* COM (94) 347. Brussels, 19 July 1994.

———. *An Industrial Competitiveness Policy for the European Union,* COM(94) 319. Brussels, 14 September 1994.

———. *Green Paper on the Liberalisation of Telecommunications Infrastructure and Cable Television Networks. Part One. Principles and Timetable.* COM(94) 440. Brussels, 25 October 1994.

———. *Green Paper on the Liberalisation of Telecommunications Infrastructure and Cable Television Networks. Part Two. A Common Approach to the Provision of Infrastructure for Telecommunications in the European Union.* COM(94) 682. Brussels, 25 January 1995.

———. "Directive 96/19/EC of 13 March 1996 Amending Directive 90/388/EEC with Regard to the Implementation of Full Competition in the Telecommunications Markets." *Official Journal* L74/13, 22 March 1996.

———. *Illegal and Harmful Content on the Internet.* COM(96) 487. Brussels, 16 October 1996.

———. *Communication on the Further Development of Mobile and Wireless Communications—Challenges and Choices for the European Union.* COM(1997) 217. Brussels, 29 May 1997.

———. "Directive 97/36/EC Amending Council Directive 89/552/EEC on the Coordination of Certain Provisions Laid down by Law, Regulation or Administrative Action in Member States Concerning the Pursuit of Television Broadcasting Activities." *Official Journal* L202, 30 July 1997.

———. *Second Report on the Application of Directive 89/552/EEC "Television Without Frontiers."* COM(1997) 523. Brussels, 24 October 1997.

———. *Green Paper on the Convergence of the Telecommunications, Media and Information Technology Sectors, and the Implications for Regulation. Towards an Information Society Approach.* COM(97) 623. Brussels, 3 December 1997.

———. *Fourth Report on the Implementation of the Telecommunications Regulatory Package.* Brussels: European Commission, 1998.

———. *DG IV Discussion Paper on the Application of Articles 90, Paragraph 2, 92 and 93 of the EC Treaty in the Broadcasting Sector.* Brussels: DG Competition, 1998.

———. *Communications on Globalisation and the Information Society,* COM(98) 50. Brussels, 4 February 1998.

———. "Commission Recommendation 98/322/EC of 8 April 1998 on Interconnection in a Liberalised Telecommunication Market. Part 2: Accounting Separation and Cost Accounting." *Official Journal* L141/41, 13 May 1998.

———. *Audiovisual Policy: Next Steps.* COM(98) 446. Brussels, 14 July 1998.

———. "Recommendation 98/511/EC of 29 July 1998 Amending Recommendation 98/195/EC on Interconnection in a Liberalised Telecommunications Market. Part 1—Interconnection Pricing." *Official Journal* L228/30, 15 August 1998.

———. *eEurope. An Information Society for All.* Brussels: European Commission, 1999.

———. *The Convergence of the Telecommunications, Media and Information Technology Sectors, and the Implications for Regulation. Results of the Public Consultation on the Green Paper COM(97)623.* COM(1999) 108. Brussels, 10 March 1999.

———. *Fifth Report on the Implementation of the Telecommunications Regulatory Package.* COM(1999) 537. Brussels, 10 November 1999.

———. *Towards a New Framework for Electronic Communications Infrastructure and Associated Services. The 1999 Communications Review.* COM(1999) 539. Brussels, 10 November 1999.

———. *State aid No. NN 88/98—United Kingdom, Financing of a 24-hour Advertising-free News Channel out of the Licence Fee by the BBC, SG(99) D/10201.* Brussels, 14 December 1999.

———. "Decision 2000/400/EC of 10 May 2000 Relating to a Proceeding Pursuant to Article 81 of the EC Treaty (Case IV/32.150—Eurovision)." *Official Journal* L151/18, 24 June 2000.

———. *Proposal for a Directive of the European Parliament and of the Council on a Common Regulatory Framework for Electronic Communications Networks and Services.* COM(2000) 393. Brussels, 12 July 2000.

———. *European Governance. A White Paper,* COM(2001) 428. Brussels, 25 July 2001.

———. *European Competitiveness Report.* SEC (2001) 1705. Brussels, 29 October 2001.

———. "Communication on the Application of State Aid Rules to Public Service broadcasting." *Official Journal* C320/5, 15 November 2001.

———. *Productivity: The Key to Competitiveness of European Economies and Enterprises.* COM(2002) 262. Brussels, 21 May 2002.

———. *State Aid No. N 631/2001—United Kingdom BBC Licence Fee, C(2002) 1886.* Brussels, 22 May 2002.

———. *Action Plan: Simplifying and Improving the Regulatory Environment.* COM(2002) 278. Brussels, 5 June 2002.

———. "Commission Guidelines on Market Analysis and the Assessment of Significant Market Power under the Community Regulatory Framework for Electronic Communications Networks and Services." *Official Journal* C165/6, 11 July 2002.

———. "Commission Decision 2002/622/EC of 2 July 2002 Establishing a Radio Spectrum Policy Group." *Official Journal* L198/49, 27 July 2002.

———. "Commission Decision 2002/627/EC of 29 July 2002 Establishing the European Regulators Group for Electronic Communications Networks and Services." *Official Journal* L200/38, 30 July 2002.

———. *Fourth Report on the Application of Directive 89/552/EEC "Television without Frontiers."* COM(2002) 778. Brussels, 6 January 2003.

———. "Commission Recommendation 2003/312/EC of 11 February 2003 on Relevant Product and Services Markets within the Electronics Communications Sectors Susceptible to ex ante Regulation in Accordance with Directive 2002/21/EC of the European Parliament and of the Council on a Common Regulatory Framework for Electronic Communication Networks and Services." *Official Journal* L114/45, 8 May 2003.

———. *Green Paper on Services of General Interest.* COM(2003) 270. Brussels, 21 May 2003.

———. "Commission Recommendation 2003/561/EC of 23 July 2003 on Notifications, Time Limits and Consultations Provided for in Article 7 of Directive 2002/21/EC of the European Parliament and of the Council on a Common Regulatory Framework for Electronic Communications Networks and Services." *Official Journal* L190/13, 30 July 2003.

———. *State Aid No. N 37/2003—United Kingdom BBC Digital Curriculum.* Brussels, 1 October 2003.

———. *The EU Economy: 2003 Review.* COM(2003) 729. Brussels, 26 November 2003.

———. *Communication on the Future of European Regulatory Audiovisual Policy.* COM(2003)784. Brussels, 15 December 2003.

———. *Facing the Challenge. The Lisbon Strategy for Growth and Employment. Report from the High Level Group Chaired by Wim Kok.* Brussels: European Commission, 2004.

———. *Proposal for a Directive of the European Parliament and of the Council on Services in the Internal Market.* COM(2004) 2. Brussels, 13 January 2004.

———. *Commission Staff Working Paper on the Interoperability of Digital Interactive Television Services.* SEC(2004)346. Brussels, 18 March 2004.

———. *Interpretative Communication on Certain Aspects of the Provisions on Televised Advertising in the "Television without Frontiers" Directive.* C(2004)1450. Brussels, 23 April 2004.

———. "Commission Decision 2004/339/EC of 15 October 2003 on the Measures Implemented by Italy for RAI SpA." *Official Journal* L119/1, 23 April 2004.

———. *Commission Proposal for a Recommendation on the Protection of Minors and Human Dignity and the Right of Reply in Relation to the Competitiveness of the European Audiovisual and Information Services Industry.* COM(2004) 341. Brussels, 30 April 2004.

———. *White Paper on Services of General Interest.* COM(2004) 374. Brussels, 12 May 2004.

———. *Decision on Measures No. C 2/2003 (ex NN 22/02) Implemented by Denmark for TV2/DANMARK, C(2004)1814.* Brussels, 19 May 2004.

———. *Communication on Interoperability of Digital Interactive Television Services.* COM(2004) 541. Brussels, 30 July 2004.

———. "Commission Decision 2004/641/EC of 14 September 2004 Amending Decision 2002/627/EC Establishing the European Regulators Groups for Electronic Communications Networks and Services." *Official Journal* L293/30, 19 September 2004.

———. "Commission Decision 2004/838/EC of 10 December 2003 on State Aid Implemented by France for France 2 and France 3." *Official Journal* L361/21, 8 December 2004.

———. *Better Regulation for Growth and Jobs in the European Union.* COM(2005) 97. Brussels, 16 March 2005.

———. "Conclusions. High-level Group of Regulatory Authorities in the Field of Broadcasting—Incitement to Hatred in Broadcasts Coming from Outside of the European Union." 17 March 2005. <http://ec.europa.eu/comm/avpolicy/docs/library/legal/conclusions_regulateurs/conclusions_regulateurs_fin_en.pdf> (1 July 2006).

———. *The Commission's Contribution to the Period of Reflection and Beyond: Plan-D for Democracy, Dialogue and Debate.* COM(2005) 494. Brussels, 13 October 2005.

———. "Commission Decision 2005/406/EC of 15 October 2003 on ad hoc Measures Implemented by Portugal for RTP." *Official Journal* L142/1, 6 June 2005.

———. *Proposal for a Directive Amending Council Directive 89/552/EEC on the Coordination of Certain Provisions Laid Down by Law, Regulation or Administrative Action in Member States Concerning the Pursuit of Television Broadcasting Activities.* COM(2005) 646. Brussels, 13 December 2005.

———. *Issues Papers for the TVWF Review 2005.* <http://ec.europa.eu/comm/avpolicy/reg/tvwf/modernisation/consultation_2005/index_en.htm> (1 July 2006).

———. *Communication on Reviewing the Interoperability of Digital Interactive Television Services Pursuant to Communications COM(2004) 541 of 30 July 2004.* COM(2006) 37. Brussels, 2 February 2006.

———. *Eleventh Report on the Implementation of the Telecommunications Regulatory Package.* SEC(2006) 193. Brussels, 20 February 2006.

———. *Amended Proposal for a Directive of the European Parliament and of the Council on Services in the Internal Market.* COM(2006) 160. Brussels, 4 April 2006.

———. *Communication on the Review of the EU Regulatory Framework for Electronic Communications Networks and Services. Commission Staff Working Document.* COM(2006) 816. Brussels, 28 June 2006.

———. *Communication on the Review of the EU Regulatory Framework for Electronic Communications Networks and Services. Impact Assessment.* SEC(2006) 817. Brussels, 28 June 2006.

———. *Draft Commission Recommendation on Relevant Product and Service Markets within the Electronic Communications Sector Susceptible to ex ante Regulation in Accordance with Directive 2002/21/EC on a Common Regulatory Framework for Electronic Communication Networks and Services.* SEC(2006) 837. Brussels, 28 June 2006.

———. *Communication on the Review of the EU Regulatory Framework for Electronic Communications Networks and Services.* COM(2006) 334. Brussels, 29 June 2006.

———. *Staff Working Document on the Review of the EU Regulatory Framework for Electronic Communications Networks and Services.* SEC (2006) 816. Brussels, 29 June 2006.

———. *Proposal for a Regulation on Roaming on Public Mobile Networks within the Community and Amending Directive 2002/21/EC on a Common Regulatory Framework for Electronic Communication Networks and Services.* COM(2006) 382. Brussels, 12 July 2006.

——. *Media Pluralism in the Member States of the European Union*. SEC(2007) 32. Brussels, 16 January 2007.

——. *Draft Audiovisual Media Services Directive. Consolidated Text*. 9 March 2007. <http://ec.europa.eu/comm/avpolicy/docs/reg/modernisation/proposal_2005/av msd_cons_amend_0307_en.pdf> (10 March 2007).

European Commission—Competitiveness Advisory Group. <http://europa.eu.int/ comm/cdp/cag/mission_en.htm> (7 March 2005).

European Commission Memos. 3 March 2005–27 February 2007. <http://europa .eu.int/rapid/setLanguage.do?language=en> (30 July 2006).

European Commission Press Releases. 14 December 1989–26 February 2007. <http:// europa.eu.int/rapid/setLanguage.do?language=en> (13 July 2006).

European Communities. *Bulletin of the European Communities*. 1970—1985.

——. *Ninth General Report on the Activities of the European Communities in 1975*. Brussels: European Commission, 1976.

European Council of American Chambers of Commerce. *Comments on the European Community Action Programme on Telecommunications*. Brussels: EC-AmCham, 1985.

European Court of First Instance. "Judgment of 15 September 1998 in Case T-95/96 Gestevisión Telecinco SA v Commission." *European Court Reports* (1998): II-3407.

——. "Judgment of 11 July 1996 in Joined Cases T-528/93, T-542/93, T-543/93 and T-546/93 *Métropole télévision SA (M6) and Others v Commission*." *European Court Reports* (1996): II-649.

——. "Judgment of 8 October 2002 in Joined Cases T-185/00, T-216/00, T-299/00 and T-300/00 *M6 and Others* v. *Commission*." *European Court Reports* (2002): II-3805.

European Court of Justice. "Judgment of 30 April 1974 in Case 155/73. Giuseppe Sacchi. Tribunale civile e penale di Biella–Italy. " *European Court Reports* (1974): 409.

——. "Judgment of 18 March 1980 in Case 52/79. Procureur du Roi v Marc J.V.C. Debauve and others." *European Court Reports* (1980): 833.

——. "Judgment of 18 March 1980 in Case 62/79. SA Compagnie générale pour la diffusion de la télévision, Coditel, and Others v. Ciné Vog Films and others." *European Court Reports* (1980): 881.

——. "Judgment of 20 March 1985. Case 41/83. Italian Republic v. Commission of the European Communities."*European Court Reports* (1985): 873.

——. "Judgment of the Court of 19 March 1991. French Republic v. Commission of the European Communities. Competition in the Markets in Telecommunications Terminals Equipment. Case C-202/88." *European Court Reports* (1991): I–1223.

——. "Judgment of the Court of 17 November 1992. Kingdom of Spain, Kingdom of Belgium and Italian Republic v. Commission of the European Communities. Competition in the Markets for Telecommunications Services. Joined Cases C-271/90, C-281/90 and C-289/90." *European Court Reports* (1992): I–5833.

——. "Judgment of 24 July 2003 in Case C-280/00, Altmark Trans GmbH and Regierungspräsidium Magdeburg v Nahverkehrsgesellschaft Altmark GmbH." *European Court Reports* (2003): I-7747.

European Parliament. *Motion for a Resolution on Radio and Television Broadcasting in the European Community*. EP Doc. 1-409/80. Brussels, September 1980.

——. *Motion for a Resolution on the Threat to Diversity of Opinion Posed by Commercialisation of New Media*. EP Doc. 1-422/80. Brussels, September 1980.

——. *Report on the Information Policy of the European Community, of the Commission of the European Communities and of the European Parliament (Schall Report)*. PE DOC 1-596/80. Brussels, 16 January 1981.

——. *Report Drawn up on Behalf of the Committee on Economic and Monterrey Affairs on the Recommendations from the Commission of the European Communities to the Council on Telecommunications*. Rapporteur: F.H.J Herman, PE71859. Brussels, 27 April 1981.

——. *Report on Radio and Television Broadcasting in the European Community on Behalf of the Committee on Youth, Culture, Education, Information and Sport. (The Hahn Report)*. PE Doc 1-1013/81. Brussels, 23 February 1982.

——. *Report Drawn on Behalf of the Committee on Youth, Culture, Education, Information and Sport on Broadcast Communication in the European Community (the Threat to Diversity of Opinion Posed by the Commercialization of New Media) (Hutton Report)*. PE 78.983., Doc. 1-1523/83. Brussels, 15 March 198.

——. *Report Drawn on Behalf of the Committee on Youth, Culture, Education, Information and Sport on a Policy Commensurate with New Trends in European Television. (Arfé Report)*. EP 1-1541/83, PE 85.902. Brussels, 16 March 1984.

——. "Position of the European Parliament of 1 March 2001 on the Proposal for a European Parliament and Council Directive on a Common Regulatory Framework for Electronic Communications Networks and Services. A5-0053/2001." *Official Journal* C277/91, 1 October 2001.

——. *Report on the Commission White Paper on European Governance*. Committee on Constitutional Affairs. Rapporteur: Sylvia-Yvonne Kaufmann. A5-0399/2001. Brussels, 15 November 2001.

——. *Resolution on Television without Frontiers (2003/2033(INI))*. P5 TA(2003)0381. Brussels, 4 September 2003.

——. *Report on the Risks of Violation, in the EU and Especially in Italy, of Freedom of Expression and Information*. A5-0230/2004. Rapporteur: Johanna Boogerd-Quaak. Brussels, 5 April 2004.

——. *Resolution on the Risks of Violation, in the EU and Especially in Italy, of Freedom of Expression and Information* (Article 11(?) of the Charter of Fundamental Rights) (2003/2237(INI)). P5_TA(2004)0373. Brussels, 22 April 2004.

——. *Position of the European Parliament Adopted at First Reading on 16 February 2006 with a View to the Adoption of Directive 2006/.../EC of the European Parliament and Council on Services in the Internal Market*. PE 369.610. Brussels, 16 February 2006.

——. *Report on the Proposal for a Directive Amending Council Directive 89/552/EEC on the Coordination of Certain Provisions Laid Down by Law, Regulation or Administrative Action in Member States Concerning the Pursuit of Television Broadcasting Activities*. Rapporteur: Ruth Hieronymi. A6-0399/2006. Brussels, 22 November 2006.

——. *Legislative Resolution on the Proposal for a Directive Amending Council Directive 89/552/EEC on the Coordination of Certain Provisions Laid Down by Law, Regulation or Administrative Action in Member States Concerning the Pursuit of Television Broadcasting Activities*. P6_TA-PROV(2006)0559. Strasbourg, 13 December 2006.

European Parliament and Council. "Directive 95/47/EC of 24 October 1995 on the Use of Standards for the Transmission of Television Signals." *Official Journal* L281/51, 23 November 1995.

——. "Directive 95/62/EC of 13 December 1995 on the Application of Open Network Provision (ONP) to Voice Telephony." *Official Journal* L321/6, 30 December 1995.

——. "Decision 128/1999/EC of the on the Co-ordinated Introduction of a Third-generation Mobile and Wireless Communications System (UMTS) in the Community." *Official Journal* C17/1, 22 January 1999.

——. "Directive 2000/31/EC of 8 June 2000 on Certain Legal Aspects of Information Society Services, in Particular Electronic Commerce, in the Internal Market." *Official Journal* L178/1, 17 July 2000.

——. "Regulation 2887/2000/EC of 18 December 2000 on Unbundled Access to the Local Loop." *Official Journal* L336/4, 30 December 2000.

——. "Decision 676/2002/EC of 7 March 2002 on a Regulatory Framework for Radio Spectrum Policy in the European Community (Radio Spectrum Decision)." *Official Journal* L108/1, 24 April 2002.

——. "Directive 2002/21/EC of 7 March 2002 on a Common Regulatory Framework for Electronic Communications Networks and Services (Framework Directive)." *Official Journal* L108/33, 24 April 2002.

European Report. "Culture/ Audiovisual Council." 25 May 2002.

European Union [EU]. *Treaty of Rome Establishing the European Economic Community.* 1957. <http://www.eurotreaties.com/eurotexts.html#rometreaty> (10 April 2006).

——. "Treaty of the European Union." *Official Journal* C191, 29 July 1992.

——. *The Amsterdam Treaty.* June 1997. <http://www.eurotreaties.com/amsterdamtreaty.pdf> (20 July 2006).

——. 1998 Telecommunications Regulatory Package. <http://europa.eu.int/information_society/topics/telecoms/regulatory/98_regpack/index_en.htm> (2 June 2006).

——. "Resolution of the Council and of the Representatives of the Governments of the Member States Meeting within the Council of 25 January 1999, Concerning Public Service Broadcasting." *Official Journal* C30/1, 5 February 1999.

——. *Comments on the 1999 Communications Review.* <http://europa.eu.int/ISPO/infosoc/telecompolicy/review99/comments/comments.html> (1 July 2006).

——. *Presidency Conclusions. Lisbon European Council. 23 and 24 March 2000.* 2000. <http://www.consilium.europa.eu/ueDocs/cms_Data/docs/pressData/en/ec/001 00-r1.en0.htm> (28 June 2006).

——. *2002 Regulatory Framework for Electronic Communications.* <http://europa .eu.int/information_society/policy/ecomm/info_centre/documentation/index_ en.htm> (24 January 2007).

——. *Comments on Draft Commission Recommendation on Relevant Markets.* 2002. <http://europa.eu.int/information_society/topics/telecoms/regulatory/publicconsult/ documents/comments_on_draft_rec_relevant_prod_service_mkts.htm> (25 June 2006).

——. *Comments on Green Paper on Services of General Interest.* 2003. <http://ec .europa.eu/services_general_interest/comments/public_en.htm> (10 July 2006).

——. *Comments on TVWF Review 2003.* <http://ec.europa.eu/comm/avpolicy/reg/ tvwf/modernisation/consultation_2003/contributions/index_en.htm> (1 July 2006).

———. *Responses to the 2004 Digital Interoperability Consultation.* <http://europa.eu
.int/information_society/policy/ecomm/info_centre/documentation/public_
consult/interoperability_idtv/index_en.htm> (1 July 2006).

———. *Comments on TVWF Review 2005.* <http://ec.europa.eu/comm/avpolicy/reg/
tvwf/modernisation/consultation_2005/contributions/index_en.htm> (1 July
2006).

———. *Consultation on 3G Extension Band.* 2005. <http://forum.europa.eu.int/
Public/irc/infso/radiospectrum/home> (21 November 2005).

———. *Second Phase Consultation on International Roaming.* March 2006. <http://
ec.europa.eu/information_society/activities/roaming/roaming_regulation/
consultation/index_en.htm> (15 March 2007).

———. *Responses to the Consultation on the Review of the 2002 Regulatory Framework for
Electronic Communications.* October 2006. <http://ec.europa.eu/information_
society/policy/ecomm/info_centre/documentation/public_consult/review_2/
index_en.htm> (15 March 2007).

European Voice. 23 November 1995–7 June 2006.

Eurostrategies and Cullen. *The Possible Value Added of a European Regulatory Authority
for Telecommunications.* Report for the European Commission, 1999.

Featherstone, Kevin, and Claudio M. Radaelli, eds. *The Politics of Europeanization.* Oxford and New York: Oxford University Press, 2003.

Ferguson, Charles. *The United States Broadband Problem: Analysis and Recommendations.* Washington, D.C.: Brookings Institution, 2002.

Fernandes, Bosco Eduardo. "The UMTS Task Force." Pp. 147–55 in *GSM and UMTS.
The Creation of Global Mobile Communication,* edited by Friedhelm Hillebrand. Chichester: John Wiley, 2002.

Financial Times. 11 December 1989–29 June 2006.

Flamm, Kenneth. *Targeting the Computer: Government Support and International Competition.* Washington. D.C.: The Brookings Institution, 1988.

Fransman, Martin. *Japan's Computer and Communications Industry.* Oxford: Oxford University Press, 1995.

Fraser, Matthew William. "Television." Pp. 204–25 in *The European Union and National Industrial Policy,* edited by Hussein Kassim and Anand Menon. London and New York: Routledge, 1996.

Freedland, Mark. "The Marketization of Public Services." Pp. 90–110 in *Citizenship, Markets, and the State,* edited by Colin Crouch, Klaus Eder and Damian Tambini. Oxford and New York: Oxford University Press, 2001.

Freeman, Christopher, and Anthony Young. *The Research and Development Effort in Western Europe, North America and the Soviet Union. An Experimental International Comparison of Research Expenditures and Manpower in 1962.* Paris: OECD, 1965.

Fuchs, Gerhard. "Integrated Services Digital Network: The Politics of European Telecommunications Network Development." *Journal of European Integration* XVI, no. 1 (1992): 63–88.

FRUS [Foreign Relations of the United States] XXXIV, "1964–1968, Energy, Diplomacy and Global Issues." Washington D.C.: Government Printing Office, 1999.

Galperin, Hernan. *New Television, Old Politics: The Transition to Digital TV in the United States and Britain.* Cambridge University Press, 2004.

Gamble, Andrew. "The New Political Economy." *Political Studies* 43 (1995): 516–30.

———. "Economic Governance." Pp. 110–37 in *Debating Governance. Authority, Steering, and Democracy*, edited by Jon Pierre. Oxford and New York: Oxford University Press, 2000.

Gannon, Paul. *Trojan Horses & National Champions: The Crisis in the European Computing and Telecommunications Industry*. London: Apt-Amatic Books, 1997.

GAP [Analysis and Forecasting Group—European Commission]. *Proposals for the Coordinated Introduction of Integrated Services Digital Networks in the Community*. Mimeo. Brussels: European Commission, 5 June 1985.

———. *Proposals for the Coordinated Introduction of Broadband Services in the Community*. Mimeo. Brussels: European Commission, 16 October 1986.

Garnham, Nicholas. "The Media and the Public Sphere." Pp. 45–53 in *Communicating Politics*, edited by Peter Golding, Graham Murdock and Philip Schlesinger. Leicester: Leicester University Press, 1986.

———. "The Broadcasting Market." *The Political Quarterly* 65, no. 1 (1994): 11–19.

———. "Comments on John Keane's 'Structural Transformations of the Public Sphere.'" *The Communication Review* 1, no. 1 (1995): 23–25.

———. "The Information Society Debate Revisited." Pp. 287–302 in *Mass Media and Society*, edited by James Curran and Michael Gurevitch. 4th ed. London: Hodder Arnold, 2005.

Gellner, Ernest. *Nations and Nationalism*. Oxford: Blackwell, 1983.

Giddens, Anthony. *Central Problems of Social Theory: Action, Structure, and Contradiction in Social Analysis*. Basingstoke: Macmillan, 1979.

Gill, Stephen. "Constitutionalising Capital: EMU and Disciplinary Neo-Liberalism." Pp. 47–69 in *Social Forces in the Making of the New Europe: The Restructuring of European Social Relations in the Global Political Economy*, edited by Andreas Bieler and Adam David Morton. London: Palgrave, 2000.

Godin, Benoît. *The Obsession for Competitiveness and Its Impact on Statistics: The Construction of High-Technology Indicators*. Project on the History and Sociology of S&T Statistics, Working Paper no. 25 (2004). <www.csiic.ca/PDF/Godin_25.pdf > (24 April 2006).

Gordon, Robert. "Does the 'New Economy' Measure up to the Great Inventions of the Past?" *Journal of Economic Perspectives* 14, no. 4 (2000): 49–74.

Grande, Edgar. "The New Role of the State in Telecommunications: An International Comparison." *West European Politics* 17, no. 3 (1994): 138–57.

Grant, Charles. *Delors: Inside the House That Jacques Built*. London: Nicholas Brealey Publishing, 1994.

Grantham, Bill. *Some Big Bourgeois Brothel: Context for France's Culture Wars with Hollywood*. Luton: University of Luton Press, 2000.

Griffiths, Richard T. "'An Act of Creative Leadership': The End of the OEEC and the Birth of the OECD." Pp. 235–56 in *Explorations in OEEC History*, edited by Richard T. Griffiths. Paris: OECD, 1997.

Groebel, Annegret. "*European Regulator Group (ERG)*." 2002. <www.regtp.de/en/international/start/in_11-02-00-00-00_m/> (12 April 2005).

Guardian. 13 January 2003. [Dominic Timms, "Learning to Fight Back," *Guardian*, 13 January 2003, 50].

Guth, Joanne. "Update on the U.S.-EU Third-Generation Mobile Phone Technology Debate: Who's Calling the Shots on Standards?" *International Economic Review* (May/June 1999): 23–25.

Guttman, Monika. "GATT: The Sequel." *U.S. News and World Report*, 27 December 1993/3 January 1994, 14.

Guzzetti, Luca. *A Brief History of European Union Research Policy.* Luxembourg: Office for Official Publications of the European Communities, 1995.

Haas, Ernst B. *The Uniting of Europe: Political, Social and Economic Forces, 1950–1957.* 2nd ed. Stanford, Calif.: Stanford University Press, 1968 [1958].

Haas, Peter. "Introduction: Epistemic Communities and International Policy Co-ordination." *International Organization* 46, no. 1 (1992): 1–35.

Habermas, Jürgen. "Citizenship and National Identity: Some Reflections on the Future of Europe." *Praxis International* 12, no. 1 (1992): 1–19.

———. "Why Europe Needs a Constitution." *New Left Review* 11 (September/October 2001): 5–26.

Hall, Peter A., and David Soskice. *Varieties of Capitalism: The Institutional Foundations of Comparative Advantage.* Oxford: Oxford University Press, 2001.

Hanson, Brian T. "What Happened to Fortress Europe? External Trade Policy Liberalisation in the European Union." *International Organization* 52, no. 1 (1998): 55–85.

Harcourt, Alison. "EU Media Ownership Regulation: Conflict over the Definition of Alternatives." *Journal of Common Market Studies* 36, no. 3 (1998): 369–89.

———. *The European Union and the Regulation of Media Markets.* Manchester: Manchester University Press, 2005.

Harcourt, Alison, and Claudio Radaelli. "Limits to EU Technocratic Regulation?" *European Journal of Political Research* 35 (1999): 107–22.

Hay, Colin. *Political Analysis: A Critical Introduction.* Basingstoke: Palgrave, 2002.

Hay, Colin, and Ben Rosamond. "Globalization, European Integration and the Discursive Construction of Economic Imperatives." *Journal of European Public Policy* 9, no. 2 (2002): 147–67.

Hay, Colin, and Matthew Watson. "Diminishing Expectations: The Strategic Discourse of Globalization in the Political Economy of New Labour." Pp. 147–72 in *A Ruined Fortress? Neoliberal Hegemony and Transformation in Europe,* edited by Alan Cafruny and Magnus Ryner. Lanham, Md.: Rowman & Littlefield, 2003.

Hayes-Renshaw, Fiona, and Helen Wallace. *The Council of Ministers.* 2nd ed. London: Palgrave Macmillan, 2005.

Held, David. "Democracy, the Nation-State and the Global System." Pp. 197–235 in *Political Theory Today,* edited by David Held. Cambridge: Polity Press, 1991.

Hennis, Marjoleine. "Europeanization and Globalization: The Missing Link." *Journal of Common Market Studies* 39, no. 5 (2001): 829–50.

Henten, Anders, Henning Olesen, Dan Saugstrup and Su-En Tan. "Mobile Communications: Europe, Japan and South Korea in a Comparative Perspective." *Info: The Journal of Policy, Regulation and Strategy for Telecommunications, Information and Media* 6, no. 3 (2004): 197–207.

Héritier, Andrienne. "The Accommodation of Diversity in European Policy-making and Its Outcomes: Regulatory Policy as a Patchwork." *Journal of European Public Policy* 3, no. 2 (1996): 149–67.

——. "Policy-making by Subterfuge: Interest Accommodation, Innovation and Substitute Democratic Legitimation in Europe—Perspectives from Distinct Policy Areas." *Journal of European Public Policy* 4, no. 2 (1997): 171–89.

——. "New Modes of Governance in Europe: Policy-Making without Legislating?" *Max Planck Project Group: Common Goods: Law, Politics and Economics*, 2001/14. <http://papers.ssrn.com/abstract=299431> (2 July 2006).

——. "Market Integration and Social Cohesion: The Politics of Public Services in European Regulation." *Journal of European Public Policy* 8, no. 5 (2001): 825–52.

——. "New Modes of Governance in Europe: Increasing Political Capacity and Policy Effectiveness?" Pp. 105–26 in *The State of the European Union, 6. Law, Politics, and Society*, edited by Tanja Börzel and Rachel Cichowski. Oxford: Oxford University Press, 2003.

Hewson, Martin, and Sinclair, Timothy J., eds. *Approaches to Global Governance Theory*. New York: State University of New York Press, 1999.

Hillebrand, Friedhelm. "The Creation of the UMTS Foundations in ETSI from April 1996 to February 1999." Pp. 184–220 in *GSM and UMTS. The Creation of Global Mobile Communication*, edited by Friedhelm Hillebrand. Chichester: John Wiley, 2002.

Hills, Jill. *Information Technology and Industrial Policy*. London: Croom Helm, 1984.

——. *Deregulating Telecoms—Competition and Control in the United States, Japan and Britain*. London: Frances Pinter, 1986.

——. "A Global Industrial Policy. US Hegemony and GATT. The Liberalization of Telecommunications." *Review of International Political Economy* 1, no. 2 (1994): 257–79.

——. *The Struggle for Control of Global Communication. The Formative Century*. Urbana and Chicago: University of Illinois Press, 2002.

Hills, Jill, and Maria Michalis. "Restructuring Regulation: Technological Convergence and European Telecommunications and Broadcasting Markets." *Review of International Political Economy* 7, no. 3 (2000): 434–64.

Hills, Jill, with Stylianos Papathanassopoulos. *The Democracy Gap: The Politics of Information and Communication Technologies in the United States and Europe*. Westport, Conn.: Greenwood Press, 1991.

Hix, Simon. "The Study of the European Union II: The 'New Governance' Agenda and Its Rival." *Journal of European Public Policy* 5, no. 1 (1998): 38–65.

——. *The Political System of the European Union*. London: Macmillan, 1999.

Hjarvard, Stig. "Pan-European Television News: Towards a European Political Public Sphere?" Pp. 71–94 in *National Identity and Europe. The Television Revolution*, edited by Phillip Drummond, Richard Patterson and Janet Willis. London: British Film Institute, 1993.

Hobsbawm, Eric, and Terence Ranger, eds. *The Invention of Tradition*. Cambridge: Cambridge University Press, 1983.

Hodges, Michael. "Industrial Policy: Hard Times or Great Expectations?" Pp. 265–93 in *Policy-Making in the European Community*, edited by Helen Wallace, William Wallace and Carole Webb. Chichester: John Wiley, 1983.

Holman, Otto, and Kees van der Pilj. "Structure and Process in Transnational European Business." Pp. 71–93 in *A Ruined Fortress?: Neoliberal Hegemony and Trans-*

formation in Europe, edited by Alan Cafruny and Magnus Ryner. Lanham, Md.: Rowman & Littlefield, 2003.

Hooghe, Liesbet, and Gary Marks. "The Making of a Polity: The Struggle over European Integration." *European Integration online Papers, European Integration online Paper* 1, no. 4 (1997). <http://eiop.or.at/eiop/texte/1997-004.htm> (20 December 2005).

———. *Multi-Level Governance and European Integration.* Lanham, Md.: Rowman & Littlefield, 2001.

House of Lords—European Union Committee. *Television without Frontiers? Report with Evidence.* London: Stationery Office, 2007.

Huber, Josef, Dirk Weiler and Hermann Brand. "UMTS, the Mobile Multimedia Vision for IMT-2000: A Focus on Standardization." *IEEE Communications Magazine* (September 2000): 129–36.

Hulsink, Willem. *Privatisation and Liberalisation in European Telecommunications. Comparing Britain, the Netherlands and France.* London and New York: Routledge, 1999.

Humphreys, Peter. *Mass Media and Media Policy in Western Europe.* Manchester and New York: Manchester University Press, 1996.

Humphreys, Peter, and Seamus Simpson. *Globalisation, Convergence and European Telecommunications Regulation.* Cheltenham and Northampton, Mass.: Edward Elgar, 2005.

Huurdeman, Anton. *The Worldwide History of Telecommunications.* N.J.: John Wiley, 2003.

ITU [International Telecommunication Union]. *Regulatory Implications of Telecommunications Convergence, Chairman's Report of the Sixth Regulatory Colloquium.* Geneva: ITU, 1997.

———. "West African Regulators Agree on Common Regulatory Framework Region Takes a Big Step Towards a Common ICT Market." *ITU Press Release* (7 October 2005). <http://www.itu.int> (10 October 2005).

Jachtenfuchs, Markus. "The Governance Approach to European Integration." *Journal of Common Market Studies* 39, no. 2 (2001): 245–64.

Jacquemin, Alexis, and Lucio Pench. "What Competitiveness for Europe? An Introduction." Pp. 1–42 in *Europe Competing in the Global Economy,* edited by Alexis Jacquemin and Lucio Pench. Cheltenham: Edward Elgar, 1997.

———, eds. *Europe Competing in the Global Economy.* Cheltenham: Edward Elgar, 1997.

Jessop, Bob. *The Future of the Capitalist State.* Cambridge: Polity, 2002.

———. "The Future of the State in an Era of Globalization." *International Politics and Society,* no. 3 (2003): 30–46. <http://www.fes.de/ipg/ONLINE3_2003/ARTJESSOP.PDF> (18 July 2006).

———. "The European Union and Recent Transformations in Statehood." 2004. <http://eprints.lancs.ac.uk/217/02/F-2004g_vienna-state-best.doc> (3 Aug. 2006).

Jones, Erik, and Amy Verdun, guest eds. "Political Economy and the Study of European Integration." *Journal of European Public Policy* 10, no. 1 (2003).

Jospin, Lionel. "L' avenir de L' Europe élargie." Speech to the Foreign Press Association, Paris, 28 May 2001. <http://www.monde-diplomatique.fr/cahier/europe/jospin> (12 July 2005).

Journal of European Public Policy. "Special Issue on Social Constructivism." 6, no. 4 (1999).

Jupille, J., and J. A. Caporaso. "Institutionalism and the European Union: Beyond International Relations and Comparative Politics." *Annual Review of Political Science* 2, no. 1 (1999): 429–44.

Kangaroo Group [European Parliament]. <http://www.kangaroogroup.org/E/032_origin_D.lasso > (21 Oct. 2005).

Kano, Sadahiko. "Technical Innovations, Standardization and Regional Comparison —A Case Study in Mobile Communications." *Telecommunications Policy* 24, (2000): 305–21.

Keane, John. "Structural Transformations of the Public Sphere." *The Communication Review* 1, no. 1 (1995): 1–22.

King, Alexander. *Science and Policy: The International Stimulus.* London: Oxford University Press, 1974.

———. "Overload: Problems of Governing in the 1970s." *Political Studies* 23, nos. 2/3 (1975): 284–96.

Kingdon, John. *Agendas, Alternatives, and Public Policies.* Boston: Little, Brown, 1984.

Knieps, Günther. "Deregulation in Europe: Telecommunications and Transportation." Pp. 72–100 in *Deregulation or Reregulation?: Regulatory Reform in Europe and in the United States,* edited by Giandomenico Majone. Pinter: London, 1990.

Knill, Christoph, and Dirk Lehmkuhl. "The National Impact of European Union Regulatory Policy: Three Europeanization Mechanisms." *European Journal of Political Research* 41, no. 2 (2002): 255–80.

Kohler-Koch, Beate, and Berthold Rittberger. "Review Article: The 'Governance Turn' in European Studies." *Journal of Common Market Studies—Annual Review* 44 (2006): 27–49.

Koski, Heli, and Tobias Kretschmer. "Entry, Standards and Competition: Firm Strategies and the Diffusion of Mobile Telephony." *Review of Industrial Organization* 26, no. 1 (2005): 89–113.

Krebber, Daniel. *Europeanisation of Regulatory Television Policy: The Decision-making Process of the Television without Frontiers Directives from 1989 & 1997.* Baden-Baden: Nomos Verlagsgesellschaft, 2002.

Krige, John, and Arturo Russo. *A History of the European Space Agency 1958–1987. Volume I: The Story of ESRO and ELDO, 1958–1973.* Noordwijk: ESA Publications Division, 2000a.

———. *A History of the European Space Agency 1958–1987. Volume II: The Story of ESA, 1973–1987.* Noordwijk: ESA Publications Division, 2000b.

Krugman, Paul. *Rethinking International Trade.* Cambridge, Mass., and London: MIT Press, 1990.

———. "Competitiveness: A Dangerous Obsession." *Foreign Affairs* 73, no. 2 (1994): 28–44.

———. *Peddling Prosperity: Economic Sense and Nonsense in the Age of Diminished Expectations.* London and New York: Norton, 1994.

Labarrère, Claude. *L' Europe des Postes et des Télécommunications.* Paris: Masson, 1985.

Laffan, Brigid. "The Politics of Identity and Political Order in Europe." *Journal of Common Market Studies* 34, no. 1 (1996): 81–102.

Laffan, Brigid, and Colin Shaw. "Classifying and Mapping OMC in Different Policy Areas." 2005. <http://www.eu-newgov.org/database/DELIV/D02D09_Classifying_and_Mapping_OMC.pdf> (7 February 2007).

Langlois, Richard N., and W. Edward Steinmueller. "The Evolution of Competitive Advantage in the Worldwide Semiconductor Industry, 1947–1996." Pp. 19–78 in *Sources of Industrial Leadership*, edited by David C. Mowery and Richard R. Nelson. Cambridge and New York: Cambridge University Press, 1999.

Lasswell, Harold D. *Politics: Who Gets What, When and How.* New York: Peter Smith, 1950 [1936].

Latzer, Michael, Natascha Just, Florian Saurwein and Peter Slominski. "Institutional Variety in Communications Regulation. Classification and Empirical Evidence from Austria." *Telecommunications Policy* 30 (2006): 152–70.

Lawton, Thomas. "Introduction: Concepts Defined and Scenes Set." Pp. 1–22 in *European Industrial Policy and Competitiveness*, edited by Thomas Lawton. London: Macmillan, 1999.

Layton, Christopher. *European Advanced Technology: A Programme for Integration.* London: Allen & Unwin, 1969.

Lembke, Johan. *Competition for Technological Leadership. EU Policy for High Technology.* Cheltenham and Northampton, Mass.: Edward Elgar, 2002.

Lenschow, Andrea. "Transformation of European Environmental Governance." Pp. 39–60 in *The Transformation of Governance in the European Union*, edited by Beate Kohler-Koch and Rainer Eising. London and New York: Routledge, 1999.

Levy, David. *Europe's Digital Revolution. Broadcasting Regulation, the EU and the Nation State.* London and New York: Routledge, 1999.

Liikanen, Erkki. "The Future of the eEurope Action Plan." Speech/02/81, delivered at the Informal Telecommunications Council, Vitoria, 22 February 2002.

Lindblom, Charles E. *The Market System: What It Is, How It Works, and What to Make of It.* New Haven and London: Yale University Press, 2001.

Lowi, Theodore J. "American Business, Public Policy, Case Studies and Political Theory." *World Politics* 16, no. 4 (1964): 677–715.

Lucas, Robert E. Jr. "On the Mechanics of Economic Development." *Journal of Monetary Economics* 22, no. 1 (1998): 3–42.

Machlup Fritz. *The Production and Distribution of Knowledge in the United States.* Princeton, N.J.: Princeton University Press 1962.

Mackintosh, Ian. *Sunrise Europe: The Dynamics of Information Technology.* Oxford: Blackwell, 1986.

Maggiore, Matteo. *Audiovisual Production in the Single Market.* Luxembourg: Office for Official Publications of the European Communities, 1990.

Majone, Giandomenico. "The Rise of the Regulatory State in Europe." *West European Politics* 17, no. 3 (1994): 77–101.

———. "The European Commission as Regulator." Pp. 60–79 in *Regulating Europe*, edited by Giandomenico Majone. London: Routledge, 1996.

———. "The New European Agencies: Regulation by Information." *Journal of European Public Policy* 4, no. 2 (1997): 262–75.

———. "The European Commission: The Limits of Centralization and the Perils of Parliamentarization." *Governance: An International Journal of Policy, Administration and Institutions* 15, no. 3 (2002): 375–92.

Maier, Charles. "The Politics of Productivity: Foundations of American International Economic Policy after Word War II." Pp. 23–49 in *Between Power and Plenty: Foreign Economic Policies of Adavnced Industrial States*, edited by Peter Katzenstein. Madison: University of Wisconsin Press, 1978.

Malik, Rex. "France's Social Agenda for Le Computer." *Computerworld*, 9 May 1983, ID/1.

Mansell, Robin, Peter Holmes and Kevin Morgan. "European Integration and Telecommunications: Restructuring Markets and Institutions." *Prometheus* 8, no 1 (1990): 50–66.

Markoski, Joseph. "Telecommunications Regulations as Barriers to the Transborder Flow of Information." *Cornell International Law Journal* 14 (1981): 287–331.

Marks, Gary. "Structural Policy and Multilevel Governance in the EC." Pp. 391–410 in *The State of the European Community. Vol. II: The Maastricht Debates and Beyond*, edited by Alan Cafruny and Glenda Rosenthal. Boulder, Colo.: Lynne Rienner; Harlow: Longman, 1993.

Mattelart, Armand, and Michael Palmer. "Advertising in Europe: Promises, Pressures and Pitfalls." *Media, Culture and Society* 13, no. 4 (1991): 535–56.

Mattli, Walter, and Anne-Marie Slaughter. "Revisiting the European Court of Justice." *International Organization* 52, no. 1, (1998): 177–209.

McGowan, Lee, and Helen Wallace. "Towards a European Regulatory State." *Journal of European Public Policy* 3, no. 4 (1996): 560–76.

McGowan, Lee, and Stephen Wilks. "The First Supranational Policy in the European Union: Competition Policy." *The European Journal of Political Research* 28 (1995): 141–69.

McGrew, Anthony. "Democracy beyond Borders?" Pp. 405–19 in *The Global Transformations Reader*, edited by David Held and Anthony McGrew. Cambridge: Polity, 2000.

McGuire, Steven. "Trade Tools: Holding the Fort or Declaring Open House?" Pp. 72–92 in *European Industrial Policy and Competitiveness. Concepts and Instruments*, edited by Thomas Lawton. London: Macmillan. 1999.

McKendrick, George. "The INTUG View on the EEC Green Paper." *Telecommunications Policy* 11, no. 4 (1987): 325–29.

Meunier, Sophie. "Trade Policy and Political Legitimacy in the European Union." *Comparative European Politics* 1, no. 1 (2003): 67–90.

Michalis, Maria. "EU Broadcasting and Telecoms: Towards a Convergent Regulatory Regime?" *European Journal of Communication* 14, no. 2 (1999): 147–71.

———. "Local Competition and the Role of Regulation: The EU Debate and Britain's Experience." *Telecommunications Policy* 15, nos. 10/11 (2001): 759–76.

———. "The Debate over Universal Service in the European Union. Plus ça Change, Plus c'est la Même Chose." *Convergence: The Journal of Research into New Media Technologies* 8, no. 2 (2002): 80–98.

———. "Broadband Communications in the European Union: Myths and Realities." Pp. 1–25 in *European Economic and Political Issues*, edited by Frank Columbus. New York: Nova, 2002.

———. "Institutional Arrangements of Regional Regulatory Regimes: Telecommunications Regulation in the Europe and the Limits to Policy Convergence."

Pp. 285–300 in *Global Economy and Digital Society*, edited by Erik Bohlin, Stanford Levin, Nakil Sung and Chang-Ho Yoon. Amsterdam: Elsevier, 2004.

Middlemas, Keith. *Orchestrating Europe. The Informal Politics of European Union 1973–1995*. London: Fontana Press, 1995.

Milward, Alan S. *The Reconstruction of Western Europe 1945–51*. London: Metheun, 1984.

———. *The European Rescue of the Nation-State*. London and New York: Routledge, 1992

———. *The European Rescue of the Nation-State*. 2nd ed. London and New York: Routledge, 2000.

Mitrany, David. *A Working Peace System*. London: Royal Institute of International Affairs, 1943.

———. "The Functional Approach to World Organisation." Pp. 65–75 in *The New International Actors: The UN and the EEC*, edited by C. A. Cosgrove and K. J. Twitchett. London: Macmillan, 1970.

Moran, Michael. "Understanding the Regulatory State." *British Journal of Political Science* 32, no. 2 (2002): 391–413.

———. *The British Regulatory State: High Modernism and Hyper-innovation*. Oxford: Oxford University Press, 2003.

Morley, David. "Media Fortress Europe: Geographies of Exclusion and the Purification of Cultural Space." *Canadian Journal of Communication* 23, no. 3 (1998). <http://www.cjc-online.ca/viewarticle.php?id=471&layout=html> (19 May 2006).

Moonman, Eric, ed. *Science and Technology in Europe*. Harmondsworth, Middl.: Penguin, 1968.

Mouly, Michel. "System Architecture." Pp. 301–308 in *GSM and UMTS. The Creation of Global Mobile Communication*, edited by Friedhelm Hillebrand. Chichester: John Wiley, 2002.

Möwes, Bernd. *Fifty Years of Media Policy in the Council of Europe—A Review*. MCM(2000)003. 2000. Strasbourg: Council of Europe. <http://www.coe.int/T/E/human_rights/media/4_Documentary_Resources/MCM%282000%29003_en.asp#TopOfPage> (23 March 2006).

Muller, Jurgen. *The Benefits of Completing the Internal market for Telecommunications Services/ Equipment in the Community. Research on the "Cost of Non-Europe", Basic Findings, vol. 10*. Luxembourg: Office for Official Publications of the European Communities, 1988.

Mueller, Milton. "Intelsat and the Separate System Policy: Toward Competitive International Telecommunications." *Cato Policy Analysis*, no. 150 (1991). <http://www.cato.org/pubs/pas/pa-150.html> (1 November 2004).

Murdock, Graham. "Rights and Representations: Public Discourse and Cultural Citizenship." Pp. 7–17 in *Television and Common Knowledge*, edited by Jostein Gripsrud. London: Routledge, 1999.

Mytelka, Lynn Krieger. "States, Strategic Alliances and International Oligopolies: The European ESPRIT Programme." Pp. 182–210 in *Strategic Partnerships and the World Economy: States, Firms and International Competition*, edited by Lynn Krieger Mytelka. London: Pinter, 1991.

Natalicchi, Giorgio. *Wiring Europe. Reshaping the European Telecommunications Regime*. Lanham, Md., and Oxford: Rowman & Littlefield, 2001.

Newsbytes News Network. "Nokia & Ericsson Backing Wideband CDMA." 9 June 1997. <http://www.newsbytes.com> (5 March 2005).

New York Times. 8 Dec. 1993—14 April 1999.

Nicolaidis, Calypso. "Mutual Recognition of Regulatory Regimes: Some Lessons and Prospects." *Jean Monnet Paper Series.* New York University School of Law Jean Monnet Center, 1997. <http://www.jeanmonnetprogram.org/papers/97/97-07.html> (18 July 2006).

Noam, Eli. *Television in Europe.* New York: Oxford University Press, 1991.

———. *Telecommunications in Europe.* New York: Oxford University Press, 1992.

Nora, Simon, and Alain Minc. *The Computerization of Society: A Report to the President of France.* Cambridge, Mass., and London: MIT Press, 1980 [1978].

OECD [Organization for Economic Cooperation and Development]. *The Residual Factor and Economic Growth.* Paris: OECD, 1964.

———. *Gaps in Technology: General Report.* Committee for Science Policy. Paris: OECD, 1968.

———. *Trends of Change in Telecommunications Policy.* Paris: OECD, 1987.

———. *New Directions for Industrial Policy. Policy Brief No. 3.* Paris: OECD, 1998.

———. *Policy and Regulatory Issues for Network-Based Content Services.* DSTI/ICCP/IE(96) 9/REV1. Paris: OECD, 1997.

———. *OECD Economic Outlook No 67.* Paris: OECD, 2000.

———. *The New Economy: Beyond the Hype.* Paris: OECD, 2001.

———. *Telecommunication Regulatory Institutional Structures and Responsibilities.* DSTI/ICCP/TISP(2005)6/FINAL. Paris: OECD, 2006. <www.oecd.org/dataoecd/56/11/35954786.pdf> (25 January 2006).

Ofcom [Office of Communications, UK]. *Online Protection. A Survey of Consumer, Industry and Regulatory Mechanisms and Systems.* London: Ofcom, 2006.

Oftel [Office of Telecommunications, UK]. *The Benefits of Self- and Co-regulation to Consumers and Industry. Statement Issued by the Director General of Telecommunications.* London: Oftel, 2001.

OHG [Operators Harmonization Group]. "Open Letter to Standard Organizations from Operators Harmonization Group On Global 3G (G3G) CDMA Standard." June 1999. <http://www.3gpp.org/ftp/tsg_ran/TSG_RAN/TSGR_04/Docs/Pdfs/rp-99358.pdf> (31 March 2005).

Ohmae, Kenichi. *The End of the Nation-State.* London: HarperCollins, 1995.

Pagden, Anthony. "Europe: Conceptualizing a Continent." Pp. 33–54 in *The Idea of Europe: From Antiquity to the European Union,* edited by Anthony Pagden. Cambridge: Woodrow Wilson Center Press and Cambridge University Press, 2002.

Palmer, Michael. "GATT and Culture: A View from France." Pp. 27–38 in *Trading Culture: GATT, European Cultural Policies and the Transatlantic Market,* edited by Annemoon van Hemel, Hans Mommaas and Cas Smithuijsen. Amsterdam: Boekman Foundation, 1996.

Paulu, Burton. *Radio and Television Broadcasting on the European Continent.* Minneapolis: University of Minnesota Press, 1967.

Pauwels, Caroline, and Jean-Claude Burgelman. "Policy Challenges to the Creation of European Information Society: A Critical Analysis." Pp. 59–85 in *The European Information Society: A Reality Check,* edited by Jan Servaes. Bristol: Intellect, 2003.

Pearce, Joan, and John Sutton. *Protection and Industrial Policy in Europe*. London: Routeldge & Kegan Paul, 1985.

Peterson, John. "The European Technology Community: Policy Networks in a Supranational Setting." Pp. 226–48 in *Policy Networks in British Government*, edited by David Marsh and R.A.W. Rhodes. Oxford: Oxford University Press, 1992.

———. *High Technology and the Competition State: An Analysis of the Eureka Initiative*. London: Routledge, 1993.

———. "The Choice for EU Theorists: Establishing a Common Framework for Analysis." *European Journal of Political Research* 39 (2001): 289–318.

Peterson, John, and Margaret Sharp. *Technology Policy in the European Union*. London: Macmillan, 1998.

Pierre, Jon. "The Marketization of the State: Citizens, Consumers, and the Emergence of the Public Market." Pp. 55–81 in *Governance in a Changing Environment*, edited by Guy B. Peters and Donald J. Savoie. Montreal and Kingston: McGill—Queen's University Press, 1995.

———, ed. *Debating Governance. Authority, Steering, and Democracy*. Oxford and New York: Oxford University Press 2000.

Pierson, Paul. "The Path to European Integration: A Historical Institutionalist Analysis." *Comparative Political Studies* 29, no. 2 (1996): 123–63.

Pollack, Mark. "Theorizing EU Policy-Making." Pp. 13–48 in *Policy-Making in the European Union*, edited by. Helen Wallace, William Wallace and Mark Pollack. 5th ed. Oxford and New York: Oxford University Press, 2005.

Porat, Marc Uri. *The Information Economy: Definition and Measurement*. Washington, D.C.: Government Printing Office, 1977.

Porter, Michael. *The Competitive Advantage of Nations*. London: Macmillan, 1990.

PR Newswire. "Wireless Operators Announce Agreement on Globally Harmonized Third-Generation (G3G) Code Division Multiple Access Standard." 8 June 1999. <http://www.prnewswire.co.uk/cgi/news/release?id=51166> (30 March 2005).

Preston, Paschal. *Reshaping Communications. Technology, Information and Social Change*. London: Sage, 2001.

Public Network Europe, "Turing Copper into Gold." November 1998, 42–45.

Puttnam, David. *The Undeclared War: The Struggle for Control of the World's Film Industry*. London: HarperCollins, 1997.

Quatrepoint, Jean-Michel, Jacques Jublin and Danielle Arnaud. *French Ordinateurs: de l' Affaire Bull à l' Assassinat du Plan Calcul*. Paris: Alain Moreau, 1976.

Quinn, James Brian. "Technological Competition: Europe vs. USA." *Harvard Business Review* (July–August 1966): 113–30.

Radaelli, Claudio M. "The Europeanization of Public Policy." Pp. 27–56 in *The Politics of Europeanization*, edited by Kevin Featherstone and Claudio M. Radaelli. Oxford and New York: Oxford University Press, 2003.

Radio Spectrum Committee. *RSC Report on the Invitation for Comments to the Use of the Band 2500-2670 MHz. RSCOM05-44rev1*. Brussels: European Commission, 28 October 2005.

RAND Europe. *Assessing Indirect Impacts of the EC Proposals for Video Regulation. Prepared for Ofcom*. Cambridge: RAND Europe, 2006.

Reding, Viviane. "The Challenges Facing a Future. European Regulatory System for Media and Communications." Speech/02/490, delivered at Medientage, Munich, 17 October 2002.

———. "Towards a True Internal Market for Europe's Telecom Industry and Consumers—The Regulatory Challenges Ahead." Speech/07/86, delivered at the 20th Plenary of the European Regulators' Group, Brussels, 15 February 2007.

"Regina v. Independent Television Commission, ex parte. TVDanmark 1 Limited, UK House of Lords, 25 July 2001." *Common Market Law Reports* (2001): 545.

Rhodes, Martin. "The Scientific Objectives of the NEWGOV Project. A Revised Framework." Paper presented at the NEWGOV Consortium Conference, Florence, 30 May 2005.

Rhodes, R.A.W. *Understanding Governance: Policy Networks, Governance, Reflexivity and Accountability.* Buckingham and Philadelphia: Open University Press, 1997.

———. "Governance and Public Administration." Pp. 54–90 in *Debating Governance. Authority, Steering, and Democracy,* edited by Jon Pierre. Oxford and New York: Oxford University Press, 2000.

Richardson, Jeremy. "Actor Based Models of National and EU Policy-Making." Pp. 26–51 in *The European Union and National Industrial Policy,* edited by Hussein Kassim and Anand Menon. London and New York: Routledge, 1996.

Richardson, J. J., and R. M. Lindley. "Editorial." *Journal of European Public Policy* 1, no. 1 (1994): 1–7.

Richardson, Keith. "Big Business and the European Agenda." *Sussex European Institute Working Paper* No. 35. Brighton: Sussex European Institute, 2000.

Risse, Thomas. "A European Identity? Europeanization and the Evolution of Nation-State Identities." Pp. 210–13 in *Transforming Europe,* edited by. Maria Green Cowles, James Caporaso and Thomas Risse. Ithaca and London: Cornell University Press, 2001.

Roe, Keith, and Gust De Meyer. "Music Television: MTV-Europe." Pp. 141–57 in *Television Across Europe,* edited by Jan Wieten, Graham Murdock and Peter Dahlgren. London: Sage, 2000.

Romer, Paul. "The Origins of Endogenous Growth." *Journal of Economic Perspectives* 8, no. 1 (1994): 3–22.

Rosamond, Ben. *Theories of European Integration.* Basingstoke and New York: Palgrave, 2000.

———. "Imagining the European Economy: 'Competitiveness' and the Social Construction of 'Europe' as an Economic Space." *New Political Economy* 7, no. 2 (2002): 157–77.

Rosenau, James N., and Ernst-Otto Czempiel, eds. *Governance without Government: Order and Change in World Politics.* Cambridge: Cambridge University Press, 1992.

Ross, George. "Sliding into Industrial Policy: Inside the European Commission." *French Politics & Society* 11, no. 1 (1993): 20–44.

———. *Jacques Delors and European Integration.* Cambridge: Polity, 1995.

RSPG [Radio Spectrum Policy Group, EU]. <http://rspg.groups.eu.int/>. (26 June 2006).

——. "RSPG 04-56. Proposal for Strengthening Further the Future Working of the RSPG." 5 November 2004. <http://rspg.groups.eu.int/doc/documents/meeting/rspg5/rspg04_56_prop_strengh_work_rspg.doc> 22 April 2005).

Sandholtz, Wayne. *High-Tech Europe: The Politics of International Cooperation*. Berkeley and Oxford: University of California Press, 1992.

Sandholtz, Wayne, and Alec Stone Sweet, eds. *European Integration and Supranational Governance*. Oxford: Oxford University Press 1998.

Sandholtz, Wayne, and John Zysman. "1992: Recasting the European Bargain." *World Politics* XLII, no. 1 (1989): 95–128.

Sawhney, Harmeet. "Wi-Fi Networks and the Rerun of the Cycle." *Info: The Journal of Policy, Regulation and Strategy for Telecommunications, Information and Media* 5, no. 6 (2003): 25–33.

Sbragia, Alberta. "The European Union as Coxswain: Governance by Steering." Pp. 219–40 in *Debating Governance. Authority, Steering, and Democracy*, edited by Jon Pierre. Oxford and New York: Oxford University Press, 2000.

——. "Governance, the State, and the Market: What Is Going On?" *Governance: An International Journal of Policy, Administration and Institutions* 13, no. 2 (2000): 243–50.

Scharpf, Fritz W. *Governing in Europe: Effective and Democratic?* Oxford: Oxford University Press, 1999.

——. "The European Social Model: Coping with the Challenges of Diversity." *Journal of Common Market Studies* 40, no. 4 (2002): 645–70.

Scharpf, Fritz W., and Vivien Schmidt, eds. *Welfare and Work in the Open Economy, Vol. 2: Diverse Responses to Common Challenges*. Oxford: Oxford University Press, 2000.

Schlesinger, Philip. "Wishful Thinking: Cultural Policies, Media and Collective Identities in Europe." *Journal of Communication* 43, no. 2 (1993): 6–17.

——. "From Cultural Defence to Political Culture: Media, Politics and Collective Identity in the European Union." *Media, Culture and Society* 19, no. 3 (1997): 369–91.

——. "Changing Spaces of Political Communication: The Case of the European Union." *Political Communication* 16, no. 3 (1999): 263–79.

Schmidt, Susanne K. "Sterile Debates and Dubious Generalisations: European Integration Theory Tested by Telecommunications and Electricity." *Journal of Public Policy* 16, no. 3 (1997): 233–71.

——. "Commission Activism: Subsuming Telecommunications and Electricity under European Competition Law." *Journal of European Public Policy* 5, no. 1 (1998): 169–84.

Schmidt, Vivien. "National Patterns of Governance under Siege. The Impact of European Integration." Pp. 155–72 in *The Transformation of Governance in the European Union*, edited by Beate Kohler-Koch and Rainer Eising. London and New York: Routledge, 1999.

——. *The Futures of European Capitalism*. Oxford and New York: Oxford University Press, 2002.

Schmitter Philippe. *How to Democratize the European Union . . . and Why Bother?* Lanham, Md.: Rowman & Littlefield, 2000.

Schneider, Volker. "The Institutional Transformation of Telecommunications Between Europeanization and Globalization." Pp. 27–46 in *Governing Telecommunications and the New Information Society in Europe*, edited by Jacint Jordana. Cheltenham: Edward Elgar, 2002.

———. "State Theory, Governance and the Logic of Regulation and Administrative Control." Pp. 25–41 in *Governance in Europe. The Role of Interest Groups*, edited by Andreas Warntjen and Arndt Wonka. Baden-Baden: Nomos Verlagsgesellschaft, 2004.

Schneider, Volker, and Raymund Werle. "International Regime or Corporate Actor? The European Community in Telecommunications Policy." Pp. 77–106 in *The Political Economy of Communications: International and European Dimensions*, edited by Kenneth Dyson and Peter Humphreys. London: Routledge, 1990.

Schneider, Volker, Godefroy Dang-Nguyen and Raymund Werle. "Corporate Actor Networks in European Policy-Making: Harmonizing Telecommunications Policy." *Journal of Common Market Studies* 32, no. 4 (1994): 473–98.

Schreyer, Paul. "The Contribution of Information and Communication Technology to Output Growth: A Study of the G7 Countries." *OECD STI Working Paper*, no. 2000/2. Paris: OECD, 2000.

Schumpeter, Joseph. *The Theory of Economic Development*. Cambridge, Mass.: Harvard University Press, 1961 [1934].

Seidman, Harold, and Robert Gilmour. *Politics, Position and Power. From the Positive to the Regulatory State*. 4th ed. Oxford: Oxford University Press, 1986.

Servan-Schreiber, Jean-Jacques. *The American Challenge*. Translated by Ronald Steel. New York: Atheneum, 1968 [1967].

Sherman, Charles E. "The International Broadcasting Union: A Study in Practical Internationalism." *EBU Review* XXV, no. 3 (1974): 32–36.

Shore, Chris. *Building Europe: The Cultural Politics of European Integration*. London and New York: Routledge, 2000.

———. "Wither European Citizenship? Eros and Civilization Revisited." *European Journal of Social Theory* 7, no. 1 (2004): 27–44.

Smith, Anthony. "National Identity and the Idea of European Unity." *International Affairs* 68, no. 1 (1992): 55–76.

———. "Television as a Public Service Medium." Pp. 62–91 in *Television. An International History*, edited by Anthony Smith. Oxford: Oxford University Press, 1995.

Solow, Robert. "A Contribution to the Theory of Economic Growth." *Quarterly Journal of Economics* 70, no. 1 (1956): 65–94.

Spaak, Paul-Henri. *Report of the Heads of Delegation to the Ministers of Foreign Affairs*. (In French) [Spaak Report] 21 April 1956. <http://aei.pitt.edu/> (10 April 2006).

Sparks, Colin. "Is There a Global Public Sphere?" Pp. 108–24 in *Electronic Empires*, edited by Daya Thussu. London Arnold, 1998.

Sparks, Colin, and Risto Kunelius. "Problems with a European Public Sphere." *Javnost/The Public* 8, no. 1 (2001): 5–20.

Stopford, John M., Susan Strange and John S. Henley. *Rival States, Rival Firms: Competition for World Market Shares*. Cambridge and New York: Cambridge University Press, 1991.

Strange, Susan. "Who Are the EU? Ambiguities in the Concept of Competitiveness." *Journal of Common Market Studies* 36, no. 1 (1998): 101–14.

――――. "Foreword." Pp. xiii-xiv in *European Industrial Policy and Competitiveness*, edited by Thomas Lawton. London: Macmillan, 1999.

Strassmann, Paul. "Facts and Fantasies about Productivity" in *Information Productivity*. Information Economics Press, 1997. <http://www.strassmann.com/pubs/fnf/factnfantasy.shtml> (24 June 2006).

Stråth, Bo. "Introduction: Europe as a Discourse." Pp. 13–44 in *Europe and the Other and Europe as the Other*, edited by Bo Stråth. Brussels: PIE-Peter Lang, 2000.

――――. "Multiple Europes: Integration, Identity and Demarcation to the Other." Pp. 385–420 in *Europe and the Other and Europe as the Other*, edited by Bo Stråth. Brussels: PIE-Peter Lang, 2000.

――――. "A European Identity: To the Historical Limits of a Concept." *European Journal of Social Theory* 5, no. 4 (2002): 387–401.

Streeck, Wolfgang. "Competitive Solidarity: Rethinking the 'European Social Model.'" *Max Planck Institute for the Study of Societies Working Paper*, no. 8 (1999). <http://www.mpi-fg-koeln.mpg.de/pu/workpap/wp99-8/wp99-8.html> (5 February 2007).

Sun, Jeanne-Mey, and Jacques Pelkmans. "Why Liberalisation Needs Centralisation: Subsidiarity and EU Telecoms." *World Economy* 18, no. 5 (1995): 635–64.

TABD [TransAtlantic Business Dialogue]. "1998 Charlotte Transatlantic Business Dialogue." 1 October 1998. <http://128.121.145.19/tabd/media/1998CharlotteCEOReport.pdf> (31 March 2005).

Telegraph. 29 January 2006.

Telò, Mario. "Introduction: Globalization, New Regionalism and the Role of the European Union." Pp. 1–17 in *European Union and New Regionalism: Regional Actors and Global Governance in a Post-Hegemonic Era*, edited by Mario Telò. Aldershot: Ashgate, 2001.

Thatcher, Mark. *The Politics of Telecommunications. National Institutions, Convergence and Change.* Oxford: Oxford University Press, 1999.

――――. "Analysing Regulatory Reform in Europe." *Journal of European Public Policy* 9, no. 6 (2002): 859–72.

Thurow, Lester. *The Zero-Sum Society*. New York: Basic Books, 1980.

Tomlinson, John D. *The International Control of Radiocommunications*. Ann Arbor, MI: J.W. Edwards, 1945.

Total Telecom. 18 June 2001–20 February 2003. <http://www.totaltele.com> (11 April 2004).

Toutan, Michel. "CEPT Recommendations." *IEEE Communications Magazine* 23, no. 1 (1985): 28–30.

Tracey, Michael. *The Decline and Fall of Public Service Broadcasting*. Oxford: Oxford University Press, 1998.

Treib, Oliver, Holger Bähr and Gerda Falkner. "Modes of Governance: Towards a Conceptual Clarification." *Journal of European Public Policy* 14, no. 1 (2007): 1–20.

Trubek, David M., and James S. Mosher. "New Governance, EU Employment Policy, and the European Social Model." New York University School of Law, Jean Monnet Chair Working Paper 15/01, 2001. <http://www.jeanmonnetprogram.org/papers/01/011501.html> (13 July 2006).

Tsoukalis, Loukas. *The New European Economy Revisited*. 3rd ed. Oxford and New York: Oxford University Press, 1997.

Tyson, Laura D'Andrea. *Who's Bashing Whom? Trade Conflict in High-Technology In-dustries*. Washington, D.C.: Institute for International Economics, 1992.

UMTS Forum. *A Regulatory Framework for UMTS*, 1997. <http://www.umts-forum .org/servlet/dycon/ztumts/umts/Live/en/umts/Resources_Reports_01_index> (29 March 2005).

Ungerer, Herbert, and Nicholas Costello. *Telecommunications in Europe*. Rev. ed. Lux-embourg: Office for Official Publications of the European Communities, 1990.

———. "Switchover of Catch-up? Applying the Modernised EC Competition Regime in the New Media Sectors." Speech delivered at the Law Society's European Group, Brussels, 5 April 2005.

UNICE [Union of Industrial and Employers' Confederations of Europe]. *A Telecom-munications Policy for Europe*. Brussels: UNICE, 1986.

———. *Releasing Europe's Potential through Targeted Regulatory Reform. The Unice Regu-latory Report*. Brussels: UNICE, 1995.

Urwin, Derek. *The Community of Europe. A History of European Integration since 1945*. London and New York: Longman, 1995.

van Apeldoorn, Bastiaan. "The Political Economy of Regional Integration: Trans-national Social Forces in the Making of Europe's Socio-Economic Order." Pp. 235–44 in *Political Economy and the Changing Global Order*, edited by Richard Stubbs and Geoffrey Underhill. 2nd ed. Don Mills, Ont., and New York: Oxford University Press 2000.

———. *Transnational Capitalism and the Struggle over European Integration*. London and New York: Routledge, 2002.

Van den Berg, D. "The European Conference of Postal and Telecommunications Ad-ministrations (CEPT)." *EBU Review* (March 1966): 28–32.

Van Waarden, Kees, and Frans van Waarden. " 'Governance' as a Bridge between Dis-ciplines: Cross-disciplinary Inspiration Regarding Shifts in Governance and Prob-lems of Governability, Accountability and Legitimacy." *European Journal of Politi-cal Research* 43 (2004): 143–71.

Vasconcelos, Antonio-Pedro. *Report by the Think Tank on the Audiovisual Policy in the European Union*. Brussels: European Commission, 1994.

Venturelli, Shalini. *Liberalizing the European Media: Politics, Regulation, and the Public Sphere*. Clarendon Press; Oxford: New York, 1998.

Wagner, Michael. "Liberalization and Public Service Broadcasting. Competition Regu-lation, State Aid and the Impact of Liberalization." 1999. <http://www.ebu.ch/ CMSimages/en/leg_p_psb_liberalization_mw_tcm6-4356.pdf> (4 July 2006).

Wallace, Helen. "Europeanisation and Globalisation: Complementary or Contra-dictory Trends?" *New Political Economy* 5, no. 3 (2000): 369–82.

———. "The Changing Politics of the European Union: An Overview." *Journal of Common Market Studies* 39, no. 4 (2001): 581–94.

———. "An Institutional Anatomy and Five Policy Modes." Pp. 49–90 in *Policy-Making in the European Union*, edited by Helen Wallace, William Wallace and Mark Pollack. 5th ed. Oxford and New York: Oxford University Press, Oxford, 2005.

Wallace, Helen, William Wallace and Mark Pollack. *Policy-Making in the European Union*. 5th ed. Oxford and New York: Oxford University Press, 2005.

Wallenborn, Léo. "From IBU to EBU. The Great European Broadcasting Crisis. (Part I)." *EBU Review—Programmes, Administrative Law* XXIX, no. 1 (1978): 25–34.

Ward, David. *The European Union Democratic Deficit and the Public Sphere: An Evaluation of EU Media Policy.* Amsterdam and Oxford: IOS Press, 2002.

———. "State Aid or Band Aid? An Evaluation of the European Commission's Approach to Public Service Broadcasting." *Media, Culture & Society* 25 (2003): 233–50.

WEF [World Economic Forum]. *WEF Global Competitiveness Reports. 2004–2006.* <http://www.weforum.org/site/homepublic.nsf/Content/Global+Competitiveness+Programme%5CGlobal+Competitiveness+Report> (28 June 2006).

Weiler, J. H. H. *The Constitution of Europe. "Do the New Clothes Have an Emperor?" And Other Essays on European Integration.* Cambridge: Cambridge University Press, 1999.

Weiss, Ernst. "25th Anniversary Reminiscences." <http://www.intug.net/background/ernst_reminiscences.html> (21 May 2006).

Werle, Raymund. "Internet @ Europe: Overcoming Institutional Fragmentation and Policy Failure." Pp. 137–58 in *Governing Telecommunications and the New Information Society in Europe,* edited by Jacint Jordana. Cheltenham and Northampton, Mass.: Edward Elgar, 2002.

Wilks, Stepehen. "The Metamorphosis of European Competition Policy." Research Unit for the Study of Economic Liberalisation, *RUSEL Working Paper* No. 9 (1992). Exeter: University of Exeter.

Williams, Roger. *European Technology: The Politics of Collaboration.* London: Croom Helm, 1973.

Wilson, Graham. "In a State?" *Governance: An International Journal of Policy, Administration and Institutions* 13, no. 2 (2000): 235–42.

Wilson, H. H. *Pressure Group: The Campaign for Commercial Television.* London: Secker & Warburg, 1961.

Wolfe, Joel D. "Power and Regulation in Britain." *Political Studies* 47, no. 5 (1999): 890–905.

Woolcock, Stephen. "Information Technology: The Challenge to Europe." *Journal of Common Market Studies* XXII, no. 4 (1984): 315–31.

———. "Competition among Rules in the Single European Market." Pp. 289–321 in *International Regulatory Competition and Coordination. Perspectives on Economic Regulation in Europe and the United States,* edited by William Bratton, Joseph McCahery, Sol Picciotto and Colin Scott. Oxford: Clarendon Press, 1996.

World Bank. *Governance and Development.* Washington, D.C.: World Bank, 1992.

Young, John W. *Britain, France and the Unity of Europe 1945–1951.* Leicester: Leicester University Press, 1984.

Zimmerman, Hubert. "Western Europe and the American Challenge: Conflict and Cooperation in Technology and Monetary Policy, 1965–1973." *Journal of European Integration History* 6, no. 2 (2000): 85–110.

Zysman, John. *Governments, Markets, and Growth: Financial Systems and the Politics of Industrial Change.* Ithaca: Cornell University Press, 1983.

Index

3G. *See* third-generation mobile system

advertising: and audiovisual media services directive, 223, 226–28; and European broadcasting channel, 119; and EU competition cases, 88, 169, 240; and liberalization of broadcasting, 158–60; and national divergences and single market, 120, 122, 158, 226–27, 240; new techniques of, 219–20; and product placement, 228; and Television without Frontiers directive, 161–62, 173, 285

AEG, 75–76, 133n45

Alcatel, 112, 152, 248

Amsterdam Protocol on public service broadcasting, 170, 172, 175, 179, 286; and state aid, 230, 232–34, 236–37, 240–41

Analysis and Forecasting Group, 113–15

Antena 3, 168, 268n190

Application Programming Interfaces (APIs), 242–46

ARD, 124, 169, 264n105, 265n119, 265n122, 266n150, 266n156

Asian Tigers, 107, 109, 122

Association of Commercial Television broadcasters in Europe (ACT), 174, 268n190, 276; and audiovisual media services directive, 222, 228, 266n150, 266n152, 266n156; and public service broadcasting, 217, 239–40

Astra, 123, 158, 162

AT&T, 108, 116, 252

auction licensing, 156, 215, 251. *See also* radio spectrum

audiovisual media services [without frontiers] directive: and advertising, 228; background of, [Television without Frontiers (second review)], 219–20; and institutional aspects, 229–30; and jurisdiction, 226–28; and quotas and cultural diversity, 228–29; scope of, 220–26

Austria: broadcasting in, 161, 227; and European cooperation in posts and telephony, 50, 53, 64n88; and European integration and organizations, 40, 60n17, 62n59, 81, 163, 174

About the Author

Maria Michalis is principal lecturer and course leader for the Masters programs in Communication, Communication Policy, and Global Media at the University of Westminster, London. She holds a B.A. in political science and international relations from Panteio University in Athens, Greece, and an M.A. and a Ph.D. in communication policy from City University, London. Her teaching and research interests are in the field of communication policy and regulation with a focus on Europe. She has participated in projects dealing with a range of communication policy-related matters around the world. She is deputy head of the Communication Policy & Technology Section of the International Association for Media and Communication Research (IAMCR).

Dr. Michalis has contributed several book chapters and articles in journals such as the *European Journal of Communication, Review of International Political Economy, Convergence, Gazette,* and *Telecommunications Policy*. Her work covers various telecommunications and media policy and regulatory issues, including digital television, public service broadcasting, internet telephony, local access competition, broadband communications, universal access, and the regulatory convergence between telecommunications and broadcasting.